Practising Transnational Politics

Practising Transnational Politics

Preparing and Participating in UN and EU Simulations

Edited by

Claudia Wiesner

Professor of Political Science, Department of Social and Cultural Studies, Fulda University of Applied Sciences, Germany

Edward Elgar
PUBLISHING

Cheltenham, UK • Northampton, MA, USA

Published by

Edward Elgar Publishing Limited
The Lypiatts
15 Lansdown Road
Cheltenham
Glos GL50 2JA
UK

Edward Elgar Publishing, Inc.
William Pratt House
9 Dewey Court
Northampton
Massachusetts 01060
USA

Authorised representative in the EU for GPSR queries only: Easy Access System Europe – Mustamäe tee 50, 10621 Tallinn, Estonia, gpsr.requests@easproject.com

A catalogue record for this book is available from the British Library

Library of Congress Control Number: 2025950538

This book is available electronically in the **Elgar**online
Political Science and Public Policy subject collection
https://doi.org/10.4337/9781035326136

MIX
Paper | Supporting responsible forestry
FSC® C013604

ISBN 978 1 0353 2612 9 (cased)
ISBN 978 1 0353 2613 6 (eBook)
ISBN 978 1 0353 9443 2 (ePub)

Printed and bound by CPI Group (UK) Ltd, Croydon, CR0 4YY

Contents

List of contributors		vii
Foreword Chaldeans Mensah		ix
Acknowledgements		xv
1	Introduction to *Practising Transnational Politics*: preparing and participating in UN and EU simulations *Claudia Wiesner*	1
PART I	MUN AND MEU: ACTIVE LEARNING AND CITIZENSHIP EDUCATION	
2	What is Model United Nations? *Chaldeans Mensah, Muriel Cathérine Wenzel and Clara Umstätter*	14
3	What is Model European Union? *Alexandru Balas*	26
4	Teaching innovations and transnational blended learning: diplomacy and peer-to-peer experiential learning *Chaldeans Mensah*	47
5	Active learning through simulations: a civic education perspective *Antonio Manuel Álvarez García, Elena García Guitián and Luis Bouza García*	67
PART II	UN, EU AND TRANSNATIONAL POLITICS	
6	The United Nations *Muriel Cathérine Wenzel and Claudia Wiesner*	84
7	The EU as an arena of politics *Claudia Wiesner*	106

8 "Of nations large and small": an overview of multilateral law-making processes in the United Nations Organisation 122
Daniel R. Quiroga-Villamarín

PART III DOING TRANSNATIONAL POLITICS: CASE STUDIES AND MATERIALS

9 Procedures, practices, politics: how institutions work 140
Claudia Wiesner and Taru Haapala

10 UN case study: the rule of law in the Security Council 159
Hannah Birkenkötter

11 EU case study: the politics of shaping EU citizenship 176
Claudia Wiesner

PART IV LEARNING TO PRACTISE TRANSNATIONAL POLITICS

12 Preparing MUN and MEU: course plan, teaching materials and teaching modules 197
Clara Umstätter, Muriel Cathérine Wenzel and Claudia Wiesner

13 Preparing and doing a UN or EU simulation 250
Muriel Cathérine Wenzel, Clara Umstätter and Claudia Wiesner

14 Tutorials, practical advice, do's and don'ts 270
Muriel Cathérine Wenzel and Clara Umstätter

Index 279

List of contributors

Antonio Manuel Álvarez García is a Predoctoral Researcher FPI-UAM and PhD Candidate at Universidad Autónoma de Madrid, Spain.

Alexandru Balas is a Professor of International Studies and Director of Clark Center for Global Engagement at State University of New York at Cortland (SUNY Cortland), United States.

Hannah Birkenkötter is an Assistant Professor of International Law at the Instituto Tecnológico Autónomo de México (ITAM), Mexico.

Luis Bouza García is an Associate Professor of Political Science at Universidad Autónoma de Madrid, Spain.

Elena García Guitián is Full Professor of Political Science and Administration in the Department of Political Science and RRII at Universidad Autónoma de Madrid, Spain.

Taru Haapala is a Tomás y Valiente Research Fellow (tenure-track) at the Department of Political Science and International Relations at Universidad Autónoma de Madrid, Spain.

Chaldeans Mensah is an Associate Professor of Political Science at MacEwan University, Canada, and Past President at National Model United Nations 2021–2023.

Daniel R. Quiroga-Villamarín is a Postdoctoral Researcher (Habilitand) in International Law and European & Global History at University of Vienna, Austria.

Clara Umstätter is a Project Manager for "Boards and Executive Affairs" at the Hamburg Sustainability Conference, Germany.

Muriel Cathérine Wenzel is a Research Assistant at the Department of Social and Cultural Sciences, Fulda University of Applied Sciences, Germany.

Claudia Wiesner is Professor of Political Science at Fulda University of Applied Sciences, Germany, Honorary Professor at University College London, Uk, and Adjunct Professor at Jyväskylä University, Finland. She directs the Jean Monnet Centre of Excellence "Europe in the World" (WorldEU).

per cent), writing (91 per cent), and team building (92 per cent). Leadership scored slightly lower than 90 per cent, with 87 per cent of the participants agreeing that the conference helped them develop their leadership skills. The same survey found that over 90 per cent agreed that the conference helped them prepare to become better global citizens (a critical component of internationalisation efforts in many universities) in the following categories (National Model United Nations 2023):

- Expanding my knowledge of political, economic, and social conditions in other countries (96 per cent).
- Increasing my understanding of the complexities of international relations (94 per cent).
- Teaching me how to understand different perspectives on global issues (93 per cent).
- Increasing my knowledge of the functions, structure, and limitations of the UN (97 per cent).

While this book includes case studies of UN and EU processes and actions (see Chapters 9, 10 and 11), the books major focus is on the UN and EU as practice, providing a hands-on approach to understanding the workings of IOs through students' use of the rules of procedure in MUN and understanding the process of negotiations and the accompanying political process embedded in the institutional architecture of the organisation. Rules of procedure for the simulation provide the normative standards for consistent behaviour and legitimacy to the outcomes produced by the actors following the rules. The aim of this book is to emphasise students' agency and offer a realistic view of international relations that helps them become active global citizens and change-makers in their communities and academic spaces. The international politics-as-practice approach encourages students to become aware of the difficult and complex task environment that diplomats deal with and gives them the appropriate negotiating tools for collaboration with representatives of other states to address issues of global governance. It is unrealistic to assume that the interactions – whether physical or through hybrid diplomacy – can adequately replicate the complexities that actual diplomats encounter in their work. What simulations offer is the experience of bringing theoretical and institutional understandings of IOs into the practical realm where they can meld the ideas of the architecture of IOs into the pragmatic level of diplomatic behaviour based on an understanding of the practices and rules that inform such behaviour.

REFERENCES

Barnett, Michael N./Finnemore, Martha (2004). Rules for the world. International organisations in global politics. Ithaca, NY, Cornell University Press.

Bergsteiner, Harald/Avery, Gayle C./Neumann, Ruth (2010). Kolb's experiential learning model: Critique from a modelling perspective. Studies in Continuing Education 32 (1), 29–46. https://doi.org/10.1080/01580370903534355

Bjola, Corneliu (2016). Diplomacy as world disclosure: A fractal theory of crisis management. The British Journal of Politics and International Relations 18 (2), 335–350. https://www.semanticscholar.org/paper/Diplomacy-as-world-disclosure%3A-A-fractal-theory-of-Bjola/1a221bfa3e48cdf30bc60f3b851aa9b5aaef344e?utm_source=direct_link

Bjola, Corneliu/Coplen, Michaela (2022). Virtual venues and international negotiations: Lessons from the COVID-19 pandemic. International Negotiation (28), 63–93. Available online at https://brill.com/view/journals/iner/28/1/article-p69_4.xml?ebody=pdf-63199 (accessed 7/11/2023).

Bjola, Corneliu/Manor, Ilan (2022). The rise of hybrid diplomacy: From digital adaptation to digital adoption. International Affairs 98 (2), 471–491. https://doi.org/10.1093/ia/iiac005

Bramsen, Isabel/Hagemann, Anine (2021). The missing sense of peace: Diplomatic approachment and virtualisation during the COVID-19 lockdown. International Affairs 97 (2), 539–560. https://doi.org/10.1093/ia/iiaa229

Coker, Jeffrey Scott/Porter, Desiree Jasmine (2015). Maximizing experiential learning for student success. Change: The Magazine of Higher Learning 47 (1), 66–72. https://doi.org/10.1080/00091383.2015.996101

Fortin, Jacon C. (2012). Role-Playing and Simulation Based Learning in Higher Education: Case Study in Model United Nations. Dissertation. The Honors Program; Senior Capstone Project. Bryant University. Available online at https://digitalcommons.bryant.edu/honors_history/15/ (accessed 7/2/2025).

Haas, Ernst B. (1990). When knowledge is power: Three models of change in international organisations. Berkeley, California, University of California Press.

Kolb, David A. (1984). Experience as the source of learning and development. Upper Sadle River, Prentice Hall.

Leib, Julia/Ruppel, Samantha (2020). The learning effects of United Nations simulations in political science classrooms. European Political Science 19 (3), 336–351. https://doi.org/10.1057/s41304-020-00260-3

Morgenthau, Hans Joachim (1993). Politics among nations. The struggle for power and peace. Hg. von Kenneth W. Thompson. New York, McGraw-Hill.

National Model United Nations (2023). NMUN•NY 2023 Survey Results. Unpublished internal document.

Stone, Randall W. (2011). A theory of international organisation. In: Randall W. Stone (Ed.). Controlling institutions. Cambridge University Press, 11–32.

Acknowledgements

Co-funded by the
Erasmus+ Programme
of the European Union

DAAD
Deutscher Akademischer Austauschdienst
German Academic Exchange Service

The creation of these resources has been (partially) funded by the ERASMUS+ grant programme of the European Union under grant no. 2020-1-DE01-KA226-HE-005758. Neither the European Commission nor the project's national funding agency DAAD are responsible for the content or liable for any losses or damage resulting of the use of these resources.

1. Introduction to *Practising Transnational Politics*: preparing and participating in UN and EU simulations

Claudia Wiesner

Model United Nations (MUN) is a worldwide practice of simulations in which participants take over the role of an international delegate in a simulated committee of the United Nations (UN). Especially in the United States of America (USA), an extended network of educational institutions organise MUNs and establish training courses within their curricula for students. Currently, thousands of people participate in MUNs each year (United Nations 2025; see Chapters 2 and 4). European Union (EU) simulations or Model European Union (MEU) are more recent and offer simulations of the political dynamics in the EU (see Chapter 3). Despite the huge interest that students and university teachers take into these simulations, few publications prepare for them.

The present volume *Practising Transnational Politics. Preparing and participating in UN and EU Simulations* aims to do so, and thus close a gap in the existing literature. It offers background information, sample case studies, and teaching material to prepare scholars, university staff, and students for simulations of the UN and the EU. The volume provides both the necessary knowledge on the UN and the EU and the related simulations, and reflections as well as concrete modules and practices for active learning. The last part of this volume contains a course plan and teaching material. In all this, we want to transmit *how political action shapes the practice of transnational politics*. The goal of our volume is thus not only to deliver knowledge and tools for understanding the rules of transnational politics, but also for *practising* them, especially with regard to the UN and the EU. For the sake of clarity, we add here that in the volume both the terms "simulation" and "conference" are used.

This volume also closes another gap: it is rare that the UN and the EU are discussed jointly. However, the political processes and decision-making mechanisms in the UN and the EU show a number of similarities. In particular, they both originated in the same time period, that is, after the Second World War, and out of the same motivation, namely to strive for peace, multilateralism and international cooperation (Chapters 6 and 7). Despite these similarities, the UN is an International Organisation (IO) based on the principle of sovereign equality of member states (Chapter 6), whereas the EU combines international (or intergovernmental) and strong supranational elements. This affects how politics is practised (Chapter 7). Moreover, EU laws are binding for the EU's member states, that is, there are no possibilities of avoiding to apply them. The EU also disposes of means of law enforcement – infringement procedures and fines, and also internal sanctions. As opposed to this, UN resolutions do not have a binding character and the UN's means to enforce international law are limited.

BACKGROUND AND DEVELOPMENT OF THE VOLUME

Besides the focus on practice, it is particularly important to understand this volume's structural background, that is, the funding and collaborations behind it. The basis was laid by the work of the Erasmus+ Project "Practising Transnational Politics" (PATRAPO)[1] that ran from March 2021 to August 2023 (grant no. 2020-1-DE01-KA226-HE-005758). The PATRAPO project was carried out by researchers from Fulda University of Applied Sciences, Autonomous University Madrid (UAM), and University of Zagreb (UNiZG), with the associate partner MacEwan University, Edmonton. This volume would not have been possible without the intense discussions and the contributions of our PATRAPO project partners – not all of them were able to contribute chapters: Đana Luša and Ana Matan from University of Zagreb, Antonio Manuel Álvarez García, Elena García Guitián, Luis Bouza García and Taru Haapala from Autonomous University Madrid, Chaldeans Mensah and the UN club from MacEwan University; Zhylien Kaja, Philip Liste, Clara Umstätter, Meike Schmidt-Gleim, Maria Keller and Muriel C. Wenzel from Fulda University, and Halyna Protsyk from Ukrainian Catholic University (UCU), Lviv. It is also the PATRAPO project budget that allowed us to publish this book Open Access.

The PATRAPO project aimed at developing and teaching hybrid tri-national MUN preparation seminars in cooperation between Madrid, Zagreb, and Fulda, and at developing the related teaching material. Based on their previous experiences both in MUN model games and in EU projects, the PATRAPO

1 https://erasmus-plus.ec.europa.eu/projects/search/details/2020-1-DE01-KA226-HE-005758

project partners jointly developed, established, and implemented the following elements in their universities:

1. a teaching kit for preparative joint blended MUN training seminars (1st semester of each academic year) at all participating institutions, including: teaching curricula, seminar plans, material, content, explanation, organisation, training video collection (see Chapters 12–14);
2. a teaching kit for joint blended or real life MUN (2nd semester of each academic year) including: procedure, technical solutions, organisational advice, and detailed description of "how-to" (see Chapters 12–14);
3. a handbook including a manual and user advice for the two teaching kits (see Chapters 12–14);
4. four short time staff training sessions: the project was a learning system
5. blended student mobility sustained the attendance of virtual and in-person MUN.

The PATRAPO project thus offered a singular opportunity to make an essential contribution to both the development of teaching curricula in the participating institutions, and the international MUN community within the European context. By implementing the PATRAPO project, the team was able to develop a best-practice teaching framework that can be obtained open access and sustainably implemented in any faculty of International Relations, Political Science, or other related fields at any university.

The project and collaboration context behind this book did not only consist of this one Erasmus+ project PATRAPO, but also of two other complementary projects and sets of activities. First, the Department of Social and Cultural Sciences at Fulda University of Applied Sciences had won a grant for internationalisation from the German Academic Exchange Service (DAAD). The project "Transnational Governance and Human Rights" ran from 2021 until 2024. One part of this comprehensive project consisted of organising and funding MUN activities jointly with project partner MacEwan University and Dr Chaldeans Mensah. Another cooperation partner was State University of New York (SUNY) at Cortland, and it was Dr Alexandru Balas from Cortland who introduced us to MEU (see Chapter 3).

Moreover, the federal state of Hesse in 2022 attributed us a grant that was destined to intensify and stabilise hybrid cooperation with Ukrainian universities in general, and UCU Lviv in particular. The funding was used to include faculty and students from UCU in our activities. This project ran until April 2025 and concluded by a delegation sent to NMUN New York.

The collaborative and networking character of these project activities was decisive for the work on what has finally been put down in this volume. In all of the abovementioned projects, we had numerous discussions about how to organise a preparatory class, a syllabus, or a research activity. Especially the PATRAPO project, but also the related activities, thus were learning systems.

Moreover, we undertook several MUN-related activities between 2021 and 2024 which included not only several excursions of Fulda delegations to MUN simulations in Erfurt, Paderborn and two times (2024 and 2025) to NMUN New York (see Chapter 2), but also two UN simulations that we organised with our Fulda team in Fulda in summer 2022 and 2023 respectively (see the Foreword and Chapter 4). The 2022 MUN was a hybrid conference, and the 2023 MUN was an in-person conference. In both conferences, students from all partner universities (including the associate partner from Edmonton and students from Ukraine) conducted a four-day MUN simulation. The conferences included a cultural programme to strengthen cooperation and allow for networking.

In sum, the project environment thus served at gaining broad knowledge both on the thereotical and institutional background of transnational politics and on the practices of preparing and doing simulations. We not only developed seminar srructures, materials, and curricula (Chapters 12–14) for preparing and organising MUN and MEU seminars at universities worldwide – we also developed a politica practice approach in which organisations such as the UN and the EU appear as arenas of politics (see Chapters 6–10).

The experiences gathered had several sustainable effects. Preparatory classes for simulations were permanently included in the Master curricula of Fulda University of Applied Sciences' Department of Social and Cultural Sciences. The exchanges fostered cooperation between the partner universities and have grown into a solid basis for further collaborations. Moreover, we became involved in the MUN and MEU worldwide network of scholars and students (see Foreword, Chapters 2, 3 and 4) that is welcoming and very willing to share knowledge and activities. The present volume is also a sustainable contribution to all this.

Last but by no means least, the fact that we were able to dispose of several funding budgets was decisive in other ways. It is impossible to think of organising a simulation in your home university if there is no extra funding for it, even if it is only a small amount and even if the simulation itself is organised by volunteers. There will always be travel costs as well as expenses for the organisation that will need to be covered. In times of budget cuts for research and teaching, it is not only vital to keep this in mind, but also extremely helpful to allocate additional funding.

PRACTISING TRANSNATIONAL POLITICS

The present volume includes, for one, the PATRAPO teaching programme which is presented in Chapters 12–14. It can be taught in a joint and blended manner in several institutions simultaneously. In the course of elaborating our experiences on teaching simulations, the first and fourth parts of the present volume were added which elaborate on our experiences and lessons learned in these respects. The second and third parts of the volume are written as background for and addition to the teaching programme. Part two explains the UN and the EU and discusses them as arenas of politics. Part three presents the micropolitical approach of the volume along with sample case studies on the UN and the EU. Parts two and three are key to understanding our approach to *transnational politics as practice*.

As said above, the aim of the volume is to introduce the practice of transnational politics. This means that the volume relies on and presents a practice-oriented approach to teaching and understanding International Relations, European integration, and Political Science, which goes far beyond simple knowledge gathering on the institutions and their legal framework. For the simulations, students need to learn how to practice transnational politics, i.e. they need to understand particular national interests, build alliances, and gain negotiation skills (Chapters 2 and 4). In a general sense, our approach to the UN and the EU therefore focuses on the micropolitics behind transnational politics (see Chapters 9 and 11), that is, the everyday workings, negotiations, strategies, and conflicts carried out in IOs and transnational organisations, and hence, the more informal and "unofficial" aspects of doing politics. Accordingly, the contributions to the volume take on a perspective of controversies and contingencies. History is discussed as non-linear, conflictual, and open to change. The chapters account for power relations and individual and collective investments in the history of the UN and international rights declarations. Transnational politics is approached with a perspective on the international power play, the role of state pressure, and the general status of law (soft and hard law). The volume also provides reflections and sample case studies on how transnational politics is practised (Chapters 9–11).

In order to be prepared to act as a delegate in a MUN or a MEU, students also need to train their capacities in speaking, writing, and negotiating. None of these come naturally, and none of these are included in most of the classical curricula of the Social Sciences or International Relations. The course material on simulation preparation thus includes teaching modules relating to these skills (Chapter 12). When it comes to speaking, students need to learn the essentials of how to speak in public, how to prepare a speech, how to structure it, how to appear on stage, or how to handle nervousness and difficult situations. Also, the writing of position papers and resolutions is not to be compared to the writing of term papers, which is due to the political role such documents play. Position papers and resolutions require command of the diplomatic procedures and a sufficient background knowledge of the respective states' interests. Finally, negotiation is a key element in diplomacy and it is also not typically taught in a standard Social Sciences or International Relations curriculum. The featured teaching material therefore contains sessions on the how-to and the practices of negotiations. This volume, finally, provides material and tools that allow students to be actively involved in their learning as it requires them to conduct research and develop solutions (see Chapters 2, 3, 4 and 5 as well as 12–14).

THE STATE OF THE ART IN THE MUN AND MEU LITERATURE AND THE GAPS WE AIM TO CLOSE

As said above, MUN is a well-established worldwide network of educational simulations in which students take on the role of delegates at the UN and, in doing so, practice international politics (Chapter 2). MEU is the younger sibling (Chapter 3). Simulations are nowadays often used didactically as an innovative teaching tool, especially in the context of International Relations study programmes. However, with regard to preparing students and university teachers for these events, there is a significant gap: very few publications prepare for simulations.

The relevant literature can be divided into three subgroups. To start with, introductory literature on the UN and the EU is relevant for the preparation of a MUN and a MEU, such as textbooks or handbooks providing an overview about the UN (e.g. Gareis 2012; Trent and Schnurr 2017; United Nations 2017; Weiss and Daws (eds.) 2018) and the EU (e.g. Costa and Brack 2019; Hix and Høyland 2022; Hodson and Peterson (eds.) 2017; Tömmel 2014) and their institutions, history, and structure.

Moreover, there are also a few more specialised and hands-on guides on participation in simulations (see e.g. Bursens et al. 2018), some of them address MUN (see e.g. American Model United Nations 2024; Hodgin 2012; Krein 2023; Mickolus and Brannan 2013; National Model United Nations 2022; Turunç 2009; United Nations 2020), others MEU (e.g. Jones 2018; Usherwood 2014). Another type of literature, mostly published as articles in academic journals, reflects on what it means to teach international politics through MUNs (see e.g. Calossi and Coticchia 2018; Cicchi et al. 2020; Coticchia et al. 2020; Engel et al. 2017; Hammond and Albert 2020; Hazen 2019; Jesuit and Strachan 2021; Kartal 2021; McIntosh 2001; Obendorf and Randerson 2012; Obendorf and Randerson 2013; Taylor 2013) and MEU (e.g. Bobot and Goergen 2010; Brunazzo and Settembri 2015; Clark et al. 2017; Elias 2014; Fink 2015; Jones 2018; Rünz 2015; Usherwood 2014; Van Dyke et al. 2000; Wulk 2018).

In all this, what is missing is literature that combines the different fields of interest and connects knowledge on the practice of micropolitics within both the UN and the EU with training tools for UN and EU simulations. This volume thus seeks to close the gap between different types of literature that would generally be of interest for preparing simulations. It provides, on the one hand, the relevant background knowledge regarding the UN and the EU, their procedures and their workings as institutions. On the other hand, it proposes active learning tools to build capacities necessary for successful participation in simulations: resolution-writing, debating, and rhetoric. The volume thus connects the rather abstract knowledge of the history and institutional structure of the UN and the EU, and hands-on guidance on how to act as a MUN or MEU participant.

As said above, the volume moreover seeks to stress the political practice aspect, regarding both the UN and the EU as *arenas of politics* and discussing them in one volume (see Chapters 6 and 7). Instead of introducing the UN and the EU as static systems with bodies such as the Security Council and the General Assembly, the Council and the Commission, as well as with certain highly institutionalised procedures, as UN and EU textbooks would do, we put the emphasis on political practice and the micropolitics at work in both these institutions (see Chapter 9).

In sum, the volume combines background and practical knowledge on the UN and the EU with a perspective that regards both the UN and EU as arenas of politics. It moreover provides a concise and practice-oriented guide to teaching and organising (hybrid) MUNs and MEUs, including concrete sample studies and proposals for a syllabus and teaching modules. The volume thus helps to fill in the blanks in the field of MUN and MEU, the UN, the EU, and the ways politics is practiced in this context. The volume therefore not only aims to provide fundamental knowledge of the UN and the EU as well as simulations, it is also destined to help build capacities of critical thinking and analytical techniques.

STRUCTURE OF THE BOOK

The volume is structured into four parts that reflect these goals. The first three parts contain chapters that introduce the themes and the teaching philosophy of simulations (part one), the background and approach to the UN and EU (part two), and sample case studies (part three). The fourth and final part includes the model course plan and syllabus, as well as good practices of teaching preparatory classes for simulations. The material aims at enabling the teaching of the necessary background knowledge as well as the necessary skills in the practice of politics in diplomacy that prepare students in order to successfully participate in MUN and MEU simulations. Students learn how to act successfully as delegates of an assigned country and gain an understanding of the different dimensions of practising transnational politics. The detailed structure of the volume is as follows:

The first part is devoted to discussing and explaining the background and the goals of MUN and MEU simulations and to discuss the specific pedagogical approach of active learning.

Chapter 2 by Chaldeans Mensah, Muriel Cathérine Wenzel, and Clara Umstätter describes MUN as a practice of transnational politics. It explains the history and background of MUN simulations, and the cooperation and practice of National Model United Nations (NMUN). Moreover, it explains the learning outcomes simulations aim for.

Chapter 3 by Alexandru Balas presents MEU. Like MUN, MEU is an experiential learning opportunity for students at both high school and university level to improve their negotiation skills while learning about the decision-making processes and major agenda items of the EU. MEU activities can also equip students with skills in research, public speaking, presentation, or leadership. Moreover, MEU teaches students about the EU's decision-making processes and the major items on the EU's agenda. The chapter also explains how MEUs can be organised and why they are very flexible in size and duration.

Chapter 4 by Chaldeans Mensah elaborates further on the practice-oriented approach to understanding IOs through active learning of diplomacy. It is an important educational tool for students to understand both the highly formalistic procedures within such organisations and the social practice of negotiations and building of consensus to address complex global problems. The chapter also reflects on the role of professors and university teachers in active learning, arguing that it rests on navigating the balance between the authoritative decision-maker and a delegating supervisor. Finally, the chapter emphasises the importance of peer-to-peer training (by students for students).

Chapter 5 by Antonio Manuel Álvarez García, Elena García Guitián and Luis Bouza García discusses simulations as active learning strategies. Active learning is a pedagogical approach that emphasises the development of students' know-how through activities that demand higher-order thinking. The learning outcomes are related to public virtue and political participation, which makes political simulations a promising tool for civic education.

Part two contextualises MUN and MEU in a wider framework, emphasising their function as an arena of politics. This part links introductions into the institutional setting and procedures of the UN and the EU with a perspective that helps to get the students acquainted with the political dimension and practices of these organisations.

Chapter 6 by Muriel Cathérine Wenzel and Claudia Wiesner focuses on the UN, explaining what the UN is, how it works and how it engages in international politics. The history of the UN, its Charter, tasks, and goals as well as the UN organs, budget, the larger UN system as well as specific fields of action and current challenges are discussed.

Chapter 7 by Claudia Wiesner describes how the EU is structured, what its institutions are, and how it works as an arena of politics. The chapter is based on the argument that the EU has characteristics of both a political system and an IO: it uses mechanisms and processes of diplomacy and intergovernmental negotiation and is based on treaties like the UN, but it is no longer a simple IO. It has many supranational elements. Moreover, the EU is to be understood in its historical perspective, as it continuously was and is still shaped by political actions of various actors, ranging from member states' governments over members of EU institutions to citizens and activists.

Chapter 8 by Daniel R. Quiroga-Villamarín explains the UN's background in international law. Founded in 1945 in the wake of the Second World War, it was created with the idea that it would serve to represent the globe's population – just as a domestic parliament can agglutinate the general will of any given nation. This "international parliament," just as the League of Nations which preceded the UN, has had the task of harmonising global plurality into a common horizon of international legal standards, while at the same time respecting the diversity of each of its member states. The chapter provides an overview of the processes of multilateral law-making that unfold within the UN.

The third section contains examples of political practices, procedures and conflicts in both the UN and the EU context.

Chapter 9 by Claudia Wiesner and Taru Haapala explains and critically discusses how political practices in inter- and supranational institutions work, focusing on the rhetorical, argumentative, and political strategies at stake, the possibilities of creative usage of rules and institutional settings, and the ways in which this is manifested in documents. The chapter ends with a sample case of EU politics which regards the extension of the European Parliament's powers via micropolitics.

Chapter 10 by Hannah Birkenkötter presents a UN case study on the rule of law in the Security Council. It discusses various understandings of the rule of law among UN member states, as articulated in a Security Council thematic debate on the topic. While the rule of law is generally considered a valuable concept, there exists fundamental disagreement as to its precise content. UN member states disagree on whether the rule of law should apply to international relations, as a principle that governs states' internal structures, or both. These different visions became visible during the first-ever thematic debate on the rule of law in the Security Council.

Chapter 11 by Claudia Wiesner presents an EU case study. It analyses exemplary political processes and controversies taking place in the EU's multilevel system, discussing how EU politics are done via documents, that is, how different interests and political goals are expressed in documents, how positions are manifested and opposed to one another, how the resulting controversies are carried out, and how the results of the political processes are laid down in documents. More specifically, the chapter focuses on a special type of micropolitics, conceptual politics, in the sense of the political moves that shape key concepts, and in this case, European Union Citizenship.

The last section of the book presents the teaching material developed in the PATRAPO project, and the knowledge we gained in organising simulations.

Chapter 12 by Clara Umstätter, Muriel Cathérine Wenzel, and Claudia Wiesner provides the material necessary to thoroughly prepare students for MUN or MEU participation. It can be used both for onsite and online training seminars. The chapter includes 16 teaching modules and material that can be adapted to various circumstances.

Chapter 13 by Muriel Cathérine Wenzel, Clara Umstätter, and Claudia Wiesner explains the requirements of organising a simulation, the tasks to be carried out, the budget and staff needed, and the general considerations to be taken into account.

Chapter 14 by Muriel Cathérine Wenzel and Clara Umstätter provides additional information, material and support for anyone teaching, organising or participating in a simulation and various practical support tools, such as a glossary, including the most important MUN-specific terms, practical tips or do's and don'ts.

REFERENCES

American Model United Nations (2024). 2024 Handbook. Available online at https://www.amun.org/handbooks/2024/handbook/full/ (accessed 6/27/2025).

Bobot, Lionel/Goergen, Andreas (2010). Case Study. Teaching European Negotiations: The EU Chocolate Directive Simulation. International Negotiation 15 (2), 301–323. https://doi.org/10.1163/157180610X506992

Brunazzo, Marco/Settembri, Pierpaolo (2015). Teaching the European Union: A Simulation of Council's Negotiations. European Political Science 14 (1), 1–14. https://doi.org/10.1057/eps.2014.34

Bursens, Peter/Donche, Vincent/Gijbels, David/Spooren, Pieter (Eds.) (2018). Simulations of Decision-Making as Active Learning Tools. Design and Effects of Political Science Simulations. Cham, Springer International Publishing.

Calossi, Enrico/Coticchia, Fabrizio (2018). Students' Knowledge and Perceptions of International Relations and the "Model United Nations": An Empirical Analysis. Acta Politica 53 (3), 409–428. https://doi.org/10.1057/s41269-017-0058-9

Cicchi, Lorenzo/Calossi, Enrico/Onderco, Michal/Coticchia, Fabrizio (2020). I Love This Game: The Interplay Between Experience and Background in Role-Playing Simulations: Insights from MUN Participants in Italy and the Netherlands. European Political Science 20, 397–412. https://doi.org/10.1057/s41304-020-00277-8

Clark, Nicholas/Van Dyke, Gretchen/Loedel, Peter/Scherpereel, John/Sobisch, Andreas (2017). EU Simulations and Engagement: Motivating Greater Interest in European Union Politics. Journal of Political Science Education 13 (2), 152–170. https://doi.org/10.1080/15512169.2016.1250009

Costa, Olivier/Brack, Nathalie (2019). How the EU Really Works. London/New York, Routledge.
Coticchia, Fabrizio/Calossi, Enrico/Cicchi, Lorenzo (2020). A Reality Check for Students? How Participating to the Model United Nations Influences Skills, IR Perceptions, and Perspectives on Future Career. Politics 40 (2), 245–261. https://doi.org/10.1177/0263395719852238
Elias, Anwen (2014). Simulating the European Union: Reflections on Module Design. International Studies Perspectives 15 (4), 407–422. https://doi.org/10.1111/insp.12009
Engel, Susan/Pallas, Josh/Lambert, Sarah (2017). Model United Nations and Deep Learning: Theoretical and Professional Learning. Journal of Political Science Education 13 (2), 171–184. https://doi.org/10.1080/15512169.2016.1250644
Fink, Simon (2015). 36 Different Chocolate Directives: How Does the Setting Influence Negotiation Outcomes in an EU Simulation? European Political Science 14 (3), 241–253. https://doi.org/10.1057/eps.2015.21
Gareis, Sven Bernhard (2012). The United Nations: An Introduction. 2nd ed. Houndmills/Basingstoke/Hampshire, Palgrave Macmillan.
Hammond, Augustine/Albert, Craig Douglas (2020). Learning by Experiencing: Improving Student Learning Through a Model United Nations Simulation. Journal of Political Science Education 16 (4), 441–458. https://doi.org/10.1080/15512169.2018.1548967
Hazen, Timothy A. (2019). Model United Nations: Review for First-Time Instructors and Advisors. Journal of Political Science Education 15 (1), 133–135. https://doi.org/10.1080/15512169.2018.1442721
Hix, Simon/Høyland, Bjørn (2022). The Political System of the European Union. 4th ed. London, Bloomsbury Academic.
Hodgin, Greg (2012). Model UN Handbook. A Preparation for MUN Conferences. Lanham, Md., Hamilton Books.
Hodson, Dermot/Peterson, John (Eds.) (2017). The Institutions of the European Union. Oxford/New York, NY, Oxford University Press.
Jesuit, David K./Strachan, J. Cherie (2021). Student Engagement and Learning Outcomes in the Model United Nations. Journal of University Teaching and Learning Practice 18 (8). https://doi.org/10.53761/1.18.8.11
Jones, Rebecca (2018). What's the EU? Achieving Learning Outcomes and Preparing US Students for EuroSim. In: Peter Bursens/Vincent Donche/David Gijbels et al. (Eds.). Simulations of Decision-Making as Active Learning Tools. Design and Effects of Political Science Simulations. Cham, Springer International Publishing, 51–61.
Kartal, Mert (2021). Facilitating Deep Learning and Professional Skills Attainment in the Classroom: The Value of a Model United Nations Course. Journal of Political Science Education 17 (supl), 148–168. https://doi.org/10.1080/15512169.2020.1854771
Krein, Anna-Theresia (2023). Model United Nations. A Practical Guide. Cham, Springer.
McIntosh, Daniel (2001). The Uses and Limits of the Model United Nations in an International Relations Classroom. International Studies Perspectives 2 (3), 269–280. https://doi.org/10.1111/1528-3577.00057
Mickolus, Edward/Brannan, J. Thomas (2013). Coaching Winning Model United Nations Teams. A Teacher's Guide. Washington, D.C., Potomac Books.

National Model United Nations (2022). Delegate Preparation Guide. National Model United Nations. Available online at https://www.nmun.org/assets/documents/nmun-delegate-prep-guide.pdf (accessed 2/7/2023).

Obendorf, Simon/Randerson, Claire (2012). The Model United Nations Simulation and the Student as Producer Agenda. Enhancing Learning in the Social Sciences 4 (3), 1–15. https://doi.org/10.11120/elss.2012.04030007

Obendorf, Simon/Randerson, Claire (2013). Evaluating the Model United Nations: Diplomatic Simulation as Assessed Undergraduate Coursework. European Political Science 12 (3), 350–364. https://doi.org/10.1057/eps.2013.13

Rünz, Paul (2015). Beyond Teaching: Measuring the Effect of EU Simulations on European Identity and Support of the EU. European Political Science 14 (3), 266–278. https://doi.org/10.1057/eps.2015.23

Taylor, Kirsten (2013). Simulations Inside and Outside the IR Classroom: A Comparative Analysis. International Studies Perspectives 14 (2), 134–149. https://doi.org/10.1111/j.1528-3585.2012.00477.x

Tömmel, Ingeborg (2014). The European Union: What It Is and How It Works. Houndsmills, Palgrave Macmillan.

Trent, John E./Schnurr, Laura (2017). A United Nations Renaissance. What the UN Is, and What It Could Be. Opladen/Berlin/Toronto, Barbara Budrich Publishers.

Turunç, Kerem (2009). The Winning Delegate. An Insider's Guide to Model United Nations. 2nd ed. New York, iUniverse.

United Nations (2017). Basic Facts about the United Nations. 42nd ed. New York, United Nations, Department of Public Information.

United Nations (2020). The United Nations Guide to Model UN. New York, United Nations Publications.

United Nations (2025). Model United Nations. Available online at https://www.un.org/en/mun (accessed 7/3/2025).

Usherwood, Simon (2014). Constructing Effective Simulations of the European Union for Teaching: Realising the Potential. European Political Science 13 (1), 53–60. https://doi.org/10.1057/eps.2013.29

Van Dyke, Gretchen/Declair, Edward G./Loedel, Peter H. (2000). Stimulating Simulations: Making the European Union a Classroom Reality. International Studies Perspectives 1 (2), 145–159. https://doi.org/10.1111/1528-3577.00014

Weiss, Thomas G./Daws, Sam (Eds.) (2018). The Oxford Handbook on the United Nations. Oxford, Oxford University Press.

Wulk, Sophie (2018). Simulating European Climate Policy Negotiations in a Teacher Training Seminar: Which Effects Can Be Detected? In: Peter Bursens/Vincent Donche/David Gijbels et al. (Eds.). Simulations of Decision-Making as Active Learning Tools. Design and Effects of Political Science Simulations. Cham, Springer International Publishing, 129–143.

PART I

MUN and MEU: active learning and citizenship education

2. What is Model United Nations?

Chaldeans Mensah, Muriel Cathérine Wenzel and Clara Umstätter

Model United Nations (MUN) – as the practice of international politics – is the name of United Nations (UN) simulations practiced around the world. In MUN, participants take on the role of an international delegation in a UN organ or committee such as the General Assembly (GA). One of its main goals is to provide realistic insights into the structures and procedures of the UN. By simulating international negotiations, participants experience International Relations and decision-making processes themselves. Furthermore, by representing a member state, students learn new perspectives and how to advance the foreign policy goals of their assigned state. Hence, through this process of experiential learning and engaging with other delegates, they develop soft skills, competences, and rhetorical skills as well as leadership and collaboration (Hammond and Albert 2020). This chapter briefly describes the history and background of MUN, and its largest expression in the National Model United Nations (NMUN). It shows how and for what purpose the conferences were developed and outlines the simulations' aspired learning outcomes in depth. Lastly, the chapter explains some MUN characteristics and roles.

HISTORY AND BACKGROUND OF MUN

MUN is a well-established approach used extensively around the world at all levels of education to teach students about how the UN as an institution and global affairs more broadly work. It is estimated that more than 200,000 high school and university students engage in over 400 annual MUN conferences in 35 countries (Fortin 2012).

Simulations and active learning of the way International Organisations (IO) operate are probably as old as the early governance innovations that preceded the formation of the UN. In the 1920s, Ivy League students introduced the Model League, and the NMUN traces its roots to the Model League of Nations simulations held at the University of Syracuse in 1927 (National Model United Nations 2024). Recently, the UN has embarked on innovative efforts to widen the MUN experience to all levels of education: for instance, the UN's interactive briefing series "The Real UN"; production of resources, such as the UN Guide to Model UNs; and the UN USA's "My Diplomat App" (United Nations 2024; United Nations Association of the USA 2025). Admittedly, while there is a growth of MUNs around the world, there is also an uneven distribution of the content and flow of the simulations, and the way participants learn about the means and ends of UN actions.

PURPOSE OF MUN: LEARNING THE RULES OF DIPLOMATS BY PRACTISING THEM

As will be further discussed in Chapter 5, what MUN does best is offer a forum for students to partake in the social experience of engaging in negotiations and creating conversational space (Baker et al. 2002; see also Chapter 5) and to bring delegates from differing cultural backgrounds to practice the niceties of international diplomacy and find solutions to global problems. MUN facilitates a learning process that helps students narrow the gap between their textbook knowledge and understanding the formalism and institutional framework of the UN by offering an immersive experience of modelling the behaviour of diplomats. Youth engagement through MUNs prepares them to deal with concrete political challenges to the UN such as future efforts to re-design the UN to address the growing power of the Global South, and the failure to deal with the crisis of multilateralism. Students learn the process of policy-making in IOs, whether through symbolic decisions or rule-creating or rule-supervisory decisions and the hierarchy within international diplomacy (Haas 1990; Pouliot 2016).

The MUN's practical approach to understanding formal organisations – established for decision-making for actors in the international system – requires more than learning about their institutional architecture. It also includes learning about the roles of diplomats by simulating their behaviour in the organisations. An important goal of a simulation of an IO, and a central concern of international politics (Stone 2011), is to help students understand the normative and material underpinnings of the organisations as a reflection of global power dynamics and the position of individual states within the system. Key to understanding diplomacy is to see the UN and other IOs as arenas of politics (see Chapters 6, 7 and 9). This requires understanding the exercise of power for agenda-setting and shaping desired outcomes. Simulations allow students to encounter the exercise of power in the context of negotiations and gain insights into how states collaborate within the constraints of global power dynamics to address issues of global governance, the challenges of multilateralism in the face of changing geopolitical realities, and the interplay of knowledge and interest in IOs (Haas 1990). While students represent states or non-state actors, depending on the committee for the simulation, the purpose of these simulations is to move away from a purely functionalist view of IOs and to see them as autonomous actors (Barnett and Finnemore 2004) that can bring their moral authority and expertise to have an impact on global governance.

The pedagogical value of simulations in terms of enhancing factual knowledge of International Relations and bolstering procedural and soft skills (Fortin 2012; Leib and Ruppel 2019) is duly acknowledged by scholars as providing an in-depth understanding of world affairs (see e.g. Calossi and Coticchia 2018; Frederking 2005; Jones and Bursens 2015; Taylor 2013). The use of simulations helps students develop an understanding of the nature of the give-and-take of negotiations to arrive at a consensus and diplomatic resolution to global problems. Indeed, there is a growing recognition of the importance of experiential learning (see Chapter 5) in enhancing student learning in areas such as civic engagement, deep learning, and practical competence (Coker and Porter 2015). Given the turmoil in our world today, simulations give students not only insights into the institutional architecture of our international order but provide an understanding of the normative basis of that order. Through a practice-oriented approach to learning, students also gain an appreciation of both the power dynamics of inter-state relations and the values of global citizenship and conflict resolution.

As noted previously, the learning opportunities of MUN are part of the vast network of such activities at different academic levels – from high school MUN to college and university level – simulations of the UN. International Relations scholars and university and college administrators should pay special attention to the educational experience and learning that takes place in the setting of a typical MUN simulation. When students attend MUN conferences there is a requirement for students to research when preparing a position paper for the country assigned to the attending delegation. The students become conversant with the foreign policy stances of the country and the mandates of the committee for simulation, as well as the relevant rules of procedure, gaining a sense of the norms that underpin the UN's work in dealing with global challenges. In addition, MUN helps students bridge the "reality gap" (Muldoon 1995) between what happens in the actual UN and the learning process in academic spaces. Unlike actual diplomats who seek authorisation or state consent for decisions, MUN delegates use insights gained from preparation and research combined with their creative thinking to model the behaviour of diplomats at the UN. The conference itself is a beehive of diplomatic activity, as delegates apply the rules of procedure and navigate the intricacies of negotiations to draft working papers for passage into resolutions. Furthermore, negotiations are an integral part of the MUN experience, as delegates navigate conflicting positions, personalities, and the international pecking orders (Pouliot 2016) of their assigned states to collaborate for optimal outcomes.

While collaboration is highlighted in many of the committees simulated in MUN and is expressed in the spirit of mutual trust, openness, and youthful creativity of the delegates as they pursue collaboration regardless of status and power, the hierarchies of international diplomacy are very much a significant part of the engagement among simulation participants. Besides these hierarchies in the real-world order, there is also the cultural diversity during MUN simulations. Delegates deal with students from diverse backgrounds with different cultural understandings of diplomatic conduct. They learn like actual diplomats to explore relationships, understand power asymmetries and break down the words of the counterparts to decipher their core interests and priorities (Gaudiosi et al. 2019).

MUN thus sets its participants on a course to understand the global power dynamics that influence the work of the UN, the procedures that undergird the work of its committees, and the legal basis and normative standards of international society within which the organisation exists. In addition to gaining knowledge of how institutions and international politics work in practice, students gain important meta-skill sets from the conference (see also Chapter 5).

MUN, as with other simulations, gives students agency and a realistic view of International Relations (Jesuit and Endless 2018) to become active global citizens and change-makers in their communities and academic spaces. Delegates become aware of the difficult and complex task environment that diplomats deal with and are given the appropriate negotiating tools for collaboration with representatives of other states to address issues of global governance. It is unrealistic to assume that the interactions – whether physical or as a form of hybrid diplomacy – can adequately replicate the complexities that actual diplomats encounter in their work. What simulations offer is to bring the practical understanding of IOs into the purview of students, where they can meld the ideas of the architecture of IOs into the pragmatic level of diplomatic behaviour based on an understanding of the practices and rules that inform such behaviour. Simulations cover formal procedures and rules that cement the notion that, regardless of the size of the country represented, participants can use these procedures to have their voices heard in the channels of multilateral diplomacy. Understanding formalisms and the rationalised operational rules of IOs must be complemented by a deeper appreciation of the underlying power dynamics and hierarchies within IOs. What is interesting in these simulations is to observe how some "diplomats" can make substantive contributions and exert influence beyond their actual diplomatic hierarchies or state capabilities. This brings into play the preparation of students for the simulation and their ability to master the game of negotiations, and highlights important social attributes to maximise their contribution to diplomatic interactions. In the complex context of simulations where differing perspectives are brought to the table, the exercise is designed to help students understand the rules of the game and the power politics that pervade multilateral diplomacy. Formalisms structure the practice of international diplomacy (see Chapter 9) and offer a context for simulation participants to engage with each other on an equal footing, but understanding such practice should not be devoid of appreciation of the structural power that is an important part of diplomacy.

NMUN AS BIGGEST MUN-CONFERENCE WORLDWIDE

While there are many organisations around the world engaged in UN simulations that provide a practice-oriented focus to understanding International Relations, NMUN is the world's largest and oldest simulation of the UN. NMUN is a Non-Governmental Organisation (NGO) recognised by the UN Department of Global Communications with headquarters in New York. The organisation traces its origins back to the 1927 simulation of the League of Nations at Syracuse University in New York, that paved the way for UN simulations after the organisation was established in 1945. In 1946 the Middle/Mid-Atlantic Model (UN) General Assembly (MGA) was the "first Model United Nations simulation to be held after the ratification of the UN Charter" (NMUN 2024). NMUN offers a cooperative, hands-on, realistic, active learning gathering of thousands of students from around the world to its annual conferences. The organisation has expanded to accommodate interest in its experiential learning programmes, including offering two conferences (A and B) in New York, a conference in Washington DC, and annual "international conferences" which have been held in venues such as Japan, Canada, Germany, Galapagos Islands in Ecuador, South Korea, China, and Italy. Except for the Second World War and COVID-19 cancellations in 1945 and 2019 respectively, NMUN (and its pre-1964 expressions) has held its conferences consistently in New York since 1964, and the period before then saw conferences held in different USA east coast cities. In 2020 and 2021, first the Washington and then the New York conference were held virtually due to COVID-19 (NMUN 2024).

One of the unique contributions of NMUN is the use of its position as a UN Global Communications-recognised NGO since 1982 to advance education about the UN and global issues. This platform gives the UN a connection to the youth from around the world, tapping into NMUN's constituency of youth delegates to advance its global youth strategy. NMUN has been a member of the UN's Academic Impact since 2013, and it helps promote the ten principles and themes at the heart of the programme through its mission statement and topics addressed during its simulations: Global citizenship; Inter-cultural Dialogue; Addressing Poverty; Capacity Building; Peace and Conflict Resolution; Sustainability; Education for All; Human Rights; Higher Education and UN Charter.

Given its relationship with the UN, as an accredited NGO, NMUN has credibility when it requests UN actors to share their experiences with delegates and requests access to UN facilities for its conference opening and/or closing ceremonies. In a reciprocal way, the organisation serves as an important conduit for the UN to reach out to a large youth cohort from colleges and universities around the world as it promotes its youth outreach. The UN recently highlighted, in a photo series entitled "From Model to the Real UN," individuals who moved on from participating in MUNs to work for the UN (United Nations 2023). As a facilitator of connections to the UN-as-practice, not just a theoretical construct, NMUN offers delegates opportunities to reach out to actual diplomats for mission briefings from assigned countries. The organisation also brings in speakers from the UN system to share their experiences with delegates. Over the years, speakers at NMUN included Secretary-Generals, including Kurt Waldheim, Kofi Annan, Boutros Boutros-Ghali, and Ban Ki Moon; Deputy Secretary-Generals Jan Eliasson and Amina Mohammed; and Permanent Representatives to the UN, including George H.W. Bush, Susan Rice, Samantha Power, and Linda Thomas-Greenfield (NMUN 2024).

In addition, the UN provides NMUN with the rules of procedure developed with the United Nations Institute for Training and Research. The UN General Assembly Handbook is an important source for details on the mandate, rules of procedure, and information on the constitutive committees of the Assembly. Rules of procedure for the simulation provide the procedural standards for consistent behaviour during the simulation. They also add legitimacy to the outcomes of the simulation.

NMUN is handled by a Board of Directors, which provides the strategic directions, oversees its overall financial sustainability, and a management team, which runs the programmes and manages the operational details of the organisation. An important feature of NMUN is its reliance on volunteer staff of former delegates to chair committees and help management with the running of the conferences. The volunteer staff reflects the diversity of the conference as well as the UN itself, which reflects the ethos of inclusion institutionalised in the recruitment practices of the organisation. In some sense, this embodies the notion of peer-to-peer leadership as volunteer staff get to offer leadership skills, model appropriate diplomatic behaviour, and offer guidance to delegates as they engage in diplomatic interactions. NMUN conferences include a faculty programme, including guest speakers, an orientation session for new faculty, and a feedback session to give management and the board input for governance of the organisation.

GOALS AND SCHEDULES OF A TYPICAL CONFERENCE

A MUN is an "operational simulation" (Obendorf and Randerson 2012) when it comes closest to simulating the role descriptions and expectations of behaviour of actual UN committees. The goal of a MUN participant, to be called delegate, is to represent the official position of the assigned member state as realistically as possible, which entails concentrating on representing the interests of this statement and abstaining from stating personal opinions.

The simulation's topics focus on current political issues which are often connected to contemporary debates in the UN. Some MUNs use the crisis-style approach by simulating current or historical events related to crises (especially in the Security Council), whereas others simulate the work of GA committees with an emphasis on the ethos of collaboration and conflict resolution (Chasek 2005; Heater and Berridge 1993).

MUN consists of formal sessions or debates based on the rules of procedure of the UN and informal sessions for negotiation and formulating working papers and draft resolutions. The specific content and agenda of MUN conferences may differ, and some offer additional activities such as cultural programmes. Therefore, the duration of a MUN simulation may range from a couple of hours to a full-blown conference, lasting several days. Using a virtual, hybrid, or in-person approach, the conference typically ends with voting on draft resolutions or a framework agreement or statement of proceedings (Barston 2013).

There is a general order in which a MUN conference proceeds (see also Chapter 13). Before the MUN officially starts, there might be a cultural programme including visits to touristic sights, sightseeing or dinner, and rules training where the rules of procedure are explained. This may help the participants to be better prepared and to refresh their knowledge, especially if it is their first simulation or if the MUN entails a specific set of rules. The conference officially starts with an opening ceremony during which speeches by faculty members, university staff, or other invited speakers (e.g. politicians, scholars, experts in the field) are held to introduce the topic(s) before the committee(s). The conference then proceeds as a formal session with a roll call by the dais, that is, the chair leading the MUN, before it moves to set the agenda. In this phase, after opening the speakers list, delegates hold agenda-setting speeches to state their preferences for the first topic to be discussed at the simulation. These topics are often chosen based on relevance and current international events but also on the preferences of the assigned member states. A vote, after closing and exhausting the speakers list, on which topic is to be discussed first ends the agenda-setting phase. Notably, smaller conferences may only have one topic. Consequently, the agenda-setting process would not take place, but the delegates would directly move to discussing the topic.

After the agenda has been set, a new speakers list will be opened. The organisational team of the conference or the dais will usually decide on the speakers time (commonly it varies from 60 to 90 seconds). Delegates add themselves to the speakers list either by raising their placard or by passing a note through the page, a person responsible for bringing notes from the participants to the dais or other delegates during the formal session. Notably, these procedures might differ depending on the character of the conference as virtual conferences require different modes of communication. Delegates will hold opening speeches which can be prepared prior to the simulation and are often based on the position papers which must be written in advance. During the main part of the conference, delegates will move back and forth from formal to informal sessions, that is, from highly formalised sessions where they stick to the script and are not allowed to leave or enter the committee room, to informal sessions in which everyone moves to look for allies, negotiate drafts, or work on documents. They will make various speeches and motions in formal sessions, while negotiating, forming alliances, writing working papers, which are then to be corrected and formatted until they become draft resolutions, all taking place in informal sessions. Hence, the majority of the time during the MUN conference will be spent in informal sessions. Within these sessions, the dais will set deadlines for handing in working papers, edit these and provide feedback which can be included by the delegates. In addition, mergers of working papers might occur if the content of two or more working papers overlaps.

The conference schedule entails breaks and usually leaves room for social activities in the evening where the students can network. These additional activities are crucial for building friendships and social interaction, as delegates must stay in character during formal and informal sessions and remain strictly professional and diplomatic during these sessions.

At some point, when there are various working papers or draft resolutions on the floor, the speakers list and the debate will be closed. The committee will then move into the voting procedure and either accept the draft resolutions to become resolutions or reject them. If there is more than one topic, the next topic will be started after the voting procedure. When all topics are discussed or when the time for the MUN is up, the committee session will be adjourned until the next year. The official end of the MUN is then the closing ceremony which commonly includes speeches by faculty members or other relevant persons. Furthermore, some conferences hand out awards for the best speech, the best position paper, or other categories. Lastly, the adopted resolutions might be made accessible publicly for everyone interested in reading them.

ROLES AT MUN

Every MUN entails different roles. However, some vital ones are usually represented at each MUN. These are (based on Krein 2023, pp. 21–30):

- *Dais*: The dais at a MUN consists of a chair and one or two rapporteur(s). They guide, moderate, and facilitate the committee through the formal sessions and enforce the rules of procedure whereby the rapporteur(s) assist the chair. The decisions of the dais may be questioned or challenged by delegates through several types of motions. The dais provides advice to the delegates, updates the speakers list, acts as a contact and information point, and is responsible for managing the time during the whole conference and ensuring decorum is maintained during the conference. The dais is often played by experienced former participants of MUN conferences.
- *Delegate*: A student who represents a member state at a MUN conference. They are either assigned or can choose a member state in a committee. Delegates prepare a position paper based on their own research on their member state's position on the topic(s) before the committee prior to the conference. During the MUN, they participate in formal and informal sessions, deliver speeches, negotiate, collaborate, work on working papers with their fellow delegates, and vote on resolutions.
- *Faculty advisor/attendee*: Most often, faculty members of the university or higher education institution the students attend accompany the students to the conference. They usually provide support and guidance before, during and after a conference; often, they also organise travel and accommodation as well as the preparation for the MUN in the form of a course or seminars. They are present during the MUN as a contact person and to safeguard their students. Faculty advisors are usually allowed to enter and leave the committee room at all times. In some conferences, they participate in feedback sessions and act as an intermediary between their students and the secretariat.
- *Head delegate*: A student participating as a delegate in a MUN who takes additional responsibilities for his/her delegation. They are either appointed or elected and act as a link between the delegates, the faculty advisor, staff, dais, and the secretariat. Often these students have previous MUN experience and can thus support their fellow delegates. However, this role is mostly represented at bigger conferences.
- *Secretariat*: Organises a MUN conference and often consists of university staff and/or students. The secretariat is responsible for logistics, the conference programme, a cultural programme (if necessary) as well as all administrative and technical issues. Depending on the size of the conference, the

organisational team may entail one or several main coordinators and other members who have different responsibilities, like taking care of the technical equipment, the internal and external communication, or the budget.

MODES OF MUN PREPARATION

To prepare for a MUN, participants not only need to know about structures, processes and negotiations going on in the UN, but must also be well informed about the topics at hand and the position and interests of their represented member state. Four different options can be used for preparation: the compulsory integration of MUN in the curriculum of a university, participation on an optional selectional or selective basis, the offer of MUN on a voluntary and extracurricular basis for students, and (M)UN clubs (Krein 2023, pp. 4–7). However, Krein (2023, p. 7) points out that participation in MUN is "often not (fully) 'institutionalized', and vital top-down support for students wishing to take part in MUN is lacking." Furthermore, students may also participate on an individual basis and are thus responsible for their own preparation. What should be kept in mind is that unexpected international events might have an impact on MUN preparation and participation. When the pandemic (see also Chapter 4) put limits on face-to-face interactions, simulations added digital diplomacy or hybrid diplomacy (Bjola and Manor 2022) to complement physical interactions, which expanded opportunities to include more participants from around the world.

UN clubs, which are usually self-organised by students, allow students to work collaboratively as a team and co-create their own experiences at the university. They can complement the classroom curriculum or offer formal co-curricular opportunities (Richardson 2023). Typically, club members, without the benefits of the scaffolding of International Relations content of their Political Science counterparts, receive the required knowledge of IOs and their internal procedures needed for successful MUN participation. UN clubs offer peer-to-peer interaction (see also Chapter 4), leadership skills, and serve as important supplements to traditional classroom teaching. In addition, they provide students with opportunities to pick up soft skills such as giving public presentations, developing creative and critical thinking abilities, and gaining cross-cultural understandings.

Clubs and classes have their own value in practising international diplomacy and gaining greater understanding of International Affairs. Traditional International Relations courses integrated with simulations (Hazleton and Jacob 1983) provide students with the practical policy-making experience of diplomats in formal institutional settings. Student-led UN clubs allow students from a variety of disciplinary backgrounds to participate in UN simulations and hence bring their specific disciplinary expertise which is crucial to grasping the complex issues addressed by the UN. However, (M)UN club might be limited in their activities through a lack of understanding of key political concepts such as power and representation, conflict and cooperation needed to provide fellow students with the crucial insights of decision-making processes at the UN. Nevertheless, the combination of clubs and classes might offer an interesting dynamic to UN simulations. It is, however, a condition that students are decided and willing to form a UN club. Experience with the PATRAPO project suggests that student club culture is much more pronounced and established in Canada or the USA than in Europe.

To conclude, in an era marked by complex global challenges and increasing political polarisation, MUN offers an urgently needed, hands-on approach to education – one that not only equips students with essential skills in diplomacy, leadership, and critical thinking, but also fosters a deeper understanding of multilateral cooperation, making it an indispensable tool for preparing the next generation of global citizens and decision-makers.

REFERENCES

Baker, Ann C./Jensen, Patricia J./Kolb, David A. (2002). Conversational Learning. An Experiential Approach to Knowledge Creation. Westport, Connecticut, Quorum Books.

Barnett, Michael N./Finnemore, Martha (2004). Rules for the World. International Organizations in Global Politics. Ithaca, NY, Cornell University Press.

Barston, Ronald P. (2013). Modern Diplomacy. 4th ed. London/New York, Routledge Taylor & Francis Group.

Bjola, Corneliu/Manor, Ilan (2022). The Rise of Hybrid Diplomacy: From Digital Adaptation to Digital Adoption. International Affairs 98 (2), 471–491. https://doi.org/10.1093/ia/iiac005

Calossi, Enrico/Coticchia, Fabrizio (2018). Students' Knowledge and Perceptions of International Relations and the "Model United Nations": An Empirical Analysis. Acta Politica 53 (3), 409–428. https://doi.org/10.1057/s41269-017-0058-9

Chasek, Pamela S. (2005). Power Politics, Diplomacy and Role Playing: Simulating the UN Security Council's Response to Terrorism. International Studies Perspectives 6 (1), 1–19. https://doi.org/10.1111/j.1528-3577.2005.00190.x

Coker, Jeffrey Scott/Porter, Desiree Jasmine (2015). Maximizing Experiential Learning for Student Success. Change: The Magazine of Higher Learning 47 (1), 66–72. https://doi.org/10.1080/00091383.2015.996101

Fortin, Jacon C. (2012). Role-Playing and Simulation Based Learning in Higher Education: Case Study in Model United Nations. Dissertation. The Honors Program; Senior Capstone Project. Bryant University. Available online at https://digitalcommons.bryant.edu/honors_history/15/ (accessed 7/2/2025).

Frederking, Brian (2005). Simulations and Student Learning. Journal of Political Science Education 1 (3), 385–393. https://doi.org/10.1080/15512160500261236

Gaudiosi, Rebecca W./Roesch, Jimena Leiva/Ye-Min, Wu (2019). Negotiating at the United Nations. A Practitioner's Guide. Milton, Routledge.

Haas, Ernst B. (1990). When Knowledge is Power: Three Models of Change in International Organizations. Berkeley, California, University of California Press.

Hammond, Augustine/Albert, Craig Douglas (2020). Learning by Experiencing: Improving Student Learning Through a Model United Nations Simulation. Journal of Political Science Education 16 (4), 441–458. https://doi.org/10.1080/15512169.2018.1548967

Hazleton, William A./Jacob, James E. (1983). Simulating International Diplomacy: The National Model United Nations Experience. Teaching Political Science 10 (2), 89–99. https://doi.org/10.1080/00922013.1983.9942346

Heater, Derek/Berridge, G. R. (1993). Crises and Diplomacy. In: Derek Heater (Ed.). Introduction to International Politics. London, Palgrave Macmillan, 44–61.

Jesuit, David K./Endless, Brian (2018). Model United Nations and Experiential Learning: An Assessment of Changes in Knowledge and Attitudes. Journal of Social Studies Education Research 9 (4), 198–213. Available online at https://jsser.org/index.php/jsser/article/view/346 (accessed 7/11/2023).

Jones, Rebecca/Bursens, Peter (2015). The Effects of Active Learning Environments: How Simulations Trigger Affective Learning. European Political Science 14 (3), 254–265. https://doi.org/10.1057/eps.2015.22

Krein, Anna-Theresia (2023). Model United Nations. A Practical Guide. Cham, Springer.

Leib, Julia/Ruppel, Samantha (2019). Studentische Lerneffekte in Simulationen der Vereinten Nationen. Zeitschrift für Friedens- und Konfliktforschung 8 (1), 99–111. https://doi.org/10.1007/s42597-019-00007-y

Muldoon, James P. (1995). The Model United Nations Revisited. Simulation & Gaming 26 (1), 27–35. https://doi.org/10.1177/1046878195261003

National Model United Nations (2024). Mission & History. Available online at https://www.nmun.org/about-nmun/mission-and-history.html (accessed 4/17/2024).

Obendorf, Simon/Randerson, Claire (2012). The Model United Nations Simulation and the Student as Producer Agenda. Enhancing Learning in the Social Sciences 4 (3), 1–15. https://doi.org/10.11120/elss.2012.04030007

Pouliot, Vincent (2016). Hierarchy in Practice: Multilateral Diplomacy and the Governance of International Security. European Journal of International Security 1 (1), 5–26. https://doi.org/10.1017/eis.2015.4

Richardson, Brock (2023). Leadership Lost. Student Clubs Are Struggling in the Pandemic's Wake. Universities Can Help Them Back On Their Feet. Available online at https://www.universityaffairs.ca/opinion/in-my-opinion/leadership-lost/ (accessed 7/11/2023).

Stone, Randall W. (2011). A Theory of International Organization. In: Randall W. Stone (Ed.). Controlling Institutions. Cambridge University Press, 11–32.

Taylor, Kirsten (2013). Simulations Inside and Outside the IR Classroom: A Comparative Analysis. International Studies Perspectives 14 (2), 134–149. https://doi.org/10.1111/j.1528-3585.2012.00477.x

United Nations (2023). From Model UN to the Real UN. Available online at https://www.un.org/en/model-united-nations/model-un-real-un (accessed 7/26/2023).

United Nations (2024). THE Real United Nations. Available online at https://www.un.org/en/mun/article/real-united-nations.

United Nations Association of the USA (2025). Model UN in the Palm of your Hand. https://unausa.org/programs/model-un/ (accessed 11/7/2025).

3. What is Model European Union?

Alexandru Balas

In the United States of America (USA) where I teach university students, I like to describe Model European Union (MEU) as a Model United Nations (MUN), except with fewer countries, with easier rules of procedure and, for pedagogical purposes, with an increased chance for student engagement given the smaller number of roles. MEU[1] is an experiential learning opportunity for students at both high school and university level to improve their negotiation skills while learning about the decision-making processes and major agenda items of the European Union (EU). Students are assigned a specific role (e.g. the head of government, a minister of foreign affairs or environment, a European Commission commissioner, a Member of the European Parliament (MEP), etc.) within a specific setting of the EU institutions (European Council, various settings of the Council of the EU, European Parliament etc.) and are asked to prepare to embody that particular role in a role play negotiation on a topic of discussion within the EU. This type of exercise is fun for the students and remains one of the most important memories in the students' academic careers in which they learn about the EU and EU policies.

While it may seem obvious that students studying in the EU should learn about the EU through Model EU role play simulations, the question is why students in other parts of the world, from Canada to Argentina and Indonesia, should care about the EU, and how can professors in these non-EU countries convince students of the importance of the EU for their daily lives? But, even within the EU, how many EU students/citizens have actually learned about the EU through such simulations which are meant to reflect the day-to-day negotiations within the EU institutions? This chapter aims to showcase the value of MEU role play simulations at the high school and university level and provide some lessons learned about how best to organise such MEU events.

1 There are many MEU conferences around the world. The website of the Administration Team of the EU Delegation to the United States (2022) has a sample of such MEU conferences organised in the United States of America.

WHY THE EUROPEAN UNION MATTERS FOR STUDENTS' LIVES?

Showing the regulatory power of the EU on students' everyday lives, while providing specific examples based on the location where the MEU is organised, can help this process of showcasing the value of the EU. A question such as "What is the impact of the EU in my daily life?" often sparks students' interest in both EU and non-EU countries. The fact that a government and system of government other than the students' national government can impact students' daily lives directly runs against almost everything they have ever been taught until that point. One strategy is to focus on the role of the EU, giving multiple specific examples. This approach has been well articulated by Anu Bradford (2020) in her article and subsequent book "*The Brussels Effect*" about the powerful positive impact of the EU on Americans' lives:

> Few Americans are aware that EU regulations determine the makeup they apply in the morning, the cereal they eat for breakfast, the software they use on their computer, and the privacy settings they adjust on their Facebook page. And that's just before 8:30 AM. The EU also sets the rules governing the interoffice phone directory they use to call a co-worker. EU regulations dictate what kind of air conditioners Americans use to cool their homes, and why their children no longer find soft plastic toys in their McDonald's Happy Meals. (Bradford 2020, p. 3)

Educators can consider providing other examples of products that are heavily regulated at the global level, owing to the EU's norm-setting standards, which are particularly relevant to their students. For example, consider the area of agricultural products. Students who live in or come from an agricultural background may be intrigued to find out that their farms need to produce goods using EU regulations rather than their country's regulations, because dairy farmers want to sell their produce on the European market. This not only impacts the farms' export operations, but the product that gets sold in their local grocery store, thus making the EU relevant in their daily lives. One role play simulation for bringing this point home focuses on chocolate, something a large number of European and non-European people enjoy: "*The European Chocolate Directive*" (Vertegenwoordiging in Nederland van de Europese Commissie 2025). Deciding what "chocolate" actually means according to the EU, teaches students about EU processes while using a daily life product. Other examples of EU regulations impacting students' daily lives around the world could be used as the topic of the MEU, such as the General Data Protection Regulation (GDPR), the legislation on artificial intelligence (AI), rules about air travel to and within the EU, or the ways in which the EU free trade agreements (FTAs) with so many countries and regions around the world impact those students' lives.

Second, in addition to bringing the EU to life through students' daily experiences, tying the EU to study abroad opportunities is another way to showcase the value of the EU: getting to know which institution governs most of the laws in the EU country a student is going to. For instance, 1.66 million students were studying abroad in the EU in 2022 (Eurostat 2022). According to data from the National Association of Foreign Student Advisers: Association of International Educators (NAFSA 2025), from the 2018–2019 to the 2022–2023 academic years, more than 63 per cent of all American students going to study abroad went to Europe (most of them, to EU member-states). Europe is the most desirable destination for students seeking to study abroad, given the many opportunities available to study in English as large numbers of universities now have programmes fully in English, and in major cosmopolitan metropolises and countries perceived as safe. Promoting MEU opportunities to this audience would get them to learn about the places they are going to study and live in, or to remember fondly the time spent in Europe.

Third, promoting the study of the EU as an experiment in regional integration is one way to promote the study of the EU beyond EU-focused courses. MEU events could extend knowledge about the EU through role play simulations to other fields such as Environmental Studies, Agricultural Studies, Economics, Health, or Education. The EU as a regional integration experiment could draw comparisons with other similar processes (East Africa in the 1970s, West Africa and East Africa currently through, e.g. ECOWAS, as well as the process taking place in South-East Asia, e.g. ASEAN, as well as in Central and South America, e.g. Mercosur etc.). Teaching the EU in a course on International Organisations (IOs) can show how the EU is much more than an IO by focusing on its supra-national governance structures. Finally, the EU can also be promoted in International Negotiation courses for multilateral negotiations and in Conflict Resolution/Peace Studies courses as peace is at the heart of the EU (see Chapter 7).

After providing suggestions about how the EU could be brought to life for students to get them interested in partaking in MEU role play simulations, next I want to take a look at what previous researchers who analysed the use of MEU as a teaching tool have to say.

LITERATURE REVIEW

Teachers have praised the benefits of using role play simulations for decades (Guetzkow and Jensen 1966; Verba 1964; Zuckerman and Horn 1973; see also the discussion in Chapters 2, 4 and 5). Simulation games are seen as providing students with an alternative way of learning by allowing for active engagement with the material, their learning process, and their classmates than typical classroom study. The simulation creates a memorable experience; students continue to reflect on the processes that took place and the ideas that were developed for days or even weeks following the end of the exercise.[2] But what does the existing research on the use of MEU experiential learning exercises tell us about the value of MEU as a teaching tool? There is some substantial body of research on the use of EU simulations (Bobot and Goergen 2010; Galatas 2006; Kaunert 2009; Van Dyke et al. 2000; Zeff 2003). This line of research was spearheaded by Gretchen Van Dyke et al. (2000), with her study of one of the three oldest MEU multi-university conferences in the USA (the Mid-Atlantic Model EU).[3] Van Dyke et al. found that the value for the students was so much more than just learning specifics about the EU, but the interactional aspects of the event:

> Students have been pleased especially with the opportunity to meet other students, to interact with a wide variety of people with different backgrounds, to demonstrate and employ many of the skills and/or theories they have learned in the classroom, and to experience, as close as possible, the "real world" of politics. In general, the students enjoy the experience, have fun, get to know faculty and peers, and [love] the drama of being in Washington, D.C., instead of the classroom. (Van Dyke et al. 2000, p. 154)

Beyond the focus on students, Van Dyke et al. reported that this type of experiential learning was also beneficial for the faculty (tools for bridging the gap between theory and practice) and for the participating departments and institutions as a whole (departments standing out positively for engaging students in hands-on activities and universities promoting these experiential learning exercises to recruit future students). A study by Galatas (2006) examined the use of a MEU Council of the EU simulation in an upper-division political science course in Georgia, USA, spread over three class sessions. Galatas found that students understood EU policy-making and intergovernmentalism better and were very much in favour of including simulations as a component of the course in the future. The fact that students engaged in extra-classroom negotiations in between the official classroom MEU negotiations suggested to Galatas that "[...] students [...] see the simulation as an opportunity to engage in learning" (Galatas 2006, p. 151).

In the same vein, a 2008 study by Jones (2008) analysed one instance of a multi-university MEU conference, the 2007 Eurosim, and found a significant

---

2 For a discussion of educators' claims regarding simulation, and a meta-review of the research surrounding this topic, see Druckman and Ebner (2013).

3 The Mid-Atlantic MEU started in 1993. There was a MEU started by five universities in New York in 1988 which has branched as of 2025 into three MEU annual conferences (Global MEU, Eurosim, and SUNY MEU), and there is also the Midwest MEU started in 1993.

increase in students' affective learning, focused on emotions, values, feelings, and attitudes in relation to learning, rather than knowledge and skills. In addition, just like with Van Dyke's study, students also reported learning other skills beyond the EU:

> It appears that students do gain more than just cognitive learning from simulations and that they appreciate the opportunity to learn and to practice negotiating skills, research skills, and speaking skills, as well as the opportunity to meet new people, not only from their own universities but from other schools and countries as well. (Jones 2008, p. 416)

This focus on the "beyond the EU knowledge" skills is also highlighted by Brunazzo and Settembri (2015, p. 12):

> [...] simulations may be useful in equipping students not only with specific knowledge about the EU but also with a number of "higher order" skills like comprehension of the complexity of the "real" world.

Other research (Clark et al. 2017; Sobisch et al. 2018) on the topic of the impact of MEU role play simulations on students' learning shows that there is no significant improvement in students' learning when comparing simulations with traditional methods, but that the simulations promote information acquisition. Rather, the added value of simulations is to be found in their ability to stimulate student engagement with the subject of EU politics (Sobisch et al. 2018, p. 32). On the other hand, Jones (2018, p. 60) reported that students participating in MEU simulations "[...] understand the workings of the EU far more clearly than they did prior to participating in the simulation [...]", providing some evidence to the hypothesis that knowledge about the EU is a by-product of these role play simulations. In addition, Jones (2018) points out that students really enjoy the leadership, negotiation, and research skills they gain through such experiences. Zeff's (2003, p. 273) study of three different MEU simulations held in a classroom environment during a semester also shows evidence for student learning, and similar to Galatas (2006), evidence of student engagement in learning: students were "[...] more actively engaged in learning the class material because they have to defend their countries' positions to the other participants." Muno and Prinz (2015, p. 384) provide support that "[...] [s]ubject specific knowledge about the EU is acquired, especially about the decision-making process of European legislation, but also knowledge about institutions and policies [...]" based on their study of the MEU in Mainz, Germany. But, "[...] [t]here is no real evidence that simulations are better in that sense [than traditional methods]" (Muno and Prinz 2015, p. 385). Most research on the impact of the MEU role play simulations provides ample evidence that "[...] the simulation game indeed left its imprint with the students

[...]" and that "[...] it is the simulation games' potential to arouse the curiosity for politics that can be considered as a strength of the method" (Wulk 2018, p. 141).

One other line of research which has not been studied as much is the one adopted by Rünz (2015), with the following research question: Do EU simulations influence European identity and political support of the EU? Rünz states

> [...] that MEU does have some small positive impact on European identity and support of the EU, but it is far from transforming these attitudes of MEU participants. (Rünz 2015, p. 276)

Overall, when considering both the knowledge of the EU and the other skills students gain through MEU simulations, such experiential learning exercises showcase useful pedagogical value.

A VARIETY OF MODEL EUROPEAN UNION MODELS

MEU events can take many forms and shapes. As Elias (2014, p. 416) points out:

> [...] simulations provide no guarantee that students will learn. For this to happen, careful consideration needs to be given to what it is students should be able to do upon completion of the simulation, how this learning can be shown, and what teachers can do to help students meet these expectations.

Like it is the case for MUNs (see Chapter 2, 12 and 13), organisers (who could be instructors, professors, administrators, student body leaders, members of the diplomatic corps, or people in many other roles) can organise MEU events in a classroom environment, as a university-wide conference, as a conference with participants from across a city or a region, or as a national or international conference. MEUs can be stand-alone events or become yearly activities. MEU events can be held in person or online (synchronously, asynchronously or a combination); in one extended session, or over many shorter meetings. The organisation procedure for each model is different, considering a wide variety of factors (see Chapters 12 and 13).

The goals of why a Model EU is organised should drive the activity's set-up process. Simon Usherwood (2014, p. 53) makes the case that

> [...] for a successful simulation there must be: learning objectives clear to all participants; alignment between those objectives, game play and assessment; and a meaningful feedback process.

An MEU event used as a way to increase interest in the EU amongst freshmen and sophomore students would be organised differently than one used to assess advanced undergraduate or graduate students' knowledge of specific EU policies or institutional processes, or one aiming to improve diplomatic, leadership, presentation, public speaking, or negotiation skills. Regardless of the format chosen, the preparation for organising an MEU event should begin well in advance. For example, for an MEU event held within a university course, preparation should begin during the semester preceding the course. For larger-scale multi-university MEU national or international conferences, preparation should begin about seven to nine months in advance.

Some of the typical formats of MEU events and guidelines for their organisation include: a) MEU event in a high school or university classroom setting; b) MEU as an institution-wide conference (high school or university-wide); c) MEU as a multi-institution city/regional conference; and d) MEU as a multi-institution national/international conference. If you consider running an MEU event in any of the settings mentioned above, here are some considerations: preparation aspects, the role of the instructors during the simulation, the topic(s) of the simulation, group size, students' preparation, rules of procedure, time concerns, debriefing, and student assessment (on these considerations see also Chapters 12 and 13).

MEU PREPARATION ASPECTS

The MEU settings mentioned above (classroom, institution-wide, city/regional-wide, national/international) use basically the same preparation aspects, with more items being added as the simulations become larger and more complex (see also Chapters 12 and 13):

1. In a classroom setting, you should start the preparation approximately four months in advance. Some of the things to consider in the process of organising a MEU include: a) thinking about matching your MEU goals to your class learning objectives; b) taking your institution's goals into account (if your institution values such experiential learning techniques or not); c) envisioning how the simulation will run in actual time; d) identifying where the MEU fits in the syllabus; e) choosing a specific simulation design (one session, multiple sessions, entire semester; what specific institution(s) you will focus on etc.); f) identifying how you plan to prepare the students to conduct the role play simulation exercise(s); g) thinking about how and to whom you assign roles; h) choosing how you will collect feedback after the simulation; i) creating the assignments you plan to use which are tied to the simulation – preparatory assignments, reflection assignments and so on; and j) planning the logistics of the simulation (how

is the room going to be set up for the simulation, what rules of engagement you plan to use, any touches of reality you plan to use – flags etc.).

2. For an MEU as an institution-wide conference, the preparation should start four to six months in advance, and attention should also be paid to the recruitment of participants and the preparatory training of participants (organising in-person or webinar meetings with participants from across campus and disciplines who have different levels of knowledge about the EU). The specific room(s) and room set-up in which the conference is to be organised should be identified. A budget should also be included. The funding for organising any MEU conferences larger than in a classroom setting could be obtained from local university funds (offices promoting internationalisation and/or experiential learning, the departments of the organising instructors, as well as offices of Deans, Provost, and President) or through a conference registration fee for larger city/regional, national, and international MEUs. Quite often, conference registration fees are also paid fully or partially by the students' universities through the same offices mentioned above.
3. For an MEU as a regional conference, the preparation should start six to eight months in advance, and the conference should take place over at least two days. Identifying participating institutions, reaching out to instructors at those institutions to recruit students to participate in the MEU, identifying a large enough venue for such an endeavour, recruiting a group of interns to help with the organisation of the event, and inviting guest speakers from the EU Delegation, nearby EU diplomatic offices, or professors with expertise on the EU, are additional aspects that need to be addressed as compared with the smaller versions of MEUs.
4. Finally, the most complex MEU could be organised as multi-university national or international conferences. For these MEU experiences, organisation should start seven to nine months in advance. In addition to aspects mentioned above, time needs to be dedicated to identifying accommodation venues, flight information and airport pick-up, and adding MEU-related activities in the evenings and throughout the three to five days of the MEU conference: organising visits/briefings to the EU Delegation in your country (if feasible, given location), to EU member states' embassies or consulates, organising other EU-related events in the evenings – a European party in which participants bring products to share from the country they represent at the MEU conference; screen a European film, visit an EU-related museum or site, and so on.

Overall, as you can see, MEUs are very flexible. They can last anywhere from an hour and half to five days, can have as little as ten students and as many as 150 students participating, one council or four to five councils running parallel at the same time, within a classroom or involving 20+ universities. If you have a large group with multiple individuals assigned to the same role (e.g. three students playing the head of government of each EU member state), an hour and a half simulation will not be enough time to allow all of them to have a meaningful experience. Instead, you should either consider organising multiple councils with one student per role or increase the time allotted to the simulation.

THE ROLE OF INSTRUCTORS DURING THE MODEL EU CONFERENCE

Instructors (university professors and/or high school teachers) are already burdened with many other roles and responsibilities, so why should we use role play simulations, which can add so much more work to our already busy schedules? The literature review evidence provides some insights into the pedagogical value for teaching and, maybe more importantly, student learning and engagement with the topic. However, if instructors were to organise such time-consuming activities as MEUs, they should either be remunerated extra or have this work count towards their portfolio evaluations. Decision-making administrators at educational institutions like to be able to showcase experiential learning opportunities like MEUs, which also come with added media exposure for such activities in the local/regional media and to potential donors.

Instructors, beyond the organiser(s), should definitely be involved for city/regional or national/international MEU conferences. For classroom or university-wide MEU conferences, only the main organiser is enough. Most of the work of the instructor takes place before the conference, making sure that their students are well prepared in terms of EU content and rules of procedure. During the conference, instructors should play as minimal a role as possible. If needed, they can explain procedural aspects and ensure that the negotiations are realistic and in accordance with EU policies. But these interventions should be kept to a minimum.

Instructors should not facilitate/manage the EU institution's meetings, but rather let the students facilitate the process themselves. If some content advice from instructors to students is needed, then it should be offered during the breaks or at the end of a session, rather than interrupting the simulation. Students might make mistakes, but they will learn from them and reflect on their conference experience. Choosing the right student-facilitators to play the presidency of the European Council and of the Council of the EU, the High Representative for Foreign and Security Affairs, European Commission, European Parliament and so on, is key to a successful student-run MEU role play simulation – just as it is key in a MUN (see Chapters 2, 4 and 12). Highly qualified students should play the roles of the country holding the rotating presidency of the EU, the president of the European Council, the European Commission, and/or similar key roles. The participants playing these roles will chair the meetings. They need to have some experience and exposure to facilitating dialogue in meetings and they should know the rules of procedure well. Such a student-led meeting also requires that the delegates for those EU member states who are most interested in the specific topics negotiated at the table be played by skilled students. Finally, you should think about students' background and language abilities. If you have students of Italian background or who can understand Polish, for example, you should consider assigning them to those roles, so that they can embrace the experience even more, and access information relevant for the MEU activity in those specific languages, too.

A student-led conference enables faculty advisors to organise faculty-specific sessions for themselves, while students negotiate in the various councils. Such sessions could be dedicated to presenting research on the EU, sharing best practices for teaching EU topics, creating faculty networks of cooperation for EU purposes (applying for joint grants from the EU, developing EU hubs in their university/city, developing EU-related events in their university/city etc.), and preparing future MEU events.

TOPIC OF SIMULATION, MATCHING TOPICS TO INSTITUTIONS, AND HOW "REAL" SHOULD THE SIMULATION BE

MEU events can focus on a wide range of topics as the EU discusses many issues. Some of the questions to consider when choosing topics for MEU events include: What topics would "sell" to the particular "audience" the organiser has in mind? Is the topic in the news? Would this group of students be able to relate to it? Dealing with topics that are close to real-life events gives participants the sense that they are dealing with the most crucial topics of their time, thus motivating them to do well.[4] On the other hand, there may be a desire to teach specific treaty negotiations or historical moments in the life of the EU and thus adopt a more historical approach to the MEU. Another option could be to develop a totally new topic, a fictional scenario or something likely to emerge in the future (e.g. Canada Applies for Membership to the EU, as created by Balas et al. (2024)). Of course, the organisers can choose topics of special interest to them, irrespective of what topics "sell" or are "hot" at that given moment in time.

Regardless of whether a MEU is based on current events, historical or set in the future, an MEU simulation always centres around a particular topic that is

---

[4] For more on this topic see Settembri and Brunazzo (2018).

to be discussed and decided by an EU institution. An issue, either pressing or routine, requires the decision-making attention of an EU institution, and MEU participants play the roles of the members of this institution, charged with deciding the issue. Which topic, though, and which institution are best for your MEU event? This is a bit complex as different considerations pertain, and each consideration affects others.

To get a sense of the initial complexity of these decisions, lets consider that certain topics might be best discussed in a particular institution. MEU event planners might not have any preferences as to the EU institution to be simulated but do want the event to focus on a particular topic. The choice of topic will, in turn, affect the choice of suitable institutions to set the simulation in. Conversely, MEU event planners might wish to have participants gain familiarity with a particular EU decision-making institution (see Chapter 7 on the EU's institutions). Preferring this institution will affect the range of suitable topics to consider. MEU event planners might have no substantive or institutional preferences at all, but they anticipate having a large group of participants, or conversely – a very small group. These elements will inform their choice between institutions. While deciding the topic and appropriate EU institution, it is best to begin by considering whether any of these are predetermined and inflexible, for example, the event takes place as part of a course focusing on a particular substantive topic (e.g. EU's Environmental Policy); or, the event is funded with the express purpose of simulating a specific EU institution. If so, use that rigid element as your anchor, and move on to make other choices that support it best.

For some of the MEU events, the organisers can pick "off the shelf" MEU role play simulations, as, for example, those provided by the EU Delegation in Washington, D.C.,[5] on topics such as European Agenda on Migration, Counter-Terrorism, negotiating an FTA with a quasi-fictional large trading partner of the EU called Tradeland, Climate Change and Security Implications, EU Digital Policy and Artificial Intelligence, or EU-U.S. Trade and Technology. There are other "off the shelf" MEU simulations out there including the famous one about the chocolate directive mentioned above, and analysed by Fink (2015), as well as simulations on the topics of European Energy Union, Common Agricultural Policy, European Defence Union, European Development Aid, EU Policy on Gender Equality, EU Policy to Combat Disinformation and False Media, European Digital Single Market, Migration and Asylum Policy, EU Arctic Policy, EU Addressing Issues Involving Russia, Ukraine, and the Caucasus, Continuing to Improve Relations with EU's Eastern Partnership, EU-China FTA, and "Global Europe? Deciding Canada's Membership Application to the

[5] See Administration Team of the EU Delegation to the United States (2022).

EU". Using "off the shelf" simulations may be an excellent way for instructors who want to use an experiential learning exercise but do not have the experience of organising MEUs or do not want to spend too much time preparing one from scratch. This solution is good for in-class or university-wide events. For larger events, city/region-wide or national/international conferences, organisers may choose to work with the student presidency teams to create an agenda topic from scratch. Chapters 9 and 11 present some sample cases and material on the workings of EU politics that can be illustrative.

CONSIDERING GROUP SIZE IN CHOICE OF SIMULATION TOPIC/INSTITUTION

Each EU institution simulation has a certain number of "natural" players – corresponding to the number of people who fill the primary representative roles in the real-world institutions. A simulation must not have the precise number of participants as the real-world institution's number of representatives. However, the closer the number of participants is to that institution's natural player number, the closer the similarity between the simulation and the institution's proceedings. If there are odd numbers of students (e.g. 32 students for a European Council meeting), then organisers should assign two students for those roles that require the most work (e.g. President of the European Council, presidency of the European Commission, EU member state which has one of the most important roles for the specific topic under discussion etc.). If two or more students are assigned per role then the organisers should clarify that students should take turns negotiating on behalf of their assigned countries during the formal and informal MEU negotiations.

There are thus 30 "natural" players in a European Council simulation, 29 "natural" players in a Council of the EU simulation, and 720 "natural" players in a simulation of the European Parliament. Clearly, all other things being equal, this makes the first two institutions a better choice for conducting MEUs with class-size groups and leaves the European Parliament as the go-to choice for massive simulations involving hundreds of participants and multiple instructors all engaging in the same activity together. For such massive MEUs, there will have to be a large number of students (seven to ten students) assigned to each political grouping, and this should mirror the proportions political groupings have in the European Parliament. Another option for large-scale MEUs is to have multiple Councils of the EU running in parallel (e.g. Foreign Affairs; Environmental; Transport, Telecommunications, and Energy; and Economic and Financial Affairs).

TOPIC-INTRODUCTION FOR MEU SIMULATIONS

Once you have selected the institution to be simulated and the topic, you need to choose a simulation-introduction format: How are participants in your simulation to receive the information they need in order to participate in the simulation? How do they learn about the issues under consideration, and their country's positions on them?

There are four primary paths to introducing the topics:

1. *Scenario-based simulations*: Participants are provided with a background story: the events leading up to the Council focusing on this topic (previous directives or policy decisions of the EU institutions), and the scope of the conclusion (i.e. the negotiated agreement) the institution seeks to achieve. In simulations using this design, it is common to provide the same background information to all participants, but you can also provide individualised background material suited to each country or each group of countries, to encourage participants to view the situation primarily from their own country's point of view. In such simulations, you can create any "reality" you like to serve as the background for the discussions, add fictional elements to the current reality, move the simulation to ten years in the future, or anything else.
2. *Decision-based simulations*: Organisers provide no background narrative, but rather the actual text of a decision, declaration, or legislation that the presidency has asked the council to discuss and decide. The focus will be largely on the text students are provided with.
3. *Hybrid simulations*: Students receive both a background narrative and a proposed decision.
4. *Participant-generated simulations*: Students receive only the most basic information about the topic, generally giving them only a subject matter area and perhaps a few lines of guidance regarding possible issues. Participants conduct their own research and decide what the meeting will focus on. This is how MUNs are usually prepared (Chapters 2 and 12).

PROVIDING INFORMATION TO THE MEU STUDENTS

Each student in the simulation will require appropriate information allowing them to plan and act in their roles in a similar way to those of the real EU officials they are supposed to embody. Below are several options for how much information organisers could provide participants, ranging from not much to a lot. The less information is provided, the more time organisers need to provide for students' self-preparation.

- *Option 1:* Provide students with the name of the role they are playing (e.g. providing a student a label identifying them as the Chancellor of Germany) and the topic under discussion (e.g. by presenting them with the draft decision, or with a short description). For example: "This Council is meeting to decide the EU policy regarding protection of fisheries off the coast of EU member states." Students should research by themselves their country's positions, interests, goals, and potential allies and opponents from amongst the EU member states. Again, this is the way MUNs are usually prepared (see Chapters 2 and 12).
- *Option 2:* Provide students with some general background information on the topic under discussion, and the parameters of what the final decision should contain (usually, one to three pages of material).
- *Option 3:* In addition to such general information as mentioned in Option 2, provide each participant with private information, for their eyes only. In it, sketch out their country's main positions, interests, and goals.
- *Option 4:* In addition to general and private information mentioned in Options 1 through 3, guide each party as to their potential allies or opponents so that they can identify which EU member states are likely to be aligned with their views or opposed to them.

It is a good idea to provide students with maps or documents that will help them to participate in the simulation, especially if they have never participated in role play simulations or lack the knowledge on the specific topic discussed during the meeting. In any case, organisers should guide students to gather more information about their assigned country, role, and topic from EU sources, governmental sources for their assigned country, newspapers and magazines from their assigned EU member state (if possible in English or a language the specific student(s) can understand), European and global newspapers, and magazines which cover the topic under discussion in the council meeting. In addition, sources on the procedure/rules of engagement of the specific council should be made available to the students, and an explanation of the voting system adopted for each council (consensus, qualified majority voting, simple majority etc.) needs to be provided to the participants, along with sources on "Euro-jargon"[6] (e.g. Copenhagen criteria, Schengen, Lisbon, Dublin, Frontex, Euro, subsidiarity, etc.).

---

[6] For an example see BBC (2016).

MEU RULES OF PROCEDURE

One of the most difficult aspects of MEU events is determining the rules of procedure to be used during the event. Many students have been exposed to MUNs before the MEU and have internalised the use of the MUN's very strict "motions"-oriented rules of procedure (see Chapters 12 to 14). Time to prepare the students well regarding the rules of procedure should be allocated before the MEU event, to make sure everyone (students playing the presidency roles and thus facilitating the discussions, and the other students participating) understands how the whole MEU process is supposed to take place.

The rules of procedure of EU institutions are simpler than those of the United Nations (UN) since MEUs do not require motions and a specialised procedural language, and thus the rules of procedure of MEUs should reflect that and be much simpler than those of MUNs. Some MEU organisers still prefer to use Robert's Rules of Order (Robert 2020) even though these are not used by the EU. I prefer to stick as close as possible to the reality, by using the rules of procedure of the EU.[7] Thus, I recommend the use of formal (structured) and informal (unstructured) negotiation meetings with the chairs having the ability to set up time limits. I use the recommendation of the EU of speeches not exceeding two minutes for the opening round, and after that the chairs can decide if they want shorter interventions. The focus of the EU rules of procedure is on dialogue-facilitation, rather than the specifics of procedure like MUN, and thus student-facilitators are advised to allow for as much dialogue as possible, either at the table (formal) or in the hallways (informal).

TIME REQUIREMENTS

The time required to conduct an MEU event can be broken down into three parts:

- *Preparation time:* This will depend on the depth of preparation expected by the organisers and how much research the students are required to do. If full guidebooks with specific individualised roles are assigned, then the preparation time could be shortened. If only the "bare-bones" of a simulation are provided and/or the topic is particularly technical or difficult, more preparation time is required.
- *Simulation time:* To conduct a full simulation, at the very least, one hour and 30 minutes is required. This can be expanded to three to five days, such

[7] See European Union (2022).

as when a simulation is conducted in the framework of an MEU national/international conference.

- *Debrief time:* This period is essential to actually have the students learn from the experience. This period can range from a 45-minute discussion to a debriefing process requiring several hours in different forums in larger events.

One of the worries that new organisers have is what happens if there is a fast agreement between the participating students (e.g. the event is planned for four hours and the students agree after 30 minutes on a specific unrealistic text), or if the students seem stuck way too long on a specific aspect without any solution in sight. Options to deal with such challenges exist, such as with the introduction of "breaking news"[8] which can either prolong the simulation or nudge the students past stumbling blocks. These "breaking news" should be thought of by the organisers in advance to see how this news could change the behaviour of the participants and then introduced during the role play simulation as needed. "Breaking news" could take the form of a simulated media announcement (e.g. a fictional event has happened which can alter the course of the EU negotiations), or of new instructions provided by specific EU member states' governments to their representatives.

Another worry is how to end the MEU simulation. If there is no obvious move towards an end of the simulation, the organisers should communicate with the students facilitating the council meeting(s), preferably via WhatsApp or electronic text (this is always a good option to have a back channel with the facilitator-students for any questions/challenges they may face), to remind them of the deadline. Voting should be held close to the end of the allotted time, and if certain points do not pass, then they could be tabled for future discussion on the agenda of the EU. For those points which have passed, a signing ceremony could be held as a way to celebrate the hard work that was done and provide a sort of ending for the MEU and transition towards the very important debriefing period.

With the start of the debriefing period, the instructor steps back into the centre of activity to guide the transition back from simulation to reality, and from the exercise into reflecting on what was done and learned throughout this experience. First, the instructor should tell students to take a deep breath and get out of their roles. This may be easier said than done, as students like to continue debating even after the simulation has ended. A small break could be

---

8 For more on this topic of "breaking news" in role play simulations, please see Ebner and Efron (2005).

useful to allow the students to get out of their roles and return to their normal selves.

DEBRIEFING GUIDE

Often overlooked, the debriefing guide is an integral part of the MEU role play simulation experience and a very important part for the students to reflect on what knowledge and skills they gained through this experience.[9] This is the same for MUN (see Chapter 12). Organisers are advised to develop their own debriefing guide depending on which learning objectives they have set up at the beginning of the activity. First, I recommend that the debriefing process starts with an in-person component. Brunazzo and Settembri (2015, p. 10) also recommend the same for MEU events:

> [...] feedback should be collective: the success of a simulation does not spring from individual performances but is a collective endeavour to be measured in terms of the quality of the outcome and of the negotiations that produced it. As a consequence, the feedback session focused on group dynamics rather than on single interventions.

Organisers should start this learning phase of the debriefing by explaining the goals of the debriefing. This is the students' opportunity to transform their experiences in the simulation into understanding and practical lessons to take away. Clearly defining the objectives of this session should help the process: for example, "Let's try to understand how the EU decision-making process actually happens" or "Let's aim to understand what skills you have improved and what skills you need improving". Starting with general questions about how students felt participating in such an experiential learning activity can help the transition from their assigned roles to the debriefing. First, students love to vent their frustrations or showcase their successes during the debriefing session. Next, the conversation could focus on a) understanding the decision-making processes of EU institutions; b) personal negotiation and conflict resolution skills; c) team and multi-party negotiation and conflict resolution skills; d) intra-EU conflict and collaboration processes; e) substantive knowledge on the specific topic of discussion; and f) research preparation, presentation, public speaking, and leadership skills. Specific questions should be developed by the organisers before the event takes place and used during the debriefing

[9] For specific questions to be used during the debriefing session please see Balas et al. (2023). For in-depth discussion of debriefing negotiation and dispute resolution simulation-games see Deason et al. (2013).

process. The debriefing process can be continued, as needed, through reflection papers.

STUDENT ASSESSMENTS

An important question when it comes to using simulations in a classroom setting is whether the simulation should be assessed or not. This is up to the instructors, but assessment is usually beneficial to ensure appropriate student participation. Quite often lately, if learning activities are not directly linked to grades, students do not seem to engage as much. If you choose to assess students on their simulation participation, then how should this be done? Which simulation components lend themselves to assessment? There is no one-size-fits-all solution and the MEU organisers should pick and choose what works for their purposes. An example of student assessments would include assessment to take place a) before the MEU activity; b) during the MEU activity; and c) after the MEU activity.

Before the MEU activity, students could be asked to write a short paper (preliminary brief) which would include their opening speech for the assigned role, and a detailed list of the role's positions, interests, goals, potential allies and opponents, and who they plan to contact during informal negotiations and specific negotiation strategies and tactics planned. Summaries of key points from assigned readings relevant to the EU role they are asked to embody and on the specific topic of negotiation in the EU institution could be asked from the students before the MEU event.

During the MEU event, organisers could rate active participation in both formal and informal settings (are the students conveying information like the EU official they are supposed to embody, are the students participating in drafting documents, are the students working "behind the scenes" to create coalitions? etc.). After the simulation, students should be assigned to write a reflection paper. This can include open-ended questions, or targeted questions to specific aspects of the whole experience such as an analysis of the negotiation process, the final agreement and how it satisfied the interests of their country, challenges they encountered during the preparation and negotiation process, whether the MEU simulation helped them to better understand the EU processes, any skills they think they improved through this experience, what they would change if they were to do this again and so on.

To sum up, this chapter explained what MEU events are, the research about the use of MEUs as a teaching tool and presented aspects that need to be considered when planning to use MEUs. MEU activities are a great experiential learning tool for instructors to increase student interest in the study of the EU and equip students with a plethora of skills such as negotiation, research, public speaking, presentation, leadership and many others. Empowering students to learn through different exercises such as MEUs rather than traditional pedagogical tools is a memorable experience for these students for many years after the event.

REFERENCES

Administration Team of the EU Delegation to the United States (2022). Educational Programs. Model EU. Live the EU Experience and Test Your Skills as an EU Negotiator! Available online at https://www.eeas.europa.eu/delegations/united-states-america/model-eu_en?s=253 (accessed 6/2/2025).

Balas, Alexandru/Ebner, Noam/Kotelis, Andreas (2023). Debriefing Guide. Available online at https://www.eeas.europa.eu/sites/default/files/documents/2024/5.%20Counter-Terrorism%20Debriefing%20Guide.pdf (accessed 5/12/2025).

Balas, Alexandru/Ebner, Noam/Kotelis, Andreas (2024). Going Global? Deciding Canada's Membership Application to the European Union. Available online at https://www.maxwell.syr.edu/research/program-for-the-advancement-research-on-conflict-collaboration/e-parcc/annual-teaching-case-simulation-competition (accessed 5/12/2025).

BBC (2016). EU Jargon: A-Z Guide to Brussels-Speak. Available online at https://www.bbc.com/news/world-europe-35920422 (accessed 5/12/2025).

Bobot, Lionel/Goergen, Andreas (2010). Case Study. Teaching European Negotiations: The EU Chocolate Directive Simulation. International Negotiation 15 (2), 301–323. https://doi.org/10.1163/157180610X506992.

Bradford, Anu (2020). The Brussels Effect: How the European Union Rules the World. Faculty Books (232). Available online at https://scholarship.law.columbia.edu/books/232 (accessed 5/12/2025).

Brunazzo, Marco/Settembri, Pierpaolo (2015). Teaching the European Union: A Simulation of Council's Negotiations. European Political Science 14 (1), 1–14. https://doi.org/10.1057/eps.2014.34

Clark, Nicholas/Van Dyke, Gretchen/Loedel, Peter/Scherpereel, John/Sobisch, Andreas (2017). EU Simulations and Engagement: Motivating Greater Interest in European Union Politics. Journal of Political Science Education 13 (2), 152–170. https://doi.org/10.1080/15512169.2016.1250009

Deason, Ellen E./Efron, Yael/Howell, Ranse William/Kaufman, Sanda/Lee, Joel/Press, Sharon (2013). Debriefing the Debrief. In: Christopher Honeyman/James R. Coben/Andrew Wei-Min Lee (Eds.). Educating Negotiators for a Connected World. Volume 4 in the Rethinking Negotiation Teaching Series. Saint Paul, MN, DRI Press, 301–332.

Druckman, Daniel/Ebner, Noam (2013). Games, Claims, and New Frames: Rethinking the Use of Simulation in Negotiation Education. Negotiation Journal 29 (1), 61–92. https://doi.org/10.1111/nejo.12005

Ebner, Noam/Efron, Yael (2005). Using Tomorrow's Headlines for Today's Training: Creating Pseudo-Reality in Conflict Resolution Simulation-Games. Negotiation Journal 21 (3), 377. Available online at https://papers.ssrn.com/sol3/papers.cfm?abstract_id=1292594 (accessed 5/12/2025).

Elias, Anwen (2014). Simulating the European Union: Reflections on Module Design. International Studies Perspectives 15 (4), 407–422. https://doi.org/10.1111/insp.12009

European Union (2022). Comments on the Council's Rules of Procedure. Luxembourg, Publications Office of the European Union.
Eurostat (2022). Statistics Explained. Learning Mobility Statistics. Available online at https://ec.europa.eu/eurostat/statistics-explained/index.php?title=Learning_mobility_statistics#:~:text=1.66%20million%20students%20from%20abroad,from%20abroad%20studying%20in%20Germany (accessed 6/2/2025).
Fink, Simon (2015). 36 Different Chocolate Directives: How Does the Setting Influence Negotiation Outcomes in an EU Simulation? European Political Science 14 (3), 241–253. https://doi.org/10.1057/eps.2015.21
Galatas, Steven E. (2006). A Simulation of the Council of the European Union: Assessment of the Impact on Student Learning. PS: Political Science & Politics 39 (1), 147–151. https://doi.org/10.1017/S104909650606029X
Guetzkow, Harold/Jensen, Lloyd (1966). Research Activities on Simulated International Processes. Background 9 (4), 261–274. https://doi.org/10.2307/3013650
Jones, Rebecca (2008). Evaluating a Cross-Continent EU Simulation. Journal of Political Science Education 4 (4), 404–434. https://doi.org/10.1080/15512160802413790
Jones, Rebecca (2018). What's the EU? Achieving Learning Outcomes and Preparing US Students for EuroSim. In: Peter Bursens/Vincent Donche/David Gijbels et al. (Eds.). Simulations of Decision-Making as Active Learning Tools. Design and Effects of Political Science Simulations. Cham, Springer International Publishing, 51–61.
Kaunert, Christian (2009). The European Union Simulation: From Problem-Based Learning (PBL) to Student Interest. European Political Science 8 (2), 254–265. https://doi.org/10.1057/EPS.2009.8
Muno, Wolfgang/Prinz, Lukas (2015). Teaching and Learning with EU Simulations: Evaluating Model European Union Mainz. Journal of Contemporary European Research 11 (4), 370–387. https://doi.org/10.30950/jcer.v11i4.681
NAFSA (2025). Trends in U.S. Study Abroad. Using Data from the Institute of International Education's Open Doors Report and the U.S. Department of Education's National Center for Education Statistics. Available online at https://www.nafsa.org/policy-and-advocacy/policy-resources/trends-us-study-abroad (accessed 5/12/2025).
Robert, Henry M., III/Honemann, Daniel H./Bachl, Thomas J./Seabold, Daniel E./Gerber, Shmuel (2020). Robert's Rules of Order Newly Revised. 12th ed. New York, PublicAffairs.
Rünz, Paul (2015). Beyond Teaching: Measuring the Effect of EU Simulations on European Identity and Support of the EU. European Political Science 14 (3), 266–278. https://doi.org/10.1057/eps.2015.23
Settembri, Pierpaolo/Brunazzo, Marco (2018). Mission Impossible? Verisimilitude in EU Simulations. In: Peter Bursens/Vincent Donche/David Gijbels et al. (Eds.). Simulations of Decision-Making as Active Learning Tools. Design and Effects of Political Science Simulations. Cham, Springer International Publishing, 63–76.
Sobisch, Andreas/Scherpereel, John/Loedel, Peter/Van Dyke, Gretchen/Clark, Nick (2018). The Costs and Benefits of Organizing a Multi-institutional Simulation on the European Union. In: Peter Bursens/Vincent Donche/David Gijbels et al. (Eds.). Simulations of Decision-Making as Active Learning Tools. Design and Effects of Political Science Simulations. Cham, Springer International Publishing, 21–34.
Usherwood, Simon (2014). Constructing Effective Simulations of the European Union for Teaching: Realising the Potential. European Political Science 13 (1), 53–60. https://doi.org/10.1057/eps.2013.29

Van Dyke, Gretchen/Declair, Edward G./Loedel, Peter H. (2000). Stimulating Simulations: Making the European Union a Classroom Reality. International Studies Perspectives 1 (2), 145–159. https://doi.org/10.1111/1528-3577.00014

Verba, Sidney (1964). Simulation, Reality, and Theory in International Relations. World Politics 16 (3), 490–519. https://doi.org/10.2307/2009585

Vertegenwoordiging in Nederland van de Europese Commissie (2025). Role-Play EU Decision-Making. Available online at https://netherlands.representation.ec.europa.eu/role-play-eu-decision-making_nl (accessed 5/12/2025).

Wulk, Sophie (2018). Simulating European Climate Policy Negotiations in a Teacher Training Seminar: Which Effects Can Be Detected? In: Peter Bursens/Vincent Donche/David Gijbels et al. (Eds.). Simulations of Decision-Making as Active Learning Tools. Design and Effects of Political Science Simulations. Cham, Springer International Publishing, 129–143.

Zeff, Eleanor, E. (2003). Negotiating in the European Council: A Model European Union Format for Individual Classes. International Studies Perspectives 4 (3), 265–274.

Zuckermann, David W./Horn, Robert E. (1973). The Guide to Simulations/Games for Education and Training. Lexington, Information Resources.

4. Teaching innovations and transnational blended learning: diplomacy and peer-to-peer experiential learning

Chaldeans Mensah

INTRODUCTION

The simulation of diplomatic processes within intergovernmental institutions or active learning of diplomacy is an important educational tool for students to understand not only the intricacies of highly formalistic procedures within such institutions but also the social practice of negotiations and building of consensus to address complex global problems (see also Chapters 2 and 5). Experiential learning exposes students to the institutional architecture of International Organisations (IO), the internal dynamics of multilateral diplomacy, and the role diplomats contribute to the process of general rule making and the containment of conflict (Barston 2013). In a sense, active learning emphasises the value of learning by doing (Bradberry and de Maio 2019) and, as inspired global citizens, students gain insights into the dilemmas of global governance. The use of active or experiential learning removes the focus away from the traditional, teacher-centred approach to the learning process, which often contributes to passivity on the part of students, to an engaging student-centred learning process that emphasises active participation, collaboration, communication, and professionalism (Cohen 1991). There is a paradigmatic shift in the teaching of International Relations (Lantis 1998) to embrace active student-centredness, whereby teachers work with students to construct knowledge about International Relations through active learning. The role of the professor, whether in the classroom or as faculty advisor for a club, rests on navigating the balance between the authoritative decision-maker and a delegating supervisor (Williams 2021). An important question is how to bridge the gap between the authoritative role of the professor in the classroom and the supervisor in a club.

In a typical International Relations course, students cover the power of states and non-state actors in the international system and the normative framework that states establish to create international order on a textbook basis. As opposed to this, in the specific context of a simulation, students must understand the structural power of their state (if applicable) to concretely influence the course of events, formal power (including voting rights and committee membership) and informal power to shape favourable outcomes (Stone 2013). With the incorporation of simulations of IOs into International Relations courses, students thus encounter the dynamics of power within these organisations combined with their own creative impulses to find idealistic solutions to world problems.

This raises the question of how to maximise the beneficial impact of simulations for students who are not in formal International Relations courses but join other classes or student clubs designed to simulate the work of IOs. My suggestion in this reflective chapter, based on my experience of teaching International Relations for over two decades and serving as faculty advisor for my university's United Nations (UN) club, is that peer-to-peer training in clubs and the inclusion of student peers as dais or in other leadership positions for traditional International Relations courses might be a fruitful pedagogical approach to enhance student learning. It could help bridge the gap between the role of the professor as authoritative decision-maker and delegating supervisor (Williams 2021) by inserting a critical role of student peers in the learning process. A neglected part of active learning (whether it is a face-to-face format or through blended learning) is creating space to complement the role of professor or faculty advisor with empowerment of student peers and using peer-to-peer training in clubs or using student leadership as dais in classes under the supervision of a faculty member to advance knowledge of international affairs. Active learning gains a greater level of student engagement when experienced peers deliver the material. Peer-to-peer delivery bridges the teacher-student power dynamic, allows students to take ownership of the learning process and relate to their peers as mentors, and offers a context in which peers can share experiences gained from participation in simulations around the world. It could be said that peer-to-peer training is part of the student-as-partner model of learning, which is described as a form of radical collegiality (Fielding 1999) or a case of intergenerational learning and democratic fellowship (Fielding 2011). When participants of a simulation are from distinct national settings with differing cultural backgrounds – connected in-person or virtually using blended learning or hybrid diplomacy (as seen during the COVID-19 pandemic) – peer-to-peer training and leadership can help enhance intercultural communication and cross-cultural learning and bring to the fore the challenges of virtual diplomacy.

This chapter discusses the importance of incorporation of peer-to-peer training into experiential learning, whether through clubs or in formal International Relations classes, in preparing students for understanding the diplomatic process within IOs. While experiential learning is indeed consistent with a student-focused learning paradigm, the use of experienced student peers to teach the essentials of diplomatic behaviour or serve on the dais for the simulation further provides avenues for engaging students in the learning process. The chapter shares the highlights of the content of the training programme used by my university's UN club, which fosters a dynamic learning environment when peer-to-peer training and leadership are included in teaching about diplomatic practices in IOs. It assesses how this peer-to-peer training for National Model United Nations (NMUN) conferences was expanded into collaboration among students and faculty from MacEwan University and two Ukrainian universities: National University of Kyiv-Mohyla Academy (NaUKMA) and Ukrainian Catholic University (UCU) under the Canada Ukraine Model UN project. The discussion focuses on the lessons learned from the collaboration – its pitfalls and benefits – and addresses the role that peer-to-peer training played to facilitate the attendance of Ukrainian delegates at two NMUN conferences in Erfurt, Germany, and New York, USA. It shows how the initial training to prepare students for conferences using virtual exchange modules spilled over into the inclusion of the peer-to-peer training model into a Collaborative Online Intercultural/International Learning (COIL) course on Model United Nations (MNU) offered by the three universities in the Winter session of 2022 – a course that was interrupted by the Russia-Ukraine war.

The major point here is that it is crucial to incorporate peer-to-peer delivery of active learning content in UN clubs or classes, including having student peers serve as dais for the simulation and give feedback on simulation preparation all under the tutelage of the faculty advisor or professor for a specific class. Peer-to-peer training creates spaces for student partnership and expands the learning process by emphasising student agency and responsibility. This model of learning reworks the lines of responsibility, giving students more responsibilities. This helps to build skills in adaptability, problem solving, public speaking, and organisation (Storey et al. 2021). Typically, simulations at NMUN are course requirements or run as extra-curricular activities by student clubs. While peer-to-peer inclusion in the learning process is vital with respect to the club-related simulations, involving peers in teaching of active learning in formal International Relations courses should not be neglected. Student peers can add value to the quality of the simulation and contribute to the achievement of academic benefits such as enhancing critical thinking, working paper review, and developing social skills, self-confidence, empathy, problem solving, research, and negotiations (Hazleton and Jacob 1983; Karns 1980; Phillips and Muldoon 1996; Williams 2021).

BACKGROUND: ACTIVE LEARNING AND TEACHING INTERNATIONAL RELATIONS

Incorporation of active learning into the teaching of International Relations started in my Introduction to International Relations course back in 1992 with a simulation of a General Assembly (GA) plenary session. The rationale for incorporating simulations and active learning in the teaching of International Relations was to engage students in the learning process of understanding the diplomatic process in IOs, and the routinised decision-making in the UN, and to move away from overreliance on traditional modes of delivery by lectures (see also Chapters 2 and 5). Through a thorough understanding of how IOs work, the goal was to help students gain an understanding of the diplomatic style of their assigned states, which contributes not only to developing knowledge of the foreign policies of the states, but also their international identity and diplomatic reputation (Barston 2013, p. 37). In situating the learning of multilateral diplomacy and International Relations within experiential learning, the objective was to model the course to make it consistent with broader efforts in the teaching of International Relations to shift instruction from traditional instructional paradigms to a new learning paradigm that focused on enhancing the role of students in the learning process (Lantis 1998). Experiential learning broadens students' learning horizons on the essential features of the "new diplomacy," one that is open, focuses on multilateralism and addresses issues of global governance, as distinct from the old diplomacy that emphasised bilateralism, secret negotiations, strict protocol, and ceremonial duties. Engagement of students in simulations – in a class context or with clubs by opening non-International Relations students to the world around them – places students in the "position" of future decision makers and contemporary diplomats. It endows them with the skill sets to succeed in the era of new diplomacy: public speaking, debating, team building or collaboration, research, negotiation, writing, and leadership (Hazleton and Jacob 1983; Karns 1980; Phillips and Muldoon 1996).

Students in my International Relations class suggested the formation of a Model UN club to extend the active learning experience to students from other disciplines. The club established the Alberta Inter-collegiate Model UN, which is a simulation that alternates between MacEwan University and universities in Calgary to bring delegates from Alberta and Western Canadian institutions to Edmonton and Calgary for a simulation of the GA. MacEwan University's UN club subsequently started attending international conferences, including sending delegations to simulations of the Organisation of American States, and beginning in the new millennium taking delegations to the world's largest simulation of the UN – the NMUN – in New York and in non-USA international venues.

It should be noted that at large simulations, including NMUN, participants attend as part of a class to meet specified course requirements or as a club. The club-class dynamic at large conferences such as NMUN introduces tensions between the imperatives for collaboration and exhibiting appropriate diplomatic behaviour versus a sense of competitiveness when, in certain limited cases, delegates are graded based on aggressive behaviour or specific interactions designed to "win awards" over authentic professional diplomatic behaviour. While I continue to use simulations in my International Relations course, and cognisant of not letting the simulation overwhelm the learning, I endorsed the idea of forming a club to bring learning about IOs, multilateralism, global governance, and related topics to a wider university audience under the extracurricular umbrella of a club. Whether it is a club or class, it is crucial to highlight the importance of understanding the diplomatic process, particularly the conduct of negotiations within the framework of multilateral diplomacy. The reality of global governance, in terms of the need for states to cooperate to address pressing global challenges, calls for students from different academic backgrounds to embark on a steep learning curve of understanding the complexities of the many issues addressed by the UN and the power that underscores diplomatic outcomes. In addition, students learn how to negotiate with their diplomatic counterparts in the simulation of the process of norm creation and elaboration.

In the first five years of the club's existence, emphasis was on my role as the authoritative decision-maker directing all aspects of the club's preparation for the NMUN conferences. As students gained more experience with each successive attendance at NMUN conferences, the club transitioned into a peer-to-peer training model, involving student peers taking ownership of the training programme for preparing delegates to attend NMUN conferences. The transition to peer-to-peer training shifts the role of the professor into one offering overall guidance, setting expectations and serving as a role model for students in terms of professionalism and ethical behaviour. When peer-to-peer leadership is offered in the context of a class, the faculty member should select the dais and secretariat (Williams 2021). Working with the club, the students and I developed teaching resources and modules for use to help students understand the essential components of the simulation and the overall process of diplomacy and the conduct of negotiations. It should be noted that after the first decade of the club's existence, it shifted completely into a student-as-producer-model (Obendorf and Randerson 2013) when the students created, revised, and delivered the content. The underlying principle of the peer-to-peer training is that it is insufficient to focus on teaching the institutional and formal aspects of the UN but to add the more significant focus on diplomacy skills, professionalism, negotiations and team building (O'Dell et al. 2023). While diplomacy skills and negotiations are an integral part of the training programme, students are reminded of the importance of having an inclusive mindset and exhibiting professionalism in line with the university and NMUN Codes of Conduct.

In addition to conference attendances around the world, the club started two strategic partnerships – working to train Ukrainian students from Ukrainian Catholic University (UCU) and National University Kyiv-Mohyla Academy (NaUKMA). The students and I collaborated with German, Spanish, and Croatian colleagues for a Model UN in Fulda as part of the project called "Practising Transnational Politics in Blended Learning" (PATRAPO), that is at the origin of this book (see Introduction). I visited Kyiv, Ukraine, before the pandemic with student trainers to prepare Ukrainian students for the NMUN Germany conference in Erfurt in 2018. In the post-pandemic period, I visited Fulda with students to participate in two Fulda MUNs in 2022 and 2023, for simulations that had students from the MacEwan UN club serve as dais and offer peer-to-peer feedback to students from Germany, Croatia, Spain, and Ukraine. In addition, the initial peer-to-peer training of student delegates in Ukraine morphed into faculty members from the three institutions (MacEwan, UCU, and NaUKMA) bringing the training methodology into a COIL course in 2022 until its interruption by the Ukraine-Russia war, which dispersed many of the students across the world. In the formal COIL course, student peers from MacEwan University and an alumna from UCU offered training to students in preparation for a simulation that was part of the course.

CLUB GOVERNANCE FOR PEER-TO-PEER TRAINING

In establishing a club, which has broadened its outreach beyond campus training to include international peers, it was critical to develop a governance structure that ensures cohesiveness of members and specifies clear aims and mechanisms for its smooth operation. It is crucial to note that successful clubs need institutional support and a culture that encourages the potential academic enrichment that they can provide to students. The absence of a culture of institutional support imperils student efforts to sustain their activities. The governance structure used in my university's UN club is framed around a leadership team, including the Secretary-General, Director-General, Vice President Operations, Vice President Fundraising, Vice President Finance, and Vice President Events. This governance team provides overall leadership for the club's activities within a culture of strong institutional support for student clubs, albeit the club operates under the overarching rules of the Students' Association. While the Secretary-General is responsible for the overall leadership of the club, the Director-General is a key actor for the effectiveness of the peer-to-peer training component of the club. As the term suggests, peer-to-peer training places the training of students for conferences squarely in the hands of their counterparts, who have gained and can share experiences from attending past conferences or teach the content of the club's training modules to their fellow students. The Director-General, under the club constitution, is the individual responsible for coordinating the peer-to-peer training programme of the club. This training programme is at the heart of the club's efforts to send delegates that are well versed in the intricacies of all that is required to be a model diplomat of an assigned country in the conference setting. Peer-to-peer training teaches all the key features of becoming effective model diplomats at international conferences. It fosters leadership skills for students, makes them accountable to each other to maintain excellence in conference preparation and performance, and creates a trail of accomplishments that others can follow to enable a general culture of responsibility. Peer-to-peer training, as the COIL course example with Ukrainian universities suggests, melds nicely into International Relations courses by having students lead simulations and train their colleagues. Through this process, the role of the faculty advisor shifts into one of a delegating supervisor in the context of club activities but maintains both roles as authoritative decision maker and delegating supervisor for formal courses in International Relations.

CONTENT OF PEER-TO-PEER TRAINING: UNDERSTANDING THE DIPLOMATIC PROCESS

It is important to view peer-to-peer training as an opportunity for students to learn from first-hand experience and understand the subtleties of theories and concepts while using role-playing to make defensible decisions (Asal and Blake 2006). What peer-to-peer training entails is giving students the opportunity to share their conference attendance experiences with their colleagues using an effective training programme based on well-developed modules designed to emphasise the acquisition of the requisite skill sets to be competent active learning participants at conferences. Student peers serve as dais sharing their experience of committee leadership. Interestingly, many MacEwan UN club members have moved on to work as volunteer staff at NMUN conferences. The peer-to-peer training has been successful in making students take ownership of the learning process and monitor each other's performances to identify deficiencies and address them before conferences. When students rely on their peers to review their performance and depend on student committee leadership for direction, it sets the frame for mutual accountability and addresses the power dynamics that often come from a typical professor-student relationship.

A significant part of peer-to-peer training involves understanding the procedural requirements typically embedded in the charters/constitutions of the organisation to be simulated (Volgy et al. 2008) and the process of negotiations, which underpins the work of diplomats in achieving consensus through multilateral diplomacy. The entire peer-to-peer training programme covers the basic model of the diplomatic process of negotiations as noted by Barston (2013). The model's schematic phases include the following (on the following see also Chapter 12):

1. Preparatory phase:
    - Preparation of national position.
    - Agree [on] venue.
    - Outline agenda approved.
    - Level at which talks are to be conducted.
2. Opening phase (procedural):
    - Confirm credentials of the parties.
    - Re-establish purpose and status of talks (e.g. whether they are informal or preliminary discussions, formal talks or whether any follow-up talks are envisaged and at what venue).
    - Working documentation.
    - Working procedures:
        - Recess (if any).
        - Language to be used.
        - Rules of procedure.
        - Agree which text or draft (if any) will be used as the basis for negotiations.
        - Whether there is to be an agreed record.
3. Opening phase (substantive):
    - Confirm or amend agenda.
    - Exposition of opening position.
4. Substantive negotiation:
    - Exploration of areas of difference.
    - Construction of areas of agreement.
5. Adjournment of the negotiation for further rounds of talks (if appropriate).
6. Framework agreement reached.
7. Legal clearance and residual drafting amendments.
8. Initialling or signature of final agreement.
9. Statement on proceedings or communique.

While Barston's (2013) diplomatic process does not apply completely to the simulation-training activities used in the MacEwan UN club's peer-to-peer training programme, it covers the major components of the model. Substantive negotiations – discussed in detail later – are tackled in the third phase of the model, but delegates must be engaged in the preparatory steps needed to become effective diplomatic representatives before things develop into the give-and-take of actual negotiations. It is instructive to point out that students must understand the important modes of diplomatic behaviour, including among others: rule following, negotiation strategising, and leadership positioning (Bjola 2015). The preparatory phase of the training typically emphasises the importance of developing research skills, and covers understanding the UN system, its history and organisational structure, and the specific mandate of the UN committee simulated. In addition, training focuses on getting delegates to become conversant with their assigned state's foreign policy stances, and the determinants of its foreign policy and its typical diplomatic partners in multilateral institutions. Of course, effective representation requires building a reservoir of knowledge about your assigned country, hence the need to become conversant with its geographical location, government structure, history and culture, key economic sectors, and its past engagement with the UN system. It is crucial for delegates to have an in-depth understanding of the topic(s) before the specific committee. Certainly, knowledge of the committee's history and mandate, its role in managing substantive operations and norm elaboration and coordination (Abbott et al. 2015) are important to determine the extent of recommended action within the committee. Similarly, having knowledge of rules of procedure of the committee sets the stage for effective participation.

Rules of procedure are the agreed-upon and enforced prescriptions (Cole 2014) or, in essence, the rules of the game. The rules of procedure and the underlying UN Charter constitute the internal law of the organisation (Bernhardt 1983). Delegates, as representatives of state actors, expect to accept as axiomatic the conference requirement of the rules of procedure (Sabel 2009). Formal rules, such as rules of procedure, provide stable and predictable policy outputs from the committee (Stone 2013). They shape diplomatic practice and generate habitual codes of behaviour (Bjola 2015). Having background knowledge of the rules of procedure sets the stage for the preparation of the position paper, which is a significant feature of the preparatory phase for NMUN conferences and class simulations. The position paper gives other delegates a sense of the quality of research undertaken to prepare for the conference or simulation. The paper must convey to readers that you have a sharp understanding of the position of your assigned state on the issue under discussion, how the UN or other intergovernmental actors have addressed the issue in the past or offered remedial and innovative solutions your country brings to the table to address the issue before the committee. Delegates must read the background guides of their committees as well as the NMUN position paper guide for details of writing an effective position paper. It is critical for faculty to provide feedback and ensure that position papers are original, not written by ChatGPT, and that they reflect the essentials taught by their peers. Faculty must not write position papers for students; albeit, as noted previously, they can offer constructive criticism in the writing process.

The conference agenda is set before the simulation, but delegates have a say in agenda-setting – that is, in determining the order of agenda items during the opening phase (substantive) of the diplomatic process. Initial focus of the peer-to-peer training programme on position papers targets the structure of position papers, the technical requirements, the do's and don'ts of position paper writing, and specific ideas on the editing process for writing an effective position paper. The research and background reading on the committee topics prepare delegates/students with a broad understanding of the issue(s) before the committee, and the remedial policies that their assigned country working collaboratively with other states can bring to bear in addressing the issue(s). Understanding the foreign policy priorities of assigned states sets delegates up to determine the order of priorities that works for their assigned country.

As noted earlier, one of the significant learning outcomes for active learning is to foster confidence in public speaking or communicating ideas. Communication is crucial for the process of negotiations (Lauren et al. 2020). A survey done by NMUN in 2023 indicates that 95 per cent of participants at the NMUN NY conference viewed public speaking as an important skill set enhanced by participating in the simulation (National Model United Nations 2023). The peer-to-peer training of the MacEwan UN club reinforces the importance of developing the skills of public speaking and building confidence in students to deliver effective and persuasive speeches in a conference setting, whether for formal or informal debates and substantive negotiations. As with position paper essentials, the basic structure of speech giving covers the formalities of the introduction, the middle content for ideas, solutions, and ongoing work on working papers, and the conclusion. The training emphasises that speeches focus on the specific phases of the simulation, setting the agenda, speeches for working papers, and speeches for draft resolutions. The speeches must highlight collaboration, convey innovative ideas, and foster the spirit of listening to the speeches of other delegations for shared ideas and areas for working together to address global problems. Emphasis is on the mechanics of effective speech delivery, including body language, maintaining eye contact, staying in character, and using diplomatic language. Additionally, delegates learn the key strategies for keeping an audience's attention and delivering cogent content to overcome boredom and avoid mistakes. Overall, in terms of best practice, peers stress the important best practices for communicating ideas at a simulation:

- Acknowledging the chair and assembly;
- adjusting the requirements of the speech for the phase of the simulation;
- conveying confidence by maintaining eye contact;

- listening to the ideas from other speeches; and
- adding your country to the speakers list as appropriate.

Acknowledging that individual negotiators and their unique negotiating skills can be consequential regardless of the country they represent is an important consideration for delegates.

In the opening phase (procedural) session of a typical simulation, there is an opportunity for delegates to record their presence at the simulation, as with confirming credentials at international meetings. Delegates are taught how to declare their presence with either "present" or "present and voting," the former denoting ability to vote affirmatively or negatively on substantive matters without abstention, whereas the latter indicates ability to vote in the affirmative, negative or abstain. This is not trivial, as it touches somewhat on the question of representation, which deals – on a larger scale – with issues around who can be a member of the IO and how their vote is counted (Haas 1990). The training programme includes a strong focus on learning the rules of procedure used at NMUN conferences. The substantive negotiating process of transforming working papers into draft resolutions and resolutions is a major preoccupation of the training programme.

THE PROCESS OF NEGOTIATIONS IN PEER-TO-PEER TRAINING

Negotiations are at the heart of modern diplomacy and must appropriately capture the essence of collaborative problem solving. Delegates must try to review posted position papers for their committees, especially those of their regional partners, blocs or even adversaries. This acquisition of knowledge is crucial for exploring differing perspectives on specific issue areas for discussion and ascertaining areas of commonality in foreign policy approaches. Understanding negotiations requires having the capacity to define clearly common interests and areas of disagreement. As Lauren et al. (2020, p. 166) point out, the two sides at the beginning of negotiations must ascertain the nature of their conflicting interests and common concerns. In general, negotiations require knowing your assigned state's maximum demand or ideal outcome, and bottom-line position or initial resistance point. The level of knowledge, as with expertise in international negotiations, is critical in negotiating meaning (McEntee-Atalianis 2008) and informing the interpretations of past resolutions and texts. The essence of negotiations is bridging the resistance points or settlement range of member states.

It is also instructive for students to understand the competing conceptions of diplomatic agency to help guide their behaviour: self-effacing bureaucrat, the two-level mediator, foreign policy shaper, and diplomat as custodian of international society. Skilful delegates are the ones able to work collaboratively with other members of their committees, avoiding confrontational or combative stances, but bringing innovative ideas and solutions to accommodate the reasonable preferences of other states in the simulation. They must do this while staying in character. While delegates may lack knowledge of the history of individuals and their personalities, they can use their encounters to learn more about their psychological predispositions that affect the negotiations process and use strategies such as negotiator's pause or momentum (Gaudiosi et al. 2019). In the context of a physical encounter, negotiators can read body language, emotional expression, and gain insights from casual conversation, something that is lost when there is sole reliance on digital diplomacy. Delegates are taught the essentials of committee dynamics for achieving the ideal outcomes of negotiations, and the archetypes of delegates one is likely to encounter in a committee setting: freeloader, passive, active, power, and leader.

Another negotiating feature that delegates are likely to encounter in a committee setting is the accommodative and optimising approaches to negotiations. The former approach adopts a minimalist posture by not asking for much more in a negotiation than is reasonable or likely to be accepted. The latter pursues a maximalist or optimising strategy by trying to achieve as much as possible using sweeping demands and by not being afraid to be combative and abusive (Lauren et al. 2020, p. 170).

FROM WORKING PAPERS TO RESOLUTIONS

In the training programme, it is made clear to delegates that, in the context of NMUN, since pre-written resolutions are discouraged, there is stress on the importance of negotiations for developing working papers that go through debate and refinement as draft resolutions until adopted by a substantive vote. The dais offers feedback to delegates and ensures appropriate formatting and there are no pre-written resolutions, so delegates must approach them with utmost professionalism. Delegates learn the distinction between sponsors and signatories of resolutions, with the former responsible for initiating and drafting the resolution text (Permanent Mission of Switzerland 2017), and the latter bringing the working paper forward for consideration. As noted in the NMUN Preparation Guide, the dais will indicate the required number of sponsors and signatories after the first roll call, albeit the typical number of signatories is equivalent to 20 per cent of the committee membership in attendance during the first session, or five – whichever is greater (NMUN 2022, p. 26).

The structure of resolutions includes "agreed language" or specific paragraphs, sentences used in previous UN resolutions for limited usage, but NMUN encourages originality in the formulating of working papers. Note that in the UN "agreed language" is a backup in case there is no agreement. Delegates must use informal sessions for negotiations and consultations to bring forward a proper version of the draft resolution. There might be cases of dais-recommended mergers of working papers, which means ramping up negotiations to achieve consensus. Unlike the actual UN, delegates at NMUN do not have to go through the "silence procedure" for a specific time while diplomats get approval from their home governments. Resolutions must have preambular paragraphs (PPs) and then operative paragraphs (OPs). The former lists applicable or relevant UN resolutions or the context of the issue, whereas the latter is the action-oriented part of the resolution that requests action by the Security Council or subsidiary bodies (Permanent Mission of Switzerland 2017).

THE CANADA UKRAINE MODEL UN PROJECT: A CASE OF PEER-TO-PEER TRAINING

In addition to the peer-to-peer training used to prepare students to embrace international politics as practice and acquire the behavioural traits for effective participation in simulations of IOs, this section provides a case of expansion of peer-to-peer training through international collaboration and the added benefit of cross-cultural learning. In 2018, the NMUN board asked me to shepherd a board scholarship programme in Ukraine designed as an outreach to bring delegates from that country to NMUN conferences and create MUN clubs in Ukrainian universities. I reached out to Larisa Hayduk, Executive Director of Ukraine Resource Development Centre at my University, which works closely with educational entities in Ukraine and the broad Ukrainian diaspora in Alberta and Canada. This eventually led to virtual meetings with students and colleagues from two Ukrainian universities – NaUKMA, and UCU – to set the foundation for collaboration between student peers and faculty members. The next step was to move from virtual interaction to a field trip with four students to Kyiv in June 2019 to train students from NaUKMA and UCU for an upcoming NMUN conference in Erfurt, Germany. This cross-cultural experiential learning allowed MacEwan UN club students to meet their Ukrainian peers in person and to benefit from the self-development and opportunity to teach as a "cross-cultural encounter" (Wilson 1986). One MacEwan student, Sean Waddingham, described the experience as follows:

> I used to naively believe that "travel expands the mind" was a bit of a silly trope, but that changed when I learned things on the trip that I otherwise wouldn't have – hearing the history of the Kievan Rus' Empire, seeing Soviet remnants in the architecture, and understanding the contemporary struggle for independent Ukraine. (URDC 2020, p. 2)

Peer-to-peer training of the content noted in the previous section prepared the NaUKMA and UCU students to send a joint delegation to the NMUN Germany conference in Erfurt, Germany, which featured a keynote speech by German President, Frank-Walter Steinmeier. Interestingly, the NaUKMA-UCU delegation performed admirably at the Erfurt conference and won an honorary mention award. A student from NaUKMA who was a participant at the Kyiv peer-to-peer training sessions, and is now a volunteer staff member for NMUN, commented:

> [T]he support of the MacEwan team (in Erfurt) was especially valuable. They were always ready to help us. Gaining experience in intercultural communication was especially useful, while it proved that even though people may have different life-perceptions and backgrounds, they can collaborate in finding effective solutions for global issues. (URDC 2020, p. 3)

PEER-TO-PEER TRAINING IN AN INTER-INSTITUTIONAL CONTEXT: LESSONS LEARNED FROM COLLABORATION

What is significant in terms of lessons from the peer-to-peer training is that the students from Ukraine who went through the training programme became trainers in setting up clubs in their respective universities. Given Ukraine's effort to bolster its diplomatic standing in the international system as a recently established democratic state from the former USSR, there is strong interest in diplomacy and International Relations as demonstrated by the expressions of interest by faculty and students beyond the original two institutions of the training exercise.

An important benefit of the training problem is the co-creation of the educational experiences in the form of the role of the initial trainees in contributing their skills to the subsequent training programme for the two virtual MUN's held since the initial Kyiv trip in 2019. Since the Germany NMUN conference, a virtual Summer School held in June 2020, featured guest speakers from the diplomatic community in Canada and Ukraine and was repeated in July 2021. This brought multiple student voices from Canada and Ukraine to dialogue and work in partnership in the context of a virtual simulation. Delegations from UCU-NaUKMA participated in NMUN NY (virtual session in 2021), where the delegation received a distinguished delegation award, and were present in person in New York for NMUN 2022, where the delegation received a resounding welcome in recognition of the effort made to travel to New York under the adverse circumstances of the Russian war against Ukraine. In 2022, a summer MUN school, originally planned to take place in Lviv, Ukraine, for peer-to-peer training, took place in Fulda, Germany, as part of Fulda University of Applied Sciences PATRAPO project, involving faculty and students from Croatia, Spain, and Germany (see Foreword and Introduction). Fulda University of Applied Sciences funded the attendance of students from UCU for the simulation that focused on the conflict in Ukraine. Three MacEwan University UN club peer trainers served as the dais for the conference, cementing the importance of incorporating student leadership in the running of the simulation. The dais had the responsibility of leading the simulation and navigating their peers through enforcement of rules of procedure and overseeing discussion of a topic with emotional import for some of the delegates. The dais demonstrated a case of the faculty relinquishing power and letting the students guide their colleagues through the simulation based on trust and respect, even if they had their own fear of not being taken seriously by their colleagues or even having a case of imposter syndrome (Parkman 2016). Overall, the dais performed effectively and steered the simulation to a successful conclusion, engaging the students to negotiate working papers on the war in Ukraine. The 2022 Fulda UN simulation is an instance of peer-to-peer leadership in a partnership of co-facilitators with faculty (Mercer-Mapstone et al. 2017) in running the simulation combined with the intermingling of cross-cultural academic influences to discuss current global crisis.

The 2022 PATRAPO project simulation used a hybrid diplomacy approach, with Ukrainian, Croatian, and German students attending in-person in Fulda, whereas students from Spain joined online. This made for a difficult situation in getting a higher level of diplomatic engagement from the online participants deprived of the interpersonal aspects of modern diplomacy. Online participants lost out on the benefits of the face-to-face interactions of their colleagues during informal sessions, albeit technology facilitated their participation in the sessions. What was lost in this hybrid diplomatic exchange was the impersonal quality of the exercise for the online participants, as they were absent from corridor conversations between in-person delegates due to the restrictions of technology. It is in recognition of the challenges of organising a hybrid simulation that the PATRAPO project opted for an in-person simulation for the second Fulda simulation in July 2023.

The topics of the 2022 simulation concerned Ukraine. Having students address the Ukrainian crisis, while involving Ukrainian participants, had its challenges, as delegates had to suppress their personal emotions to stay in character for their respective countries. The collaboration amongst peers under peer leadership helped alleviate any power dynamics and contributed to a constructive diplomatic process and authentic partnership (Clancy et al. 2019). Management of the relationship between the Russian and Ukrainian representatives and the sensitivities of the students from Ukraine was a delicate exercise carefully handled by the dais and helpful faculty. While the benefits of exposing students from non-English speaking backgrounds to simulations are obvious, it is problematic that students from universities without a strong facility in English are disadvantaged in the opportunity to attend NMUN simulations, where English is the mode of communication. There is the added challenge of having the financial resources to attend international simulations to reap the benefits of close inter-cultural contact with peers.

PEER-TO-PEER TRAINING IN A COIL COURSE: LIMITS OF DIGITAL DIPLOMACY

The COIL course entitled "International Organizations and Global Governance" involved students from MacEwan University, UCU and NaUKMA from early February to 30 March 2022. Among other learning outcomes, the COIL emphasised the beneficial impact of intercultural interactions, the ability of students to understand the UN's rule of procedure, legal standards and official documents, and oral and written communication of the simulation content in a logical, coherent and consistent diplomatic manner. It embedded a peer-to-peer training component, including former NMUN attendees and students with NMUN staff experience delivering parts of the simulation modules and serving as dais for the simulation. Delegations included students from the three universities to maximise collaboration and encourage dialogue between students from the two countries as they prepared for work on position papers and the simulation.

The first challenge of organising the COIL course was the scheduling of the courses to fit the time difference and content requirements of the three institutions. MacEwan University began the Winter session earlier than the Ukrainian universities; the first four weeks of my course were devoted to building conceptual and procedural knowledge of the UN, including a detailed overview of the major theoretical perspectives on IOs. The plan was to have a combined six-week module of content, including a simulation of the GA Committee 3. The session started with an introductory overview of the training session and an address by Hon. Douglas Roche, Canada's Ambassador to the UN on Disarmament. The following sessions thrust the student peers into action. Peer-to-peer training covered the next four weeks of the session, including the basics of Model UN, the UN architecture, the process of research for the MUN, position papers, speeches and negotiations, and resolutions. The final session of the training was devoted to the actual simulation. The faculty agreed to MUN evaluation criteria that covered public speaking, resolution writing, active participation and negotiations, rules of procedure and resolution voting.

There were initial hiccups with getting communication going among the members of the selected delegations, largely a consequence of the differing schedules of students. This changed quickly as students used social media and other online communication tools to connect, and they were in contact with each other by the second week of the training session.

Unfortunately, after the second week of the training module, Russia invaded Ukraine on 24 February 2022, which completely upended the course, as many students had to flee the country to escape the attacks. Many Canadian students from the COIL course received updates from their colleagues about the unfolding developments. Others requested help in addressing disinformation and support for Ukraine. The wartime conditions simply made the COIL course untenable as originally planned.

As universities closed in Ukraine or moved to alternate modes of delivery, the COIL course ended, but the training programme continued as originally designed. MacEwan University students continued the training model using student peers for the training while recording the sessions for later use by the two Ukrainian universities. The use of student peers in a formal International Relations course did enhance the learning process, but the true intercultural benefit was difficult to assess due to the unexpected intrusion of the Russian attack on Ukraine and its attendant disruption of the learning process in the country. The COIL programme did not conclude as planned due to the Russia-Ukraine war, but the important lesson from the course was that incorporation of peer-to-peer training was beneficial. As with combining virtual and face-to-face learning environments, hybrid diplomacy faced technological challenges and the benefits of intercultural learning truncated by the onset of the war. COIL courses offer the prospect of sharing experiences across sovereign jurisdictions mediated by technology, but such virtual settings are problematic for diplomatic interchange and limit the advancing of a negotiating agenda and building of face-to-face relationships.

CONCLUSION

UN simulations are important vehicles for teaching students the institutional environment of IOs, while immersing them in the complex behavioural aspects of diplomacy through understanding and practice of the working procedures of diplomatic institutions. This practice approach to understanding IOs can incorporate student peers in the training of their counterparts in the formalisms of IOs as well as in giving them basic information on the history, structure and power hierarchies embedded in these organisations. This convergence of institutional understanding of IOs with hands-on immersion in diplomatic practice is effective in building important skills and student learning in a changing world. The benefits of including students-as–trainers in this peer-to-peer training model are important for developing student leadership skills and for the sharing of experiences among peers. Student peers can contribute to the practice approach to international politics by teaching formalisms, rules of procedure and behavioural expectations of diplomacy to their colleagues. This is a student-as-producer-of-knowledge approach and frames the teaching and learning philosophy from a professor-centric teaching approach to one that embraces a philosophy that benefits from the empowerment of student peers in the inculcation of the knowledge and experience of IO as practice. Teaching the diplomatic process of negotiations by peers is an effective way to share their leadership and conference experiences with colleagues in an interactive environment. When peer training or conference leadership takes place in a situation that combines virtual and physical settings, there must be an understanding that hybrid diplomacy or blended learning has serious limitations as it can lead to students in virtual environments missing contextual differences of face-to-face interactions that are important in the practices of negotiations.

In addition, when learning the elements of the diplomatic process outlined in Barston's (2013) model for negotiations that was detailed above, student peers must not gloss over the power hierarchies in IOs that could inform the negotiating stances of countries and change the dynamics of the negotiation process. This is where faculty can facilitate sessions to add to the content on building diplomatic skills with specific sessions to highlight the power dimensions of international politics for students. While student peers can make an important contribution to the teaching and learning of international politics as practice, it is crucial for faculty to work as co-facilitators to highlight the overhang of power politics that shapes the application of rules and norms, and the way actors act within IOs. This is significant, especially for student clubs, where students might not have a deep understanding of the basics of power in International Relations.

REFERENCES

Abbott, Kenneth W./Genschel, Philipp/Snidal, Duncan/Zangl, Bernhard (2015). International Organizations as Orchestrators. Cambridge, Cambridge University Press.

Asal, Victor/Blake, Elizabeth L. (2006). Creating Simulations for Political Science Education. Journal of Political Science Education 2 (1), 1–18. https://doi.org/10.1080/15512160500484119

Barston, Ronald P. (2013). Modern Diplomacy. 4th ed. London/New York, Routledge Taylor & Francis Group.

Bernhardt, Rudolf (1983). International Organizations, Internal Law and Rules. In: Rudolf L. Bindschedler/Thomas Burgenthal/Helmut Strebel (Eds.). International Organizations in General Universal International Organizations and Cooperation. Elsevier B.V., 142–145.

Bjola, Corneliu (2015). Diplomacy as World Disclosure: A Fractal Theory of Crisis Management. The British Journal of Politics and International Relations 18 (2), 335–350. https://doi.org/10.1111/1467-856X.12076

Bradberry, Leigh A./de Maio, Jennifer (2019). Learning By Doing: The Long-Term Impact of Experiential Learning Programs on Student Success. Journal of Political Science Education 15 (1), 94–111. https://doi.org/10.1080/15512169.2018.1485571

Clancy, Tracey L./Ferreira, Carla/Thompson, Paige (2019). Student-Faculty Partnership as a Foundation for Authentic Learning. Papers on Postsecondary Learning and Teaching 3, 144–149. https://doi.org/10.11575/pplt.v3i1.53079.

Cohen, Mel (1991). Bringing Life to the Classroom: Making Class Participation a Reality. PS: Political Science and Politics 24, 699–703.

Cole, Daniel H. (2014). Formal Institutions and the IAD Framework: Bringing the Law Back In. SSRN Electronic Journal. https://doi.org/10.2139/ssrn.2471040

Fielding, Michael (1999). Radical Collegiality: Affirming Teaching as an Inclusive Professional Practice. The Australian Educational Researcher 26 (2), 1–34. https://doi.org/10.1007/BF03219692

Fielding, Michael (2011). Patterns of Partnership: Student Voice, Intergenerational Learning and Democratic Fellowship. In: Nicole Mockler/Judyth Sachs (Eds.). Rethinking Educational Practice Through Reflexive Inquiry. Essays in Honour of Susan Groundwater-Smith. Dordrecht, Springer Netherlands, 61–75.

Gaudiosi, Rebecca W./Roesch, Jimena Leiva/Ye-Min, Wu (2019). Negotiating at the United Nations. A Practitioner's Guide. Milton, Routledge.

Haas, Ernst B. (1990). When Knowledge is Power: Three Models of Change in International Organizations. Berkeley, California, University of California Press.

Hazleton, William A./Jacob, James E. (1983). Simulating International Diplomacy: The National Model United Nations Experience. Teaching Political Science 10 (2), 89–99. https://doi.org/10.1080/00922013.1983.9942346

Karns, Margaret Padelford (1980). Teaching International Organization through Model U.N.'s. Washington, D.C., Distributed by ERIC Clearinghouse.

Lantis, Jeffrey S. (1998). Simulations and Experiential Learning in the International Relations Classroom. International Negotiation 3 (1), 39–57. https://doi.org/10.1163/15718069820848094

Lauren, Paul Gordon/Craig, Gordon Alexander/George, Alexander L. (2020). Force and Statecraft. Diplomatic Challenges of Our Time. 6th ed. Oxford, Oxford University Press.

McEntee-Atalianis, Lisa (2008). Diplomatic Negotiation in an International Organisation: An Exploration of Expert Status and Power. The International Journal of Diversity in Organizations, Communities, and Nations: Annual Review 8 (3), 265–272. https://doi.org/10.18848/1447-9532/CGP/v08i03/39594

Mercer-Mapstone, Lucy/Dvorakova, Lucie Sam/Groenendijk, Lauren J./Matthews, Kelly E. (2017). Idealism, Conflict, Leadership, and Labels: Reflections on Co-facilitation as Partnership Practice. Teaching and Learning Together in Higher Education (21). Available online at https://repository.brynmawr.edu/tlthe/vol1/iss21/8/ (accessed 2/26/2025).

National Model United Nations (2022). Delegate Preparation Guide. National Model United Nations. Available online at https://www.nmun.org/assets/documents/nmun-delegate-prep-guide.pdf (accessed 7/3/2025).

National Model United Nations (2023). NMUN•NY 2023 Survey Results. Unpublished internal document.

Obendorf, Simon/Randerson, Claire (2013). Evaluating the Model United Nations: Diplomatic Simulation as Assessed Undergraduate Coursework. European Political Science 12 (3), 350–364. https://doi.org/10.1057/eps.2013.13

O'Dell, Roni Kay M./Scott, Ariana B./Nealon, Mark J./Franzino, Brianna N. (2023). Training for the United Nations in the Twenty-First Century; Professionalism Training on Leadership, Negotiation, and Gender for Model United Nations Simulations. International Studies Perspectives, 1–19. https://doi.org/10.1093/isp/ekad011

Parkman, Anna (2016). The Imposter Phenomenon in Higher Education: Incidence and Impact. The Imposter Phenomenon in Higher Education: Incidence and Impact 16 (1), 51–60. Available online at https://articlegateway.com/index.php/JHETP/article/view/1936 (accessed 7/11/2032).

Permanent Mission of Switzerland (2017). The GA Handbook. A Practical Guide to the United Nations General Assembly. New York.

Phillips, Mary Jones/Muldoon, John P. (1996). The Model United Nations: A Strategy for Enhancing Global Business Education. Journal of Education for Business 71 (3), 142–146. https://doi.org/10.1080/08832323.1996.10116774

Sabel, Robbie (2009). Rules of Procedure and International Law. In: Robbie Sabel (Ed.). Procedure at International Conferences. A Study of the Rules of Procedure at the UN and at Inter-governmental Conferences. Cambridge University Press, 31–50.

Stone, Randall W. (2013). Informal Governance in International Organizations: Introduction to the Special Issue. The Review of International Organizations 8 (2), 121–136. https://doi.org/10.1007/s11558-013-9168-y

Storey, Angela/Eckel-Sparrow, Hannah/Ransdell, Henrietta (2021). Cultivating Student Agency and Responsibility Through Peer-to-Peer Teaching. International Journal for Students as Partners 5 (1), 97–106. https://doi.org/10.15173/ijsap.v5i1.4478

URDC (2020). Newsletter. MacEwan University. Bring MacEwan to the World, 2020. Available online at https://www.macewan.ca/c/documents/urdc_newsletter_winter2020.pdf (accessed 4/2/2025).

Volgy, Thomas J./Fausett, Elizabeth/Grant, Keith A./Rodgers, Stuart (2008). Identifying Formal Intergovernmental Organizations. Journal of Peace Research 45 (6), 837–850. Available online at https://www.jstor.org/stable/27640772 (accessed 2/26/2025).

Williams, Mark S. (2021). The Role of the Faculty Advisor for a Model United Nations Conference: 5 Lessons Learned from Practice. Journal of Political Science Education 17, 275–283. https://doi.org/10.1080/15512169.2019.1678481

Wilson, Angene H. (1986). Cross-Cultural Experiential Learning for Teachers. Theory Into Practice 26, 519–527.

5. Active learning through simulations: a civic education perspective

Antonio Manuel Álvarez García, Elena García Guitián and Luis Bouza García

Since the first League of Nations simulation in 1927, the Model United Nations (MUN) has been an inspiration for countless higher education programmes that have adopted simulations as their method to guarantee active learning in Political Science and International Relations. During the last decade, these simulation programmes have gained attention in pedagogical literature, and much work has been done in examining the learning results that can be obtained through simulations of international relations. In this regard, most of the recent publications consist of empirical assessments of political simulations (Baranowski and Weir 2015). In contrast, this chapter will provide a more theoretical insight into MUN simulations' potential, relying on both the pedagogical and the political fields of knowledge. In the first section of the chapter, we will discuss active learning, the pedagogical approach on which political simulations like the MUN need to be based. This section will discuss: a) what are the epistemological fundamentals of active learning; b) what educational outputs can be obtained through active learning; and c) how these outputs are actually achievable in political simulations. The second section reflects on the learning outcomes previously exposed, but this time relating them to a wider, civic-education strategy. This reflection will include: a) the influence of doing simulations in the acquisition of a cosmopolitan perspective; and b) the outcomes of simulations regarding the ability to think politically in a constrained, highly institutionalised framework.

ACTIVE LEARNING: THE PEDAGOGICAL APPROACH OF SIMULATIONS

Epistemological Fundamentals of Active Learning

Active learning is an educational approach that has acquired great attention since the late 1980s and early 1990s, when a significant amount of literature was produced to conceptualise a set of different active methodologies that were rising in secondary and higher education classrooms. In this regard, the work of Bonwell and Eison (1991) was especially influential. In a rather prosaic way, these authors defined active learning strategies as "[...] instructional activities involving students in doing things and thinking about what they are doing [...]" (Bonwell and Eison 1991, p. 3). From then on, other scholars have made new contributions on the theoretical basis of active learning, though always emphasising the two elements already highlighted by Bonwell and Eison: doing things and reflecting on what has been done.

However, active learning is not a product of the 1990s. In fact, its fundamentals can be traced back to the early twentieth century, when American pragmatic philosophers – especially John Dewey ([1938] 1998) – developed an epistemological theory that would challenge traditional pedagogies by emphasising the relation between knowledge and personal experience. Therefore, though "active learning" is a relatively new signifier in the literature, the concept itself consists of different, not so new epistemological principles. These principles can be summarised as follows:

- Experience – rather than memory – is the foundation and the stimulus for learning. Traditional pedagogy assumed that the best way of achieving learning outcomes was through the memorisation of a set of closed, standardised, declarative knowledge. As for active learning, it is not memory, but *experience* that is the main stimulus for learning. Active learning approaches assume that knowledge is achievable when students live certain experiences and, after reflecting on them, deduce new learnings that may be applicable in future occasions. This starts a virtuous circle in which experience is present in both the acquisition and the application of knowledge: first, the student faces and experiences; then, she reflects on what can be observed, trying to make sense of the stimulus that she is facing; afterwards, a deduction is made regarding what inferences can be obtained from the experience; finally, these inferences will result in a set of generalisable laws that the student may apply in future occasions, where the learning circle finds its closure. This all means that active experiences such as political simulations are not designed to put into practice a set of knowledge previously memorised in the classroom; on the contrary, experiences should be the learning moment *par excellence*, the main vehicle through which knowledge is both acquired and reinforced. This is why active learning can be also addressed as "experimental learning" (Boud et al. 1993).

- Knowledge is a result of a meaning-construction process. Active learning approaches are, by definition, based on constructivist epistemology. According to constructivism, knowledge cannot be taken as isolated, unrelated propositions. Instead, a holistic, systemic perspective is adopted, where knowledge is understood as a construction taking place in students' minds. Through this construction, students actively give meaning to new experiences by fitting them into their already existing mental frames, which had already been constructed during previous experiences, and so on (Bonwell and Eison 1991).
- As opposed to "surface learning", active learning seeks *deep learning*. Surface learning implies remembering isolated facts (or even details) of every subject. This may include declarative knowledge such as "Beijing hosted the 2008 Olympic Games" or "The capital of Nigeria is Abuja". By contrast, deep learning involves students in higher order thinking so that they construct meaningful knowledge that allows them to compute what they are experiencing. This is closely related to the constructivist approach on which active learning is based. As new learning needs to be constructed via previous mental frameworks, it goes beyond the acquisition of isolated propositions. In fact, deep learning is only acquired when pupils assimilate knowledge through higher order thinking, which includes the *analysis* of what is being experienced, the *evaluation* of it, and the *synthesis* of what can be made of all the process (Smith and Colby 2007).
- As meaning construction and deep learning always need to be done by students themselves, active learning approaches emphasise the students' role in the pedagogical process. Of course, during active learning students are involved in something more than listening. The point is that students must create their own meaning through experience, which results in exploring and developing their own mindset, skills, and personal attitudes. This has implications for the teachers, as their role is no longer being just proposition messengers, but also – and more importantly – guides and facilitators of intellectual development (Barr and Tagg 1995). In Chapter 4 of this book, the benefits of peer-to-peer strategies to ensure active learning were discussed; this may switch the role of the professor into that of a coach offering overall guidance, so that students themselves become the main source of each other's learnings. However, it is important to keep in mind that this "overall guidance" from teachers still includes crucial tasks, such as providing *fundamental knowledge*: knowledge that should serve as a

first step to facilitate the construction of meaningful learning during students' peer-to-peer experiences.

Active Learning Outputs

Active, deep learning approaches do not only seek factual or declarative knowledge (also known as "knowing-that"). Though factual knowledge is also a necessary condition for proper meaning construction, it is not sufficient. In fact, deep learning implies many more kinds of knowledge, which David R. Krathwohl (2002) summarises as follows:

- Factual knowledge (knowing-that): Knowledge that can be presented in declarative sentences that do not imply conceptual difficulty or contestation. One example of factual knowledge is "South Africa hosted the football World Cup in 2010".
- Conceptual knowledge: The meaningful understanding of those ideas that are too abstract and complex to be easily pinned down in factual, declarative sentences. For example, in Political Science, conceptual knowledge includes all those theories that serve as an intellectual arsenal to make sense of reality: Liberalism, Feminism, Nationalism, and so on. Also, conceptual knowledge may include just concepts by themselves, such as "freedom" or "legitimacy".
- Procedural knowledge (knowing-how): The set of attitudes and skills that are required to do something, such as shooting a football, swiping the floor, or proceeding during a political negotiation. People who own certain skills may not be able to put them into words like they do with factual knowledge; however, they still have said skills and are able to put them into practice, even without noticing it. Some examples of specific skills are persuasion or team organisation skills.
- Metacognitive knowledge: The ability of students to grasp their own learning process. Usually, metacognitive knowledge implies being able to convert one's procedural and conceptual knowledge into declarative propositions, for example: "During the last course, I have developed emotional skills thanks to being involved in team-work assignments".

Active Learning Outputs in Simulations

Having discussed the fundamentals and goals of active learning, we can now take a closer look at simulations as a specific active learning methodology. By reflecting on deep learning's different kinds of knowledge, we can briefly summarise the learning outcomes that should be accomplished in preparation courses for simulations and during the simulation itself (Calossi and Coticchia 2018; Coticchia et al. 2020; Engel et al. 2017; Hammond and Albert 2020):

- Factual knowledge: Simulation participants acquire factual knowledge when learning about the United Nations (UN) and the European Union (EU), their history, institutions, or rules of procedure. Factual knowledge also includes some national characteristics of the corresponding country of each delegate: political system, most common religions, or climate. This kind of knowledge is expected to be learned mainly during simulation preparation courses. However, active simulations serve as an opportunity for reinforcing old factual knowledge and acquiring new learnings. For example, it is expected that a delegate will assimilate more deeply her country's political system once she has to adhere to it during a simulation.
- Conceptual knowledge: Conceptual knowledge related to simulations offers the possibility to better and more concretely understand International Relations theories such as Realism, Liberalism, Constructivism, Feminism, and so on – in case students are familiar with them. In this regard, the delegate will construct her interpretation of international relations while facing the positions of different delegates or trying to make sense of the different political alliances that take place around her (Martini 2022). The simulation will also provide conceptual knowledge by forcing participants to reflect on specific, crucial political concepts such as interests, culture, ideology, or power. Importantly, simulations also facilitate some of the conceptual knowledge aimed at in UN *Global Citizenship Education*. This education strategy longs for the understanding of key universal values such as peace, human rights, diversity, justice, democracy, caring, and tolerance. The point is that these values cannot be assimilated through factual propositions but require conceptual, higher-order thinking in order to be applied by students in their understanding of local, national, and global issues (UNESCO 2013; UNESCO 2015). All these conceptual learnings can be obtained during preparation courses, but they are more likely to be assimilated during the simulation when participants try to make (conceptual) sense of the political reality they face first-hand.
- Procedural knowledge: There are many skills that are achievable through simulations. This includes the ability to work in a team, capacity for analysis, writing synthesis, and countless skills related to public speaking and persuasion. Also, simulations can provide many of the skills included in the Global Citizenship Education strategy, such as: critical, creative and innovative thinking, problem-solving, decision-making, and some emotional abilities like openness to other perspectives and empathy, which is especially crucial in role-playing (UNESCO 2013; UNESCO 2015). Additionally, many of these skills are closely related to the wider key

competences recognised by the United Nations Educational, Scientific and Cultural Organization (UNESCO) in its 2017 report by "Future competences and the future of curriculum", these include *self-agency* (entrepreneurship, responsibility, creativity), *interacting with others* (respect, open-mindedness, sensitivity) and *interacting with the world* (being glocal) (Marope et al. 2017). During simulations, participants will use all their skills repertoire, but they will also obtain new abilities along the way, especially those that are unlikely to be mastered beforehand. One good example of this is the adaptability required to manage constraints in the highly institutional framework of MUN and Model European Union (MEU).

- Metacognitive knowledge: Briefing and debriefing sessions during preparation courses allow students to grasp what they have learned. This provides a self-conscious dimension that will help students to apply their learning in future, non-MUN or MEU related experiences.

Several empirical articles have confirmed that political simulations are indeed more effective than non-active methods regarding deep learning achievements (Calossi and Coticchia 2018; Coticchia et al. 2020; Engel et al. 2017; Hammond and Albert 2020). However, it is fair to say that other authors state that there is not enough evidence in the literature to objectively conclude that, *ceteris paribus*, active learning simulations are more effective than other teaching methods (Baranowski and Weir 2015). Regarding these inconclusive results on the effectiveness of simulations, it is important to note the difficulties implied in evaluating political simulations or any other active learning strategy. During active learning experiences, learning outcomes are personally constructed by each student individually, which means that those outcomes can only be properly evaluated through individually designed assessments. Also, while the acquirement of declarative knowledge is easy to evaluate, it is more difficult to grasp students' personal progress on conceptual, procedural, and metacognitive knowledge. These considerations remind us that every simulation preparation course needs to integrate ambitious evaluation strategies, such as individual assignments, personalised interviews, or debriefing sessions.

LEARNING OUTCOMES APPLIED TO A CIVIC EDUCATIONS STRATEGY

In the following section we will link some of the learning outcomes of simulations to a wider civic education perspective. This perspective will consist of highlighting those aspects of the simulations that can be especially useful when it comes to educating *citizens* and preparing them for the present political world. We argue that political simulations can contribute to civic education through two fundamental lines: 1) providing participants with a cosmopolitan perspective in which their unity of solidarity transcends their nation-states; and 2) giving students an opportunity to experience actual institutional politics, with all the complexities and constraints that this implies.

A Cosmopolitan Perspective

Our reality has become cosmopolitan. There are global rights and international institutions beside nation-states and regional organisations and the different political entities and communities are interconnected. All of this generates the necessity for global moral responsibility based on a global public consciousness. That is why it is essential to change the way we analyse our societies and review the framework established by the nation-state model. This is what is proposed by political visions identified as "cosmopolitan".

In fact, the rise of cosmopolitanism was taking place in an already globalised world that had been breaking down the model of nation-states. For this reason, authors such as Beck (2005) considered that cosmopolitanism was not only a set of theories that define a specific position in philosophical or political debates, but also a perspective that can provide us with a true understanding of global interdependencies and how they influence the nation-state paradigm.

As Brown and Held (2010) point out, the common element of cosmopolitan thought is the conviction that there are moral obligations towards all human beings. These obligations are based on a shared humanity, and not on belonging to the same state or political community. This common ethical concept forms the basis of a political theory that involves three normative commitments. The first commitment is to adopt an individualistic vision, since the individual is placed as the first source of moral obligations, above states or other forms of political association; this does not mean that other types of obligations should be rejected, but they must be accepted as plural and coexist alongside the moral value of individuals, which must always prevail. The second normative commitment is to assume that this moral view of individuals should be recognised by all people equally, as every person deserves equal respect. Finally, the third cosmopolitan commitment would be to accept a universalist view that treats individuals as if they were all citizens of the world (Brown and Held 2010; García Guitian 2016).

The main features of humanity would thus be reason and moral capacity, which unite and ground human fraternity and universal community. This implies that our reflections should focus on addressing the human problems of people who find themselves in a particular situation. That is why the cosmopolitan point that Martha C. Nussbaum draws from Stoicism is that we all owe a moral community that is composed of all human beings. This translates into the ideal of treating with equal respect the dignity of reason and the capacity for moral choice that exists in all human beings. This is the principle that should inspire and regulate our moral and political conduct (Nussbaum 2009).

In the opinion of these authors, the characteristic feature of the cosmopolitan gaze would be to defend an egalitarian and universalist foundation, but one that is also articulated as a moral and political project, incorporating a series of principles that should inspire the reform of the structures of global institutions. This moral perspective is therefore projected onto discourses of global justice, human rights, the reform of the international system and, most critically, the reform of education programmes around the world.

In her classic book *Cultivating Humanity* (1997), Nussbaum diagnosed the main educational needs in the world during the change of century. Nussbaum points out that we live in a multicultural and multinational world that requires problem resolution through dialogue with "the other". This implies being able to put yourself in "the other" shoes, understanding her emotions, thoughts and way of life. The point is that, in an interdependent, globalised reality, this "other" does not only include our fellow national citizens, but also the rest of humankind. Therefore, it is essential to obtain the ability to see oneself as a global citizen, not just belonging to a specific region or group, but related to other human beings by ties of recognition and concern.

During the last decade, some political movements have been contesting "globalism", producing a regressive discourse that highlights national identity over any other form of citizenship (Sparke 2022). Although these discourses are influential, we argue that our world is growing increasingly interdependent and Nussbaum's thesis should still be considered up to date. In fact, in recent years UNESCO has followed Nussbaum's steps by formulating the term "Global Citizenship Education" (UNESCO 2024). According to Nussbaum, we need to promote an education for human development producing decent world citizens who can understand global problems and have the practical competencies to do something about them. This should be based on (Nussbaum 2009):

1. Criticism and critical thought about one's traditions, testing their logic and concepts while imagining alternatives to them.
2. Ability to see oneself as a member of a heterogeneous nation inserted in a diverse world. This is achieved through the understanding of the history and character of different groups and nationalities. In this regard, one should also acknowledge how differences in gender, race, and religion have been associated with different life opportunities.
3. Narrative imagination. This means the cultivation of sympathy towards other realities through moral imagination. This can be cultivated through literature, music, or fine arts, which provide a cultural insight into the experience of different groups.

In this regard, especially a MUN, but also a MEU, is a perfect example of a cosmopolitan education activity that transcends the state as the only unit of awareness and solidarity. The most crucial implication in this matter is role-playing: the *identification* of participants with a random foreign country. This identification does not only imply learning about a country's history or recent political positions on a given subject but also involves entering the cultural and conceptual frames that enable the rational understanding of that country's reality. When we talk about "rational understanding" we mean that the student does not limit herself to acquiring declarative knowledge about her assigned country but also acquires sufficient conceptual knowledge to draw critical conclusions about why her country is positioned in a certain way in a geopolitical debate. This identification between the student and her assigned country is vital to fulfil Nussbaum's cosmopolitan ideal, which does not pursue a mere tolerance or global coexistence but rather requires citizens to understand and find the rational meaning of the different sensitivities that abound in the different countries of the planet (García Guitián 2006; Nussbaum 2009). In fact, the role-playing in simulations is a perfect example of the cultivation of what Nussbaum calls "narrative imagination" (see above).

It is worth insisting on the difference between the rational understanding that simulations facilitate and the mere idea of "tolerance" promoted by some civic education programmes designed in national frameworks. As Janmaat (2013) points out, "ethnic tolerance" is a recurring objective within this kind of programme, in addition to being one of the main concerns of the specialised literature on the subject. However, we must not ignore that the concept of "tolerance" can imply ignoring the rational foundations of the people or values that are being tolerated (Vallespín 2021). That means that to "tolerate" a nation or the actions of its state would not imply knowing its history, its institutions, its culture, or the different reasons that may explain its geopolitical positions. On the other hand, the cosmopolitan education that simulations offer does facilitate a critical approach to all these elements, so that the student is not limited to "tolerating" the different realities with which she establishes contact in the simulation but rather acquires a critical knowledge of each of them.

Identifying with different groups and states is also an opportunity to relativise the cultural perspectives and political positions of one's own country, which connects with Nussbaum's ideal of cosmopolitan critical thought. Additionally, it is important to note that MUN operates through a transnational logic. This means that its specific design and rules of procedure are independent from any decision taken by individual member states in their national curriculum. This independence from national curricula is also an essential value when it comes to cosmopolitan perspective promotion, as this allows the programme to be disassociated from the ethnocentric nature of most national educational systems, which tend to be based on nation-building strategies that normalise states as the natural unit of solidarity, prioritising national standard knowledge over potential individual, personal concerns and interests.

Finally, it is worth highlighting a recurring characteristic among most national civic education programmes that, fortunately, is not found in simulations: the community approach that these national programmes usually adopt. For many decades, the individualisation of society, the constant growth of the private sphere, and the loss of social capital in Western countries have been the main concerns of the literature and of most national programmes on civic education. In the 1970s, many authors were already pointing out this sort of problem, including Richard Sennett with his book *The Fall of the Public Man* (1977). Since then, the gradual disappearance of public life has been systematically pointed out as a great threat against democracy. It was argued that the loss of community feeling, the systematic decrease in electoral turnout, or the gradual disappearance of political and social associations could lead, in the long run, to the loss of legitimacy of the power exercised by democratic institutions. That was the main enemy to be combated in classrooms through civic education. This way, the paradigm of the active citizen and the promotion of community engagement soon became the ideal desired by most specialists in the area (Advisory Group of Citizenship 1998; Galston 2001). An example of this perspective is found in the famous Crick Report (Advisory Group of Citizenship 1998), which marked the direction that civic education would eventually take in the United Kingdom (UK) and in other Western countries. This report repeatedly recommends the participation of students in a series of outdoor activities: volunteering, work experiences, events organisation, and so on. These activities encourage young citizens to integrate into the public sphere of their closest community.

According to some authors, the problem with this perspective is that many countries limit their civic education strategies to a series of "community involvement programmes", as shown by Hanna Borhan (2025) in her Organisation for Economic Co-operation and Development (OECD) working paper. These community involvement programmes try to promote among young people a certain sense of belonging and responsibility towards their closest community – usually their town or city – but sometimes this does not provide students with any kind of broader political perspective that allows them to question critically the *status quo* of their near community. In fact, some authors point out a conservative bias in some community involvement programmes, since they reinforce the students' sense of responsibility towards a community endowed with certain identities and common values that are presented as unalterable (Hinchliffe 2020; Janmaat 2013). On the other hand, simulations provide a global vision that helps students consider their identity and role as citizens within a broader political order, not limited to the specific community in which they live. In other words, simulations encourage critical thinking about one's own society and traditions through the international contextualisation of countries and communities. This is not easily achievable through national, civic education programmes based on local community activities.

Of course, simulations do not fully guarantee this "global vision" either, as some of its activities develop under a highly competitive framework where students are strongly tied to specific national interests. However, identifying with a different nation-state than their own and interacting with other national sensibilities do provide students with a strong global sensibility. Moreover, the fact that this sensibility is acquired in a highly competitive context is not a problem, but a virtue (as the next section shows).

CONFLICT-ORIENTED AND POLITICAL APPROACH TO POLITICS

Another problem derived from a community bias in national civic education programmes is the lack of political perspective. Fortunately, apart from encouraging a cosmopolitan mindset, MUN and MEU also stand out for providing a first-hand, reliable simulation that is both highly political and highly institutionalised. In this regard, simulations foster a specific kind of participation that is intrinsically *political*, in the sense that it highlights the strategic, conflict dimensions of public international struggles; concurrently, this political participation takes place in an extremely *institutionalised* context, where students learn how to integrate and use the complex formalities and rules of procedure of simulation conferences.

The political interaction in simulations forces participants not only to think about politics, but also to *think politically* (Freeden 2008). While thinking about politics implies factual and conceptual knowledge related to the meaning of concepts, theories or political systems (as we should always do in any traditional Political Science class), thinking politically is a know-how procedural ability that we all need to practice at some point in our daily lives, even without noticing: for example, when we think about our relations with the treasury or when we design our best argument to convince our boss to give us a raise. Although thinking about politics may be perfected through different kinds of pedagogical approaches, thinking politically is by definition a know-how skill that is better encouraged through active learning experiences such as simulations. Thanks to this training in "thinking politically", simulations stand out among most civic national education programmes, which insist on a loose moral dimension, fostering a communitarian commitment that is usually "apolitical". Consequently, most national programmes seem to teach young people that they should develop a moral voice within their community, without reflecting on the relations of power and authority present in everyday political life (García Guitián 2006; Hinchliffe 2020). This apolitical commitment to the community is closely related to the "active citizenship" ideal, which fosters political participation as if it had an intrinsic value, without considering how, when, and why people should participate in public life.

Unlike most national programmes, simulations highlight the conflictive and strategic condition of politics. Thus, the value of simulations does not lie in creating "active citizens" as such, but in providing students with a political literacy that allows them to understand the elements that characterise every political conflict: which actors make up the conflict board, what alliances and confrontations exist between them, what is the role of political values in the negotiation, what is the role of political interest, how values and interests interact in the formation of political positions, and so on (see also Chapter 9).

Highlighting the political nature of simulation conferences does not mean that the simulation will establish a cynical, ultra-realistic vision of international relations among young people. It is true that several studies have shown that, once the MUN experience is completed, students do tend to adopt more realistic perspectives on politics and international relations. For example, some authors define MUN as a "reality check" for students, who after the conference would become more sensitive to the conflict, discard idealistic positions and lose confidence in the capacity for international cooperation – as defended by liberal institutionalism (Calossi and Coticchia 2018; Coticchia et al. 2020). However, becoming aware of the political dimension of conflicts can be compatible with preserving a moral sensitivity that allows students to determine which situations are just or unjust. In other words, political literacy acquired during MUN may allow students to distinguish which exercises of power are legitimate in relation to certain UN principles, such as multilateralism, self-determination, sovereignty, or equality of peoples.

Another special element provided by simulations in comparison to other political simulations is the highly institutionalised context in which the participants are embedded. This allows students to familiarise themselves with all the procedural and time constraints that characterise institutions. Several civic education programmes consist of an idealised model that does not correspond to the complexity of political, institutionalised reality. This may end up generating a rejection and disbelief in the political integrity of actual institutions, which in the long term can foster political disengagement or even the emergence of populist and pro-authoritarian sensibilities (Galston 2001, García Guitián 2006). By contrast, the strict formal guidelines in simulations seek to make students understand the role that institutions play in ensuring, not only *efficient*, but also *just* political interaction.

One of the dimensions of civic education that has generated the most attention – both in the literature and in national educational programmes – is *political efficacy*. Specifically, we speak of "*internal political efficacy*" when students have the feeling that their political activity can have real effects on the social reality that surrounds them. On the other hand, we speak of "*external political efficacy*" to indicate the belief that politicians and political institutions are responsive to citizens' demands, being able to change things for the better (Barrett and Pachi 2019). The problem with most educational programmes is that they focus exclusively on a narrow vision of *internal* political efficacy, offering students community activities through which they can easily feel that their actions have an immediate impact on their close social environment. However, there are not many programmes – like MUN and MEU – that fuel external political efficacy among young people. During MUN conferences, participants can identify with these "external" political elites, and they experience first-hand the complex institutional logics that govern among senior diplomats when trying to direct political action in one direction or another.

Some authors point out that the fact of experiencing these complex institutional logics during a simulation can have a negative impact on external political efficacy among youngsters. Thus, after completing the simulation, students would end up with the feeling that in international associations like the UN the possibilities for action and political change are very limited, mainly due to the formal and institutional constraints that govern the conferences: time limits, session interruptions, text formalities, and so on (Engel et al. 2017). However, we argue that this effect can be a positive first step that might lead to understanding the meaning and necessity of institutions and of all the formal constraints that operate in them. This way, the participant may be "disappointed" with the limited scope of action imposed by all the institutional obstacles of the UN or the EU, but this disappointment is compatible with understanding and accepting the need for said obstacles. Therefore, the student might become aware that, without those obstacles or formalities, it is impossible to establish a fair political interaction based on principles such as equity, non-domination, or legal efficacy. This process of institutional understanding can, in the long run, have a positive impact on what the literature calls "*institutional trust*": the belief that political institutions are fair and trustworthy, and that their level of political efficacy is reasonable within the limits that must prevail in any fair political process (Barrett and Pachi 2019).

CONCLUSION

In this chapter we have shown the pedagogical value of political simulations like MUN and MEU. In this regard, we have recapitulated the epistemological foundations of active learning and we have linked them to the educational outcomes that can be acquired through simulations. These outcomes include factual knowledge related to the history of the UN and the EU and their constituent states, conceptual knowledge about International Relations theories and key political concepts, procedural knowledge related to numerous skills and competencies, and, finally, metacognitive knowledge that allows participants to understand their own learning process. Subsequently, we have argued that the pedagogical benefits of a simulation can be integrated into a civic education perspective. Here we have highlighted two civic elements that simulations can promote more successfully than most national civic education programmes: the first element is the adoption of a cosmopolitan attitude in the interpretation of global reality; the second element is the awareness of the political dimension of social conflicts and the importance of institutional constraints in guaranteeing just and efficient interactions.

It is important to understand that the civic benefits of simulations are directly related to the pedagogical foundations of the programme, that is, the active learning approach. The acquisition of a cosmopolitan perspective and the awareness of the political dimension of conflicts are results that are acquired thanks to the pedagogical logic of active learning theory. For example, in MUN simulations students acquire a cosmopolitan narrative imagination only through *experience*, as they take part in a role play dynamic where they need to identify with foreign cultures, institutions and political orientations. Also, this type of learning is acquired through knowledge *construction* because, as predicted by constructivist theory, participants build their own knowledge as the simulation progresses and they face several unpredicted stimuli: negotiations with other participants, improvisation of arguments to justify one's country's position, time and protocol management, and so on. In this dynamic, students need to actively give meaning to every new experience they face.

In short, the simulation procedure itself is strongly linked to the learning outcomes provided by simulations. This is because, as active learning theory shows, knowledge is not an *a priori* substance that students apply in their experiences *a posteriori*. On the contrary, knowledge is also *acquired* through experience, especially through demanding and stimulating experiences like MUN and MEU.

REFERENCES

Advisory Group of Citizenship (1998). Education for Citizenship and the Teaching of Democracy in Schools. London, Qualification and Curriculum Authority.

Baranowski, Michael K./Weir, Kimberly A. (2015). Political Simulations: What We Know, What We Think We Know, and What We Still Need to Know. Journal of Political Science Education 11 (4), 391–403. https://doi.org/10.1080/15512169.2015.1065748

Barr, Robert B./Tagg, John (1995). From Teaching to Learning — A New Paradigm For Undergraduate Education. Change: The Magazine of Higher Learning 27 (6), 12–26. https://doi.org/10.1080/00091383.1995.10544672

Barrett, Martyn/Pachi, Dimitra (2019). Social and Demographic Factors Linked to Youth Civic and Political Engagement. In: Martyn Barrett/Dimitra Pachi (Eds.). Youth Civic And Political Engagement. New York, Taylor & Francis Group, 45–75.

Beck, Ulrich (2005). The Cosmopolitan State: Redefining Power in the Global Age. International Journal of Politics, Culture, and Society 18 (3–4), 143–159. https://doi.org/10.1007/s10767-006-9001-1
Bonwell, Charles C./Eison, James A. (1991). Active Learning: Creating Excitement in the Classroom. ASHE-ERIC Higher Education Report. Washington, D.C., School of Education and Human Development, George Washington University.
Borhan, Hannah (2025). Civic Education as a Pathway to Inclusive Societies: Exploring the Role of Education in Fostering Civic and Social Engagement. OECD Education Working Papers (No. 326). https://doi.org/10.1787/3f128be8-en
Boud, David/Cohen, Ruth/Walker, David (1993). Introduction: Understanding Learning from Experience. In: David Boud/Ruth Cohen/David Walker (Eds.). Using experience for learning. Buckingham/Bristol, Open University Press; Society for Higher Education, 1–17.
Brown, Garrett W./Held, David (Eds.) (2010). The Cosmopolitanism Reader. Cambridge/Malden, Polity Press.
Calossi, Enrico/Coticchia, Fabrizio (2018). Students' Knowledge and Perceptions of International Relations and the "Model United Nations": An Empirical Analysis. Acta Politica 53 (3), 409–428. https://doi.org/10.1057/s41269-017-0058-9
Coticchia, Fabrizio/Calossi, Enrico/Cicchi, Lorenzo (2020). A Reality Check for Students? How Participating to the Model United Nations Influences Skills, IR Perceptions, and Perspectives on Future Career. Politics 40 (2), 245–261. https://doi.org/10.1177/0263395719852238
Dewey, John ([1938] 1998). Experience and Education. New York, Rowman and Littlefield.
Engel, Susan/Pallas, Josh/Lambert, Sarah (2017). Model United Nations and Deep Learning: Theoretical and Professional Learning. Journal of Political Science Education 13 (2), 171–184. https://doi.org/10.1080/15512169.2016.1250644
Freeden, Michael (2008). Editorial: Thinking Politically and Thinking Ideologically. Journal of Political Ideologies 13 (1), 1–10. https://doi.org/10.1080/13569310701828120
Galston, William A. (2001). Political Knowledge, Political Engagement, and Civic Education. Annual Review of Political Science 4 (1), 217–234. https://doi.org/10.1146/annurev.polisci.4.1.217
García Guitián, Elena (2006). La Educación Cívica como Educación Política. Zaragoza, Fundación Jiménez Abad.
García Guitián, Elena (2016). Cosmopolitismo. In: Joan Antón/Xavier Torrens (Eds.). Ideologías y Movimientos Políticos Contemporáneos. Madrid, Technos, 249–260.
Hammond, Augustine/Albert, Craig Douglas (2020). Learning by Experiencing: Improving Student Learning Through a Model United Nations Simulation. Journal of Political Science Education 16 (4), 441–458. https://doi.org/10.1080/15512169.2018.1548967
Hinchliffe, Geoffrey (2020). Civic Republicanism, Citizenship and Education. In: Andrew Peterson/Garth Stahl/Hannah Soong (Eds.). The Palgrave Handbook of Citizenship and Education. Cham, Springer International Publishing, 53–65.
Janmaat, Jan Germen (2013). Civic Competences. Some Critical Reflections. In: Murray Print/Dirk Lange (Eds.). Civic Education and Competences for Engaging Citizens in Democracies. Rotterdam, SensePublishers, 51–64.
Krathwohl, David R. (2002). A Revision of Bloom's Taxonomy: An Overview. Theory Into Practice 41 (4), 212–218. https://doi.org/10.1207/s15430421tip4104_2

Marope, Mmantsetsa/Griffin, Patrick/Gallagher, Carmel (2017). Future Competences and the Future of Curriculum: A Global Reference for Curricula Transformation. Available online at https://learningportal.iiep.unesco.org/en/library/future-competences-and-the-future-of-curriculum-a-global-reference-for-curricula (accessed 5/12/2025).
Martini, Alice (2022). Deconstructing Geopolitics in the Classroom. Grasping Geopolitical Codes Through Active Learning. Revista Española de Ciencia Política 60, 145–173. https://doi.org/10.21308/recp.60.05
Nussbaum, Martha C. (1997). Cultivating Humanity. A Classical Defense of Reform in Liberal Education. Cambridge, MA, Harvard University Press.
Nussbaum, Martha C. (2009). Education for Profit, Education for Freedom. Liberal Education 95 (3), 6–13.
Sennett, Richard (1977). The Fall of Public Man. New York, Alfred A. Knopf.
Smith, Tracy Wilson/Colby, Susan A. (2007). Teaching for Deep Learning. The Clearing House: A Journal of Educational Strategies, Issues and Ideas 80 (5), 205–210. https://doi.org/10.3200/TCHS.80.5.205-210
Sparke, Mattew (2022). Reactionary Anti-Globalism: The Crisis of Globalization. In: Richard Ballard/Clive Barnett (Eds.). The Routledge Handbook of Social Change. London, Routledge, 19–33.
UNESCO (2013). Outcome Document of the Technical Consultation on Global Citizenship Education: Global Citizenship Education: An Emerging Perspective. ED/2013/PSD/PHR/PI/4. Available online at https://unesdoc.unesco.org/ark:/48223/pf0000224115 (accessed 6/2/2025).
UNESCO (2015). Global Citizenship Education: Topics and Learning Objectives. Available online at https://unesdoc.unesco.org/ark:/48223/pf0000232993 (accessed 6/2/2025).
UNESCO (2024). What You Need to Know About Global Citizenship Education. Available online at https://www.unesco.org/en/global-citizenship-peace-education/need-know (accessed 11/26/2024).
Vallespín, Fernando (2021). La sociedad de la intolerancia. Madrid, Galaxia Gutenberg.

PART II

UN, EU and transnational politics

6. The United Nations

Muriel Cathérine Wenzel and Claudia Wiesner

The United Nations (UN) is an International Organisation (IO) – different from the European Union (EU) that also has supranational elements (see Chapter 7). The members of IOs are sovereign states. IOs are established by treaties under international law that provide legal status to them and allow them to enter into agreements with member states or with other IOs (Klabbers 2009, p. 9; Seyersted 2008, pp. 8–26, 51).

The UN was founded by the UN Charter (United Nations 2025a) in San Francisco on 26 June 1945, shortly after the Second World War ended. The UN Charter is part of international law. As such, it is legally binding for the member states of the UN. Currently, 193 states are members of the UN, which makes it the biggest IO worldwide. Established democracies as well as autocracies are UN members, as the organisation is in principle open to all sovereign states worldwide and does not differentiate between types of government (see UN Charter, Article 4) in contrast to the North Atlantic Treaty Organisation (NATO) or the EU, which link membership to the fact that a state is a liberal democracy.

The UN consists of several bodies and part institutions. It takes action in a number of areas and policy fields such as peace and development (see below). Moreover the UN, as well as persons and institutions near to it, such as the UN Peacekeeping Forces in 1988, Secretary-General Dag Hammarskjöld in 1961, or the United Nations Children's Fund (UNICEF) in 1965, have been awarded the Nobel Peace Prize 12 times (United Nations 2025b).

In comparison to other IOs such as the World Trade Organisation (WTO) or the World Health Organisation (WHO) the UN is one of the most formalised ones. This means that the UN has its own organs and a relatively autonomous bureaucracy. These are based on a Charter signed by all member states (Alvarez 2018, pp. 81–83; Scheuermann 2021, pp. 7–8). Furthermore, specific UN rules of procedure are to be adhered to by the member states and their representatives, for example, the Rules of Procedure of the General Assembly that were lastly reissued in 2022 with resolution A/520/Rev.20 (General

Assembly 2022). The UN's legal status was affirmed by an advisory opinion, a non-binding legal advice possible under Chapter IV of the Statute of the International Court of Justice, given by the International Court of Justice (ICJ) in the Reparations case in 1948. In this advisory opinion, the Court affirmed the UN's legal personality as well as its abilities to accord protection to its agents, to bring claims against national states, and its right to offer diplomatic protection (International Court of Justice 1948; for a discussion see Alvarez 2018, p. 81; Chesterman et al. 2016, pp. 113–115; Ku 2018, pp. 197–199).

This chapter aims to provide an insight into the UN system. It will explain what the UN is, how it works, and how it engages in international politics. To do so, the history of the UN will be briefly explained. Then the UN Charter and the tasks and goals of the organisation will be discussed, as well as the UN organs, budget, and the larger UN system. After that, we will sketch specific fields of action and conclude the chapter with an outlook into the future.

HISTORY: BUILDING THE UNITED NATIONS

The UN's predecessor was the League of Nations which was based on an idea of Woodrow Wilson, President of the United States of America (USA) from 1913 to 1921. The League was funded by 32 victorious states of the First World War and 13 neutral states on 28 April 1919 in Geneva. The statutes of the League of Nations came into force on 10 January 1920 (Scheuermann 2021, p. 20; The United Nations Office at Geneva 2025). All in all, the League of Nations remained relatively ineffective. It was not able to fulfil its main tasks and, in particular, it could not prevent the Second World War. This was mainly because the member states of the League of Nations were not interested in recognising it as a world political forum for negotiating. The League of Nations officially ended on 18 April 1946 (Chesterman et al. 2016, p. 3; Gareis 2012, p. 5; Koskenniemi 1995, pp. 333–334; Scheuermann 2018b, p. 2; Scheuermann 2021, pp. 24–25, 34–35).

The UN, then, has its roots in the Second World War and immediate post-war history. Franklin D. Roosevelt, President of the USA from 1933–1954, and Winston S. Churchill, British Prime Minister from 1940 to 1945 and 1951 to 1955, met in August 1941 to form an alliance against Germany. They agreed on the Atlantic Charter, which includes in its eight principles the right of self-determination of peoples and the willingness to build a comprehensive peace order (Morris 2018, pp. 41–42; Scheuermann 2021, pp. 26–27). During the Arcadia Conference, which was held in Washington, D.C., from 22 December 1941 to 14 January 1942, Churchill and Roosevelt agreed on the "Declaration by United Nations" (Secretary of State for Foreign Affairs 1942). This declaration was not yet the start for the UN, but an assurance of the signatories, Churchill, Roosevelt, and 24 signatories of the Anti-Hitler Coalition. They underlined their willingness to stand together in the fight against the members of the Three Power Pact (Germany, Italy and Japan), and not to conclude a separate peace with either Germany or Japan (Scheuermann 2021, pp. 27–28).

The Union of Soviet Socialist Republics (USSR) – even though it had been cooperating with Germany for some time – and China became members of the USA-British alliance in 1942 and 1943. China, the United Kingdom of Great Britain and Northern Ireland (UK), the USA, and the USSR signed four Moscow Declarations in 1943. The first Moscow Declaration, the Declaration of the Four Nations on General Security, includes in its fourth Article a joint declaration that laid the basis for the UN as an IO (Governments of the United States of America, Great Britain, the Soviet Union, and China 1943):

> That they recognize the necessity of establishing at the earliest practicable date a general international organisation, based on the principle of the sovereign equality of all peace-loving states, and open to membership by all such states, large and small, for the maintenance of international peace and security.

After these initial steps, government experts were then responsible for writing draft statutes for the UN. These were assembled in the Dumbarton Oaks Proposals, which consist of 12 chapters (Washington Conversations on International Peace and Security Organization 1944). The chapters describe the UN's main organs and the five permanent members of the Security Council: USA, UK, USSR, China, and France. Details, such as the question of a veto for the permanent members in the Security Council on non-procedural issues but not on procedural ones, were discussed at the Yalta Conference in February 1945. This conference took place among UK, the USA, and the USSR. Its goal was to structure the Post-War World Order (Bundeszentrale für politische Bildung 2020). It also fixed 25 April 1945 as the date for a conference to prepare the founding of the UN (Gareis 2012, pp. 6–7; Morris 2018, pp. 46–47; Scheuermann 2021, pp. 28–31).

The constituent session of the UN, to which 45 more states were invited, took place after the Second World War had ended on 8 May 1945. On 26 May 1945 the UN was officially founded in San Francisco (United Nations 2025c). The UN Charter was unanimously adopted on 25 June 1945 by the heads of 50 states and signed the next day. The Charter entered into force on 24 October 1945, with Poland as the 51st founding state (Gareis 2012, p. 1; Morris 2018, pp. 48–49; Scheuermann 2021, p. 32; United Nations 2017, p. 3).

As the founding history above indicates, the history of the UN is directly related to the experience of the Second World War and the shaping of a Post-War World Order. All major powers after the Second World War could agree on the goals of peace, security and multilateralism. But besides this general agreement, the interests of the winning powers UK, the USA, and USSR differed with regards to the shape the Post-War World Order should take on. While the USA wanted to move closer to its idea of a cultural and ideological world community with the help of the UN, the USSR wanted security in general and UK strove for economic and military security (Scheuermann 2021, p. 33).

The conflicting interests of the major world powers were most prominently underlined by the foundation of NATO that united 12 founding members, all of them Western states sided along the Atlantic. NATO was a defence organisation that was founded with the "North Atlantic Treaty" on 4 April 1949 (NATO 2023). Even though NATO was declared open for other states, its founding de facto marked one key starting point for the Cold War. NATO subsequently developed into the defence organisation known today (NATO 2022). In reaction to NATO founding, the USSR together with its Eastern European allies signed the Warsaw Pact declaration in 1955 (Dembinski 2025).

The years between 1949 and 1951 thus mark the beginning of the Cold War between an Eastern and a Western Bloc in the world. This is reflected also in the European post-war experience. The founding of the UN happened almost in parallel to the founding of the Council of Europe in 1949 and the European Coal and Steel Community (ECSC) in 1951 (see Chapter 7). But the Council of Europe also had Eastern European member states and aimed at peace and multilateralism in the whole of Europe. As opposed to this, the ECSC only consisted of six Western European founding members (Belgium, France, Italy, Luxembourg, the Netherlands, Western Germany). Even though it was also founded on the principles of peace and multilateralism, it led to an economic and political cooperation of the Western European states only.

UN CHARTER, TASKS, AND GOALS

The Charter of the UN builds the basis for the UN's work. Its goals, principles, tasks, and organisational structure are codified in a Preamble, 19 Chapters, and 111 Articles in a treaty under international law that is binding for all signatory states and is not limited in time (Scheuermann 2021, pp. 39–40; United Nations 2017, p. 3; see Chesterman et al. 2016, pp. xxxiii–xliii on the question of whether the Charter is a constitution or not).

The UN Charter has been reformed several times. Initiatives to reform the Charter were successful in 1966 and 1968 when Articles 23, 27, 61, and 109 were formally revised to respond to changes in the membership structure of the UN main bodies. A similar initiative was unsuccessful in 2005 when the General Assembly (GA) tried to change Articles 53, 77, and 107 on the UN Charter's Enemy State Clause, the Board of Trustees, and the General Staff Committee. A de jure enforcement of these approved changes never happened

(Chesterman et al. 2016, p. 643; Scheuermann 2021, pp. 41–41; United Nations 2017, p. 5).

But even though the Charter's text has remained largely unchanged from the 1945 version, over time it has been interpreted differently (Chesterman et al. 2016, p. 4). Furthermore, its principles and purposes have often been criticised for being too many, too ambiguous, sometimes even conflicting and lacking textual constraint (Koskenniemi 1995, p. 327).

Article 1 of the Charter covers the purposes or aims of the UN, which include the maintenance of international peace and security, the prevention and removal of threats to the peace by taking collective measures, and the goal:

> To develop friendly relations among nations based on respect for the principle of equal rights and self-determination of peoples [...]. (UN Charter, Article 1)

Article 1 of the Charter also declares the goal to achieve international cooperation in order to solve international problems in various areas, to protect human rights, and to contribute to the harmonisation of the actions of the UN member states.

Article 2 of the Charter sets the rules for government action in international relations. It states that the UN works on the basis of the sovereign equality of its member states, which means that every sovereign member state has the same weight in the GA, for example, in voting, and is treated equally regardless of, for example, economic differences. The article also underlines the goal of peaceful conflict settlement that all signatories commit to (UN Charter, Article 2). The UN's member states, following Articles 3 and 4 of the UN Charter, are its 51 founding members and other sovereign states that accept, are able to, and will carry out the obligations that the Charter contains (UN Charter, Articles 3–4).

The UN Charter's goals have been specified by the 2000 Millennium Declaration of the General Assembly. In Article 1 (2) of the Millennium Declaration (General Assembly 2000) the GA stated:

> We reaffirm our commitment to the purposes and principles of the Charter of the United Nations, which have proved timeless and universal. Indeed, their relevance and capacity to inspire have increased, as nations and peoples have become increasingly interconnected and interdependent.

The signatories name the following fundamental values as essential ones for the UN: freedom, equality, solidarity, tolerance, respect for nature, and shared responsibility (General Assembly 2000). The Millennium Declaration, all in all, marks an extension of the UN's goals. The aims discussed now include the preservation of positive and negative peace as well as the aim to preserve nature in sustainable ways. This is a decisive complement to classical and human security. The Millennium Declaration is directed not only at states but also mentions amicable relations to civil society. Finally, it mentions the aim to shape globalisation as a positive force and to establish the UN as an actor (see also Gareis 2012, pp. 18–19; Scheuermann 2018b, p. 2). Moreover, women and children are named explicitly as target groups for UN action. It is mentioned that women must enjoy equal rights and gender equality is named as a goal (General Assembly 2000, Article III (20)). It is also underlined that equal rights for all humans are to be granted irrespective of race, sex, language or religion (General Assembly 2000, Article I (4)).

THE UN'S BUDGET

The UN's budget is assembled via member states' mandatory contributions and via voluntary payments to the UN's programmes, funds, and special organisations. The GA decides annually (until 2019 in a two-year cycle) on the budget and the member states' contributions. The latter are based on the per capita gross national income (GNI) of the respective states, including the values of the last six years in the calculation. These "scales of assessment" are adopted by a yearly resolution of the UN's GA (e.g. General Assembly 2024a). An upper level of 22 per cent and a lowest level of 0.001 per cent of the per capita GNI is set to ensure that the UN does not depend on one single member state and that the least developed member states do not carry too much of a burden. Among the five biggest UN donor states the USA have been the most imporant for many years, as they contributed 22 per cent of the UN budget. However, payment discipline of the USA has not been stable. They currently owe 1.5 billion US$ to the UN, which amounts to 181 per cent of its planned contribution for 2025 (International Service for Human Rights 2025). It is currently open to what extent the USA will contribute to the UN in the future. The UN is therefore currently expecting budget cuts of up to 20 per cent and aims at creating cost-effective measures, relocating staff to less expensive cities, and improving efficiency across the UN to prepare for potential budget cuts (Fassihi 2025). The second biggest donor is China (15.25 per cent; 685,733,248 US$ in 2025), followed by Japan (8.03 per cent; 237,231,585 US$ in 2025), and Germany (6.11 per cent; 194,851,686 US$ in 2025) (Auswärtiges Amt 2024; Committee on Contributions 2025; Scheuermann 2018b, p. 6). For 2025, the GA approved a regular budget of 3,717,379,600 Billion US$ (Mishra 2024).

Peacekeeping operations and international tribunals are not covered by the regular budget. Instead, the member states make compulsory contributions to fund peace missions. These contributions are based on a modified distribution formula, which divides the member states into ten different country groups and grants additional deductions to developing countries with a low per capita income. This results in the total contributions to peace missions being borne by the five permanent members of the Security Council as a surcharge on their basic contribution rates (Auswärtiges Amt 2024). For the period from 1 July 2024 to 30 June 2025, the budget for peacekeeping was about 5.6 billion US$. The main contributors were the USA (26.95 per cent), who reduced their contributions to peacekeeping efforts in Trump's first term 2017–2021, China (18.69 per cent), Japan (8.03 per cent), Germany (6.11 per cent) and the UK (5.36 per cent) (United Nations Peacekeeping 2025). UN programmes, funds, offices, and specialised agencies have separate, voluntary budgets (Fassihi 2025; United Nations 2017, p. 30). Here, the USA, with Donald J. Trump becoming President in January 2025, has withdrawn, with an executive order signed in February, from several UN bodies and scaled back or frozen funding (Jefford 2025).

MAIN BODIES

The UN system consists of six principal organs (General Assembly, Security Council, Economic and Social Council (ECOSOC), Trusteeship Council, ICJ, Secretariat) and numerous subsidiary organs that can be established as necessary according to Article 7 of the Charter. In addition, it has 17 specialised agencies and many programmes and funds (see below). The six principal organs will be explained in the following.

The General Assembly

The **GA** is the UN's "chief deliberative, policymaking, and representative organ" (United Nations 2017, p. 5). In the GA, every member state of the UN has one vote. This means each state has the same weight in a decision on a resolution. GA decisions are taken with the majority of the member states' votes. They carry important political and moral clout even though they are mostly non-binding. Decisions in the GA require a two-thirds majority of the member states who are present and voting when they concern questions such as recommendations on international peace and security, the suspension of rights or privileges of membership, the expulsion of member states, or the budget as well as the admission of new member states, or elections, such as the election of the non-permanent members of the Security Council or of members of the ECOSOC. All other decisions require a majority of the member states that are present and voting (UN Charter, Article 18). Votes can be recorded or done by a show of hands or a roll-call (United Nations 2017, p. 7). The GA can be understood as a parliamentary body (see Peterson 2018, p. 120; Wiesner et al. 2017; as well as Chapter 9 in this volume).

Around three-quarters of all GA votes are adopted by consensus (Luck 2018, p. 808). Since GA votes are thus often taken with a huge majority, their language is often vague and sometimes inconsistent. According to Article 10 of the Charter, the GA discusses questions and matters that fall within the scope of the Charter or are related to powers or functions the Charter provides to UN organs. Excluded are only those topics that the Security Council is already discussing (UN Charter, Article 12; Scheuermann 2018b, p. 5).

The GA mainly serves as a forum of interstate diplomacy, because its decisions are non-binding, although they have a high symbolic value. The GA can only issue recommendations either to the member states or to the Security Council, or to both of them (UN Charter, Article 10; Alvarez 2018, p. 79). Therefore, the GA has been discussed as "moralist, admonisher or initiator" (Scheuermann 2018b, p. 5). The UN itself states about the decisions of the GA:

> While the decisions of the Assembly have no legally binding force for governments, they carry the weight of world opinion and the moral authority of the world community. (United Nations 2017, p. 7)

In consequence, the UN is described as having a lot of "soft power" which includes normative and communicative power, but only little "hard power" (Alvarez 2018, pp. 85–87, 94–95; Scheuermann 2021, pp. 12–13).

However, the GA disposes of some relatively "hard power" in that it is tasked to consider and approve the UN finances and budget (UN Charter, Article 17). In this respect, it is able to make legally binding decisions for the member states (Chesterman et al. 2016, p. 151; Luck 2018, p. 806). Furthermore, the proceedings in the GA, as in other UN bodies, are marked by the member states' interests. Member states try to influence GA majorities and follow UN decisions in their own strategic interests, for example, by blocking decisions or funding.

The GA meets yearly in the third week of September and holds a General Debate. The GA session is usually accompanied by numerous high-level meetings in the UN headquarters in New York. The GA sessions give the UN a high visibility via the related media reports and the symbolic power of the decisions the GA takes. Moreover, a high number of state and government representatives are present at the sessions (Hecht and Steffek 2024, p. 288). In addition to the General Debate, the GA meets upon request of the Security Council, of a majority of member states, or of one member state if the majority of member states concurs. Emergency special sessions are also possible (United Nations 2017, p. 6).

The operative work of the GA takes place in its six main committees, i.e. the First Committee (Disarmament & International Security), Second Committee (Economic & Financial), Third Committee (Social, Humanitarian & Cultural),

Fourth Committee (Special Political & Decolonisation), Fifth Committee (Administrative & Budgetary), and Sixth Committee (Legal). Each member state sends one representative as well as advisers, technical advisers, experts or persons of similar status as members of the committee (Scheuermann 2018b, p. 5; United Nations 2024b).

The Security Council

The **Security Council** consists of 15 member states, among them five permanent members (China, France, Russia, UK, USA) and ten member states as non-permanent members elected by the GA for a term of two years. Each member state sends one representative to the GA (UN Charter, Article 23). In contrast to the GA, decisions of the Security Council are legally binding for the UN member states (UN Charter, Article 25; Chesterman et al. 2016, p. 144). Accordingly, the Security Council has an immediate impact in world politics on the one hand. On the other hand, decision-making in the Security Council can be difficult at times because its members have a veto right: the five permanent members – as said above, these are China, France, Russia, UK, USA – do have the right to veto non-procedural votes, which then require a vote of at least nine members and the absence of such a veto. This has led to the Security Council being unable to condemn the Russian attack against Ukraine. However, the veto was used extensively during the Cold War but less often since the 1990s (UN Charter, Article 17; Scheuermann 2018b, pp. 4–5; for details on the history of the veto see Morris 2018, pp. 51–54). Meanwhile, an affirmative vote of at least nine members is necessary for procedural matters (United Nations 2017, p. 7).

Following alphabetical order, each member state holds the presidency of the Security Council for one month (United Nations 2017, p. 7). The Security Council meets periodically, not only in the UN headquarters but in different places worldwide (UN Charter, Article 28). However, one representative of each member state must be present in the UN headquarters in New York at all times (United Nations 2017, p. 8).

The Security Council is responsible for the maintenance of international peace and security (UN Charter, Article 24; von Einsiedel and Malone 2018, p. 140). It decides if a certain situation poses a risk or a breach of peace. If it decides so, it can then authorise collective (non-)military measures which include mediation, sanctions, the deployment of UN peacekeeping forces as well as authorised humanitarian intervention (Scheuermann 2018b, p. 4). The Security Council has to be sensitive to changing conditions in armed conflicts and to varying geopolitical conditions (Luck 2018, p. 809).

Comparing the GA to the Security Council, Koskenniemi (1995, p. 336) states:

> This dichotomy between hard UN (political activities for which the Security Council is mainly responsible) and soft UN (activities for which the General Assembly – through the ECOSOC – is mainly responsible) is functionally and ideologically the most significant structuring feature of the organization.

The Economic and Social Council

The **Economic and Social Council** (ECOSOC) is one of the six main UN organs. Its members are elected among the members of the GA, which means it is de facto under the authority of the GA (Rosenthal 2018, p. 165). As specified in Article 61 of the UN Charter, the ECOSOC is tasked with discussing and formulating policy recommendations on specific issues, for example, economic or educational matters. As defined in Article 61 of the Charter, the ECOSOC consists of representatives of 54 member states. Eighteen states per year are elected by the GA for a duration of three years and based on geographical representation (United Nations 2017, p. 12). Each member has one vote and decisions are made by a majority of the member states who are present and voting, like in the GA (UN Charter, Article 67). According to Article 62 of the Charter, the ECOSOC can ask for or produce studies and reports about international economic, social, cultural, educational, health, or related matters. It can furthermore make recommendations to the GA, the member states, or specialised agencies on these matters and with regard to the promotion of respect or observance of human rights. In addition, it can prepare draft conventions and hold international conferences on the matters mentioned before (UN Charter, Article 62). The ECOSOC furthermore grants consultative status to Non-Governmental Organisations (NGOs) which allows them to observe its meetings and to submit written statements (UN Charter, Article 71; United Nations 2017, p. 15). The ECOSOC mostly serves as a coordinating and steering body (Rosenthal 2018, p. 166; Scheuermann 2018b, p. 6).

The Trusteeship Council and the International Court of Justice

The **Trusteeship Council** was founded to transitionally manage the former colonies. It stopped working after Palau's independence by a resolution in 1994 (UN Charter, Article 87; Scheuermann 2018b, p. 6; United Nations 2017, p. 1, 7). However, the Trusteeship Council has never been formally terminated. It does not have a budget anymore; in 2013, it met to elect a new president and vice president, and it was lastly used to speak with the candidates to become Secretary-General in 2016 (Luck 2018, pp. 817–818).

The **International Court of Justice** (ICJ) is the principal judicial organ of the UN. It was already part of the League of Nations and has since been integrated into the UN. The ICJ Statute is an integral part of the Charter and is defined in Article 92 onwards (UN Charter, Articles 92–96; see also Ku 2018, p. 190; Scheuermann 2021, p. 35; United Nations 2017, p. 16). The ICJ is today situated in The Hague, the Netherlands, and consists of 15 judges from 15 different states. These judges act as independent magistrates and are elected by the Security Council and the GA for a period of nine years (International Court of Justice 1920, Articles 2–13; United Nations 2017, p. 16). The ICJ is not responsible for individuals – cases relating to individuals are subject to the actions of the International Criminal Court (ICC) since 2002 – but only for disputes among states (Ku 2018, p. 190; Scheuermann 2018b, p. 6; United Nations 2017, p. 16). Article 93 of the UN Charter states that all UN member states are parties to the ICJ Statute. Non-UN members can become a party to its Statute, but the GA needs to determine the conditions of adhesion individually, and membership can only take place upon recommendation of the Security Council. This allows for non-UN members to call to the ICC, too. The Court's judgments are binding and there is no appeal for the parties concerned by them (UN Charter, Articles 92–96; United Nations 2017, p. 16). In addition to the settlement of legal disputes on all matters that are included either in the Charter or in other international treaties or conventions, the GA, the Security Council, organs, and specialised UN agencies can request advisory opinions on legal questions from the ICJ (UN Charter, Article 96; United Nations 2017, p. 16; see also Ku 2018, pp. 197–201).

The Secretariat and the Secretary-General

The **Secretariat** carries out the UN's day-to-day operations. It is defined in Article 97 of the UN Charter, which does not outline its scope of action in detail. The Secretariat comprises one Secretary-General and the UN staff. It serves as the administration of the UN and employs around 41,000 people in various departments or offices with distinct responsibilities and areas of action in different places worldwide (Scheuermann 2018b, p. 5; United Nations 2017, p. 17). Its headquarters are based in New York, and there are three regional headquarters in Geneva, Nairobi, and Vienna (United Nations 2017, p. 17). The **Secretary-General** is the UN's "chief administrative officer" as well as the voice and the face of the UN (Scheuermann 2018b, p. 5; UN Charter, Article 97).

Importantly, the Secretary-General and the related staff act independently from the member states. This means that they do not follow instructions from anyone outside the UN and that they are not allowed to perform any action which might reflect on their position as international officials who are solely responsible to the UN (UN Charter, Article 100; Newman 2018, p. 235). However, the Secretary-General depends on the member states who grant legitimacy and resources to the UN, which can lead to tensions between his role as a secretary or as a general (Chesterman et al. 2016, p. 164; Newman 2018, pp. 246–247).

Former Secretary-Generals followed their own political visions and extended the political weight of the office. Kofi Annan, for example, advanced the concept of Responsibility to Protect (R2P) and the Millennium Development Goals (MDGs). He was granted a Nobel Peace Prize. Boutros Boutros-Ghali created the agenda for peace in 1992, and Dag Hammarskjöld invented the "preventive diplomacy" and was posthumously awarded the Nobel Peace Prize (Newman 2018, pp. 240–246; Scheuermann 2018b, p. 5). Since 2017, António Guterres has been the ninth Secretary-General of the UN.

Article 99 of the Charter allows the Secretary-General to bring matters that could threaten international security and peace to the Security Council, thereby putting matters on the agenda (Newman 2018, p. 234). The United Nations describes

> "[...] the use of his good offices – steps taken publicly and in private, drawing on his impartiality – to prevent and resolve international disputes" as one of the Secretary-General's "most vital roles". (United Nations 2017, p. 19)

In 2016 the GA changed the nomination and voting procedure for the Secretary-General. Now the procedure foresees that candidates have to answer questions in public hearings of the GA and other committees (Chesterman et al. 2016, pp. 167–168; Luck 2018, pp. 799–802; Scheuermann 2018b, p. 6).

OTHER BODIES OF THE UN AND UN ACTIVITIES

The UN's principal organs have their own subsidiary bodies, funds and programmes (such as UNICEF), functional or regional commissions, departments and offices, as well as research and training institutes. In addition the UN has a number of specialised agencies which are autonomous IOs. Among these are the Food and Agriculture Organisation of the United Nations (FAO), the International Labour Organisation (ILO), the International Monetary Fund (IMF), the WHO, and the World Bank Group (United Nations 2024f). All of these have their own area of work, leadership and budget. While the programmes and funds are funded by voluntary contributions, the specialised agencies are funded by both voluntary and assessed contributions of the UN member states (United Nations 2024f; see also Gareis 2012, pp. 3–4).

The UN is mainly active in the areas of international peace and security, economic and social development, and human rights. It maintains international peace and security, for instance, by working in conflict prevention or by deploying peacekeepers. It coordinates humanitarian aid, for example, in humanitarian health emergencies or when natural disasters occur. The UN also supports sustainable development and climate action by advocating for the global environment or helping to implement the Sustainable Development Goals (SDGs) (Department of Economic and Social Affairs 2025). The UN is furthermore active in human rights protection using legal instruments or on-the-ground activities based on the Universal Declaration of Human Rights (UDHR) (United Nations 2025d). Some of its activities will be described in more detail in the following.

Peace

Regarding peace and security, Chapter VI of the UN Charter includes details on the Pacific Settlement of Disputes. It stresses in Article 33 that parties of any dispute should try to solve it by peaceful means first, which could for example be done via negotiations, mediations, conciliations or judicial settlements. Articles 41 and 42 of the Charter, however, include other measures to be taken by the Security Council only. Such measures range from the complete or partial interruption of economic relations or communication to the severance of diplomatic relations. If these measures are not sufficient, the Security Council can call for further actions which could either be demonstrations or blockades, or "other operations by air, sea, or land forces" (UN Charter, Articles 41–42).

Chapter VII of the UN Charter provides details on how the Security Council can take the mentioned enforcement measures to maintain or restore international peace and security (Chesterman et al. 2016, pp. 319–320). Usually, the Security Council adopts a resolution to establish a peacekeeping operation based on a report by the Secretary-General, while the GA can determine the budget of the operations (Koops et al. 2015a, p. 3). Peacekeeping operations, which include military and/or police personnel, are carried out by the UN Department of Peacekeeping Operations (DPKO), while civilian peacekeeping or political missions fall under the responsibility of the UN Department of Political Affairs (DPA) (Koops et al. 2015a, p. 1).

The UN disposes of special envoys and political missions in the field for conflict prevention, engages in peacebuilding activities, and deploys UN peacekeeping operations. There are currently 11 peacekeeping operations running, and a total of 71 have been going on since 1948 (United Nations 2025e; for details on UN peacekeeping operations see contributions in de Coning and Mateja 2019 or in Koops et al. 2015b). The UN also coordinates the global fight against terrorism by elaborating 18 universal instruments against international terrorism and is active on disarmament, pursuing regulation of arms as well as the elimination of nuclear and mass destruction weapons (United Nations 2017, pp. 105–108; United Nations 2024c). Furthermore, the UN provides electoral assistance, for example, technical assistance or financial and material support, to its member states (United Nations 2017, pp. 66–67).

Development

In 2015, the UN adopted the 2030 Agenda for Sustainable Development, including 17 SDGs to be met until 2030, a Declaration, means of implementation, and a review and follow-up framework (Department of Economic and Social Affairs 2025). The SDGs officially came into force in January 2016. Until 2015, the eight MDGs which were launched in 2002 had been targeted (United Nations 131; United Nations 2024a). The new SDGs are broader in scope than the MDGs were. They comprise 169 targets and 230 indicators, including goals such as "No Poverty", "Zero Hunger", "Gender Equality", and "Sustainable Cities and Communities". However, they are not legally binding for the UN member states. This is fertile ground for political conflict, as any concrete measure needs to be debated and decided upon by the UN member states.

Concrete policies and actions to implement the SDGs are written down in the Addis Ababa Action Agenda. An annual SDG Progress Report to be prepared by the Secretary-General and annual meetings of the High-level Political Forum on sustainable development are used to monitor the implementation (United Nations 2017, pp. 132–133; United Nations 2024e). In evaluation of the SDGs, progress towards achieving the SDGs has been judged insufficient. There is concern that the targets might not be met by 2030. This might be due to the fact that the goals were not adequate to achieve the intended outcomes (Sorooshian 2024, p. 1).

UN Conferences

The Committee on Conferences is responsible for conference management at the UN. It was established in UN resolution 2239 (XXI) on 20 December 1966 (General Assembly 1966a), re-established in resolution 3351 (XXIX) on 18 December 1974 (General Assembly 1974) and confirmed as a permanent subsidiary organ in resolution 43/222 on 21 December 1988 (General Assembly 1988). Its tasks include managing the UN's calendar of conferences and meetings and the use of conference-servicing resources and facilities as well as matters related to documentation, publication, translation, and interpretation (United Nations 2024h).

The UN organises conferences regularly, most often in relation to issues that have worldwide relevance such as development or climate. These conferences take place in addition to the regular sessions of the UN organs. According to the GA's resolution 40/243, UN bodies can hold sessions in member states on invitation, when the (in-)direct costs are defrayed by the member state (General Assembly 1985). Examples of such UN conferences are the First World Population Conference in Rome, Italy, in 1954, the World Summit for

Social Development in Copenhagen, Denmark, in 1995, or most recently the United Nations Framework Convention on Climate Change, 29th Conference of the Parties in Baku, Azerbaijan, and the Summit of the Future in New York, USA, both in 2024.

UN conferences like these, and especially conferences that relate to topics of such impact as climate change, show a high level of visibility and are highly politicised. They certainly are key events of what can be termed a global public sphere (Hecht and Steffek 2024, pp. 286–287). It is however questionable who belongs to such a global public sphere and how many people except the Western interested public take the conference into account. UN conferences last approximately two weeks. Usually, they are concluded with an outcome document that is the result of tough negotiations (e.g. see United Nations Climate Change 2025).

Universal Declaration of Human Rights

The Universal Declaration of Human Rights (UDHR), which was adopted by the GA in 1948 (United Nations 2025f), is probably the most well-known UN document. The declaration is considered to be "customary international law" (Scheuermann 2018b, p. 2) because of its wide acceptance (United Nations 2017, p. 198). Concretely, many national courts refer to the UDHR. The UDHR is usually discussed jointly with the International Covenant on Economic, Social and Cultural Rights (General Assembly 1966b) and the International Covenant on Civil and Political Rights (United Nations 1967). These Covenants were both adopted in 1966 by the GA. The three documents build the International Bill of Human Rights, which is legally binding to its signatories and monitored by treaty bodies.

The coordination of efforts protecting and promoting human rights lies with the United Nations High Commissioner for Human Rights, who is appointed for four years. In addition, every body of the UN is involved to a certain degree in dealing with human rights (Chesterman et al. 2016, pp. 477–479; United Nations 2017, pp. 197–204). The Human Rights Council was established in 2006 and has particular responsibilities in this respect. It addresses violations of human rights, makes recommendations, develops international norms, provides an international forum in which concerns can be voiced, and publishes a universal periodic review on human rights records of UN member states every four years to ensure universality and equal treatment of each member state (United Nations 2017, pp. 203–204). The Human Rights Council is supported by a Human Rights Council Advisory Committee, which is composed of 18 independent experts from different professional backgrounds, of which five come from Africa, five from Asia, two from Eastern Europe, three from Latin America and the Caribbean, and three from Western Europe and other member states. These experts are nominated by their governments and elected by the Human Rights Council, usually in September, for three years with one possible re-election (United Nations 2017, p. 204; United Nations Human Rights Council 2024). The UN described its role with regard to human rights as being a "global conscience", a "lawmaker", a "monitor", a "nerve centre", a "defender", a "researcher", a "forum of appeal", a "fact-finder", and a "discreet diplomat" (United Nations 2017, pp. 206–207).

THE EU IN THE UN

The UN and the EU not only originated in the same period after the Second World War, they also share support for the principles of peace and multilateralism.

> The EU is committed to multilateralism, with a strong and effective UN at its core. The Council of the EU adopts the EU's priorities annually at the UN and the UN General Assembly. (European Council and Council of the European Union 2025)

This orientation is also institutionally reflected. Based on the GA's resolution 65/276, the EU enjoys an enhanced observer status in the UN (General Assembly 2011; see in detail European Union 2025). This allows the EU to participate and speak in the GA, as well as to submit proposals and amendments to draft resolutions (Hosli and Kantorowicz 2024, p. 2; for details on the relation of the EU and UN regarding peacekeeping see Koops and Tardy 2015, pp. 63–64). However, the EU does not have a right to vote in the UN. Since 2011, the presidency of the European Council speaks for the EU alongside its member states in the General Debate (European Council and Council of the European Union 2025; Hosli and Kantorowicz 2024, p. 2; Scheuermann 2018a, p. 2). Moreover, the EU member states use the General Debates to present their own position as UN member states, thereby articulating national priorities and views based on their own national perspectives (Hosli and Kantorowicz 2024, p. 16).

The EU has a delegation at the UN that is present at the New York headquarters. The staff there coordinate the positions of the EU member states to create common positions for the EU (Hosli and Kantorowicz 2024, p. 4). Such increasing coordination is expected to lead to more convergence of the member states and the official EU position and a higher level of overall cohesion on positions and voting patterns on UN resolutions (Hosli and Kantorowicz 2024, p. 4). The UN-EU cooperation is also publicised. Both the EU's External Action Service, which is linked to the European Commission under the directorship of the High Representative for Foreign and Security Policy, and the European Council emphasise the UN representation on their websites.

FUTURE

Looking at the future and current challenges for the UN, the need for reforms and adaptations to a changing global order are apparent. The UN faces new challenges and threats, for example, worldwide diseases such as COVID-19, rising interpersonal and gang violence, intrastate wars, and migration, as well as technological developments. New actors such as NGOs, businesses, and the media on the international level make discussions at the UN somewhat more pluralistic and lead to decisions reflecting a wider array of perspectives (Weiss and Daws 2018, pp. 4–6). However, the legitimacy of NGOs – who usually are not elected but act on behalf of their members or stakeholders – may be rightfully questioned. Another challenge is the expected budget cuts by the largest donor, the USA. The UN expects a 20 per cent reduction of its budget for 2025 and faces financial problems which also result from member states other than the USA who are not paying their annual dues on time and in full. It aims to draw up plans for budget cuts to be added to the 2026 budget (Fassihi 2025).

Various actors and researchers have made proposals to reform the UN. Nine recent and popular ideas include: 1) building a more legitimate Security Council; 2) having a more balanced and focused GA; 3) transforming ECOSOC into an Economic, Social and Environmental Council; 4) reconfiguring the Human Rights Council; 5) improvements in the UN's staffing and management practices; 6) autonomous emergency services for the UN; 7) reforms on financing the UN; 8) clearer principles and criteria for the R2P; and 9) changing the dispersion and control of global power (Trent and Schnurr 2021, pp. 130–143).

At the 2024 Summit of the Future, after long and complicated negotiations the GA adopted the resolution A/RES/79/1 named "Pact for the Future" that includes a "Global Digital Compact" and a "Declaration on Future Generations" (General Assembly 2024b). This pact includes 56 actions as well as five objectives in the Digital Compact. In the area of peace and security, the member states agreed on a reform of the Security Council (General Assembly 2024b, Action 39). Such a reform is found to be long overdue, but no agreement has been reached in the past (Chesterman et al. 2016, pp. 644–646). The declaration also includes a "multilateral recommitment to nuclear disarmament" (General Assembly 2024b, Action 25) and it contains an agreement "on the need for reform of the international financial architecture" (General Assembly 2024b, Actions 47–52). Regarding climate change, the declaration confirmed the "need to keep global temperature rise to 1.5°C above pre-industrial levels and to transition away from fossil fuels in energy systems to achieve net-zero emissions by 2050" (General Assembly 2024b, Action 9). With regards to digital cooperation, not only "the first comprehensive global framework for digital cooperation and AI governance" but also "the first global commitment to data governance" was declared (United Nations 2024g). With regards to youth and future generations, the member states made the first Declaration on Future Generations (Action x), and with regards to human rights and gender, they signalled "the importance of engagement of other stakeholders in global governance, including local and regional governments, civil society, private sector and others" (United Nations 2024g). Follow-up and reviews are integrated in the resolution to ensure the implementation of the declaration on future generations (United Nations 2024d; United Nations 2024g).

REFERENCES

Alvarez, José E. (2018). Legal Perspectives. In: Thomas G. Weiss/Sam Daws (Eds.). The Oxford Handbook on the United Nations. Oxford, Oxford University Press, 79–103.

Auswärtiges Amt (2024). Hintergrund: Beiträge zum Haushalt der Vereinten Nationen. Available online at https://www.auswaertiges-amt.de/de/aussenpolitik/regelbasierte-internationale-ordnung/uno/01-grundlagen-uno/01-haushalt-uno/274848 (accessed 11/28/2024).

Bundeszentrale für politische Bildung (2020). Vor 75 Jahren: Konferenz von Jalta. Available online at https://www.bpb.de/kurz-knapp/hintergrund-aktuell/304640/vor-75-jahren-konferenz-von-jalta/ (accessed 4/1/2025).

Chesterman, Simon/Johnstone, Ian/Malone, David (2016). Law and Practice of the United Nations. Documents and Commentary. Oxford/New York, NY/Auckland, Oxford University Press.

de Coning, Cedric/Peter, Mateja (Eds.) (2019). United Nations Peace Operations in a Changing Global Order. Cham, Palgrave Macmillan.

Dembinski, M. (2025). Warschauer Pakt. Available online at https://www.bpb.de/kurz-knapp/lexika/das-europalexikon/177358/warschauer-pakt/ (accessed 4/1/2025).

Department of Economic and Social Affairs (2025). The 17 Goals. Available online at https://sdgs.un.org/goals (accessed 4/1/2025).

European Council/Council of the European Union (2025). EU Cooperation with the United Nations. Available online at https://www.consilium.europa.eu/en/policies/eu-un-cooperation/ (accessed 4/1/2025).

European Union (2025). Delegation of the European Union to the United Nations in New York. Available online at https://www.eeas.europa.eu/delegations/un-new-york_en?s=63 (accessed 4/1/2025).

Fassihi, Farnaz (2025). UN Orders Agencies to Find Budget Cuts, Including via Staff Relocations From N.Y. The New York Times. Available online at https://www.nytimes.com/2025/04/29/world/un-budget-cuts-trump.html (accessed 5/19/2025).

Gareis, Sven Bernhard (2012). The United Nations: An Introduction. 2nd ed. Houndmills/Basingstoke/Hampshire, Palgrave Macmillan.

Hecht, Catherine/Steffek, Jens (2024). Salient Discourses in International Society: When and How have United Nations Global Conferences Acted as Catalysts? Journal of International Relations and Development 27 (3), 283–314. https://doi.org/10.1057/s41268-024-00324-7

Hosli, Madeleine O./Kantorowicz, Jaroslaw (2024). The European Union in the annual United Nations General Assembly Debates. Contemporary Politics, 1–26. https://doi.org/10.1080/13569775.2024.2387424

International Service for Human Rights (2025). UN Liquidity Crisis: Analysis of Contributions Paid by UN Member States by Date of Payment (2019–2025). Available online at https://ishr.ch/latest-updates/un-liquidity-crisis-analysis-of-contributions-paid-by-un-member-states-by-date-of-payment-2019-2025/ (accessed 11/13/2025).

Jefford, Kasmira (2025). Will Trump Continue to Fund the UN? Available online at https://genevasolutions.news/global-news/will-trump-continue-to-fund-the-un (accessed 5/19/2025).

Klabbers, Jan (2009). An Introduction to International Institutional Law. Cambridge, Cambridge University Press.

Koops, Joachim A./MacQueen Norrie/Tardy, Thierry/Williams, Paul D. (2015a). Introduction: The United Nations and Peacekeeping. In: Joachim A. Koops/MacQueen Norrie/Thierry Tardy et al. (Eds.). The Oxford Handbook of United Nations Peacekeeping Operations. Oxford, Oxford University Press, 1–9.

Koops, Joachim A./MacQueen Norrie/Tardy, Thierry/Williams, Paul D. (Eds.) (2015b). The Oxford Handbook of United Nations Peacekeeping Operations. Oxford, Oxford University Press.

Koops, Joachim A./Tardy, Thierry (2015). The United Nations' Inter-organizations Relations in Peacekeeping. In: Joachim A. Koops/MacQueen Norrie/Thierry Tardy et al. (Eds.). The Oxford Handbook of United Nations Peacekeeping Operations. Oxford, Oxford University Press, 60–77.

Koskenniemi, Martti (1995). The Police in the Temple Order, Justice and the UN. A Dialectical View. European Journal of International Law (6), 325–348.

Ku, Charlotte (2018). International Court of Justice. In: Thomas G. Weiss/Sam Daws (Eds.). The Oxford Handbook on the United Nations. Oxford, Oxford University Press, 190–211.

Luck, Edward C. (2018). Prospects for UN Renovation and Reform. In: Thomas G. Weiss/Sam Daws (Eds.). The Oxford Handbook on the United Nations. Oxford, Oxford University Press, 796–822.

Mishra, Vibhu (2024). General Assembly Approves $3.72 Billion UN Budget for 2025. Available online at https://news.un.org/en/story/2024/12/1158531 (accessed 3/21/2025).

Morris, Justin (2018). Origins of the United Nations. In: Thomas G. Weiss/Sam Daws (Eds.). The Oxford Handbook on the United Nations. Oxford, Oxford University Press, 40–58.

Newman, Edward (2018). Secretary-General. In: Thomas G. Weiss/Sam Daws (Eds.). The Oxford Handbook on the United Nations. Oxford, Oxford University Press, 231–249.

Peterson, M. J. (2018). General Assembly. In: Thomas G. Weiss/Sam Daws (Eds.). The Oxford Handbook on the United Nations. Oxford, Oxford University Press.

Rosenthal, Gert (2018). Economic and Social Council. In: Thomas G. Weiss/Sam Daws (Eds.). The Oxford Handbook on the United Nations. Oxford, Oxford University Press, 165–177.

Scheuermann, Manuela (2018a). Die Europäische Union und die Vereinten Nationen. UN-Basis-Informationen 42. Deutsche Gesellschaft für die Vereinten Nationen e. V. Available online at https://dgvn.de/veroeffentlichungen/publikation/einzel/die-europaeische-union-und-die-vereinten-nationen (accessed 9/17/2024).

Scheuermann, Manuela (2018b). Die Vereinten Nationen im Überblick. UN-Basis-Informationen 57. Deutsche Gesellschaft für die Vereinten Nationen e. V. Available online at https://dgvn.de/veroeffentlichungen/publikation/einzel/die-vereinten-nationen-im-ueberblick (accessed 9/17/2024).
Scheuermann, Manuela (2021). Die Vereinten Nationen. Eine Einführung. 2nd ed. Wiesbaden/Heidelberg, Springer VS.
Seyersted, Finn (2008). Common Law of International Organizations. Leiden/Boston, Martinus Nijhoff Publishers.
Sorooshian, Shahryar (2024). The Sustainable Development Goals of the United Nations: A Comparative Midterm Research Review. Journal of Cleaner Production 453, 142272. https://doi.org/10.1016/j.jclepro.2024.142272.
The United Nations Office at Geneva (2025). The League of Nations. Available online at https://www.ungeneva.org/en/about/league-of-nations/overview (accessed 3/21/2025).
Trent, John E./Schnurr, Laura (2021). Renaissance der Vereinten Nationen. Gegenwart und Potentiale im 21.
United Nations (2017). Basic Facts About the United Nations. 42nd ed. New York, United Nations, Department of Public Information.
United Nations (2024a). Background. Available online at https://www.un.org/millenniumgoals/bkgd.shtml (accessed 10/7/2024).
United Nations (2024b). General Assembly of the United Nations. Main Committees. Available online at https://www.un.org/en/ga/maincommittees/ (accessed 9/18/2024).
United Nations (2024c). Maintain International Peace and Security. Available online at https://www.un.org/en/our-work/maintain-international-peace-and-security (accessed 10/7/2024).
United Nations (2024d). Summit of the Future Outcome Documents. September 2024. Pact for the Future, Global Digital Compact, and Declaration on Future Generations. Available online at https://www.un.org/en/summit-of-the-future (accessed 10/10/2024).
United Nations (2024e). The Sustainable Development Agenda. Available online at https://www.un.org/sustainabledevelopment/development-agenda/ (accessed 10/7/2024).
United Nations (2024f). UN System. Available online at https://www.un.org/en/about-us/un-system (accessed 9/16/2024).
United Nations (2024g). United Nations Adopts Ground-Breaking Pact for the Future to Transform Global Governance. GA/12641. Available online at https://press.un.org/en/2024/ga12641.doc.htm?_gl=1*vli8te*_ga*MTk2NTM3Mjk2OC4xNzI4NTUyNDUx*_ga_TK9BQL5X7Z*MTcyODU1MjQ1MC4xLjEuMTcyODU1MjQ5My4wLjAuMA (accessed 10/10/2024).
United Nations (2024h). Committee on Conferences. Available online at https://www.un.org/dgacm/en/content/coc (accessed 11/28/2024).
United Nations (2025b). Nobel Peace Prize. Available online at https://www.un.org/en/about-us/nobel-peace-prize (accessed 4/1/2025).
United Nations (2025c). The San Francisco Conference. Available online at https://www.un.org/en/about-us/history-of-the-un/san-francisco-conference (accessed 4/1/2025).
United Nations (2025d). Our Work. Available online at https://www.un.org/en/our-work (accessed 3/24/2025).
United Nations (2025e). United Nations Peacekeeping. Available online at https://peacekeeping.un.org/en (accessed 4/1/2025).
United Nations Climate Change (2025). Outcomes of the Baku Climate Change Conference - Advance Unedited Versions (AUVs). Available online at https://unfccc.int/cop29/auvs (accessed 4/1/2025).

United Nations Human Rights Council (2024). Advisory Committee. Available online at https://www.ohchr.org/en/hr-bodies/hrc/advisory-committee/hrcac-index (accessed 11/28/2024).

United Nations Peacekeeping (2025). How We Are Funded. Available online at https://peacekeeping.un.org/en/how-we-are-funded (accessed 3/21/2025).

von Einsiedel, Sebastian/Malone, David M. (2018). Security Council. In: Thomas G. Weiss/Sam Daws (Eds.). The Oxford Handbook on the United Nations. Oxford, Oxford University Press, 140–164.

Weiss, Thomas G./Daws, Sam (2018). The United Nations. In: Thomas G. Weiss/Sam Daws (Eds.). The Oxford Handbook on the United Nations. Oxford, Oxford University Press, 2–40.

Wiesner, Claudia/Haapala, Taru/Palonen, Kari (2017). Debates, Rhetoric and Political Action. Practices of Textual Interpretation and Analysis. London, Palgrave Macmillan UK; Imprint Palgrave Macmillan.

UN Documents

Committee on Contributions (2025). Contributions Received for 2025 for the United Nations Regular Budget. Available online at https://www.un.org/en/ga/contributions/honourroll.shtml (accessed 11/13/2025).

General Assembly (1966a). 2239 (XXI). Pattern of Conferences. A/RES/2239. Available online at https://www.worldlii.org/int/other/UNGA/1966/108.pdf (accessed 4/1/2025).

General Assembly (1966b). International Covenant on Economic, Social and Cultural Rights Adopted and opened for signature, ratification and accession by General Assembly resolution 2200A (XXI) of 16 December 1966 entry into force 3 January 1976, in accordance with article 27. Available online at https://www.ohchr.org/en/instruments-mechanisms/instruments/international-covenant-economic-social-and-cultural-rights (accessed 4/1/2025).

General Assembly (1974). 3351 (XXIX). Pattern of Conferences. A/RES/3351(XXIX). Available online at https://documents.un.org/api/symbol/access?j=NR073953&t=pdf&i=A/RES/3351(XXIX)_0590527.

General Assembly (1985). 40/243 Pattern of Conferences. A/RES/40/243. Available online at https://www.unccd.int/sites/default/files/inline-files/A-RES-40-243_0.pdf (accessed 4/1/2025).

General Assembly (1988). 43/222. Pattern of Conferences. A/RES/43/222. Available online at https://documents.un.org/api/symbol/access?j=NR053201&t=pdf&i=A/RES/43/222_0136108 (accessed 4/1/2025).

General Assembly (2000). Resolution Adopted by the General Assembly [Without Reference to a Main Committee (A/55/L.2)] 55/2. United Nations Millennium Declaration. A/RES/55/2. Available online at https://www.un.org/en/development/desa/population/migration/generalassembly/docs/globalcompact/A_RES_55_2.pdf (accessed 4/1/2025).

General Assembly (2011). Resolution Adopted by the General Assembly on 3 May 2011 [Without Reference to a Main Committee (A/65/L.64/Rev.1)] 65/276. Participation of the European Union in the work of the United Nations. Available online at https://docs.un.org/en/A/RES/65/276 (accessed 6/6/2025).

General Assembly (2022). Rules of Procedure of the General Assembly (Embodying Amendments and Additions Adopted by the General Assembly Up to and Including its Seventy-Fifth Session). A/520/Rev.20. Available online at https://digitallibrary.un.org/record/3986976?ln=en&v=pdf (accessed 4/1/2025).

General Assembly (2024a). Resolution Adopted by the General Assembly on 24 December 2024 [On the Report of the Fifth Committee (A/79/390/Add.1, para. 13)] 79/249. Scale of assessments for the apportionment of the expenses of the United Nations. A/RES/79/249. Available online at https://documents.un.org/symbol-explorer?s=A/RES/79/249&i=A/RES/79/249_1736795822113 (accessed 4/1/2025).

General Assembly (2024b). Resolution Adopted by the General Assembly on 22 September 2024 [Without Reference to a Main Committee (A/79/L.2)] 79/1. The Pact for the Future. A/RES/79/1. Available online at https://documents.un.org/api/symbol/access?j=N2427222&t=pdf&i=A/RES/79/1_1727105983267 (accessed 4/1/2025).

Governments of the United States of America, Great Britain, the Soviet Union, and China (1943). Joint Four-nation Declaration. Available online at https://www.legal-tools.org/doc/910354/ (accessed 4/1/2025).

International Court of Justice (1920). Statute of the International Court of Justice. Available online at https://legal.un.org/avl/pdf/ha/sicj/icj_statute_e.pdf (accessed 4/1/2025).

International Court of Justice (1948). Advisory Opinion of 28 May 1948. 003-19480528-ADV-01-00-EN. Available online at https://www.icj-cij.org/node/103739 (accessed 4/1/2025).

NATO (2022). Founding Treaty. Available online at https://www.nato.int/cps/en/natohq/topics_67656.htm (accessed 4/1/2025).

NATO (2023). The North Atlantic Treaty. Washington D.C. - 4 April 1949. Available online at https://www.nato.int/cps/en/natohq/official_texts_17120.htm (accessed 4/1/2025).

Secretary of State for Foreign Affairs (1942). Declaration by United Nations. Treaty Series No. 5 (1942). Available online at https://treaties.fcdo.gov.uk/data/Library2/pdf/1942-TS0005.pdf (accessed 4/1/2025).

United Nations (1967). International Covenant on Civil and Political Rights. Available online at https://treaties.un.org/doc/Treaties/1976/03/19760323%2006-17%20AM/Ch_IV_04.pdf (accessed 4/1/2025).

United Nations (2025a). United Nations Charter (Full Text). Available online at https://www.un.org/en/about-us/un-charter/full-text (accessed 4/1/2025).

United Nations (2025f). Universal Declaration of Human Rights. Available online at https://www.un.org/en/about-us/universal-declaration-of-human-rights (accessed 4/1/2025).

Washington Conversations on International Peace and Security Organization (1944). Dumbarton Oaks: Proposals for the Establishment of a General International Organization. Available online at https://www.dipublico.org/doc/instrumentos/163.html (accessed 4/1/2025).

7. The EU as an arena of politics

Claudia Wiesner

This chapter describes not only how the European Union (EU) is structured and what its institutions are, but also how it works as an arena of politics (see also Chapter 9). In doing so, it enters into a field that is contested in Political Science and EU Studies: there are traditional conceptual controversies on the question of what the EU actually is. A classical position is to describe the EU as an International Organisation (IO) (see e.g. Klabbers 2009; Magnette 2005). Another one is to understand it as a "polity sui generis" – as a new type of polity that has no precedent and that in consequence cannot be described based on established categories. Other authors see the EU as a political system without being a state (Hix and Høyland 2022; Tömmel 2014). But can the EU be understood in the classical categories of comparative politics and systems analysis, that is, asking for legislative, judicative, and executive dimensions? Or does this entail an analogy of the EU and a nation state, when the EU is not a nation state (Wiesner 2019, p. 26)?

This chapter is based on the argument that the EU is a polity that can be understood only partly if one tries to grasp it as either a political system or an IO. The EU has a bit of everything: it uses mechanisms and processes of diplomacy and intergovernmental negotiation and is based on treaties like the United Nations (UN) (see also Chapter 9) – but, and importantly, the EU is no longer a simple IO. It has many supranational elements. This is why in this chapter the EU is, first, understood as a political system that has similarities and differences to other political systems.

Two more dimensions of the EU are in focus in this chapter. The EU needs to be understood in its historical perspective, as its political system has been changing decisively over the years. EU integration has been a long-term historical and political process. This process was shaped via conflicts, controversies and contingencies, and it led to changing institutional realities and practices over time (Wiesner 2019, pp. 2–3). Contingency entails that actors can never exactly predict what the outcomes of their actions will be (Palonen 1998). Third, the EU continuously was and still is shaped by political actions of various actors, ranging from the member states governments over members of EU institutions to citizens and activists. The following therefore describes the EU as an arena of politics (see also Wiesner 2019, pp. 1–22, 165–184; Chapter 9). Concretely, as argued elsewhere, to see the EU as an arena of politics means to shift the focus

> [...] on the actors and their strategies, and the contingencies and pitfalls of inventing and shaping the EU system—rather than searching for a straight path of history and clear definitions. (Wiesner 2019, pp. 2–3)

The next section will discuss European integration history – or rather histories in the plural. After that, I will present the EU's key institutions as they are fixed in the Treaties and the principal aspects of EU law making in this system. The next section will, in the tradition of comparative analysis of political systems within Political Science, discuss how to characterise the EU's institutions. After that I will briefly introduce the EU's *interinstitutional micropolitics*, that is, the way the EU system is shaped from within by the institutions and their members. Chapter 9 will then focus in detail on these mechanisms.

HISTORIES AND CONTROVERSIES OF EUROPEAN INTEGRATION

As discussed in Chapter 6, European integration began at the same time and has the same historical roots as the formation of the UN. It is insightful to recapitulate how the institutional framework of the EU developed from an IO to the complicated institutional setting in today's EU. Importantly, there is not one history of integration but histories – and there are controversies.

European integration and the development of the EU's political system since its early days has been shaped by controversies around the conflicting principles of intergovernmentalism and federalism (Wiesner 2014; Wiesner 2019, p. 26). The principle of *intergovernmentalism* refers to institutions that are structured by the nation states, their governments, and their interests, while *federalism* and *supranationalism* refer to institutions and processes that are structured above or beside the nation states and rely more on the citizens. These conflicting principles are closely related to the two strands of activists, the "Federalists" and the "Unionists", who both campaigned for a unified Europe in and after the Second World War, albeit with different goals and different membership. While the federalists were mainly activists and resistance fighters who campaigned for a federal Europe, the Unionists, led mainly by national politicians and future heads of government, wanted to see the nation states in the centre of an integrating Europe (for further detail see Wiesner 2014).

As outlined in Chapter 6, the first predecessor of the EU, the European Community of Coal and Steel (ECSC), was founded in the same time period as the UN, that is, after the Second World War and at the beginning of the Cold War. In 1951, France, Italy, Germany, Luxembourg, the Netherlands, and Belgium founded the ECSC (the Treaty was signed in 1951 and came into force in 1952) and integrated their coal and steel industries which were key for both economic development and military production. The ECSC was based on the six participating nation states and their governments (for further detail see Wiesner 2019, pp. 97–102).

The ECSC founding marked the Unionist success in the controversy around intergovernmentalist and federalist integration concepts: the ECSC was based on nation states and their governments, where integration should be fuelled by their economic and political self-interests. The Federalists, instead, had aimed at a supranational democratic federation. But visibly, the European unification process did begin with the aim to create a balance of powers in Europe, to centralise control over the core industries of coal and steel, and to insert a Western Germany that was thus controlled durably into the West. Economic integration was the tool for all this (for further detail see Wiesner 2014).

Nevertheless, the question of a federal and more democratic European integration was back on the agenda in 1952 and 1953 in debates on a *European Community of Defence*. The respective concepts explicitly foresaw the creation of a *European Political Community* (EPC) with a full-fledged two-chamber parliament, one chamber to be directly elected by the citizens, the other to be based on the Council. A draft constitution had even been developed on the initiative of the ECSC Foreign Ministers (Europäische Politische Gemeinschaft 1953). But the project had to be abandoned after the French National Assembly did not ratify the EPC Treaty in a 1954 vote. Afterwards, European integration was based on the two pillars of intergovernmental cooperation and economic integration for many years to come, even if several politicians, especially European Parliament (EP) parliamentarians, advanced proposals for EU democratisation several times (European Parliament 2009, pp. 111–128).

The next key step of integration was the founding of the European Economic Community (EEC) in the framework of the Treaties of Rome (they were signed in 1957 and valid from 1958). The Treaties of Rome comprise the EEC Treaty (known as Treaty of Rome) and the Euratom Treaty on a European Atomic Community. From 1957 onwards, three European Communities existed: the ECSC, the EEC, and the Euratom Community. After 1967, they were officially called the "European Communities".

This historical background also provides a crucial reason for the EU's policy orientation. European unification has been focusing on market integration and economic liberalisation. The Treaties of Rome and the ones that followed them make a strong point of abolishing all obstacles to a free-market economy and a successful inner market in the EU (or former EEC). Based on the Treaties and namely on the classical four freedoms (free movement of trade and goods, services, labour, and capital), obstacles to the free market were successively abolished. In other words, the EU's core competence is to be an inner market (see Wiesner 2019, pp. 97–102).

In the course of integration, the application of the *méthode Monnet* (designed by Jean Monnet, the first president of the ECSC Commission) did have its effects over time. Monnet believed that economic integration would lead to *spill-over effects* into non-economic areas and bring with it a political integration by and by (for further detail see Niemann and Schmitter 2009). The idea worked, even if it took some decades to clearly show an effect: from the second half of the 1980s on, one Treaty change followed another.

After EEC funding and until the 1980s, the institutional system of the developing polity experienced relative stability. The EU's political system is defined by the Treaties that work as a quasi.constitution. These Treaties were not changed for about thirty years following the Treaties of Rome. The first big reform Treaty, the Single European Act (SEA), was then concluded in 1987. The SEA built the base for a series of reform Treaties in the 1990s and 2000s: the Maastricht Treaty in 1993, the Amsterdam Treaty in 1999, the Nice Treaty in 2001, and the Lisbon Treaty in 2009. The Lisbon Treaty contains most of the contents of the draft Constitutional Treaty, which was never ratified after negative referenda in the Netherlands and France in 2005. The series of Treaty changes means that the EU's quasi-constitution and hence the competencies and setting of the EU's institutions has been changing continuously over a relatively short period of time. All of these Treaty changes preserved a key role of the member states – but all of them developed the EU towards a more democratic supranational system as well (Wiesner 2019, pp. 97–102).

The EU's development and the EU's institutional design reflect the tension between the principles of intergovernmentalism and federalism: the intergovernmental elements are dominant in the Council, and they are predominant in the European Council (EC). Federal elements dominate in the EP, but can also be traced in the other institutions (Monnet 1955; Palonen 2016). The EU's system is a system of cooperative federalism where no clear-cut division of power between the two levels of government exists but where the state-level actors and the federal-level actors both have legislative powers in most policy fields (Dann 2003; Hix and Høyland 2022; for further detail see Tiilikainen and Wiesner 2016).

The above also indicates that the EU is a political system in perpetual change: there has been a continual development, and no *finalité* of European integration is in view so far. EU institutions since the beginning of integration change their character, competencies, and members; moreover, they interact with each other, often via power struggles aiming at strengthening or not losing positions and influence.

The changes in the EU's system and the balance between the institutions thus occurred on one hand via Treaty changes which represent large, formalised steps. Besides the Treaty changes, they have been driven by the institutions themselves – the continual changes and dynamics of the EU's system are also shaped from within. As said above, the EU is an *arena of politics* in which not only the policies, but also the system and its institutions themselves are shaped by institutions and their members who act politically (Palonen 2003). In that, they use the possibilities for action offered by the regulations of the Treaties and the rules of procedure of the institutions. These fix the procedural roles and the margins of political action and manoeuvre. All EU institutions interpret these rules in their acting, and mostly to their respective advantage, in particular when encountering ambiguities in regulations or when facing situations and challenges not covered by the existing rules and established practices. Acting politically in the context of shaping the EU system thus means to act within pre-defined rules and eventually to change or re-interpret them. This is particularly important since the EU system is still in the making and neither its rules nor its routines are as well established as they are in most nation states. Shaping them and thus the roles and influences of the EU institutions is an important part of EU *interinstitutional micropolitics* (for further detail see Wiesner 2018; Wiesner 2023).

The history of EU integration offers many small and big examples of such processes. Some of the most telling are related to the EP, which repeatedly used competencies it already possessed to enlarge its powers in the EU system (see Chapter 9). In particular, the EP regularly used its budgetary rights as a lever (European Parliament 2009, pp. 16, 61, 147–148). Moreover, it deliberately and continually tried to widen the limits set by the Treaties.

As a result of both Treaty changes and interinstitutional politics, out of the original setting of the ECSC and the EEC, only three bodies have kept most of their characteristics: the Commission, the Court of Justice of the European Union (CJEU), which has to interpret ECSC and EEC laws, and the Council of Ministers. The EP experienced the farthest-reaching changes. The EEC already had a parliamentary assembly of delegates from the member states that had only a consultative function. In 1979 direct EP elections were introduced. With the Treaties of Maastricht, Amsterdam, Nice, and Lisbon, the EP became subsequently an institutional counterweight to the Commission and the Council (see Wiesner 2015).

In addition to the Treaty changes, European integration was also marked by several waves of enlargement. The number of member states increased from the original setting of six to 28 until the United Kingdom left the EU. Today, the EU comprises 27 member states.

LOOKING AT THE EU FROM THE OUTSIDE: THE EU'S INSTITUTIONAL SYSTEM AFTER LISBON

The Treaty of Lisbon defines a multiplicity of institutions – there are more of them than in most classical national political systems, as an analysis of the formal powers granted to the EU bodies shows. The Treaty on European Union (afterwards TEU, see European Union 2016) states:

> The Union's institutions shall be:
>
> - the European Parliament,
> - the European Council,
> - the Council,
> - the European Commission (hereinafter referred to as 'the Commission'),
> - the Court of Justice of the European Union,
> - the European Central Bank,
> - the Court of Auditors.

Compared to a classical model of a political system consisting of a head of state or a president, a parliament with a first and second chamber, and a government, the EU's system is not only more complex but also characterised by mixed functions. The EP, for instance, is a parliament with most parliamentary characteristics such as legislative rights, budgetary rights, and government oversight, but its role is slightly different from parliaments in parliamentary systems (see section 3 below).

Article 14 TEU states on the EP:

> 1. The European Parliament shall, jointly with the Council, exercise legislative and budgetary functions. It shall exercise functions of political control and consultation as laid down in the Treaties. It shall elect the President of the Commission.
> 2. The European Parliament shall be composed of representatives of the Union's citizens. They shall not exceed seven hundred and fifty in number, plus the President. Representation of citizens shall be degressively proportional, with a minimum threshold of six members per Member State. No Member State shall be allocated more than ninety-six seats.
>
>   The European Council shall adopt by unanimity, on the initiative of the European Parliament and with its consent, a decision establishing the composition of the European Parliament, respecting the principles referred to in the first subparagraph.
> 3. The members of the European Parliament shall be elected for a term of five years by direct universal suffrage in a free and secret ballot.
> 4. The European Parliament shall elect its President and its officers from among its members.

The EC unites the heads of state and government in the EU. It is the most recent of the EU's institutions. It only became one of the seven official EU institutions with the Lisbon Treaty (TEU, Article 13). The EC now disposes of a permanent president, elected by qualified majority for a term of two and a half years, renewable once. The EC meets twice every six months, convened by its President. Except where the Treaties provide otherwise, decisions of the EC are taken by consensus. They determine the general political direction of the EU. Article 15 TEU states:

> 1. The European Council shall provide the Union with the necessary impetus for its development and shall define the general political directions and priorities thereof. It shall not exercise legislative functions.
> 2. The European Council shall consist of the Heads of State or Government of the Member States, together with its President and the President of the Commission. The High Representative of the Union for Foreign Affairs and Security Policy shall take part in its work.

The EC may not act as a legislative body. This role belongs to the *Council* that unites the ministers of the member states (informally called the "Council of Ministers"). The Council is the second legislative chamber. Article 16 TEU defines:

> The Council shall, jointly with the European Parliament, exercise legislative and budgetary functions. It shall carry out policy-making and coordinating functions as laid down in the Treaties.

The Council meets in different configurations, depending on the policy matters that are discussed. This means that ministers of different policy fields, such as, for example, the ministers of Economics and Finance (ECOFIN), will unite in different Council sessions. It mostly decides by a qualified majority as defined in Article 16 (4) TEU:

> As from 1 November 2014, a qualified majority shall be defined as at least 55% of the members of the Council, comprising at least fifteen of them and representing Member States comprising at least 65% of the population of the Union.

Article 16 (8) TEU includes a decisive new provision introduced by the Lisbon Treaty, namely, it declares that Council meetings shall now be public when the Council legislates. This is in keeping with a classical characteristic of a parliament – public deliberation:

> The Council shall meet in public when it deliberates and votes on a draft legislative act. To this end, each Council meeting shall be divided into two parts,

dealing respectively with deliberations on Union legislative acts and non-legislative activities.

The *Commission* shows characteristics of an EU government, as laid out in Article 17 (1) TEU:

> The Commission shall promote the general interest of the Union and take appropriate initiatives to that end. It shall ensure the application of the Treaties, and of measures adopted by the institutions pursuant to them. It shall oversee the application of Union law under the control of the Court of Justice of the European Union. It shall execute the budget and manage programmes. It shall exercise coordinating, executive and management functions, as laid down in the Treaties. With the exception of the common foreign and security policy, and other cases provided for in the Treaties, it shall ensure the Union's external representation. It shall initiate the Union's annual and multiannual programming with a view to achieving interinstitutional agreements.

The President of the Commission is in a decisive position, laying down guidelines for the work of the Commission, deciding on the internal organisation of the Commission, appointing Vice-Presidents among the members of the Commission, and having the right to request commissioners to resign.

Article 17(7) TEU accords the EP the right to elect the Commission president upon proposal of the EC. Article 17(7) also claims that both shall take "[...] into account the elections to the European Parliament". This clause refers to the idea that the Commission president shall represent the party group that won the majority at the EP elections and hence relates to the head candidate ("Spitzenkandidaten") idea (European Union 2016; see also below).

Each member state nominates one commissioner. The EC adopts a list of persons, and the list is proposed to the EP. MEPs then hold extensive hearings – these are laid out not in the Treaties but in a framework agreement (see Chapter 9). After this, the Commission proposal as a whole is subject to a vote of consent in the EP. The Commission as a body is responsible to the EP which may vote on a motion of censure. If such a motion is successful, the Commission resigns as a body. There is also an indirect right for the EP to claim individual commissioners to resign (see section 3 and Chapter 11).

The Court of Justice of the European Union, as according to article 18 (3) TEU has the following tasks:

> (a) rule on actions brought by a Member State, an institution or a natural or legal person;
> (b) give preliminary rulings, at the request of courts or tribunals of the Member States, on the interpretation of Union law or the validity of acts adopted by the institutions;
> (c) rule in other cases provided for in the Treaties.

As will be discussed in Chapter 11, these sentences sound dry, but the Court is a key player in the EU.

LAW-MAKING AND THE EU INSTITUTIONS

Creation, interpretation and implementation of EU laws are shaped by the EU's institutional context. There are different ways in which EU laws come about.

First, there are EU treaties. Similar to other international treaties or the UN Charter, EU treaties are, on one hand, international treaties between the member states. As said above, EU treaties on the other hand have a constitution-like function, as they rule the organisation of the EU as a polity. As outlined above, the treaties, and hence the quasi-constitution of the EU, have been changing over the decades. In the cases before the Lisbon Treaty, new treaties have been voted upon by the EC, consisting of the EU's heads of state and government. The EP did not have much of a say in treaty changes. However, the Convention, which drafted the Constitutional Treaty before 2005 (the Constitutional Treaty is in most parts identical to the Lisbon Treaty), delegates from both the EP and national parliaments have been present for the first time.

Second, EU laws are based on these treaties. Formally, EU law initiatives can only be issued by the European Commission. In practice, both the Council, consisting of the Ministers of the member states, and the EP can exercise some influence on the Commission, and the EP can even induce it to make law proposals.

Third, in the early days of integration, EU laws were voted upon only by the Council, as it was the sole legislative body.

With the adoption of the Treaty of Maastricht, the EP obtained co-decision rights in a limited range of policy fields of the inner market. This means that both the Council and Parliament now had to vote upon a law jointly in these fields. Since the Treaty of Lisbon, co-decision is the ordinary legislative procedure and most laws are adopted by both the Council and the EP. Apart from such laws, which are called directives, the European Commission may issue directly binding laws (regulations).

To understand the political controversies related to EU laws and their implementation (see Chapters 9 and 11), it also has to be taken into account that EU directives are transferred into national laws, and then executed by the member states' governments as well as regional and local institutions. Accordingly, there is some margin for different interpretation of the EU directives, as well as for political manoeuvre in their realisation. The European Commission at this stage functions as the "guardian of the treaties", which means that it controls the correct implementation of EU law and can start infringement procedures against member states via the Court of Justice of the EU in case of non-compliance. The Court is an important agent in developing EU laws further when it interprets them in its judgements. Importantly, the Court has a margin; it can interpret laws in a rather broad or a rather narrow manner, and it often interpreted EU laws in the broadest possible sense – or just the opposite. There often is a political direction visible in the judgements (Grimm 2017). EU documents can be read as indicators of the interrelations and the power struggles between the different EU institutions, as well as between EU institutions and the member states (see Chapter 9).

THE EU'S SYSTEM IN THE CATEGORIES OF COMPARATIVE SYSTEMS ANALYSIS

Political systems typologies outline the specific characteristics and the balance of powers between the different institutions in different political systems. System typologies are based on specific interpretations of three clusters of concepts that represent variations or dimensions of the three elements of the classical balance of powers:

1) executive, government, head of state, head of government;
2) legislative, parliament; and
3) judicative, courts.

These three mark any liberal representative democratic system, albeit in different configurations. Three more classifications serve to distinguish different systems of shares of power: presidentialism, in which a president is usually head of state and head of government; semi-presidentialism, in which a strong president shares powers with a strong parliament; and parliamentarism, in which parliament is the power centre of the political system (Duverger 1980, Sartori 1994). I will in the following discuss how to understand the EU's institutions in such a typology.

When analysing the EU's institutional setting, at first sight it does not seem to fit easily into the classical categories of political system analysis. It is maybe due to this fact that many scholars systematically discuss the EU as a "sui generis" system (for a discussion of this see Lietzmann 2011). However, the "sui generis" categorisation ignores that the EU is a political system that combines elements of national systems and their institutions in a new way. EU institutions combine different modes of operation and legitimisation (for further detail see Costa and Brack 2019; Hix and Høyland 2022; Tiilikainen and Wiesner 2016; Tömmel 2014).

First, who is the head of state or fulfils the respective functions? The immediate candidate is either the EC's president or the EC as such. The Treaties state the EC to

> [...] provide the Union with the necessary impetus for its development and [to] define the general political directions and priorities thereof [...],

and also that

> [...] it shall not exercise legislative functions [...]. (TEU, Article 15 (1))

In this, the EC seems to take on the functions of a head of state, and namely those of a president. The fact that it nominates the candidates for the new Commission and plays a decisive role in Common Foreign and Security Policy (CFSP; see Tiilikainen and Wiesner 2016) also fits into this picture, while the fact that the EC can neither dismiss the Commission nor its President speaks against an interpretation of the EC and its President as head of state.

A closer look at the Lisbon Treaty shows that more than any other institution the EC embodies a mixture of governmental principles: it can be interpreted as a "congress of ambassadors" similar to the UN GA, a federal presidency, or an EU government (for further detail see Palonen and Wiesner 2016). In the shape of the EC, the former meetings of the heads of state were given a constitutional role in the EU. The founding of the EC therefore emphasises the *intergovernmental* diplomatic logic behind European integration.

The institutionalisation of the EC also transports a strong notion of *presidential* power and symbolism. But it may be questioned whether the role of President belongs to the EC as a body, or whether it is bicephalous, that is, split between the permanent president and the rotating member country presidency (Tiilikainen and Wiesner 2016). The permanent EC president has the function to "represent" the EC before the EP and to "report" regularly to the EP (TEU, Article 15 (6)). The EC's relations to the EP thus are distant, as it would be the case in a presidential or semi-presidential system. In that the EC defines the EU's general political direction, it also has a governmental dimension.

When it comes to the dimension of *government*, the most susceptible candidate, however, is the Commission. The EU's system here shows several elements of a parliamentary government, in particular because the cabinet – the Commission – is accountable to the EP, and it is also the EP that votes the Commission into office.

First, the Commission president is elected by the EP upon a proposal of the EC. As said above, the Lisbon Treaty claims that the results of the EP elections must be "taken into account" when nominating and electing the President of the Commission. This notion refers to the head candidate that led the big party families in the EP election campaign. After 2014 when the head candidate Jean Claude Juncker became Commission president, 2019 saw a breach of this principle. Key players in the EC such as French president Emmanuel Macron did not support the conservative head candidate Manfred Weber and suggested conservative politician Ursula von der Leyen instead. Von der Leyen was elected, and in 2024 she then became the conservative head candidate.

Second, as stated above, the election of the Commission members is also predetermined by the member states represented in the EC. This process is similar to political parties in nation states that predetermine the candidates for minister positions. Member state governments nominate the Commissioner candidates, who are then subjected to extensive hearings in the EP prior to the vote of approval. This procedure is similar to what happens in the United States (USA) congress, and therefore to the proceedings in a presidential system. If MEPs in the hearings do not approve of commissioner candidates, they can enforce the Commission president and the EC to exchange them (see Chapter 11).

Parliament is obviously to be located at the EP. The EP's powers have been constantly reinforced in the EU's institutional setting. The Lisbon Treaty strengthened the EP's legislative powers in that the co-decision procedure between the EP and the Council was turned into the ordinary legislative procedure, that is, it became the rule. The present EP has legislative powers equal to those of the Council in most policy fields. Moreover, the EP received new budgetary powers and a more formalised role in amending the fundamental treaties and the formalisation of the convention mechanism.

There are various mechanisms of parliamentary control of the Commission. Besides the right to dismiss the Commission by a vote of censure, the EP also has to formally approve of the Commission's actions. In terms of fully fledged parliamentarism, however, the EP would decide on the Commission's political agenda based on its political majorities. This is not the case in the EP.

The Council [of Ministers] has in general been treated as one part of the EU's dual executive (Hix and Høyland 2022). However, after the discussion above, it rather appears as the second, the federal, parliamentary chamber. In the EU's system of executive federalism (Dann 2003) the Council serves as the meeting point between the two levels of government.

All in all, the EU neither fully fits into the type of parliamentarism, nor the USA type of presidentialism that is based on a separation of powers between the main political bodies. The division of powers in the EU rather follows a model of semi-presidentialism, that is, it falls between parliamentarism on the one hand and presidentialism on the other. It combines a parliamentary government with the powers of a rather independent president (Duverger 1980; Sartori 1994).

IN CONCLUSION

First, the EU's system is a result of a development over some decades, and a development that has been influenced by conflicting principles. Above all, there has been a conflict between the principles of intergovernmentalism and federalism, which both indicate different directions for institutional developments and reforms. While the intergovernmental principle conforms to the aim of safeguarding or strengthening the position of the member states and their governments in the EU system, the federal principle conforms to strengthening the federal and supranational institutions like the EP or the Commission. Both of these logics are at play in MEU simulations: while Council simulations will follow the intergovernmental logic and interests of the member states will be predominant, EP simulations will follow the supranational logic and hence the interests of the EU will be in the main focus.

Second, besides those principles, the EU's development has been shaped by the necessities linked to carrying out the EU policies supported an ever-closer integration. In addition, they strengthened the roles of two supranational (but not so much federal) institutions: the Commission and the Court of Justice. While the first is responsible for the policies to be carried out, the second interprets the EU laws in its judgments. This means that the Court plays a crucial political role within the EU's arena – any MEU simulation needs to be aware that the Court is at least a hypothetical player on the field.

Third, the EU's system has been shaped both by the large formalised steps of Treaty changes and by the interinstitutional micropolitics (see Chapter 9). Those micropolitics together with the increasing role of the federal and supranational bodies and the creation of the conventions that today have to prepare Treaty changes have been reducing the importance of the intergovernmental principle. This is an observation that is of decisive importance for MEU simulations. They will be focusing on and simulating micropolitics – and it is important to keep in mind that these micropolitics not only shape legal acts, but the EU's institutional system itself.

Fourth, it is crucially important to take into account the developing character of the EU's system. What it is today in terms of political system analysis cannot be compared with what it was in the 1950s – and it is not to be expected that this development is finished right now. Every judgement on the EU's system therefore is a judgement of a momentary state of the art. In this, the EU is more fluid and more in development than the UN.

Fifth, having come from a strongly intergovernmental model of integration at the outset, the EU has been going a considerable distance towards a supranational democratic federation especially since 1993. EU democratisation has de facto led to the development of a middle ground between federalist and unionist ideas: based on sovereign nation states, more and more elements of a supranational, representative democratic federation developed, including a representative democratic supranational parliament and supranational institutions having a say over the nation states and cooperating with them. For MEU simulations this means that – different from most UN legal acts – the decisions taken by EU institutions have a direct impact on EU member states and EU citizens, also in their everyday life.

Sixth, and finally, in sum, the EU's political system as it currently stands indeed represents a mixture of different governmental principles. It disposes of the functions of the classical elements head of state, government, and parliament – but those functions are spread among the institutions in a manner that has inspired numerous scholars to criticise the lack of a balance of powers. Legislative, executive, and judicial functions (the Commission disposes of the latter, too) are mixed. The balance of powers in the EU is thus incomplete. In terms of political system typologies, the EU can best be understood as a kind of semi-presidential system. For an MEU simulation, this means taking into account the fact that the EP is not the EU's single power centre – but that it is one of three decisive institutions along with the Council and the Commission and must not be neglected.

REFERENCES

Costa, Olivier/Brack, Nathalie (2019). How the EU Really Works. London/New York, Routledge.

Dann, Philipp (2003). European Parliament and Executive Federalism: Approaching a Parliament in a Semi-Parliamentary Democracy. European Law Journal 9 (5), 549–574. https://doi.org/10.1046/j.1468-0386.2003.00192.x

Duverger, Maurice (1980). A New Political System Model: Semi-Presidential Government. European Journal of Political Research 8 (2), 165–187. https://doi.org/10.1111/j.1475-6765.1980.tb00569.x

European Parliament (2009). Building Parliament: 50 Years of European Parliament History 1958–2008. Office for Official Publications of the European Communities. Luxembourg. Available online at https://op.europa.eu/en/publication-detail/-/publication/67991291-12ef-45d5-a7a9-85bb5c4c3ff7 (accessed 7/4/2025).

Grimm, Dieter (2017). The Constitution of European Democracy. Oxford, United Kingdom, Oxford University Press.

Hix, Simon/Høyland, Bjørn (2022). The Political System of the European Union. 4th ed. London, Bloomsbury Academic.

Klabbers, Jan (2009). An Introduction to International Institutional Law. Cambridge, Cambridge University Press.

Lietzmann, Hans J. (2011). European Constitutional Politics and Contingency. The European Union as a "Sui Generis" Political Entity. In: Claudia Wiesner/Tapani Turkka/Kari Palonen (Eds.). Parliament and Europe. Rhetorical and conceptual studies on their contemporary connections. Baden-Baden, Nomos, 93–107.

Magnette, Paul (2005). What is the European Union? Nature and Prospects. Basingstoke, Palgrave Macmillan.

Monnet, Jean (1955). Les États-Unis d'Europe ont commencé: La Communauté européenne du charbon et de l'acier. Discours et allocutions, 1952–1954. Paris, Laffont.

Niemann, Arne/Schmitter, Philippe C. (2009). Neofunctionalism. In: Antje Wiener/Thomas Diez (Eds.). European Integration Theory. 2nd ed. Oxford, Oxford University Press, 45–65.

Palonen, Kari (1998). Judging Politics – A Temporal Perspective. Redescriptions (Finnish Yearbook of Political Thought) 2, 5–11.
Palonen, Kari (2003). Four Times of Politics: Policy, Polity, Politicking, and Politicization. Alternatives: Global, Local, Political 28 (2), 171–186. https://doi.org/10.1177/030437540302800202
Palonen, Kari (2016). Thinking of Politics in a Parliamentary Manner: Perspectives on the Conceptual History of Parliamentarism. In: Pasi Ihalainen/Cornelia Ilie/Kari Palonen (Eds.). Parliament and Parliamentarism. A Comparative History of a European Concept. New York/Oxford, United Kingdom, Berghahn Books, 228–242.
Palonen, Kari/Wiesner, Claudia (2016). Second Chamber, "Congress of Ambassadors" or Federal Presidency. Parliamentary and Non-Parliamentary Aspects in the European Council's Rules of Procedure. Parliaments, Estates and Representation 36 (1), 71–89. https://doi.org/10.1080/02606755.2015.1038130
Sartori, Giovanni (1994). Comparative Constitutional Engineering: An Inquiry Into Structures, Incentives, and Outcomes. Basingstoke, Macmillan.
Tiilikainen, Teija/Wiesner, Claudia (2016). Towards a Political Theory of EU Parliamentarism. In: Pasi Ihalainen/Cornelia Ilie/Kari Palonen (Eds.). Parliament and Parliamentarism. A Comparative History of a European Concept. New York/Oxford, United Kingdom, Berghahn Books, 292–310.
Tömmel, Ingeborg (2014). The European Union: What It Is and How It Works. Houndsmills, Palgrave Macmillan.
Wiesner, Claudia (2014). From Safeguarding Peace in Europe to Financial Crisis: Old Questions and New Challenges of EU Integration. In: Claudia Wiesner/Meike Schmidt-Gleim (Eds.). The Meanings of Europe. Changes and Exchanges of a Contested Concept. London, Taylor & Francis, 91–106.
Wiesner, Claudia (2015). The European Parliament as Special Parliament and Political Actor: Dissensus, Debate and Deliberation as Tools. In: Kari Palonen/Jose María Rosales/Tapani Turkka (Eds.). The Politics of Dissensus: Parliament in Debate. Santander, Ediciones Universidad de Cantabria; McGraw Hill, 101–126.
Wiesner, Claudia (2018). The Micro-Politics of Parliamentary Powers: European Parliament Strategies for Expanding Its Influence in the EU Institutional System. Journal of European Integration 40 (4), 375–391. https://doi.org/10.1080/07036337.2018.1462351
Wiesner, Claudia (2019). Inventing the EU as a Democratic Polity. Concepts, Actors and Controversies. Cham, Springer International Publishing; Imprint Palgrave Macmillan.
Wiesner, Claudia (2023). Actors, Concepts, Controversies: The Conceptual Politics of European Integration. Political Research Exchange 5 (1), 145. https://doi.org/10.1080/2474736X.2023.2258173

EU Documents

Europäische Politische Gemeinschaft (1953). Entwurf zu einem Vertrag über die Satzung der Europäischen (Politischen) Gemeinschaft (EPG). Available online at http://www.politische-union.de/epg1.htm (accessed 2/5/2013).
European Union (2016). Consolidated versions of the Treaty on European Union and the Treaty on the Functioning of the European Union – Consolidated version of the Treaty on the Functioning of the European Union – Protocols – Annexes

– Declarations annexed to the Final Act of the Intergovernmental Conference which adopted the Treaty of Lisbon, signed on 13 December 2007 – Tables of equivalences. Official Journal C 326, 26/10/2012 P. 0001 – 0390. Available online at https://eur-lex.europa.eu/eli/treaty/tfeu_2012/oj/eng (accessed 6/6/2025).

8. "Of nations large and small": an overview of multilateral law-making processes in the United Nations Organisation

Daniel R. Quiroga-Villamarín

> In fact, it is customary to talk about the post-1945 world order and to imbricate multilateralism with the system of the United Nations. It is true that multilateralism witnessed an unprecedented growth after that time, a trend that was made possible by the proliferation of international organizations, both within the United Nations Organization itself with the creation of many technical institutions, or beyond the system —for instance, regional political organizations.
>
> (Daudet 2019, p. 39).[1]

> [Demography] has always been a sensitive and classic stake of the democratic tradition. How far beyond a certain number of citizens can a republic still claim to be a democracy? If this becomes problematic well beyond the canonical examples of Athens, Corsica, Geneva, or Poland [...] what will be said, beyond the billions, of a universal democratic model which, if it does not regulate a world State or super-State, would still command an international law of European origin?
>
> (Derrida 2020 p. 101).

INTRODUCTION: "WE THE PEOPLES OF THE UNITED NATIONS"

Where can one, if at all, locate the nebulous notion of "the international community" (Johns 2024)? One cannot find it on a political map. There, instead,

[1] Author's own translation. Thereafter, any material in Castilian, French, or German will be treated in the same way.

one finds neatly bounded nation-states, which clash as if they were "billiard balls or chess figures" over the Earth's territory (Wolfers 1962, p. 82). And yet, when one thinks of "the international," it is likely that at least one place comes to mind: the main Headquarters building used by the United Nations Organisation (henceforth, the UN) in New York City (Quiroga-Villamarín 2025b). This is, of course, only one of the many venues that claim to serve as the dwellings of "the international" (Quiroga-Villamarín 2024a). But the UN Headquarters in Manhattan remains perhaps the most important of them in folk imaginaries of international law and institutions – and not in vain, it has been called a veritable "international territory" (Bartos and Hitchens 1994). While rather imprecise from a legal or technical point of view, this moniker carries some weight. For it is in this very building where every North Atlantic fall, around September or October, the international community comes together to deliberate. It does so in the form offered by this institution's General Assembly (henceforth GA) – a tradition that can be traced all the way to the first Assembly of the League of Nations (which was the UN's institutional predecessor), held in November 1920 (Gregory 1921).

In the GA, the voice (and vote) of every single state has the same importance (see also Chapters 6 and 9): one is reminded of de Vattel's (2008, p. 75) famous quip on the equal sovereignty of dwarves and giants in what was once called the law of nations – the immediate predecessor to today's international law. The UN stands, as the preamble of its Charter puts it, for "[...] the equal rights of men and women and of nations large and small." This is a logic of deliberation that we cannot afford to take for granted. For centuries in European and global history, decisions related to international affairs were, by and large, taken by Great Powers in secluded rooms – and, in a way, perhaps some important geopolitical decisions are still taken in this manner (Quiroga Villamarín 2025a)! But since the wake of the Great War of 1914–1918, one of the promises of the so-called liberal international rules-based order was that henceforth "[...] diplomacy shall proceed always frankly and in the public view [...]" – to put it in the terms of one of the famous points issued by the United States President Woodrow Wilson to end the conflict (Throntveit 2011). This has also been called the turn towards a "new diplomacy" (Géraud and Pertinax 1945) and has been followed, at least in principle, with a corresponding prohibition on secret law-making processes under international law (Donaldson 2017). The League Assembly, and the GA, embody this promise: they allow all states to come together and, *as peers*, to address international matters and codify common normative standards following the principle of sovereign equality (Klein 1974). This has also been called "parliamentary" (Götz 2005) or "conference" diplomacy (Hankey 1946; Kaufmann 1996), as these new global assemblies operate following the rules of parliamentary procedure. Another way of understanding the logic of these democratic law-making forms is through the label of *multilateralism* (Alvarez 2000; Boyle and Chinkin 2007, pp. 98–162).

And yet, how do these multilateral law-making processes actually – if at all – work? It is well known, after all, that a camel is but a horse designed by committee (Goldman 1966, p. 57). As such, one can understand why so many critics deeply suspect that any matter, let alone a truly complicated or technical problem of a global scope, could be effectively addressed by a two- or three-week long meeting where 193 states participate as equals. And in any case, who speaks on behalf of the UN as a whole? Does this capability to represent the institution belong to its permanent staff? Or to its member states? Or, perhaps, its donors? To answer this difficult question, scholars of international affairs have long argued that the best way to understand this institution is as a nebulous space where parallel worlds meet and work in tandem: there is a "first UN" constituted by its staff; a "second UN" composed of its member states; and even a "third UN" made up of the efforts of civil society organisations (Weiss et al. 2009). Hurd (2024, pp. 17–43), moreover, has helpfully distinguished that the UN can: act as an international *actor* in its own right; be a *source* of resources for other players (such as states or civil society organisations); or serve as a *forum* for international disputes. Just as states are not, in fact, homogenous "black boxes" but rather "configurations of individual and group interests who then project those interests into the international system through a particular kind of government" (Slaughter and Hale 2013, para. 17), the same is true for the UN itself. There are many different actors, organs, and processes colliding and colluding under the common "UN blue" flag. Indeed, the mere fact that the colour of the flag was originally named after Edward Stettinius Jr. – head of the USA delegation in the institution's constitutional conference held in San Francisco back in 1945 – already tells us that there are layers of history and politics behind its façade of apolitical, humanitarian, and universal aspirations (Gowan 2003; Mazower 2009).

With this in mind, in this chapter I provide an introductory overview of the way in which this universal organisation that purports to represent "we the peoples" operates (Schermers 1997). To do so, (1) after this introduction, (2) I first review its different organs, placing especial attention on the hierarchies and delegation of law-making competences between them (Colombos 1947). This, in turn, (3) allows me to trace the main processes of international law-making within this international institution – distinguishing between those used for "hard" *vis-à-vis* "soft" normative standards (Abbott and Snidal 2000). Finally, (4) I conclude on some remarks on what can the exercise of simulating the "new Leviathan" – as Crawford (2014, p. 302) once called the UN's Security Council – teach us about power, and powerlessness, in global governance today (Quiroga-Villamarín 2023, pp. 18–23).

ORGANISING THE ORGANISATION: AN OVERVIEW OF THE UN'S INSTITUTIONAL HIERARCHIES

To understand how a state works, one must study its national constitution. For International Organisations (IOs), this role is fulfilled by its constitutive treaty – that is, the international instrument subscribed by nation-states to create this institution (Brölmann 2020). For the League of Nations, this was its Covenant – subscribed in 1919, in the wake of the end of the Great War and the subsequent peace negotiations held in Paris. The UN's constitutive treaty, in turn, is its Charter of 1945, negotiated after the Second World War (see Chapter 6). While one does not have to agree with the proposition put forward by Tomuschat (1995), Fassbender (1998a), and others to understand such a Charter as a global constitution, this treaty does serve as the institutional framework for the everyday operations of the UN. It establishes its organs, assigns jurisdictional competences, and empowers actors to carry out certain operations within the bounds of what has now been called "UN law" (Conforti 2005). To successfully pursue their law-making goals within this institution, lawyer-diplomats (regardless of whether they are affiliated with the institution itself, or if they represent the interests of a member state or Non-Governmental Organisation (NGO)) need to master this body of regulations (Conforti 1969).

Following an institutional design that was, by and large, taken from the experience of the League of Nations, the UN is composed of several "principal organs," which may in turn create further "subsidiary organs" (UN Charter, Article 7; see also Chapter 6). As we noted above, at the very heart of the institution lies the GA: a global plenary body which meets at least once a year and has a very broad series of competences that are regulated by Articles 9–22 of the Charter. Each member has one vote – and most matters are decided following a simple majority rule (UN Charter, Article 18). However, on "important questions," a two-thirds majority is required: this includes all matters related to peace and security; the election of members for the other principal organs of the UN; budgetary questions; and the issues related to membership (admission, expulsion, suspension of rights). By a simple majority vote, moreover, any issue can be elevated to this category of "important question" and require a two-thirds majority for decision- and law-making purposes (Bailey 1966). Changes in the composition of the UN as a whole have changed the voting patterns within the institution and its history is full of controversial discussions about voting blocs or "automatic majorities" (Nurullayev and Papa 2023; Rowe 1969, p. 232).

Pursuant to Article 21, the GA can adopt its own rules of procedure, which were last amended in 1984 (A/520/Rev.15). To facilitate the herculean task of this rather unruly global parliament, the GA is in turn subdivided into six

Main Committees with different thematic mandates. Their names and competences are as follows:

- First: matters of disarmament & international security.
- Second: economic & financial questions.
- Third: social, humanitarian, & cultural matters.
- Fourth: special political issues and those related to decolonisation.
- Fifth: administrative & budgetary concerns.
- Sixth: legal questions.

Additionally, the GA also counts on a Credentials Committee and a General Committee. The former examines the legal standing of each delegation to represent its nation-state, while the latter oversees the general work of this body. This means, for instance, that the first deliberation of any given issue occurs before a small group of states within a Main Committee before it is then forwarded for a review of the plenary body of the GA as a whole (Alger 1966) – once again, following standard parliamentary practice in comparative domestic law (Jameson 1894). For instance, for the purposes of international law-making, the Sixth Committee of the GA plays a salient role as it is the body that first studies any juridical matter before the UN and as such fosters the development of "new law" (Hazard 1963). Another important subsidiary organ which was established by the GA in 1947 and that works quite closely with the Sixth Committee in this regard is the International Law Commission (thereafter, ILC). This latter body is composed of individual experts – most of them law professors or lawyer-diplomats – who have the task of initiating studies and making recommendations for the progressive development and codification of international law (United Nations 2021). Previous landmark efforts in international law-making – take, for instance, the UN Vienna Convention on the Law of Treaties of 1969 – were made possible because of the close interrelation of work between the ILC, the Sixth Committee, the GA, and an additional treaty-making conference – see, generally Bianchi and Zarbiyev (2024, pp. 49–84).

This last step is important because, as we will see with more detail below, the GA does not generally have – by itself – the competence to make *binding* law or decisions which are directly enforceable. Instead, within the UN system, these sorts of powers are – for better or worse – entrusted solely to the UN Security Council (henceforth, SC). Pursuant to Articles 23–32 of the Charter, this later organ functions as a smaller (and hence more exclusive) body, which is generally tasked with the maintenance of international peace and security – following, by and large, the distribution of competences between the Council and Assembly of the League of Nations (Quiroga Villamarín 2025a). And for those purposes, this body is given a series of powers duly regulated in Chapters

VI and VII of the Charter. This division is important because, generally, only measures adopted in the framework of Chapter VII are legally binding and directly opposable to all states (de Wet 2024, pp. 1578–1622). Indeed, the logic behind this division of competences between these two principal organs is that only the SC could act as the World's "policeman" (Schlesinger 1994) while the GA would be mainly devoted to global deliberation (Touloumi 2024). For that reason, the SC has reserved seats for five "permanent members": which were the Great Powers that created the organisation in the wake of their victory in the Second World War (Bosco 2009). In addition, the Council counts on the participation of ten non-permanent members which are elected by the GA following a logic of geographical representation. Given the unequal nature of this body, there has been much discussion about reforming it (see Fassbender 2020).

While these two bodies have a clear precedent in the structure of the League of Nations, in the making of the UN two additional Councils were created (Ravndal 2023). In a way, they stand halfway between the GA and the SC in their composition and mandate. They have the advisory and deliberative nature of the GA, but with a more limited membership to allow for the more detailed study of technical issues. These are the Economic and Social Council (thereafter, ECOSOC) and the Trusteeship Council – regulated, respectively, by Articles 61–72 and 75–85 of the Charter. While the latter no longer has a substantive function (as, technically, all of the UN's trust territories have now achieved independence), it was an important forum during the decades of formal decolonisation (Higgins et al. 2017). The ECOSOC, in turn, continues to have an important role in the inner workings of the UN (Trent and Schnurr 2017, pp. 71–97) and has established a plethora of programmes and subsidiary organs as it was a broad mandate that includes "human rights and fundamental freedoms" along with any "international economic, social, cultural, educational, health, and related matters" (UN Charter, Article 62). In addition, the so-called "UN family" is also composed of a series of Specialised Agencies (Dahl et al. 2020, pp. 293–308). These are separate IOs who nonetheless work closely with the UN, in terms specified by inter-institutional relationship agreements (Urueña 2022). They are too vast to review here, but they are an indispensable component of the "alphabet-soup of UN bodies" (Sharma 2007, p. 220).

But these organs cannot operate on their own. To assist the member state delegations in their law-making activities, the UN Secretariat was also established as a principal organ in its own right under Articles 97–101 of the Charter. A vast network of international civil servants is overseen by the Secretary-General (SG): the UN's "chief administrative officer" (UN Charter, Article 97), who is appointed by the GA in tandem with the "recommendation" of the SC. As Chesterman (2007) has aptly noted, this difficult position sometimes requires its officeholder to act as a mighty "general" while at other times to pretend *he* —and yes, the post has only been occupied by men so far— is but a modest "secretary." The SG has the capacity to act in all meetings of the principal organs and to execute the missions entrusted to him by them (UN Charter, Article 98). He may even refer matters related to "international peace and security" directly to the attention of the SC (UN Charter, Article 99). The SG also runs the staff of the organisation and prepares a yearly report of its functions (Troy 2021). These more technical powers allow the SG to have an enormous power of framing in relation to how the institution conceives its agenda and its priorities.

Finally, the UN has another principal organ which sits in the city of The Hague, operating somewhat aloof from its other institutional bodies. That is the International Court of Justice – or as international lawyers like to call it, the World Court – which is regulated by Articles 92–96 of the Charter (Gross 1967). It was created following the experience of the interwar Permanent Court of International Justice and serves as the institution's highest judicial body (Knaap 2023). As such, much of its work pertains to the solution of international disputes – often bilateral in nature. However, for the purposes of our overview, it is important to note that the World Court also has the competence to deliver advisory opinions on any legal questions if it is asked to do so by either the GA or the SC (UN Charter, Article 96 (1)). Moreover, any other organ of the UN or its Specialised Agencies can also request such opinions, so long as these relate to "legal questions arising within the scope of their activities" (UN Charter, Article 96 (2)). In the last few years, the advisory function of the World Court has gained a special salience in global governance (Galbraith 2023).

None of these organs exist in splendid isolation. If one studies the way the UN has addressed – or has failed to engage with – any given international issue, one will see a complex interplay of its different bodies and other actors. Take, for instance, the UN's involvement in the partition of the Mandate of Palestine in 1947–1948: a pressing issue which the first SG rightly identified as the institution's "first major test" (Ravndal 2016) and that continues to haunt international law and institutions to this very day (PARISS Collective 2025; Zarbiyev 2024). Indeed, the UN has been involved in this issue by: issuing recommendations adopted within GA; establishing subsidiary organs that report to the Secretariat; addressing the conflict as a threat to international peace and security in the deliberations of the SC (including, for instance, adopting a truce supervision operation); or even through the emission of advisory opinions by its World Court (Quiroga-Villamarín forthcoming). As such, it is difficult to speak of UN action – or inaction – as if it were a monolithic entity. In practice, the UN is better understood as a tripartite entity (functioning as an *actor*, *resource*, and *forum*) whose operations are already embedded in a very dense inter- and extra-institutional context. As we saw above, this is important because each UN organ has a different authority and mandate – and only a few of them can take binding decisions or make "new law." We turn to these normative hierarchies now.

SPEAKING AS ONE: THE UN AS A VENTRILOQUIST LAW-MAKER AND ENFORCER

Given that there is no such thing as an "international constitution," the cornerstone of our modern system of public international law is the consent of states to be bound to multilateral rules (Bodansky and Watson 1992). Indeed, even the UN Charter's highly debated claim to act as a global constitution of sorts is anchored on the fact that it has been widely ratified and adopted by almost all "peace-loving states" and has "universal" acceptance (Peters 2009). Given that there is no international authority above sovereign states, all law must have been accepted (expressly or tacitly) by them. By the same token, there is no single ultimate "enforcer" of international legal obligations – a fact that has created much debate and anxiety in the discipline (Quiroga-Villamarín 2024b). This fact places IOs in a rather awkward situation: they exist as independent legal creatures, but they can only create "new law" or enforce it to the extent that they were authorised to do so by states, as the main subjects of international law, themselves (Quiroga-Villamarín and Mansouri 2025). For this reason, Donaldson's (2021) use of the metaphor of ventriloquism to refer to the League of Nations is quite fitting, and it could be extended in a different way to think about the UN today. This organisation can have law-making powers or enforce obligations insofar as it "speaks" on behalf of its founding member states.

But not every organ or decision-making procedure within the UN is authorised to speak with such a *hard*, thundering voice (see also Chapters 6 and 9). In most cases, the UN's work is reduced to *soft* whispers: recommendations and expressions of concern. For that reason, scholars of global governance have distinguished between *binding* decisions or norms and those of a *soft* nature (Goldmann 2012). But this is not to say that the latter are irrelevant (Krisch 2014; Merry 2014; Peters 2011). There has been a rich debate in the literature in relation to how non-binding standards, despite their "liquidness," have managed to become very influential in global governance (Krisch 2017). I will not review these debates here due to a lack of space, but see Quiroga-Villamarín (2020). What matters, for the purposes of our overview, is that a fair assessment of the UN's operations in relation to any given matter must bear into account these differential normative and enforcement-related competences. Or, to put it in terms of a popular proverb used in my polity of birth and other Castilian-speaking jurisdictions: you cannot ask the elm tree to give pears. In other words, one cannot demand – as a concerned global citizen but especially as a state delegate or NGO representative engaging with the UN's operations – for an organ to speak with a voice that it is not legally authorised to use. A competent legal or diplomatic operator must engage, productively and creatively, with the possibilities that exist within these boundaries.

In practice, this means that the powers of this IO are heavily slanted towards the SC (Simpson 2004). Only this body – and only on certain occasions – can speak on behalf of the international community and use its imperative voice to issue orders and establish binding norms. But this robust normative and executive authority comes at a very high cost. To do so, the SC requires the "concurring votes of the permanent members" (UN Charter, Article 27 (3)). In reality, this gives these five founding member states the right to effectively veto any law-making effort or executive decision – an issue which has been hotly debated in the literature since the very inception of the organisation itself (Fassbender 1998b; Gifkins 2021; Lee 1947; Quiroga Villamarín 2025a). For that reason, on many occasions in which the UN needed to act it has found itself paralysed by Great Power rivalry and disagreement. As Moyn (2022) or Peters (2023) have noted, on many occasions the permanent members have used their veto privilege to shield themselves from scrutiny – exposing the Achilles heel of a system that was premised on the idea that these Great Powers would use their "policeman" function for the common good. Indeed, on many occasions much anger and frustration against the UN for its (in)action ought to be directed to the stubbornness of specific SC permanent members. And yet, on some occasions the SC has been able to effectively come together to speak with a single voice and exercise its "muscular humanitarianism" pursuant to Chapter VII of the Charter (Orford 1999). Indeed, during a brief window of Great Power reconciliation after the end of the Cold War, there was much hope – and anxiety – in relation to its role as a "world legislature" of sorts (Talmon 2005).

The GA and the SG do not have the competence to invoke the powers regulated in that chapter and are instead relegated to the mechanisms established in Chapter VI in relation to the pacific settlement of disputes. To address the gap created by the situations in which political tensions impeded the SC from speaking with a single voice, the GA and SG have sought to adopt peacekeeping operations of their own – in what has been called, following a former SG, "Chapter Six and a Half" (Groom 2004, pp. 152–153; Tudor 2023). But these operations, as they are not undertaken under the terms of Chapter VII, are always precarious and depend on the consent of the host state and the active and cooperative participation of member states (Duursma et al. 2024). We see, once again, that much of the UN's power depends on its ability to act as a ventriloquist: to be backed in its talk by other member states who are actually willing, and able, to also do the walking (Kapur 2015).

But this does not mean that the GA – including its subsidiary organs or other similar bodies with mere "soft" powers – are irrelevant in global governance. An important competence they have, in particular in relation to law-making, is to lay the groundwork for a posterior conclave of states to adopt "new" law – consenting to it and endorsing it in their own voice. Perhaps the most famous example of this is the Universal Declaration of Human Rights, which was adopted by a non-binding resolution of the GA in late 1948 after a complicated process of negotiation which included this body, the ECOSOC, and other subsidiary organs (Quiroga-Villamarín 2019). On its own, this resolution is quite soft. But it paved the road for a subsequent flurry of law-making initiatives that culminated not only in the two binding – and thus, *hard* – International Human Rights Covenants of 1966 (Cole 2005), but to a plethora of human rights-related normative initiatives, both hard and soft (see Moeckli et al. 2022). On many occasions, the UN has been able to solidify its efforts with the crystallisation of its soft recommendations or guidelines into a hard treaty subscribed by states in a special codification conference.

A similar role has been played by the World Court in relation to its advisory opinions. While its contentious judgements are, in principle, only opposable to the bilateral parties in dispute (following, once again, the principle of state consent to international adjudication), scholars have long recognised these non-binding opinions as rich materials that cannot – on their own – create "new law" but can help states or actors accurately identify already existing norms (Mayr-Singer and Mayr 2016). Take, for instance, the World Court's advisory opinion in relation to the legality of nuclear weapons (see Matheson 1997). It was originally requested by the World Health Organisation, but the World Court decided that such a Specialised Agency did not have the mandate to request such a broad opinion (Klabbers 2009). Instead, it answered the call of the GA and reiterated fundamental principles of public international law in what has been a widely cited decision. Ultimately, the World Court concluded – in what has been a very controversial opinion – not to pronounce a definitive (and thus, *hard*) conclusion on the legality of these weapons, deferring implicitly to the haunting presence of state consent (Falk 1997). But along the way, it expressed many *soft* opinions that have since become widely accepted, following the interplay of several UN organs. In this way, while the UN (*qua actor*) declined from prohibiting nuclear weapons, it served as a *forum* for discussion and provided *resources* for further law-making efforts. It might have been a softer approach than most expected – but it is certainly not the same as silence or inaction. Ultimately, the strength of the UN's voice depends on that of its member states (see also Chapter 6).

CONCLUDING REMARKS: THE NEW LEVIATHAN?

In our rather dark times, I am tempted to sometimes share the "hackneyed popular conceptions [...] which see the UN as incompetent and malevolent at worst" (Sharma 2007, p. 220). While Rome and the rest of the world burns, it is not unfair to wonder if so much attention, and resources, should be devoted to the theatrical antics of the GA in Manhattan (Ball 2020). What is the use, a concerned citizen or scholar might wonder, of having such a global "talking shop" (Panke 2014)? And if there have been increasing concerns about the UN's operations in the "Headquarters," the same can be said of its (in)actions out in "the field" – to use a dichotomy central to the work of this and other international institutions (Quiroga-Villamarín 2025b). Indeed, the last couple of decades have been marked by very important debates on how to render the UN accountable for its failures and omissions – and of those, there are plenty of examples all around the world (Klabbers 2017). If Borges (1975) would rewrite his *Universal History of Infamy* today, one would imagine that the names of several catastrophic failures of the UN might find themselves included. Just think of Rwanda, Srebrenica, the Democratic Republic of the Congo, or Haiti – to name a couple of salient instances (Howard and Dayal 2018).

Criticism of the UN, by and large, oscillates around two poles: it is either *powerless* (and just a mere space for lofty rhetoric in Manhattan, Geneva, or Vienna) and/or it fails to aptly exercise its *powers* when push comes to shove "in the field." The disjointed nature of these two prongs already hints at the fact that the reality of the UN can only lie somewhere in the middle. It is neither a powerful supra-state nor an empty shell of deliberation: the UN can only be what its member states decide to make it. Participating in its inner life – either as an actual delegate or as a student simulating its operations – can be a humbling experience because of this. At the end, no technical plan – however well-crafted or needed – can make its way from the blueprint to implementation without the support of its member states (and in some cases, of the concurring alignment of the Great Powers). And such a plan can only be adopted if it is aligned with the inter- and intra-rules, rhythms, and rationales of the UN's complex hierarchy of organs. At the end of the day, a successful lawyer-diplomat must not only master the substance of the matter at hand but also learn to navigate the troubled waters of UN law – and international institutional law, more broadly understood.

And in our dire times, competence and sensibility in these arcane arts of multilateral diplomacy are needed more than ever. For even if the UN – or more specifically, the GA – is a just "talk shop," we should remember what the promise of deliberative parliamentary diplomacy meant in the previous century. For a generation scared by the Great War of 1914 (which was caused, to a large degree, by a dark web of bilateral negotiations and the obligations enshrined in secret alliance treaties), the opening of the League of Nations' Assembly in 1920 meant the promise of a new dawn in multilateral diplomacy. This was especially true for small states, which participated – for the very first time – in global governance as equals (Rappard 1934). The years that followed in the so-called interwar period witnessed the collapse of that so-called liberal rules-based order, as Great Powers rivalries led to the slow partition and annexation of many of their smaller neighbours. Bilateral and secret negotiations, moreover, did little to "appease" the hunger of such Great Powers and eventually led to another, even greater, Second World War (Wieviorka 2023). Those were the painful memories which haunted the horizon of the men and women who came together in San Francisco "to save succeeding generations from the scourge of war, which twice in our lifetime has brought untold sorrow" (UN Charter, Preamble). In our own times of increased geopolitical tensions, marked once again by the return of secretive diplomatic negotiations between Great Powers that exclude the "smaller" states whose fate lies in the balance, we should not forget the painful lessons of the twentieth century. For all of its flaws, the UN still offers a *forum* based on the equal rights "of nations large and small," which can provide *resources* to the latter – and maybe even act as a protective *actor* on their behalf. It was only until the outbreak of the Second World War that the League of Nations closed its Assembly in Geneva (Biltoft 2020). Let's hope the UN never closes its "talking shop" in Manhattan – for the alternative, surely, can only be worse.

REFERENCES

Abbott, Kenneth W./Snidal, Duncan (2000). Hard and Soft Law in International Governance. International Organization 54 (3), 421–456. https://doi.org/10.1162/002081800551280

Alger, Chadwick F. (1966). Interaction in a Committee of the United Nations General Assembly. Midwest Journal of Political Science 10 (4), 411–447. https://doi.org/10.2307/2108921

Alvarez, José (2000). Multilateralism and Its Discontents. European Journal of International Law 11 (2), 393–411.

Bailey, Sydney D. (1966). U.N. Voting: Tyranny of the Majority? The World Today 22 (6), 234–241.

Ball, James R. (2020). Theater of State: A Dramaturgy of the United Nations. Evanston, Northwestern University Press.

Bartos, Adam/Hitchens, Christopher (1994). International Territory: The United Nations, 1945–95. London, Verso.

Bianchi, Andrea/Zarbiyev, Fuad (2024). Demystifying Treaty Interpretation. Cambridge, Cambridge University Press.

Biltoft, Carolyn N. (2020). Decoding the Balance Sheet: Gifts, Goodwill, and the Liquidation of the League of Nations. Capitalism: A Journal of History and Economics 1 (2), 379–404. https://doi.org/10.1353/cap.2020.0006

Bodansky, Daniel/Watson, J. Shand (1992). State Consent and the Sources of International Obligation. Proceedings of the Annual Meeting (American Society of International Law) 86, 108–113.

Borges, Jorge Luis (1975). A Universal History of Infamy. London, Pinguin Books.

Bosco, David L. (2009). Five to Rule Them All: The UN Security Council and the Making of the Modern World. Oxford, Oxford University Press.

Boyle, Alan E./Chinkin, Christine (2007). The Making of International Law. Oxford, Oxford University Press.

Brölmann, Catherine (2020). Specialized Rules of Treaty Interpretation: International Organizations. In: Duncan B. Hollis (Ed.). The Oxford Guide to Treaties. 2nd ed. Oxford, Oxford University Press, 524–542.

Chesterman, Simon (2007). Secretary or General?: The UN Secretary-General in World Politics. Cambridge, Cambridge University Press.

Cole, Wade M. (2005). Sovereignty Relinquished? Explaining Commitment to the International Human Rights Covenants, 1966–1999. American Sociological Review 70 (3), 472–495.

Colombos, C. John (1947). The United Nations Charter. Some Introductory Notes on Its Main Functions and Organs. The International Law Quarterly 1 (1), 20–33.

Conforti, Benedetto (1969). The Legal Effect of Non-Compliance with Rules of Procedure in the U.N. General Assembly and Security Council. American Journal of International Law 63 (3), 479–489. https://doi.org/10.2307/2198867

Conforti, Benedetto (2005). The Law and Practice of the United Nations. Leiden, Martinus Nijhoff Publishers.

Crawford, James (2014). Chance, Order, Change: The Course of International Law; General Course on Public International Law. Leiden, Brill.

Dahl, Arthur Lyon/López-Claros, Augusto/Groff, Maja (2020). Global Governance and the Emergence of Global Institutions for the 21st Century. Cambridge, Cambridge University Press.

Daudet, Yves (2019). 1919–2019, le flux du multilatéralisme. The Hague, Recueil des cours de l'Académie de La Haye.

de Vattel, Emer (2008). The Law of Nations, or, Principles of the Law of Nature, Applied to the Conduct and Affairs of Nations and Sovereigns, with Three Early Essays on the Origin and Nature of Natural Law and on Luxury. Edited by Bela Kapossy and Richard Whatmore. Indianapolis, Liberty Fund.

de Wet, Erika (2024). Introduction to Chapter VII: The General Framework. In: Bruno Simma/Daniel-Erasmus Khan/Georg Nolte et al. (Eds.). The Charter of the United Nations. 4th ed. Oxford, Oxford University Press, 1578–1622.

Derrida, Jacques (2020). The Politics of Friendship. London, Verso.

Donaldson, Megan (2017). The Survival of the Secret Treaty: Publicity, Secrecy, and Legality in the International Order. American Journal of International Law 111 (3), 575–627. https://doi.org/10.1017/ajil.2017.60

Donaldson, Megan (2021). Ventriloquism in Geneva: The League of Nations as International Organisation. In: Annabel Brett/Megan Donaldson/Martti Koskenniemi (Eds.). History, Politics, Law. Cambridge, Cambridge University Press, 253–282.

Duursma, Allard/Lindberg Bromley, Sara/Gorur, Aditi (2024). The Impact of Host-State Consent on the Protection of Civilians in UN Peacekeeping. Civil Wars 26 (1), 16–40. https://doi.org/10.1080/13698249.2023.2196185

Falk, Richard A. (1997). Nuclear Weapons, International Law and the World Court: A Historic Encounter. American Journal of International Law 91 (1), 64–75. https://doi.org/10.2307/2954141

Fassbender, Bardo (1998a). The United Nations Charter As Constitution of the International Community. Columbia Journal of Transnational Law 36, 529–619.

Fassbender, Bardo (1998b). UN Security Council Reform and the Right of Veto: A Constitutional Perspective. Leiden, Martinus Nijhoff Publishers.

Fassbender, Bardo (2020). Key Documents on the Reform of the UN Security Council 1991–2019. Leiden, Brill Nijhoff.

Galbraith, Jean (2023). Introduction to Symposium on the Contours and Limits of Advisory Opinions. American Journal of International Law Unbound 117, 274–276. https://doi.org/10.1017/aju.2023.48

Géraud, André/Pertinax (1945). Diplomacy, Old and New. Foreign Affairs 23 (2), 256–270. https://doi.org/10.2307/20029892

Gifkins, Jess (2021). Beyond the Veto: Roles in UN Security Council Decision-Making. Global Governance: A Review of Multilateralism and International Organizations 27 (1), 1–24.

Goldman, Richard Franko (1966). Arts and Letters: The Wonderful World of Culture: Or: A Strictly Highbrow and Artistic Subject. The American Scholar 35 (3), 517–520.

Goldmann, Matthias (2012). We Need to Cut Off the Head of the King: Past, Present, and Future Approaches to International Soft Law. Leiden Journal of International Law 25 (2), 335–368. https://doi.org/10.1017/S0922156512000064

Götz, Norbert (2005). On the Origins of "Parliamentary Diplomacy": Scandinavian "Bloc Politics" and Delegation Policy in the League of Nations. Cooperation and Conflict 40 (3), 263–279.

Gowan, Peter (2003). US: UN. New Left Review 24, 5–28.

Gregory, Charles Noble (1921). The First Assembly of the League of Nations. American Journal of International Law 15 (2), 240–252. https://doi.org/10.2307/2187684

Groom, A.J.R. (2004). UN Peacekeeping: From Hammarskjold to Brahimi and Beyond. Studia Diplomatica 57 (1), 149–158.

Gross, Leo (1967). The International Court of Justice. Malaya Law Review 9 (1), 10–19.

Hankey, Maurice (1946). Diplomacy by Conference: Studies in Public Affairs, 1920–1946. London, E. Benn Limited.

Hazard, John N. (1963). The Sixth Committee and New Law. American Journal of International Law 57 (3), 604–613. https://doi.org/10.2307/2196084

Higgins, Rosalyn/Webb, Philippa/Akande, Dapo/Sivakumaran, Sandesh/Sloan, James (2017). The Trusteeship Council. In: Rosalyn Higgins/Philippa Webb/Dapo Akande et al. (Eds.). Oppenheim's International Law: United Nations. Oxford, Oxford University Press, 100–112.

Howard, Lise Morjé/Dayal, Anjali Kaushlesh (2018). The Use of Force in UN Peacekeeping. International Organization 72 (1), 71–103. Available online at https://www.jstor.org/stable/26569462 (accessed 5/13/2025).

Hurd, Ian (2024). International Organizations Politics, Law, Practice. 5th ed. Cambridge, Cambridge University Press.

Jameson, J. Franklin (1894). The Origin of the Standing-Committee System in American Legislative Bodies. Political Science Quarterly 9 (2), 246–267. https://doi.org/10.2307/2140190

Johns, Fleur (2024). Connection in a Divided World: Rethinking "Community" in International Law. The Hague, T.M.C. Asser Press.

Kapur, Suvir (2015). United Nations Peacekeeping Operations: An Overview. The Indian Journal of Political Science 76 (1), 127–134.

Kaufmann, Johan (1996). Conference Diplomacy: An Introductory Analysis. 3rd ed. Basingstoke, Macmillan.

Klabbers, Jan (2009). Global Governance before the ICJ: Re-reading the WHA Opinion. Max Planck Yearbook of United Nations Law Online 13 (1), 1–28. https://doi.org/10.1163/18757413-90000035

Klabbers, Jan (2017). Reflections on Role Responsibility: The Responsibility of International Organizations for Failing to Act. European Journal of International Law 28 (4), 1133–1161. https://doi.org/10.1093/ejil/chx068

Klein, Robert A. (1974). Sovereign Equality Among States: The History of an Idea. Toronto, University of Toronto Press.

Knaap, Aden (2023). Judging the World: International Courts and the Origins of Global Governance, 1899–1971. Cambridge, Doctoral dissertation, Harvard University Graduate School of Arts and Sciences. Available online at https://dash.harvard.edu/bitstream/handle/1/37375694/Knaap%20-%20JTW.pdf?sequence=1&isAllowed=y (accessed 5/13/2025).

Krisch, Nico (2014). The Decay of Consent: International Law in an Age of Global Public Goods. American Journal of International Law 108 (1), 1–40. https://doi.org/10.5305/amerjintelaw.108.1.0001

Krisch, Nico (2017). Liquid Authority in Global Governance. International Theory 9 (02), 237–260. https://doi.org/10.1017/S1752971916000269

Lee, Dwight E. (1947). The Genesis of the Veto. International Organization 1 (1), 33–42.

Matheson, Michael J. (1997). The Opinions of the International Court of Justice on the Threat or Use of Nuclear Weapons. American Journal of International Law 91 (3), 417–435. https://doi.org/10.2307/2954181

Mayr-Singer, Jelka/Mayr, Teresa F. (2016). Keep the Wheels Spinning: The Contributions of Advisory Opinions of the International Court of Justice to the Development of International Law. ZaöRV [Heidelberg Journal of International Law] 76 (2), 425–449.

Mazower, Mark (2009). No Enchanted Palace: The End of Empire and the Ideological Origins of the United Nations. Princeton, Princeton University Press.

Merry, Sally Engle (2014). Global Legal Pluralism and the Temporality of Soft Law. The Journal of Legal Pluralism and Unofficial Law 46 (1), 108–122. https://doi.org/10.1080/07329113.2014.882103

Moeckli, Daniel/Shah, Sangeeta/Sivakumaran, Sandesh/Harris, D. J. (2022). International Human Rights Law. Oxford, Oxford University Press.

Moyn, Samuel (2022). The "rules-based international order" doesn't constrain Russia — or the United States. The Washington Post of 2022. Available online at https://www.washingtonpost.com/outlook/2022/03/01/ukraine-international-order-un/ (accessed 5/13/2025).

Nurullayev, Dmitriy/Papa, Mihaela (2023). Bloc Politics at the UN: How Other States Behave When the United States and China–Russia Disagree. Global Studies Quarterly 3 (3), 1–11. https://doi.org/10.1093/isagsq/ksad034

Orford, Anne (1999). Muscular Humanitarianism: Reading the Narratives of the New Interventionism. European Journal of International Law 10 (4), 679–711. https://doi.org/10.1093/ejil/10.4.679

Panke, Diana (2014). The GA—A Talking Shop? Exploring Rationales for the Repetition of Resolutions in Subsequent Negotiations. Cambridge Review of International Affairs 27 (3), 442–458. https://doi.org/10.1080/09557571.2014.931354

PARISS Collective (2025). On the Symbolic Force of International Law: The Case of Gaza. Political Anthropological Research on International Social Sciences 5 (2), 167–188. https://doi.org/10.1163/25903276-bja10065

Peters, Anne (2009). The Merits of Global Constitutionalism. Indiana Journal of Global Legal Studies 16 (2), 397–411.

Peters, Anne (2011). Soft Law as a New Mode of Governance. In: Udo Diedrichs/Wulf Reiners/Wolfgang Wessels (Eds.). The Dynamics of Change in EU Governance. Cheltenham, Edward Elgar Publishing.

Peters, Anne (2023). The War in Ukraine and Legal Limitations on Russian Vetoes. Journal on the Use of Force and International Law 10 (2), 162–172. https://doi.org/10.1080/20531702.2023.2264085

Quiroga-Villamarín, Daniel R. (2019). "An Atmosphere of Genuine Solidarity and Brotherhood": Hernán Santa-Cruz and a Forgotten Latin American Contribution to Social Rights. Journal of the History of International Law 21 (1), 71–103. https://doi.org/10.1163/15718050-12340103

Quiroga-Villamarín, Daniel R. (2020). Normalising Global Commerce: Containerisation, Materiality, and Transnational Regulation (1956–68). London Review of International Law 8 (3), 457–477. https://doi.org/10.1093/lril/lrab003

Quiroga-Villamarín, Daniel R. (2023). Simulando al "Gran Leviatán": La Educación Jurídica Experiencial y los Estudios Globales. Imprenta: Publicación Divulgativa de la Facultad de Ciencias Sociales 3, 18–23.

Quiroga-Villamarín, Daniel R. (2024a). "Architects of the Better World"; Democracy, Law, and the Construction of International Order (1919–1989). PhD thesis in International Law and History. Geneva, Graduate Institute of International and Development Studies.

Quiroga-Villamarín, Daniel R. (2024b). Enforcement. In: Sué González Hauck/ Raffaela Kunz/Max Milas (Eds.). Public international law: a multi-perspective approach. Abingdon, Routledge, 47–53.

Quiroga-Villamarín, Daniel R. (2025a). Challenging the Global Herrenhaus: The Undending Quest to Democratize International Relations Within, and beyond, the United Nations. University of Vienna Law Review 9 (2), 21–49. https://doi.org/10.25365/vlr-2025-9-2-21

Quiroga-Villamarín, Daniel R. (2025b). International Law, Internationally: Meditations on an Organizational Pilgrimage into the Disciplines of Global Law and Policy. [preprint]. Max Planck Institute for Social Anthropology Working Papers No. 214.

Quiroga-Villamarín, Daniel R. (forthcoming). "The Principal Judicial Organ": The Defence of the United Nations' Inter-Institutional Operations in the Gaza Strip Provisional Measures Orders of 2024. Groningen Journal of International Law.

Quiroga-Villamarín, Daniel R./Mansouri, Negar (2025). Ways of Seeing International Organisations: New Perspectives for International Institutional Law. Cambridge, Cambridge University Press.

Rappard, William E. (1934). Small States in the League of Nations. Political Science Quarterly 49 (4), 544–575. https://doi.org/10.2307/2143465

Ravndal, Ellen Jenny (2016). "The First Major Test": The UN Secretary-General and the Palestine Problem, 1947–9. The International History Review 38 (1), 196–213. https://doi.org/10.1080/07075332.2015.1023212

Ravndal, Ellen Jenny (2023). In the Beginning: Secretary-General Trygve Lie and the Establishment of the United Nations. Bristol, Bristol University Press.
Rowe, Edward T. (1969). Changing Patterns in the Voting Success of Member States in the United Nations General Assembly: 1945–1966. International Organization 23 (2), 231–253.
Schermers, Henry G. (1997). We the Peoples of the United Nations. Max Planck Yearbook of United Nations Law 1 (1), 111–128.
Schlesinger, Stephen (1994). FDR's Five Policemen: Creating the United Nations. World Policy Journal 11 (3), 88–93.
Sharma, Patrick (2007). Interests and Ideas at the United Nations. The SAIS Review of International Affairs 27 (2), 219–223.
Simpson, Gerry J. (2004). Great Powers and Outlaw States: Unequal Sovereigns in the International Legal Order. Cambridge, Cambridge University Press.
Slaughter, Anne-Marie/Hale, Thomas (2013). International Relations, Principal Theories. Max Planck Encyclopedias of International Law. Available online at https://opil.ouplaw.com/display/10.1093/law:epil/9780199231690/law-9780199231690-e722 (accessed 5/13/2025).
Talmon, Stefan (2005). The Security Council as World Legislature. American Journal of International Law 99, 175–193.
Throntveit, Trygve (2011). The Fable of the Fourteen Points: Woodrow Wilson and National Self-Determination. Diplomatic History 35 (3), 445–481. https://doi.org/10.1111/j.1467-7709.2011.00959.x
Tomuschat, Christian (1995). The United Nations at Age Fifty: A Legal Perspective. Leiden, Brill Nijhoff.
Touloumi, Olga (2024). Assembly by Design: The United Nations and its Global Interior. Minneapolis, University of Minnesota Press.
Trent, John/Schnurr, Laura (2017). A United Nations Renaissance: What the UN is, and What it Could Be. Opladen, Verlag Barbara Budrich.
Troy, Jodok (2021). The United Nations Secretary-General as an International Civil Servant. The International History Review 43 (4), 906–927. https://doi.org/10.1080/07075332.2020.1828139
Tudor, Margot (2023). Blue Helmet Bureaucrats: United Nations Peacekeeping and the Reinvention of Colonialism, 1945–1971. Cambridge, Cambridge University Press.
United Nations (2021). Introductory Remarks by Eduardo Valencia-Ospina. In: United Nations (Ed.). Seventy years of the International Law Commission: Drawing a Balance for the Future. Leiden, Brill, 49–50.
Urueña, Rene (2022). Interaction between International Organizations. In: Jan Klabbers (Ed.). The Cambridge Companion to International Organizations Law. Cambridge, Cambridge University Press, 222–243.
Weiss, Thomas G./Carayannis, Tatiana/Jolly, Richard (2009). The "Third" United Nations. Global Governance 15 (1), 123–142.
Wieviorka, Olivier (2023). Histoire Totale de la Seconde Guerre mondiale. Paris, Perrin.
Wolfers, Arnold (1962). Discord and Collaboration: Essays on International Politics. Baltimore, John Hopkins University Press.
Zarbiyev, Fuad (2024). Did the International Community die in Gaza? Available online at https://www.graduateinstitute.ch/communications/news/international-community-gaza (accessed 5/13/2025).

PART III

Doing transnational politics: case studies and materials

9. Procedures, practices, politics: how institutions work

Claudia Wiesner and Taru Haapala

INTRODUCTION: PROCEDURES, DEBATES AND POLITICAL PROCESSES

It is the aim of this chapter to explain and discuss how politics and political practices in inter- and supranational institutions and assemblies work and how they can be analysed and understood. A specific focus will be set on deliberative assemblies, that is, institutions of a parliament-like type, such as the European Parliament (EP) and the United Nations (UN) General Assembly (GA). They represent an ideal type of institution in a number of respects. First, they assemble delegates or representatives – in a nation state these would be sent from their constituencies. In international settings, they are sent by their states. In a supranational setting, such as the EP, they represent party families, constituencies and nation states. Second, assemblies adopt the principles of parliamentary debate and decision-making, which is a historically paradigmatic form (Wiesner et al. 2017, p. 25). Debates and decision-making are structured according to specific rules that are largely similar for deliberative assemblies of any kind. Third, these principles of deliberative assemblies are also the ones that structure decision-making in the UN (and also EU) bodies to a large extent.

In the following, we will discuss which generalities of the political processes are at stake in inter- and supranational institutions and assemblies, and how political conflicts are carried out. In order to do so, it is vital to understand micropolitics, that is, the everyday political practices, strategies and negotiations. We understand micropolitics (for further detail see Wiesner 2018) as the conflicts, struggles, political and rhetorical moves, debates and their actors that coin, shape or reflect the actions and practices of politics and the policies (as outcomes). Micropolitics are carried out via and inside the rule-based institutions and assemblies and their written and unwritten framework, and they are also carried out between different institutions. This framework is shaped by legal documents that range from highly formalised treaties and laws over more infomal rules to unwritten rules (for further detail see Palonen 2014; Palonen 2019).

We will in the following discuss the framework and procedures of micropolitics in and between the institutions and/or assemblies of the European Union (EU) and the UN. As mentioned in Chapters 6 and 7, the UN and the EU as organisations show differences when it comes to their legal status. The UN is an International Organisation (IO), which means it is based on the principle of sovereign equality of its member states. The EU, different from the UN, has both supranational and international or intergovernmental characteristics. Our argument is, however, that the UN and the EU show a great number of similarities when it comes to the everyday political practices that shape negotiation and decision-making, especially in their assembly-like bodies. In the following, we will discuss the frameworks, rules and political processes in the assemblies and institutions of the UN and EU and how they shape, have transformed and are being transformed by political practices, and in what circumstances. We also address the question of how their dynamics manifest and what the role of different bodies in the EU and the UN and their interinstitutional interplay is. The chapter thus does not simply show how institutions and assemblies work on the practical level, but it tries to explain the political dynamics inside inter- and supranational institutions overall.

The next section introduces our understanding of politics as political action. It is followed by a discussion of the concept of micropolitics and the function of rules, debates and documents. The second part of the chapter briefly highlights the framework that the UN and EU set for micropolitics. The third part presents an example.

MICROPOLITICS IN INSTITUTIONS

What is Politics?

Importantly, to understand political practices in inter- and supranational institutions and assemblies, we first focus on the concept of politics that is the basis of the following considerations. Politics can respectively be understood as action, conflict, sphere, field, arena and system (Kauppi et al. 2016).

The most widespread understanding in Political Science is that politics is a system or a sphere. In that sense, IOs and their bodies would be considered part of an international political system. If politics is understood as a system or sphere, it is understood as a spatially determined area or field. Actors or issues can enter or leave the system, or area, of politics. Definitions of the system of politics can differ, ranging from merely the classical political system with parties and institutions to broader understandings. But such an understanding of politics entails a decisive conceptual difference to an action-understanding of politics. In a political system view, the realm of politics is conceptualised with borders and hence remains limited. Only actors and issues in the system are part of politics.

As opposed to this, politics can take place anytime and anywhere if it is seen as activity. What is more, any issue can become political, at whatever level and group of (global) society. Against this backdrop, we understand politics as a contingent and controversial activity (Wiesner et al. 2017, pp. 9–12). Building on Kari Palonen's distinction of four sub-dimensions of politics – *politics, polity, politicisation and politicking* (Palonen 2003, p. 171) – politics is the activity, polity is the institutionalised arena or form politics relates to (this can be the political system, but also another institutional form), policy refers to the regulating aspect of politics, politicking means the doing of politics, and politicisation is understood as the act of marking, or naming something as political.

Politics-as-action in this sense can take place virtually at any time, any place, and in any situation, and anything can be marked as political (see Wiesner et al. 2017; on the following for further detail see Wiesner 2021a; Wiesner 2021b). Understanding politics as an activity therefore means that politics has no spatial boundaries. Everything and everyone can be part of politics at all times. And, importantly, *politics is also shaped by what actors do*, and not mainly by the system or sphere in which they act. Politics is also contingent – it is always possible to act otherwise, even if the results of the alternatives may be the same. Politicisation in this understanding means an active use of contingency, of rendering something contested or controversial (Haapala and Oleart 2022; Wiesner 2021c). This, importantly, is not an extension of the margins of the activity of politics itself, but rather constitutive of politics. In this sense politicisation constitutes politics, not vice versa, and all politics is a result of politicising moves (for further detail see Kauppi et al. 2016; Palonen 2003). This also means that politics as activity can take place both inside the classical political system and institutions as well as outside. Our understanding of micropolitics builds on the understanding of politics as activity. The political activity at stake in this chapter takes place in the UN and EU institutions and assemblies.

Micropolitics and Their Rules

Politics as an activity means that individual actors literally *do* politics. In return, this also entails that it is not the body or the organisation itself that does politics, but the individuals that are active in the organisation or its body. Strictly speaking, it is thus not the UN's GA that takes a decision, but the decision is the product of debates and negotiations carried out by individual actors in the GA, that is then channelled into a vote. The voting result then presents the decision made by the GAas an institution, as a collective of representatives.

While the collective decision-making outcomes can be understood as macropolitics, the individual political actions and their interplay can be understood as micropolitics. This also means that decision-making in all kinds of institutions and also IOs such as the UN or the EU follows a pattern of micropolitics (Wiesner 2018).

The concept of micropolitics considers the fact that the institutions at stake are not unitary actors, but consist of different bodies – GA, Security Council and so on – and different members – delegates, ministers, or members of parliament. The individual members or delegates not only belong to different states or political camps, but also take initiative and become politically active, both as individuals and in their existence as a collective body. These micropolitics take place both within the bodies of an IO or supranational polity (such as the GA or the EP) and with regard to other bodies, such as the Security Council and its members or the European Council.

Micropolitics are thus carried out via and inside the rule-based institutions and assemblies and their written and unwritten framework. To understand micropolitics, it is therefore first decisive to understand their framework, that is, to analyse what rules and institutional settings shape and impact the micropolitics and how. This framework is set by legal documents that range from highly formalised written rules, that is, by rules that are laid down in treaties, laws or other documents, to unwritten or even unspoken rules (for further detail see Palonen 2014; Palonen 2019).

The most formalised rules are constitutions, treaties or charters. They are founding documents that specify the functions and competencies and also the principles of work of a polity or organisation. In the case of the UN and the EU, their founding documents are treaties (EU) and an international charter (UN). These documents have been the result of international negotiations of heads of state and governments and their teams, and of votes in international settings. Laws and resolutions are both highly formalised rules and outcomes of politics in institutions. In comparison to treaties or charters, it is, however, easier to change them. Changing or making a law usually requires simple majorities in assemblies such as the GA or the EP, while most treaties or charters require either unanimous votes, or at least decisive majorities such as two-thirds majorities.

Besides these formalised rules, there are the lesser formalised ones such as rules of procedure of certain institutions. Rules of procedure are usually voted upon by the institution in question itself, and can mostly be changed by simple majorities. Even though they are less formalised documents such as rules of procedure are important because they directly set the rules for the political processes in institutions and hence structure the political debates and micropolitical processes. Rules of procedure are documents that literally lay down the rules of the political game, such as speech times, speech rules, timings of motions and draft motions, necessary majorities and voting procedures. In order to understand the micropolitics at play and thus in order to act in a Model United Nations (MUN) or Model European Union (MEU), understanding the rules of procedure and how to act in this framework is absolutely essential.

The framework for micropolitics is complemented by half-informal rules that can be written or unwritten, such as agreements between actors or institutions. Agreements, such as interinstitutional agreements in the EU (see the last section and Wiesner 2018), are usually negotiated within one institution or between several institutions. They also rule how the institutional micropolitics and the everyday political practices are organised and carried out. While agreements are usually formally voted upon, they can be changed relatively easily and with simple majorities.

Two other categories of rules are much more informal and mostly unwritten or even unspoken – practices and routines as well as "dos and don'ts". Practices and routines exist in any institution, and it is vital for all actors to know them and act accordingly. However, they will in most cases not be written down. Nevertheless, when working in the institution newcomers will soon realise what they are. An example would be that in a parliament a newly elected member of a political group will not be able to choose his or her committee, but will either be assigned to one by the whip, or he or she will have to fight in order to obtain the committee seat he or she wishes for. The underlying informal routine is seniority: longstanding members of parliament usually have the first say when it comes to choosing committees or positions.

Finally, there are the "dos and don'ts". In complementarity to practices and routines, they will neither be written down nor, in most cases, made explicit. They are also to be discovered and observed. Following the example that was just sketched, the new parliamentary member would respect the "do" of patiently waiting to be assigned to a committee; or then, he or she would deliberately choose to make a claim or even have a vote on the question – the "don't" in such a case would mean that it would be unwise to enter into a conflict in the matter unless the newcomer has the support of a considerable number of actors in his or her group, because he or she would otherwise lose the case right away. Last but not least, what has been said means that personal interactions are key at the level of micropolitics.

Micropolitics, Debates and Documents

If politics is seen as activity, debate is one of its major forms. In political institutions, debates take place in a structured and regularised form. Parliamentary debate is a historically paradigmatic form of institutionalised debate (Wiesner et al. 2017, p. 25). Parliamentary debate as an ideal type is characterised and structured by its rules and procedures, the agenda-setting and the items on the agenda, the participants in the debates, the regulating of debates, its stages and layers and, more generally, the political times of debates (Wiesner et al. 2017, p. 41; for further detail see Palonen 2014; Palonen 2019). Furthermore, debates are a key means to carry out micropolitics. Debate is an institutionalised and ritualised form of political action. Understanding debates not only entails studying the rhetorical, argumentative and political strategies that are applied, and focusing on the ways discussions are led, but it also means understanding the basic principle of debates in assemblies, that is, in institutionalised parliament-like settings.

The first point to underline in this respect is that debates, as all micropolitics, are structured by the institutional frameworks and rules described above, and in particular the rules of procedure. This means that institutionalised debates are structured by specific rules laid down for this purpose that regulate who may speak, under which circumstances, on what topic and for how long. The rules of procedure are usually executed by the chair or president (dais in a MUN). They regulate the speaking times and the occasions of speaking (or not), that is, they regulate the participants and the course of a debate in an assembly. Not just anyone present in the room is allowed to speak, but only participants that are formally delegated to this function. In IOs and their assemblies this usually means that they represent a state and speak on its behalf. The debate is thus strongly regulated and formalised. Appearing in a debate means to appear on stage, in the role and position the speaker is taking on or representing, and in line with the rules of procedure that regulate time and character of the appearance.

Second, debates in deliberative assemblies are based on the principle of speaking *pro et contra* (Palonen 2019, pp. 1–15) on a proposal (motion, draft resolution) or on an analysis of the situation at hand. This means that any speaker – literally – entering on stage does so in order to perform his or her argument *pro et contra* a decision which will be taken (usually by a vote) after the debate. In debates in deliberative assemblies, this exchange of arguments *pro et contra* is structured by the rules of procedure that ensure all sides will be treated fairly. The other actors, representing other camps in the debate, are confronted verbally, but have to be respected. Not only the debating but also the speaking time is well regulated. Usually, verbal and physical attacks are forbidden and will be sanctioned if they appear (Wiesner et al. 2017, pp. 12–23). It is important to understand that these rules themselves are an object of politics: when one party, for instance, does not want a vote to take place, it will be in their interest to formally interrupt the debate for an informal session, as this will prolong the time until the vote.

Thirdly, a debate does not simply start, but is led and structured in relation to an agenda that is determined previously, usually by a president or chair of the session or body in question. The politics of the agenda are another key factor: Which topic is set on the agenda, and at what point in time? It is decisive, for example, whether a topic is debated first or last in the order of the day. When debates can last for several hours, the first topic will have the freshest and clearest attention of the participants, whereas the last item on the agenda may easily suffer from one sole desire, the one to end the day. It is important that all this takes place in time – this does not only concern the questions of whether a long debating day has to end at some moment and what topics are discussed before the end, but it also concerns the question of adjournments of a debate, which generally aim at gaining time – time for further internal discussion in a delegation, for instance (Wiesner et al. 2017, pp. 12–23).

Documents such as motions, draft resolutions and resolutions represent the outcomes and outputs of political processes. These outcome documents are formally voted upon. The formalised votes always follow certain procedural rules. They will be directed by the chair or dais and taken after the debates, and the votes will be formally counted. Debates are usually recorded in protocols, as are the votes. The protocols today are mostly available online. Protocols of speeches and debates, or "frozen" debates, document the micropolitical processes (Wiesner et al. 2017, pp. 13, 20).

In terms of understanding micropolitics, the key link between the debate and the vote is whether a respective motion, draft resolution or position obtains a majority or not, and what is the distribution of votes. In the UN, a key question is how big or small a majority is, who voted in favour of a motion or resolution, who voted against and who abstained. Votes in institutions such as the UN often express political alliances. For instance, on 2 March 2022, in the GA, 141 states voted in favour of the resolution that condemned the Russian attack against Ukraine. Russia, Syria, North Korea, Belarus and Eritrea, that is, five states, voted against. However, it is decisively important to note which states abstained. A total of 35 states did so – among them China and Cuba, but also numerous important emerging powers such as India, Pakistan, South Africa and Bangladesh, as well as most of the Central Asian states, that is, Russia's immediate neighbours (tagesschau 2022). This indicates that there is not a simple "Western" majority against the War, but that decisive emerging powers refuse to stand with the "West" (Wiesner 2024).

The above means that documents are key in understanding and analysing micropolitics. Documents such as rules of procedures, motions, draft resolutions and resolutions all structure the political debates and micropolitical processes in institutions and assemblies, and represent their outcomes and outputs. Understanding micropolitics requires considering not only the institutional frameworks and the spoken debate but also the written debate in the form of protocols, motions, resolutions and other documents. Depending on the interest, documents of any kind can become a means of micropolitics and/or express micropolitics – and will, in turn, express them to the analyst: parliamentary protocols, committee reports, press articles, interview protocols, laws, policy documents, resolutions, official records, administrative statements, white papers, party manifestos, constitutions, or peace treaties. They can be part of political conflicts and debates themselves or merely indications of these (Wiesner et al. 2017, pp. 19–21).

The different types of documents mentioned above are also objects of research for understanding the way politics is carried out in institutions and between them. Documents carry important and detailed information on the political actions that have been taking place. They not only represent frozen debates, but also the results of past debates, indicating turning points in ongoing political conflicts, and they are the end products of political processes and debates. In each case, documents show which issues were regarded as controversial or remained unquestioned. It can be important to understand why something is missing in such a document when it would have been expected to be in it (Wiesner et al. 2017, pp. 19–21). An example of documents reflecting micropolitics is presented in the concluding section of this chapter.

It is the basis of our argument that not only a parliamentary assembly would work along these principles, but also most institutions that are based on debating and/or votes in their decision-making. The political dynamics in IOs and their bodies (see section 3 below) are shaped by such micropolitics. Understanding micropolitics requires focusing on the actors, their strategies and their moves. This perspective enables a dynamic and process-oriented approach, helping to make visible intervening factors that remain hidden when only focusing on the results of decision-making or votes (Wiesner 2018). If one focuses on the micropolitics that take place, the similarities between any kind of institution, whichever political level they are based on, are striking. In any organisation, whether it is the UN or the EU, and in any deliberative assembly, whether it is the German Bundestag or the GA, micropolitics, that is, debates, strategies, playing with rules of procedure, advancing statements and so on, shape the way decisions are made. If the organisation is inter- or supranational, micropolitics becomes more complex.

Against this backdrop, we will discuss in the following the commonalities of micropolitical processes and practices in international and supranational institutions, focusing on the frameworks, politics, procedures and political practices taking place in both the UN and the EU.

INTERNATIONAL INSTITUTIONS AND THEIR RULES

The UN and the EU and Their Institutional Framework

As has been said, our argument is that the UN and the EU show a great number of similarities when it comes to the everyday political practices that shape negotiation and decision-making in their bodies and deliberative assemblies. This might seem counterintuitive at first sight since the UN and the EU can be said to show a number of differences when it comes to their legal status. The institutional frameworks of the UN and the EU differ to some extent, as will be discussed below. Nevertheless, the principles of micropolitics that have been outlined above are at work in similar ways in the different frameworks of the UN and the EU, especially when it comes to their deliberative assemblies (EP, GA).

Both the UN and the EU have been founded as IOs within the framework of international law and multilateral treaties. In the case of the EU, the international or intergovernmental elements have over the years been complemented by supranational elements, as discussed in depth in Chapter 7 and below. However, the EU still shows traces of an IO. International Law scholar Jan Klabbers (2009, p. 14) underlines this. To understand his argument, it is illustrative to trace Klabbers' definition of an IO. He states that they are social constructions, which means that they are

> [...] created by people in order, presumably, to help them achieve some purpose, whatever that purpose may be. (Klabbers 2009, pp. 7–8)

Klabbers (2009, p. 8) continues by saying that IOs do not have a predefined character when they are founded. He defines four characteristics of IOs: they are based on international law, usually created between states, based on a Treaty, and finally, they have a will distinct from their member states (Klabbers 2009, pp. 9–10). Moreover, their founding

> [...] was not brought about by some legal act under some domestic legal system, but was done in the form of a treaty, which international law in general terms defines as a written agreement, governed by international law. And as the treaty will be governed by international law, so too will the organisation. (Klabbers 2009, p. 10)

The last criterion he mentions is that the IO "must possess at least one organ that is distinct from the will of its member states" (Klabbers 2009, p. 11). This, he continues, puts the IO into a specific tension. On the one hand, it is a creation of the member states; on the other hand, it possesses a distinctive will independent of them. Moreover, IOs are essentially entities defined by their own practices, which vary considerably according to the actors, the aims and the functions of the organisations.

The EU, following this pattern, upon its foundation was based on international law, created between states, based on a Treaty (Klabbers 2009, p. 10), and has a will distinct from its member states. The same goes for the UN. Both UN delegates and individual actors within the EU's organisational framework, such as Members of the European Parliament (MEPs), engage in an international (or supranational) rules-based system and its institutions with practices that are formalised by rules. The resulting practices are the ones that shape politics and decision-making procedures in all institutions that rely on mechanisms of assemblies or parliaments, that is, representation and deliberation of formally equal members. For that matter, the fact that the UN has member states that are not democratic does not make a difference, as *within* the UN, these states are formally equal members when it comes to membership as defined in the Charter and their votes in the GA. However, both the EU and the UN have their own political underpinnings and dynamics.

The Origins and Political Framework of the UN and the EU

Both the UN and the EU will only be discussed briefly here, as this has been done at some length in Chapters 6 and 7. The UN is based on the principle of sovereign equality of its member states. As an IO, the UN has been established by a charter (Klabbers 2009, p. 9). Political practices in the UN are guided by this founding document, the Charter of the UN (United Nations 2024, see Chapter 6).

The UN Charter also outlines the different duties and responsibilities of various organs and bodies of the UN. As discussed in Chapter 6, Article 7 of the Charter declares that the principal organs of the UN are: GA, Security Council, Economic and Social Council, Trusteeship Council, International Court of Justice and Secretariat. Importantly, the different character of the Security Council and the GA needs to be highlighted. While the GA is the body that consists of delegates of the UN member states and is based on the principle of "one state, one vote" and majority voting, the Security Council reflects the real existing power relations in the world and requires unanimity for decision-making (Koskenniemi 1995). In order to understand the political dynamics of decision-making in the UN, it is therefore highly important to see that the GA is structured and works as a parliament-like assembly, while the Security Council is marked by international negotiations and power politics. This means that debate and negotiation, as well as the need to find a majority, are much more important in the GA.

As its member states, the UN includes a full range of political regimes, ranging from representative democracies to full-fledged autocracies. This means that the institutional framework accommodates delegations from a wide range of polities with their own interests and challenges. It is also important to note that the UN membership is only for nation states that have been recognised as such by the international community. This is why, for example, Palestine does not have a formal delegation as it is not recognised as a nation state by the UN.

As discussed in Chapter 7, today's EU is the outcome of a process of Treaty changes and several enlargement rounds since 1951. It now has 27 member states and for several decades is no longer a simple IO. The EU has a mixed character, that is, shows international/intergovernmental and supranational elements. Due to the supranational elements and institutions, the interinstitutional interplay in the EU is different and highlights a variety of supranational political modalities that are not present in the UN.

The EU's institutions comprise the legislative bodies EP and Council of the EU, the European Commission as executive, the European Council that takes on the function of head of state, and the Court of Justice of the EU as judicative. While in policy fields such as the Common Foreign and Security Policy (CFSP), political decisions are taken in unanimity in the intergovernmental body of the Council, in the fully integrated policy fields of the common market, decisions are taken in co-decision between the EP and the Council. EU laws are implemented in the member states and via their executive. The EU is thus marked by its multilevel character and by the interplay between national, intergovernmental and supranational institutions.

Differences between EU and UN

While we claim that the generalities of political practices, processes and micropolitics in institutions, deliberative assemblies, and between them, are the same in both the EU and UN, we would like to highlight the differences between both organisations again, as they also indicate where they work differently.

The UN is solely an IO, which means it is based on the principle of sovereign equality of member states. The EU has both supranational and international characteristics. This means that there are differences in voting procedures, decision-making and negotiations. While the politics of the European Council are structured between nation states and their governments just as in the UN, the politics in the EP and the European Commission address the supranational level. This difference regards the legal framework for the politics that takes place and the rules of procedures. In the EP, for instance, it is not necessary to obtain a majority of member states as in the GA, but a majority of seats in the EP. In the EP, then, seats are distributed according to both party affiliation and national affiliation.

Moreover, decision-making procedures in the EU's supranational policy fields differ from those in the intergovernmental fields. In the EU's fully integrated policy fields, such as the Common Market, decision-making and policies are also supranationally organised. Member states have lost their full sovereignty. Decisions in the fully integrated supranational policy fields are taken in the so-called "ordinary legislative procedure", a procedure of co-decision between the Council of the EU and the EP. In the Council, the principle of qualified majority is at work, and in the EP, the simple majority of the MEPs. EU-led legislation in the key area of the common market is decided in co-decision by the Council and the EP, and then implemented at the national level. The main difference to the UN is that decisions have direct and concrete policy implications in the member states.

Despite these differences, however, many similarities remain. The majority principle that is applied in the EP is also at work in the GA. The unanimity principle that works in the Security Council also works in the European Council. This means that decision-making procedures are not generally different in the EU and UN. Moreover, as has been claimed throughout this chapter, the political practices and procedures in these bodies work along similar principles. The different positions, internal orders and interests of member states, as well as their relative political weight in the world order, matter in both organisations. First, bodies such as the Security Council and the Council are not based on the principle of one state – one vote, but on the political weight its members have in real life. In the European Council, this different weight is literally expressed in the voting procedure that grants more votes to states that have more citizens. The Treaties distinguish a simple majority (14 member states vote in favour), a qualified majority (55 per cent of member states, representing at least 65 per cent of the EU population, vote in favour) and the unanimous vote (all votes are in favour; see Article 16 Treaty on European Union (TEU), European Union 2016). Second, the political weight of a state influences its capacity to find allies for their position, and hence also the decision-making outcomes. Third, different interests and positions influence the way negotiations go about, and their outcomes.

THE CASE OF THE EP'S GAINS IN POWER: A MACROPOLITICAL AND MICROPOLITICAL PERSPECTIVE

To further illustrate how micropolitics work, it is useful to contrast it with what can be termed as macropolitics, that is, institutional developments via Treaty changes as large, formalised steps. The development of the EP is a case in point (on the following, for further detail see Wiesner 2019, pp. 97–102, 104–108).

The Macro-Perspective: EP Power Gains via Treaties

As discussed in Chapter 7, the organisation of the European Community of Coal and Steel (ECSC) in the early 1950s and then that of the European Economic Community (EEC) founded with the *Treaty of Rome* in 1958 had followed an inter-governmental model. In the EEC, the Commission already had strong executive powers that put limits on the inter-governmental powers of the state. The status of the Commissioners resembles that of ministers, and in the supranational policy fields of the *acquis communautaire*, the Commission soon developed independent powers. In sum, the Commission possesses many characteristics of a government since the early days of the ECSC.

The EP's history also began with the *Treaty on the European Community of Coal and Steel (ECSC)* that set up a first parliamentary institution, the Common Assembly of the ECSC which consisted of 78 delegates of the – then only six – member states' parliaments and did not have law-making powers. It did, however, already possess the right to censure the Commission and force it to resign, and also consultative functions. With the *Treaty of Rome*, the Common Assembly in 1958 went over into the European Parliamentary Assembly (EPA). In 1962, the EPA changed its name to European Parliament (EP). But for many years after this, the EP remained a representative and consultative body consisting of delegates from the member state parliaments (European Communities 2009, p. 13).

From the 1970s onwards, the powers of the EP continually increased (for further detail see European Communities 2009; Rittberger 2005). A decisive step was obtained with the EP obtaining budgetary power – a change which had been fought for by the EP for some time. The *Treaty of Brussels* in 1975 granted the Parliament the formal power to reject the budget by a two-thirds majority of its members and to co-decide on the budget with the Council (European Communities 2009, pp. 16, 61, 147–148).

The next decisive step was the introduction of a direct election procedure for the EP in 1979. Valéry Giscard d'Estaing, who was elected French President in 1974, supported a direct election of the EP and hence the Council in Paris in December 1974 decided that it should be introduced. After a lengthy process of approval in the member states, the first direct EP elections took place from 7 to 10 June 1979, where 410 MEPs were elected. One hundred and eighty-five million EEC citizens had taken part in the election, and the polling rate was almost 63 per cent (European Communities 2009, pp. 35–40).

The next decisive steps in the EP's development were again related to Treaty changes. The *Treaty of Maastricht* in 1993 was the crucial step that led to a development away from the intergovernmental structure and towards the supranational elements. It created today's EU and united the three communities ECSC, EEC and Euratom under one common roof. The Maastricht

Treaty also institutionalised cooperation in the policy areas of CFSP and Joint Policies of Justice and Home Affairs. Moreover, it introduced possibilities for co-decision between the EP and the Council of Ministers; in certain policy areas, the EP now acted as co-legislator. The EP's co-decision rights were subsequently enlarged to more policy fields by the *Treaties of Amsterdam* (signed 2 October 1997) and *Nice* (signed 26 February 2001; European Communities 2009, pp. 17–20, 118, 163).

The *Lisbon Treaty*, which entered into force on 1 December 2009, named the EP "the body representing the EU citizens" and made co-decision the ordinary legislative procedure with only a few exceptions. This, again, is a decisive move, as it de facto defines the EP as the first chamber of legislation and created a two-chamber system between the EP and Council (TEU, Article 14; for further detail see Tiilikainen and Wiesner 2016). With the *Lisbon Treaty*, the EP also obtained increased budgetary powers and the competence to vote on the approval of the European Commission President (whereas before it could only approve the whole collegium of a new Commission; European Communities 2009, p. 25; European Parliament 2025; Tiilikainen and Wiesner 2016).

These Treaty changes decisively developed the EU's institutional system and the powers of the EP: the EP over the years has thus become more of an independent political actor and a counterpart of the Council and Commission. It exercises a full-fledged parliament's role.

The Micropolitics of Extending the EP's Powers

While the EP has thus been extending its powers via Treaty changes as large, formalised steps, it has also been using micropolitics. In the following, we will briefly sketch an example of micropolitics in the EP. The example used is a summary of the findings of a study of micropolitics (for further detail see Wiesner 2018; Wiesner 2019; Wiesner 2023) that focused on the research question: Why has the EP gained new powers throughout the decades and how are these powers to be assessed? Two crucial cases that led to increasing the EP's powers in Commission investiture and scrutiny were studied, namely, the events preceding the votes of approval for the Prodi and Barroso Commissions in 1999 and 2004. Based on a material sample of quality press articles and legal documents, the course of events, the actors and their actions can be outlined. It turned out that in both cases, MEPs managed to enlarge their competences via their political actions.

The first case is the fall of the Santer Commission and the nomination of the Prodi Commission in 1999. All in all, three phases can be distinguished here:

Phase 1 (December 1998 – March 1999): The underlying political conflict dates back to a report that scandalised intransparent activities in the Commission in 1998. The EP then first refused to vote on the approval of the

Commission's actions and voted on no confidence later. Even if there was no majority for the no confidence vote, the Santer Commission resigned. So, in sum, the EP forced the Commission to publicly take on the political responsibility for the mismanagement, which finally led to its resignation.

In *Phase 2 (March 1999 – May 1999)*, the EP urged the Council to prepare a new Commission, which the Council did, starting by nominating Romano Prodi as Commission president. This meant the EP would have to vote upon approval of the new Commission. MEPs mandated a negotiation committee and agreed with designated Commission president Romano Prodi to have individual hearings of further Commissioners before the EP. MEPs thus had negotiated a series of compromises with Prodi that concretise the EP's parliamentary rights and created a new practice for the EP's parliamentarism.

In *Phase 3 (June 1999 – September 1999)*, related to the hearings, the EP successfully negotiated and established new rules as a condition for a vote of approval. Prodi promised he would seriously take into account claims for the resignation of a Commissioner issued by MEPs, and also the EP's ideas when drafting law initiatives.

Importantly, the outcome of micropolitics was institutionalised: these new rules were later formalised in an Interinstitutional Agreement (IIA) between the EP and the Commission that was published in Summer 2001, that is, a legal document. It fixes the core of an EP right to investiture, stating, among other points in its "General principles", that

> 4. The Commission shall take account of any requests [...] by the European Parliament [...] to submit legislative proposals, and undertakes to provide a prompt and sufficiently detailed reply to any such request [...].
> 9. Without prejudice to the principle of Commission collegiality, each Member of the Commission shall take political responsibility for action in the field of which he or she is in charge.
> 10. The Commission accepts that, where the European Parliament expresses lack of confidence in a Member of the Commission [...] the President of the Commission will consider seriously whether he should request that Member to resign. [...]
> 12. [...] In all fields where the European Parliament acts in a legislative capacity, or as a branch of the budgetary authority, it shall be informed, on a par with the Council, at every stage of the legislative and budgetary process. (European Union 2000, p. 3)

Those new rules had a huge practical impact. First, the EP had increased its influence in nominating a new Commission by the new informal right to reject individual candidates. Second, MEPs obtained a right to claim individual Commissioners to resign. Third, the EP obtained a right that comes close to a legislative initiative power, and fourth, especially in the crisis, the EP directly interacted with the Council, thus underlining its weight in the Commission investiture. Fifth, it showed that the hearings are both a means of pressure in the interinstitutional struggle with the designated Commission president and represent an intervention into the Commission selection procedure and hence into the Council's domain.

The EP used the new powers laid down in the 2001 IIA in the second case, before the Barroso Commission was approved in 2004. There was a power struggle between the designated Commission president, the Council and especially some of its members, and the MEPs. The conflict between the three institutions had four phases:

In *Phase 1 (Spring 2004)*, the Council nominated Barroso as designated Commission president. He was approved by the EP in June, negotiated his Commission with the Council members, and announced his proposal for a new Commission in August 2004.

In *Phase 2 (June 2004 – October 2004)*, designated Commission President Barroso presented his Commission. But before the candidates were even able to have their hearings in the EP, it became evident that doubts about some of them were so serious that a clear majority in favour of an approval of the Commission was not assured. The criticism focused on the designated Commissioner for Justice, Rocco Buttiglione. In interviews, he had openly criticised homosexuals and single mothers, which was met with indignation by several MEPs, in particular as he was designated Commissioner for Justice and anti-discrimination matters. Most political groups in the EP claimed changes in the proposed Commission, and it became evident there would not be a majority. Barroso refused changes as long as possible until the EP majority finally shifted in favour of a No vote.

In *Phase 3 (October – November 2004)*, Barroso drew back his proposal for a new Commission, and the Prodi Commission stayed in office longer than originally planned. The designated Commission president renegotiated candidates with the Council. Berlusconi offered a withdrawal of Buttiglione, but required that Italy not be the only country to accept an exchange of Commissioner. In consequence, the Council put pressure on the Italian and Latvian governments, and, ultimately, the Italian and the Latvian candidates were exchanged.

In *Phase 4 (November 2004)*, Barroso presented the new Commission to the EP and it received a high approval score in the voting. The vote of approval was again coupled with the vote on a motion that laid down the new negotiation results on interinstitutional relations and hence built the ground for a new IIA (European Communities 2009, p. 190; Moury 2007; Wiesner 2018) that was concluded in 2005:

2. Each Member of the Commission shall take political responsibility for action in the field of which he or she is in charge, without prejudice to the principle of Commission collegiality. [...]
3. If Parliament decides to express lack of confidence in a Member of the Commission, the President of the Commission, having given serious consideration to that decision, shall either request that Member to resign, or explain his or her decisions to Parliament. (European Parliament 2005, pp. 5–6)

This means that the outcome of micropolitics was again institutionalised via a new document. These quotes underline that the right to control the Commission, as well as individual Commissioners, had been strengthened in comparison to the 2001 IIA. They also signal an increased right to scrutiny over the Commission and its actions by the Parliament. The terms quoted above have been retained in the most recent IIA, concluded in 2010 (European Union 2010).

In conclusion, the above example illustrates how to understand micropolitics at work in international assemblies and institutions and between them. Using the possibilities given by the formalised rules in debates, negotiations and political actions, the MEPs managed to obtain new competencies that they also managed to formalise in documents in relation to votes. What has been sketched is a prototypical example of how new documents that entail a decisive policy change come about in a setting of international or supranational insti- with different bodies and different interests at stake. The following part of this book will present further examples.

REFERENCES

European Communities (2009). Building Parliament: 50 Years of European Parliament History 1958–2008. Office for Official Publications of the European Communities. Luxembourg. Available online at https://op.europa.eu/en/publication-detail/-/publication/67991291-12ef-45d5-a7a9-85bb5c4c3ff7 (accessed 7/4/2025).

European Parliament (2025). Treaties and the European Parliament. Available online at https://www.europarl.europa.eu/about-parliament/en/in-the-past/the-parliament-and-the-treaties (accessed 5/13/2025).

Haapala, Taru/Oleart, Alvaro (Eds.) (2022). Tracing the Politicisation of the EU. The Future of Europe Debates Before and After the 2019 Elections. Cham, Palgrave Macmillan.

Kauppi, Niilo/Palonen, Kari/Wiesner, Claudia (2016). The Politification and Politicisation of the EU. Redescriptions: Political Thought, Conceptual History and Feminist Theory 19 (1), 72–90. https://doi.org/10.7227/R.19.1.5

Klabbers, Jan (2009). An Introduction to International Institutional Law. Cambridge, Cambridge University Press.

Koskenniemi, Martti (1995). The Police in the Temple Order, Justice and the UN. A Dialectical View. European Journal of International Law (6), 325–348.

Moury, Catherine (2007). Explaining the European Parliament's Right to Appoint and Invest the Commission. West European Politics 30 (2), 367–391. https://doi.org/10.1080/01402380701239889

Palonen, Kari (2003). Four Times of Politics: Policy, Polity, Politicking, and Politicisation. Alternatives: Global, Local, Political 28 (2), 171–186. https://doi.org/10.1177/030437540302800202

Palonen, Kari (2014). Politics of Parliamentary Procedure: The Formation of the Westminster Procedure as a Parliamentary Ideal Type. Leverkusen, Barbara Budrich.

Palonen, Kari (2019). Parliamentary Thinking: Procedure, Rhetoric and Time. Cham, Springer International Publishing.

Rittberger, Berthold (2005). Building Europes Parliament. Democratic Representation Beyond the Nation-State. Zugl.: Oxford, Univ., Diss., 2004. Oxford, Oxford University Press.

tagesschau (2022). UN-Resolution gegen Russland: "Ein Historisches Ergebnis". Available online at https://www.tagesschau.de/ausland/amerika/un-vollversammlung-ukraine-105.html (accessed 9/22/2022).

Tiilikainen, Teija/Wiesner, Claudia (2016). Towards a Political Theory of EU Parliamentarism. In: Pasi Ihalainen/Cornelia Ilie/Kari Palonen (Eds.). Parliament and Parliamentarism. Berghahn Books, 292–310.

Wiesner, Claudia (2018). The Micro-Politics of Parliamentary Powers: European Parliament Strategies for Expanding Its Influence in the EU Institutional System. Journal of European Integration 40 (4), 375–391. https://doi.org/10.1080/07036337.2018.1462351

Wiesner, Claudia (2019). Inventing the EU as a Democratic Polity. Concepts, Actors and Controversies. Cham, Springer International Publishing; Imprint Palgrave Macmillan.

Wiesner, Claudia (2021a). Introduction: Rethinking Politicisation in Politics, Sociology and International Relations. In: Claudia Wiesner (Ed.). Rethinking Politicisation in Politics, Sociology and International Relations. Cham, Springer International Publishing, 1–15.

Wiesner, Claudia (2021b). Politicisation, Politics and Democracy. In: Claudia Wiesner (Ed.). Rethinking Politicisation in Politics, Sociology and International Relations. Cham, Springer International Publishing, 19–42.

Wiesner, Claudia (Ed.) (2021c). Rethinking Politicisation in Politics, Sociology and International Relations. Cham, Springer International Publishing.

Wiesner, Claudia (2023). Actors, Concepts, Controversies: The Conceptual Politics of European Integration. Political Research Exchange 5 (1). https://doi.org/10.1080/2474736X.2023.2258173

Wiesner, Claudia (2024). The War Against Ukraine, the Changing World Order and the Conflict Between Democracy and Autocracy. In: Claudia Wiesner/Michèle Knodt (Eds.). The War Against Ukraine and the EU. Facing New Realities. Cham, Springer Nature Switzerland; Palgrave Macmillan, 83–109.

Wiesner, Claudia/Haapala, Taru/Palonen, Kari (2017). Debates, Rhetoric and Political Action. Practices of Textual Interpretation and Analysis. London, Palgrave Macmillan UK; Imprint Palgrave Macmillan.

EU/UN Documents

European Parliament (2005). P6_TA(2005)0194 Framework Agreement on EP-Commission Relations and European Parliament Decision on the Revision of the Framework Agreement on Relations Between the European Parliament and the Commission (2005/2076(ACI)). Available online at http://www.europarl.europa.eu/sides/getDoc.do?pubRef=-//EP//NONSGML+TA+P6-TA-2005-0194+0+DOC+PDF+V0//EN (accessed 5/8/2012).

European Union (2000). European Parliament/Commission Framework Agreement C5-0349/2000. Available online at http://eur-lex.europa.eu/LexUriServ/LexUriServ.do?uri=OJ:C:2001:121:0122:0126:EN:PDF (accessed 5/8/2012).

European Union (2010). Framework Agreement on Relations Between the European Parliament and the European Commission. Available online at http://eur-lex.europa.eu/LexUriServ/LexUriServ.do?uri=OJ:L:2010:304:0047:0062:EN:PDF (accessed 6/23/2016).

European Union (2016). Consolidated versions of the Treaty on European Union and the Treaty on the Functioning of the European Union – Consolidated version of the Treaty on the Functioning of the European Union – Protocols – Annexes – Declarations annexed to the Final Act of the Intergovernmental Conference which adopted the Treaty of Lisbon, signed on 13 December 2007 – Tables of equivalences. Official Journal C 326, 26/10/2012 P. 0001 – 0390. Available online at https://eur-lex.europa.eu/eli/treaty/tfeu_2012/oj/eng (accessed 6/6/2025).

United Nations (2024). United Nations Charter (Full Text). Available online at https://www.un.org/en/about-us/un-charter/full-text (accessed 3/15/2024).

10. UN case study: the rule of law in the Security Council

Hannah Birkenkötter

INTRODUCTION

In many Model United Nations (MUN) conferences, the Security Council is seen as the "crown jewel" of simulations. Delegations tend to send their most experienced delegates or best speakers to the Security Council. Chairing or directing the Security Council is often reserved for experienced volunteer staff members. This mirrors, to some extent, public perception: often, the United Nations (UN) is identified with the work of the Security Council, despite the fact that the Council is only one of the UN's main organs. This is of course due to the special tasks assigned to the Council within the UN system, most notably its capacity to authorise the use of force as one of the very few exceptions to the prohibition of the use of force, codified in Article 2 (4) of the UN Charter and arguably one of its most important norms. Due to its prominent role, the Security Council is an important forum where states engage in high-level debates and where states' diverse visions of international order become apparent.

The case study in this chapter provides a glimpse into debates in the real-life Security Council. It examines different perceptions of a core principle of the international order, namely the rule of law. The rule of law is a perennially contested principle: while most people agree that it is an essential value in any legal system, it remains elusive (Tamanaha 2004, p. 3) and there is fundamental disagreement over its content (Waldron 2002). Such disagreement is also visible in the UN system. The rule of law, unlike other core principles of international law, such as the protection of human rights, is not mentioned in the text of the UN Charter.[1] It first became an agenda item in a UN principal organ, the General Assembly (GA), in 1993, as a follow-up to the World

[1] In fact, an attempt by the Australian delegation to amend Article 1 (2) UN Charter to insert the term "rule of law" failed (Birkenkötter 2024, p. 375).

Summit on Human Rights (General Assembly 1993), which conceptualised the rule of law as a condition for the full implementation of human rights (Birkenkötter 2024).

The rule of law is currently a recurring agenda item in the GA, where it is debated annually in the Sixth Committee ("The Rule of Law at the National and International Levels", latest resolution at the time of writing General Assembly 2024) and in the Human Rights Council ("Human Rights, Democracy and the Rule of Law", latest resolution at the time of writing Human Rights Council 2025). It has been the subject of several thematic debates in the Security Council between 2003 and 2023. The last thematic debate on the rule of law was held in 2023 during Japan's Council Presidency, under the title "The promotion and strengthening of the rule of law in the maintenance of international peace and security" (Security Council 2023).

The case study primarily focuses on the first thematic debate on the rule of law in the Security Council, which took place in 2003, when the topic was introduced to the Council's agenda. This debate is selected due to the novelty of the agenda item, which required states to adopt a clear stance on a new topic for the first time. The rest of the chapter is organised as follows: Section 2 briefly explains some key developments in the Security Council's recent history, serving as a background for the debate, and provides a short introduction to thematic debates as opposed to country-specific situations. Section 3 then examines the varying understandings of the rule of law among member states, as reflected in their statements during the 2003 thematic debate. It also includes an overview of how the agenda item evolved over the past two decades. Section 4 concludes with a brief outlook for MUN conferences.

THE SECURITY COUNCIL IN THE UN SYSTEM

The Security Council through the Ages: a Brief Overview of the Council's Recent History

Article 24 (1) of the UN Charter confers upon the Security Council the "primary responsibility for the maintenance of international peace and security." Its work is generally divided into a Cold War and a post-Cold War period (von Einsiedel and Malone 2018, p. 141). The post-Cold War period is characterised by fewer blockages among the five veto powers, an ensuing increase in the number of resolutions adopted by the Council, and many more country situations addressed by the Security Council than during the Cold War. It is also marked by the authorisation, beginning in the late 1980s, of so-called "multidimensional peacekeeping missions," which were tasked with organising and observing elections and assisting in rebuilding civilian administration, human rights institutions, and legal institutions, notably a domestic judiciary and legal profession (von Einsiedel and Malone 2018, pp. 142–143). Between 1987 and 1992, 13 new peacekeeping missions were mandated – the same number of missions that had previously been mandated over a period eight times as long, namely between 1945 and 1987 (General Assembly and Security Council 1992, p. 14). Until 1998, an additional 21 missions were authorised (Koops et al. 2015, p. 262).

The general political euphoria after the end of the Cold War soon dwindled when the UN Security Council failed to prevent the genocide in Rwanda against the Tutsis in 1994 and could not put an end to the Yugoslav war, which witnessed numerous war crimes and a genocide against the Bosnian Muslim population in 1995 (von Einsiedel and Malone 2018, pp. 144–145). These failures led to a yearlong debate on the duties of the Security Council and those of the international community *vis-à-vis* atrocity crimes and whether such crimes trigger a "responsibility to protect" that might constitute an exception to the prohibition of the use of force. This debate resulted in several important documents, chiefly a report by the International Commission on Intervention and State Sovereignty (ICISS 2001). The responsibility to protect as a norm was codified in the World Summit Outcome, but the World Summit Outcome also clarified that it did not constitute an exception to the prohibition of the use of force and that any such use needed to be authorised through the Security Council under Chapter VII of the Charter (General Assembly 2005, paras 138–140). The debate on the "responsibility to protect" and its specific duties remains contentious to this date (Thakur 2018).

Another consequence of the peacekeeping failures in the former Yugoslavia and Rwanda was a reflection process on how to improve peacekeeping operations. Kofi Annan, who became UN Secretary-General in 1997, launched this reflection process, which led to the establishment of a high-level panel chaired by UN veteran peace mediator Lakhdar Brahimi (Gowan 2018, p. 425). The panel issued the "Brahimi report" in 2000. This report was considered to contain the accumulated wisdom of the previous decade and would go on to mark peacekeeping for years to come (Chesterman 2004, p. 98; Koops et al. 2015, pp. 608–610). The report put the rule of law squarely on the agenda of the Security Council for the first time: it recommended "a doctrinal shift in the use of civilian police, other rule of law elements and human rights experts [...] to reflect an increased focus on strengthening rule of law institutions" (Brahimi 2000, p. 8). The report provides the backdrop for Annan's efforts to centre Security Council debates on the concept of the rule of law as a key concept for UN peacekeeping and peacebuilding efforts in the new millennium. This was challenging insofar as the term "rule of law" had not been standard vocabulary in the UN Security Council in the 1990s: as of 1996, the rule of law was not even an indexed keyword in the Security Council's archival records (United Nations Dag Hammarskjöld Library 1996).

Thematic Debates in the Security Council

The Security Council's normal working method is to address individual country situations, not general thematic debates. As its primary duty is the maintenance of international peace and security, specifically in situations that pose a threat to international peace or security, the vast majority of meetings in the Council are dedicated to individual country situations.

There are, however, some exceptions. First, the Security Council has additional duties, such as recommending the admission of new members to the organisation (UN Charter, Article 4 (2)) or, jointly with the GA, filling vacancies in the International Court of Justice (ICJ) (ICJ Statute, Articles 4 et seq.). Second, some thematic issues were added to the agenda starting in the mid-1980s, with "terrorism" being the first cross-cutting issue not limited to a specific country situation (Sievers and Daws 2014, p. 45). Thematic debates became more frequent after the end of the Cold War. The increase in peacekeeping missions led to the introduction of a new agenda item in the Council in 1990, titled "United Nations peacekeeping operations," and throughout the 1990s, several aspects of peacekeeping, such as demining or civilian police in peacekeeping missions, became their own agenda items (Sievers and Daws 2014, p. 45).

Starting in the late 1990s, substantive thematic issues began to emerge on the Council's agenda. Three thematic agenda items are of particular importance: the issue of "Children and armed conflict", first put on the agenda in 1998, "Protection of Civilians", on the agenda since 1999, and "Women and peace and security", first introduced in the Security Council in 2000 (Sievers and Daws 2014, pp. 46–48). These agenda items have led the Council to systematically integrate, for example, protection mandates in peacekeeping missions, or to call upon states to include women in peace processes, thus radically changing the face of the international peace architecture. Thematic debates have also led to a more open Security Council: most thematic debates are conducted as "open debates," which means that any interested UN member state may participate with speaking rights in the Council (Sievers and Daws 2014, p. 49), although decision-making power remains limited to Council members.

Thematic debates have an impact on the Security Council's work. The three aforementioned agenda items, "Children and armed conflict", "Protection of Civilians" and "Women and peace and security" have each resulted in several thematic resolutions, that is, resolutions that are not specifically tied to a country situation, but address the topic from a generalist point of view. This has led to some states raising concerns that the Security Council is increasingly encroaching on the mandate of the GA (Sievers and Daws 2014, p. 48; Chapter 9). In addition, the thematic debates on international terrorism and non-proliferation of weapons of mass destruction resulted in resolutions that were adopted under Chapter VII of the UN Charter (Security Council 2001; Security Council 2004b), resulting in a debate on whether the Security Council has the faculty to act as a "quasi-legislator" by issuing binding resolutions on topical issues (Talmon 2005).

However, not all thematic debates result in resolutions. Sometimes, thematic debates are either so contentious or not considered to be politically salient enough for a resolution to be adopted. In this case, the Council tends to adopt Presidential Statements which, whilst formally of the same legal value as a resolution, are often considered to be less authoritative or carrying less weight (Sievers and Daws 2014, pp. 375–376). This does not, however, mean that such thematic debates remain without impact. Thematic debates' results and topics are often taken up in subsequent country-specific resolutions. For example, in the field of "Women and peace and security", there has been an overall increase in gender-related considerations since the topic was introduced (UN Women 2025). Similarly, in the field of the rule of law – the subject of our case study – the number of resolutions using the term "rule of law" increased dramatically after the 2003 thematic debate. Between 1945 and 2002, a total of 24 resolutions contained the term "rule of law." In 2013, 25 resolutions adopted in that year alone had a reference to the term "rule of law." This illustrates the impact thematic debates can have on the Council's practice.

CASE STUDY: THE RULE OF LAW IN THE SECURITY COUNCIL – POSITIONS IN THE 2003 THEMATIC DEBATE

On 24 September 2003, the Security Council held its first-ever thematic debate on the rule of law, titled "Justice and the Rule of Law: the United Nations role" (Security Council 2003a). This meeting was called by that month's Council Presidency, the United Kingdom (UK), and chaired by the then-Foreign Minister of the UK, Jack Straw. At the end of the meeting, the Council adopted a short Presidential Statement (Security Council 2003b). No resolution was adopted on the topic, despite the Council having, by that time, already established a practice of adopting thematic resolutions on several issues, as mentioned in the previous section. This underscores that the rule of law was a rather contentious issue amongst Council members, and not one on which agreement in the form of a resolution was possible.

The thematic debate amongst Council members was followed by an Open Debate six days later, in which 25 additional states that were not members of the Council participated (Security Council 2003c). Here, we can observe a higher representation of states from some regional groups over others: of the 25 additional states, 11 were from the Western European and Others Group, compared to five states from the group of Asia-Pacific States, four states from the Eastern European States and Latin American and Caribbean States each, and only two states from the African group, which has the most members of all regional groups.[2] This is a clear indicator that the topic did not meet all member states' interests alike.

Throughout both debates, two very different understandings of the term "rule of law" were brought forward. On the one hand, several delegates advocated for the rule of law as a normative demand for states' internal organisation. In this understanding, the rule of law signifies that a state needs to put into place a number of institutions and organisations, such as courts, a functioning administration, and so on, in order to establish the rule of law within states. Within this understanding, states disagreed about the necessary institutions for the rule of law to exist, and also about the importance of economic development for the rule of law. On the other hand, several states advocated for the rule of law to not only or primarily apply to the internal order of states, but rather as a principle that governs international relations and applies to states' behaviour *vis-à-vis* each other. The following sections will focus on statements made during the first thematic debate that was limited to the 15 Security Council members (Security Council 2003a). These statements are formal speeches prepared in advance and delivered by the representatives of the 15 members of the Council. During formal public meetings, it is customary that all 15 members deliver a statement on their country's position. This applies to both thematic and country-specific debates. Such meetings are recorded in verbatim records and published after each meeting as official UN documents (Sievers and Daws 2014, pp. 25–28). The thematic debate on the rule of law was held at ministerial level and most members were represented by their Foreign Minister or their Permanent Representative, that is, the highest-ranking diplomat of a state at the UN headquarters. This underlines the importance that states accorded the topic.

Many of the speeches share certain points: virtually all members congratulated the UK on convening the meeting and underscored the importance of the

---

2 The regional group representation in the 2003 Debate was as follows (Security Council 2003c, p. 2):

- African States: Democratic Republic of the Congo, Sierra Leone
- Asia-Pacific States: Bahrain, Japan, Jordan, the Philippines, the Republic of Korea
- Eastern European States: Azerbaijan, Romania, Serbia, Montenegro
- Latin American and Caribbean States: Argentina, Brazil, Trinidad and Tobago, Uruguay
- Western European and Other States: Australia, Austria, Canada, Denmark, Finland, Italy, Liechtenstein, New Zealand, San Marino, Sweden, Switzerland

See the regional group distribution United Nations (2025a).

rule of law. However, a close reading of the verbatim record reveals different understandings of the rule of law. In the following, I provide an overview of the speeches delivered during the thematic debate that can broadly be classified into two understandings: one that views the rule of law primarily as a normative demand for states' internal organisation, and one that considers the rule of law to be an important principle for governing international relations. Amongst those states that addressed the rule of law within states, African representatives in particular emphasised the importance of poverty eradication as part of efforts to build the rule of law.

The Rule of Law as a Normative Demand for States' Internal Organisation

UK representative Jack Straw opened the meeting by stating that:

> Justice and the rule of law are vital for the proper functioning of States. They are essential elements in creating and sustaining stable, peaceful and democratic States. (Security Council 2003a, p. 2)

This makes clear that the Council Presidency, which had organised the meeting, intended for states to focus on how the rule of law could be fostered in post-conflict societies, and therefore within states. The representatives of France, Bulgaria, and the United States of America (USA) made similar statements. The French representative started his speech by stating that "Justice and the rule of law are emerging as the cornerstones of building peace and democracy [...]", echoing almost word for word the UK's opening statement, and identified constitutional assistance and the building of institutions such as national police forces and a judicial system as crucial elements of the rule of law (Security Council 2003a, p. 6). Similarly, the USA representative stated that "[...] the process of securing the rule of law is multifaceted [...]" and mentioned police forces, a functioning judiciary staffed by qualified judges, prosecutors and lawyers, reviewing legal codes, and reforming the prison system as elements of a functioning rule of law in post-conflict situations as key (Security Council 2003a, p. 20). Setting up law enforcement and effective judicial institutions were also emphasised as key by the Bulgarian representative (Security Council 2003a, p. 12).

Not all states, however, considered rebuilding police forces, the judiciary, and other parts of civilian administration as the key priority in post-conflict states. This is particularly true for non-European or Western states. The two Latin American states focused on transitional justice: Mexico highlighted "[...] the national reconciliation of States emerging from conflicts [...]" as a key priority (Security Council 2003a, p. 9). Similarly, the Chilean representative underscored the role of truth and reconciliation commissions (Security Council 2003a, p. 22). Several state representatives emphasised that the rule of law would be elusive if people lived in poverty. The Chinese representative stated that "[…] without development, justice and the rule of law are merely a mirage […]" (Security Council 2003a, p. 8). This sentiment was shared by the African representatives in the Council. The Angolan representative requested that:

> […] in order to…better promote peace, justice and the rule of law, the international community should address important challenges such as extreme poverty, […][and] support country-led economic and social initiatives focusing on poverty reduction. (Security Council 2003a, p. 18)

The Guinean representative asked:

> Can we truly imagine a world of justice, however, without of necessity taking into account the rights and interests of the economically weak countries in the globalisation process manifest in today's world economy? Do not poverty, the great pandemics and inequity in the international trading system represent an injustice with respect to developing countries? (Security Council 2003a, p. 13)

With this statement, the Guinean delegate also suggested that the rule of law at the national level could not be considered independently of rule of law considerations at the international level and in inter-state relations. This view was shared by several other delegations, as shown in the following section.

The Rule of Law as a Normative Demand for the International Community

While the UK representative had made clear in his opening statement that his delegation intended to focus the debate on the rule of law within states and in post-conflict situations, several delegations seized the opportunity of the formal debate to emphasise the importance of the rule of law governing international relations. There is a long-standing debate that dates back to the early days of the Charter and is visible in the Charter text itself: on the one hand, the Charter contains references to human rights and economic development of states; on the other hand, Article 2 (7) of the Charter prohibits the UN from intervening in matters essentially within the domestic jurisdiction of states. This creates a tension, and there have been several states that have long insisted on an understanding of international law that is limited to regulating relations between sovereign states (Ginsburg 2020, p. 226). Two such states are the Russian Federation and the People's Republic of China. The Chinese representative, in addition to focusing on the economic dimensions of the rule of law, specifically stated that:

> Governing a country requires the rule of law, as does managing international relations [...]. (Security Council 2003a, p. 8)

The Russian delegation posited that:

> [...] issues of justice and the rule of law cannot be considered in isolation from the more general problem of ensuring the rule of law in international relations [...]. (Security Council 2003a, p. 5)

However, it was not only these two permanent members, who traditionally advocate for an understanding of international law based on non-interference and non-intervention, that focused on the importance of the rule of law in international relations. Several delegations from amongst the elected members seized the opportunity of the open debate to voice their concerns about the unequal enforcement of Security Council decisions. The Pakistani representative reminded Council members that:

> [...] selective implementation [of Security Council decisions] creates an unjust environment, deepening conflicts...and undermines the credibility of the United Nations [...]. (Security Council 2003a, p. 4)

Several representatives were particularly concerned about the unequal application of the prohibition of the use of force, a core norm of the UN Charter, codified in its Article 2 (4). The Mexican delegate emphasised that:

> [...] as a result of the events of recent years, the Council has debated the scope of the use of force [...] no provisions exist in the Charter that authorise delegating the powers conferred on the Security Council under Chapter VII to a State or to a group of States. (Security Council 2003a, p. 9)

The Guinean representative added that the UN's efforts to strengthen multilateralism

> [...] have at times been compromised by the clear determination of certain parties to exploit international law by violating its fundamental principles [...]. (Security Council 2003a, p. 13)

These statements must be read against the historical context of the debate: only a few months earlier, the USA had unilaterally invaded Iraq as part of its so-called "Operation Iraqi Freedom," without a mandate from the Security Council. The Mexican delegation's statement is clearly, although not openly, directed at this violation of a key principle of the UN Charter (Rodiles 2013).

This second understanding of the rule of law as a principle that ought to govern international relations is one that neither the Council presidency nor the Secretariat had primarily in mind, as becomes obvious from then-Secretary-General Kofi Annan's introductory statement to the Council. While he acknowledged that the rule of law "[...] applies both internationally and in rebuilding shattered societies [...]", he clarified that "[...] it is the latter that I wish to speak about today [...]" (Security Council 2003a, p. 2). Nonetheless, several states chose to focus on the international dimension of the rule of law. This highlights that states may use thematic debates to exchange views and clarify their positions on diverging understandings of contentious concepts, such as the rule of law, and how it relates to the Security Council's work. The absence of a clear consensus on what the rule of law means and which relationships it should govern is also evident in the Presidential Statement that the Council adopted. In this Statement, the Council notes that member states "[...] expressed their respective views and understandings on, and reaffirmed the vital importance of these issues [...]", but without further specifying beyond some examples what the topic should cover (Security Council 2003b).

The Rule of Law: a View from the Secretariat

This case study closes with a brief view on the Secretariat's role in framing debates in the Security Council. While the Security Council is often perceived as particularly member-state driven, the debate on the rule of law is a good example of how the Secretariat has some measure of influence in framing topics – but also, how states use the forum of the formal debate to push back against conceptualisations proposed by the Secretariat. This is not unlike the division of labour practiced at many MUNs where "Secretariat" (volunteer staff) members provide an initial framing of an agenda item through a "background guide" that provides important background information on a given topic, but also to a certain extent *sets* the agenda and frames how a topic will be debated at the conference.

In the 2003 thematic debate, Kofi Annan explicitly offered to write a report to the Council on the rule of law in post-conflict situations. The Council took this up in the Presidential Statement and "[...] welcomed in particular the offer by the Secretary-General to provide a report which could guide and inform further consideration [...]" (Security Council 2003b). Annan presented this report, titled "The rule of law and transitional justice in conflict and post-conflict societies" (Security Council 2004a) one year later, at a second thematic debate on "Justice and the Rule of Law", again convened under the UK's Council Presidency (Security Council 2004c). In this report, Annan presented various "lessons learned" from a decade of peacekeeping in post-conflict states and proposed a "common understanding" of the rule of law as a

> [...] principle of governance in which all persons, institutions and entities...including the State itself, are accountable to laws that are publicly promulgated, equally enforced and independently adjudicated, and which are consistent with international human rights norms and standards [...]. (Security Council 2004a, p. 4)

This "common language" is remarkable for two reasons: first, it contains a thick definition of the rule of law that defines human rights protection as a definitional element of the rule of law.[3] This is by no means an uncontested definition of the rule of law, neither in theory (Craig 1996) nor in practice, as evidenced by the emphasis on, for example, development and poverty eradication during the 2003 thematic debate. Nonetheless, the definition of the rule of law thus proposed by Kofi Annan in 2004 has proven to be sticky: it is still used on the UN's rule of law website to date, over two decades after the original report was issued (United Nations 2025b).

Follow-up in the Security Council and Other Parts of the UN System

Annan's 2004 report did not address the tension between the rule of law at the national and international levels. This tension was never directly addressed in the Security Council, although various states reiterated points that had already been mentioned in the 2003 debate during the 2004 Open Debate, when the report was presented to the Council. Several African states highlighted the issue of poverty as a root cause of conflict, thereby undermining the rule of law, and explicitly called for better international rules and international law as a means to tackle international economic inequity. The representative of Benin, for example, underlined

> [...] the importance of promoting economic and social rights as an integral part of the rule of law [...]. (Security Council 2004c, pp. 18–19)

The Ugandan delegate asserted that:

> [...] the causes of conflict should be addressed, poverty in particular [...]

---

[3] Rule of law theory distinguishes between formal, or thin, conceptions of the rule of law that look at properties of the law, but not its substantive content, and substantive, or thick, conceptions of the rule of law that include in their understanding of the rule of law considerations of morality and justice (Craig 1996; Tamanaha 2004; Chapters 7 and 8). Tamanaha (2004, p. 91) describes these different rule of law conceptualisations as running on a spectrum from thin to thick. Rule of law understandings that comprise human rights standards as an inherent component of the rule of law are considered to be a thick conception.

and that:

> [...] the rule of law mean[s] that all nations, big and small, developed and developing, should benefit equally from the benefits of globalisation. For developing countries, this implies, for instance, access to international markets [...] trades, not loans, should be at the centre of the international development agenda. (Security Council 2004c, Resumption 1, p. 10)

The international dimension of the rule of law was also mentioned by several delegates, even if it was perhaps less prominent in the 2004 Debate than in the 2003 Debate. The delegate from Pakistan stated that:

> [...] the United Nations must build its capacity to uphold the rule of law, both at the national and – even more importantly – the international level [...]. (Security Council 2004c, p. 10)

The Peruvian representative stated that:

> [...] the rule of law at the national level translates into a State based on the rule of law. At the international level, it is the multilateralism we find in the Charter of the United Nations. It promotes stability and predictability in the international system. (Security Council 2004c, Resumption 1, p. 28)

The Nigerian representative emphasised that:

> [...] the concept of justice, the rule of law and equity [...] needs to be replicated at the global level. In this regard, it will be necessary for the United Nations and the international community to foster an international system that truly and genuinely upholds the principle of the equality of States [...] there is a need to ensure rule-based, open and transparent participation by all sovereign States. (Security Council 2004c, Resumption 1, p.37)

The delegate of Belarus suggested that:

> major emphasis should be placed on the issues of the rule of law in international relations and the role of the Security Council in securing this rule. (Security Council 2004c, Resumption 1, p. 15)

The Permanent Observer of Palestine also pointed to the unequal application of international legal standards with regard to his own country, stating that:

> [...] in the case of Palestine, the law has been elusive. At best it has been side-lined, and at worst it has been transgressed in the most egregious manner [...]. (Security Council 2004c, Resumption 1, p. 16)

Even though there was a clear interest in the rule of law in international affairs, it was not present in Annan's 2004 report. The Security Council's role in upholding the international rule of law and the extent to which it is bound by international legal rules was in turn taken up by an Austria-led initiative in subsequent years, though not as a topic in any thematic debate in the Council (Bühler 2008; Chesterman 2008).

The rule of law was taken up in the 2005 World Summit Outcome, an important document that, as mentioned, also codified the responsibility to protect. In the World Summit Outcome, the GA recognised "[...] the need for universal adherence to and implementation of the rule of law at both the national and international levels [...]" (General Assembly 2005, at para. 134). In the wake of the World Summit, Liechtenstein and Mexico introduced a new agenda item, "The rule of law at the national and international levels" in 2006 (General Assembly 2006). The two states suggested that the item be included in the GA's Sixth Committee, that is, the Legal Committee, instead of the Assembly's Third Committee (on Human Rights), and they emphasised in their memorandum that while "[...] the international and national dimensions of the rule of law are strongly interlinked [...]" the UN "[...] still lacks the appropriate tools to promote it in a coherent manner, especially with regard to its international dimension [...]" (General Assembly 2006, p. 2). However, an attempt to agree on a definition of the rule of law beyond post-conflict contexts failed definitively in 2012, when the GA's Declaration of the high-level meeting of the GA on the rule of law at the national and international levels renewed a "[...] commitment to the rule of law" and to an "international order based on the rule of law", and also recognised that "the rule of law applies to all States equally [...]", but failed to define what the rule of law meant (General Assembly 2012).

The Security Council would hold further thematic debates on the rule of law under a slightly relabelled agenda item, "The promotion and strengthening of the rule of law in the maintenance of international peace and security", in 2006, 2010, 2012, 2014, 2019, 2020, and 2023. The rule of law is today a part of the standard toolbox of peacekeeping and peacebuilding, with several entities in the UN system serving this cause, most importantly the Office of Rule of Law and Security Institutions (OROLSI) in the Department of Peace Operations, the UN Rule of Law Unit in the Secretary-General's Executive Office, and the Rule of Law Resource and Coordination Group, an inter-agency mechanism to coordinate rule of law assistance across different agencies, programmes, and funds of the UN system.

CONCLUSION

The previous case study illustrates that formal thematic debates in the Security Council are a place where states express comparatively clear positions on thematic issues. While the language in the Council is always diplomatic in tone, significant disagreements about core concepts, such as the rule of law, exist among member states and can be inferred from formal statements.

The case study highlights that the rule of law has traditionally been understood in two ways: on the one hand, as a principle that applies to the organisation of legal systems within states, and on the other hand, as a principle that governs international relations. In the Security Council, the Secretariat aimed to focus primarily on the first understanding. However, states did not limit themselves to this interpretation and raised issues regarding the international rule of law throughout their debates. Formal meetings in the Security Council, and particularly thematic debates, therefore provide an important arena for states to clarify their positions, make claims, and insert their own preferences into the agenda.

For MUN planning, thematic debates in the Security Council allow for innovative and creative thinking. In the real-world Security Council, thematic debates have led to innovative thinking about the maintenance of international peace and security as it relates to other issues, such as climate change. Here, a first thematic debate on "Energy, Security and Climate" took place in 2007 (Security Council 2007a; Security Council 2007b). Some existing thematic debates, such as women and peace and security, children in armed conflict, or climate change and international peace and security, have been a regular staple on the agendas of Model Security Councils. But as students plan future conferences, they might also think of topics that have a security nexus, yet are not currently on the Council's agenda.

REFERENCES

Birkenkötter, Hannah (2024). The United Nations and the Rule of Law. In: Michael Sevel (Ed.). Routledge Handbook of the Rule of Law. London, Routledge, 372–392.

Bühler, Konrad G. (2008). The Austrian Rule of Law Initiative 2004–2008–The Panel Series, the Advisory Group and the Final Report on the UN Security Council and the Rule of Law. Max Planck Yearbook of United Nations Law 12 (1), 409–446.

Chesterman, Simon (2004). You, the People: The United Nations, Transitional Administration, and State-Building. Oxford, United Kingdom, Oxford University Press.

Craig, Paul P. (1996). Formal and Substantive Conceptions of the Rule of Law: An Analytical Framework. Public Law, 467–487.

Ginsburg, Tom (2020). Authoritarian International Law? American Journal of International Law 114 (2), 221–260. https://doi.org/10.1017/ajil.2020.3

Gowan, Richard (2018). Peace Operations. In: Thomas G. Weiss/Sam Daws (Eds.). The Oxford Handbook on the United Nations. Oxford, Oxford University Press, 419–445.
International Commission on Intervention and State Sovereignty (ICISS) (2001). The Responsibility to Protect. Report of the International Commission on Intervention and State Sovereignty. Ottawa, Canada, International Development Research Centre.
Koops, Joachim A./MacQueen, Norrie/Tardy, Thierry/Williams, Paul D. (2015). Oxford Handbook of United Nations Peacekeeping Operations. Oxford, United Kingdom, Oxford University Press.
Rodiles, Alejandro (2013). Non-Permanent Members of the UN Security Council and the Promotion of the International Rule of Law. Goettingen Journal of International Law 5, 333–373.
Sievers, Loraine/Daws, Sam (2014). The Procedure of the UN Security Council. 4th ed. Oxford, Oxford University Press.
Talmon, Stefan (2005). The Security Council as World Legislature. American Journal of International Law 99 (1), 175–193. https://doi.org/10.2307/3246097
Tamanaha, Brian Z. (2004). On the Rule of Law. History, Politics, Theory. New York, Cambridge University Press.
Thakur, Ramesh (2018). Humanitarian Intervention. In: Thomas G. Weiss/Sam Daws (Eds.). The Oxford Handbook on the United Nations. Oxford, Oxford University Press, 387–403.
UN Women (2025). Facts and figures: Women, peace, and security. Available online at https://www.unwomen.org/en/articles/facts-and-figures/facts-and-figures-women-peace-and-security (accessed 5/19/2025).
United Nations (2025a). Regional groups of Member States. Available online at https://www.un.org/dgacm/en/content/regional-groups (accessed 5/19/2025).
United Nations (2025b). United Nations and the Rule of Law – What is the Rule of Law. Available online at https://www.un.org/ruleoflaw/what-is-the-rule-of-law/ (accessed 5/19/2025).
von Einsiedel, Sebastian/Malone, David M. (2018). Security Council. In: Thomas G. Weiss/Sam Daws (Eds.). The Oxford Handbook on the United Nations. Oxford, Oxford University Press, 140–164.
Waldron, Jeremy (2002). Is the Rule of Law an Essentially Contested Concept (in Florida)? Law and Philosophy 21 (2), 137–164.

UN Documents

Brahimi, Lakhdar (2000). Report of the Panel on United Nations Peace Operations. UN Doc. A/55/305 – S/2000/809. Available online at https://docs.un.org/en/A/55/305 (accessed 5/19/2025).
Chesterman, Simon (2008). The UN Security Council and the Rule of Law: The Role of the Security Council in Strengthening a Rules-Based International System. UN Doc. A/63/69 – S/2008/270, Annex. Available online at https://www.researchgate.net/publication/30505404_The_UN_Security_Council_and_the_Rule_of_Law (accessed 5/20/2025).
General Assembly (1993). Report of the World Conference on Human Rights. UN Doc. A/CONF.157/24. Available online at https://docs.un.org/en/A/CONF.157/24 (accessed 5/19/2025).

General Assembly (2005). World Summit Outcome. Resolution adopted by the General Assembly on 16 September 2005. UN Doc. A/Res/60/1. Available online at https://docs.un.org/en/A/Res/60/1 (accessed 5/19/2025).
General Assembly (2006). The rule of law at the national and international levels. Request for the inclusion of an item in the provisional agenda of the sixty-first session. UN Doc. A/61/142. Available online at https://docs.un.org/en/A/61/142 (accessed 5/19/2025).
General Assembly (2012). Declaration of the high-level meeting of the General Assembly on the rule of law at the national and international levels. Resolution adopted by the General Assembly on 24 September 2012. UN Doc. A/RES/67/1. Available online at https://docs.un.org/en/A/RES/67/1 (accessed 5/19/2025).
General Assembly (2024). The rule of law at the national and international levels. Resolution adopted by the General Assembly on 4 December 2024. UN Doc. A/RES/79/126. Available online at https://docs.un.org/en/A/RES/79/126 (accessed 5/19/2025).
General Assembly/Security Council (1992). An Agenda for Peace. Preventive diplomacy, peacemaking and peace-keeping. Report of the Secretary-General pursuant to the statement adopted by the Summit Meeting of the Security Council on 31 January 1992. UN Doc. A/47/277 – S/24111. Available online at https://docs.un.org/en/A/47/277 (accessed 5/19/2025).
Human Rights Council (2025). Human rights, democracy and the rule of law. Resolution adopted by the Human Rights Council on 2 April 2025. UN Doc. A/HRC/RES/58/8. Available online at https://docs.un.org/en/A/HRC/RES/58/8 (accessed 5/19/2025).
Security Council (2001). Resolution 1373 [on threats to international peace and security caused by terrorist acts]. UN Doc. S/RES/1373. Available online at https://digitallibrary.un.org/record/449020?ln=en&v=pdf (accessed 5/19/2025).
Security Council (2003a). 4833rd meeting, Wednesday, 24 September 2003. UN Doc. S/PV.4833. Available online at https://digitallibrary.un.org/record/502709?ln=en&v=pdf (accessed 5/19/2025).
Security Council (2003b). Statement by the President of the Security Council. UN Doc. S/PRST/2003/15. Available online at https://docs.un.org/en/S/PRST/2003/15 (accessed 5/19/2025).
Security Council (2003c). 4835th meeting, Tuesday, 30 September 2003. UN Doc. S/PV.4835. Available online at https://digitallibrary.un.org/record/503913?ln=en&v=pdf (accessed 5/19/2025).
Security Council (2004a). The rule of law and transitional justice in conflict and post-conflict societies. Report of the Secretary-General. UN Doc. S/2004/616. Available online at https://docs.un.org/en/S/2004/616 (accessed 5/19/2025).
Security Council (2004b). Resolution 1540 [on non-proliferation of nuclear, chemical and biological weapons]. UN Doc. S/Res/1540. Available online at https://digitallibrary.un.org/record/520326?ln=en&v=pdf (accessed 5/19/2025).
Security Council (2004c). 5052nd meeting, Wednesday, 6 October 2004. UN Doc. S/PV.5052. Available online at https://docs.un.org/en/S/PV.5052 (accessed 5/20/2025).
Security Council (2007a). Letter dated 5 April 2007 from the Permanent Representative of the United Kingdom of Great Britain and Northern Ireland to the United Nations addressed to the President of the Security Council. Annex: Energy, Security and Climate. Security Council open debate: United Kingdom concept paper. UN Doc. S/2007/186. Available online at https://docs.un.org/en/S/2007/186 (accessed 5/19/2025).

Security Council (2007b). 5663rd meeting, Tuesday, 17 April 2007. UN Doc. S/PV.5663. Available online at https://docs.un.org/en/S/PV.5663 (accessed 5/19/2025).
Security Council (2023). 9241st meeting, Thursday, 12 January 2023. UN Doc. S/PV.9241 and Resumption 1. Available online at https://digitallibrary.un.org/record/4000418?ln=en&v=pdf (accessed 5/19/2025).
United Nations Dag Hammarskjöld Library (1996). Index to Resolutions of the Security Council 1946–1996, UN Doc. ST/LIB/SER.H/5/Rev.1.

11. EU case study: the politics of shaping EU citizenship

Claudia Wiesner

The institutional and procedural regulations that shape politics in the European Union (EU) system have been discussed at some length in Chapters 7 and 9. This chapter analyses some of the political processes and controversies that take place in the EU's multilevel system.[1] The following presents an example of how EU politics are done via documents, that is, how different interest and political goals are expressed in documents, how positions are manifested and opposed to one another, how the resulting controversies are carried out, and how the results of the political processes are laid down in documents. More specifically, the chapter focuses on a special type of micropolitics (see Chapter 9), conceptual politics in the sense of the political moves that shape key concepts, and in this case, EU Citizenship. I will study the political controversies related to the creation, interpretation and implementation of EU Citizenship rights, analysing the respective processes as *conceptual politics* in the sense of

> [...] the political and rhetorical moves, strategies, debates and their actors, that coin, shape or reflect political concepts in institutional and social reality and its perception, as well as over time. (Wiesner 2023, p. 2)

The conceptual politics of EU Citizenship are reflected in the documents that fix the processes and the outcomes of the related controversies – in the case of EU Citizenship, these documents were Treaties, laws, judgements of the Court of Justice of the European Union (CJEU), reports, and communications. The actors in these controversies are on the one hand the EU's institutions and on the other hand the individuals within these institutions – as discussed in Chapter 9, the EU's institutions are not unitary actors, but consist of individuals that may have different positions in a matter. The examples studied present

[1] For earlier versions of parts of the following see Wiesner 2014, 2018, 2019a, 2019b, 2022, 2025; Wiesner et al. 2017.

the legal and political processes that shaped EU Citizenship laws and also EU Citizenship practice at key moments.

Importantly, as discussed in Chapter 7, the EU Treaties that build the base for all EU Citizenship rights have been evolving over time while partly keeping their names. The Treaty of Rome discussed below is also known as the European Economic Community (EEC) Treaty, and the Treaty of Maastricht that is discussed below as well is the first Treaty that introduced the name "European Union" and is split into a part that is called "Treaty on European Union" (TEU) and another one that is called "Treaty on the Functioning of the European Union" (TFEU). However, and importantly, the content of both these Treaties has been changing with the subsequent Treaty reforms of Nice, Amsterdam, and Lisbon. This means that the text of the Maastricht TEU and TFEU (discussed below) is not identical to the text of today's TEU discussed in Chapter 7, because additions and changes have been made in between. The following focuses on the development these additions and changes brought with regard to citizenship.

Before entering into the case, it is important to discuss the context some more, that is, the contemporary practices of citizenship in the EU's member states, and the ways of law-making and policy-making in the EU.

CITIZENSHIP AND REPRESENTATIVE DEMOCRACY[2]

Citizenship is a key concept in representative democracies: citizenship and the related nationality laws create the formal link between a polity and its demos; that is, citizenship defines the sovereign. Citizenship laws also contain the rights and conditions that allow the demos members to participate in the social and political life of a state.

Importantly, despite citizenship having these key functions, it is not understood as a set concept that always means the same. As many key concepts in Political Science and Politics, the concept of citizenship has always been contested, interpreted and practised differently in both political theory and also in political practice. Moreover, citizenship concepts and citizenship practices differ according to different national regulations and different cultural contexts (Koselleck 2006; Skinner 1993).

Both citizenship conceptions and citizenship practice have changed over centuries and decades. For instance, one could assume that all adult persons adhering to a polity would be citizens – however, this is by no means the case. In the Greek polis, for example, only a small part of the population, namely adult free men with a certain wealth, possessed full citizenship rights (Pocock

---

[2] On the following see also Wiesner et al. (2018).

1998). Women, children, and slaves were not citizens; that is, they were subordinated in status to the male adult citizens. For these few male adult citizens, citizenship practice was very intense.

The example underlines a case of exclusionary citizenship. Such exclusions from citizenship continued to exist throughout the centuries. Women and less wealthy persons, for most of the history of modern citizenship, either did not possess citizenship rights at all, or they had a limited citizenship status. Non-nationals also were not citizens. In the history of Western nation states, citizenship rights were at the core of democratisation processes; many fights were fought around them, and numerous heated political and parliamentary debates took place (Wiesner 2008).

For example, for most of the time since nation states developed in Europe and modern representative democracies were built, women did not have the right to vote. Female suffrage was only introduced in the course of the twentieth century in the European states. When it was introduced, it often happened in historical windows of opportunity in which the political systems had been overthrown anyway, namely after the first and the Second World War. In most of these cases, women activists had been campaigning for female suffrage for a long time. Finland was the first state to introduce female suffrage after it obtained independence from Russia in 1906; Germany followed in 1918, that is, after the First World War and the breakdown of the German Empire. Many other states only introduced female suffrage after the Second World War (Wiesner 2008).

Citizenship remained exclusionary. Moreover, for many centuries people could only be citizens of a nation state. Since nation states not only granted political rights but also protection rights, as Hannah Arendt famously put it, the "right to have rights" (Arendt 1973, pp. 296, 298) has been linked to nation states.

National conceptions and regulations of citizenship differ (see below), but despite the national specificities, a few generalisations can be made: in today's national representative democratic systems, citizenship defines the democratic subject, the *demos*, or the sovereign in a legal and political sense. Four sub-dimensions shape the formalities and the practice of nation state citizenship: access, rights, duties and the active content of citizenship in the sense of political activity. These four dimensions are covered by most national citizenship regulations. These usually define conditions of *access*, that is, the nationality laws, citizens' *rights* and *duties*; and they define the political rights and hence set a framework for citizens' *political activity*. The sovereignty of the nation states has been closely linked to citizenship. The classical triad of the theory of the state (see e.g. Weber 1978, pp. 54, 56) links state nationals, state territory, and the monopoly of violence of a state. Hence, nation states decided who was to be admitted into the state's sovereign territory and who was to be expelled; they also decided on the treatment and the benefits of their nationals.

As will be discussed in detail below, the EU added a new level and layer of citizenship to these national models and practices. Since the beginning of integration and in particular since the Treaty of Rome or EEC Treaty (1957), citizens of member states possess rights that do not exclusively relate to the nation state of which they are nationals, but to the EU. European integration thus brought about changes to the conception and the practices of citizenship.

The most decisive step in this development was brought about by the Maastricht Treaty. Since 1993, all nationals of an EU member state are also "Union Citizens". Citizenship in the EU is multilevel citizenship. EU citizens possess several EU-related rights in addition to their national rights. However, EU Citizenship differs in many decisive respects from the established form of nation state citizenships. In particular, there is no proper EU nationality and there are no EU citizen duties. As EU-related rights are put into practice in the EU's multi-level system, the classical nexus between sovereignty and citizenship has been changing: it is no longer the EU member states, that is, the nation states, alone that decide who may enter and who may leave a state. EU citizens and also third country nationals that have a residence permit can travel and reside freely within all EU states. This means that the member states have lost their former core competence of determining who may reside in their territory (see below).

Contrary to national democratisation processes, EU-related citizenship rights were not introduced as a consequence of political controversies and ruptures. Citizens-to-be did not actively fight for their rights. EU-related citizenship rights were introduced and shaped in a rather top-down manner by the different Treaties, policy documents, and laws. These have been mostly suggested by the European Commission, voted upon by the Council or the Council and the European Parliament (EP), and interpreted by the CJEU (see in detail Wiesner 2007, pp. 338–355), as will be discussed below.

SHAPING EU CITIZENSHIP

The political struggles related to the creation, interpretation and implementation of EU Citizenship rights are closely related to the EU's institutional context described in Chapter 7, and they are to be interpreted against this background. There are, however, different ways in which the laws in question came about. In order to understand the respective decision-making processes, it is important to underline the following two points:

1) Most of the legal acts discussed in the following did not come about in co-decision procedures, except for one case. Hence, most of the relevant

laws were suggested by the European Commission and voted upon by the Council. The last legal act discussed was decided upon in 2004 in co-decision of the EP and the Council.

2) In order to understand the political controversies around EU Citizenship it is especially important that EU laws are put into practice by national laws and national authorities. In establishing practices of EU Citizenship in the member states, they used their margin for interpretation, as will be discussed below. Importantly, the European Commission at this stage functions as the "guardian of the treaties", which means that it controls the correct implementation of the law and can start infringement procedures against member states before the European Court of Justice in case of noncompliance – which happened in EU Citizenship politics at decisive stages.

As discussed in Chapters 7 and 9, EU documents can be read as documentation of these political controversies, and as indicators of the interrelations and the power struggles between the different EU institutions, as well as between EU institutions and the member states. The following analyses EU documents to describe how creating and implementing EU Citizenship rights was crucially linked to such power struggles, and it was also linked to a battle on the interpretation and the implementation of the concept of citizenship. This battle of EU Citizenship politics (Wiesner 2007, p. 23) was carried out by Treaties, declarations, policy documents, and laws.

CITIZENSHIP RIGHTS IN THE TREATY OF ROME AND THE MEANING OF THE DEFRENNE CASE

As discussed in Chapter 7, EU Treaties are international Treaties between the member states and function as a constitution. The EU Treaties organise the EU as a polity. Importantly, the EU's Treaties have been changing over the decades – and the citizenship regulations in the Treaties have progressed with them.

The Treaty of Rome or EEC Treaty in 1957, as discussed in Chapter 7, was the second of the EU's founding Treaties. It had been preceded by the European Coal and Steel Treaty (ECSC). As this one, the Treaty of Rome had been prepared by negotiations and suggestions from both national and ECSC officials. Just like the Charter of the United Nations, the Treaty of Rome is an outcome of negotiations (European Commission 1985; Küsters 1990).

The Treaty of Rome founded the EEC and it represents the beginning of EU-related citizenship rights. The Treaty of Rome defined several quasi-citizen rights – they are quasi-citizenship since they were not yet valid for all citizens of the member states, but only for market participants. There was a right to free movement, but it was linked to market participation, as it was valid for persons working or providing services in another member state. This right to free movement was part of the four freedoms of the inner market, that is, free circulation of goods, services, capital, and labour.

The right to free movement of employees and service providers is defined in Articles 48 and 59 of the Treaty of Rome (all quotes taken from European Council 1957). Article 48 states:

> 1. Freedom of movement for workers shall be secured within the Community by the end of the transitional period at the latest.
> 2. Such freedom of movement shall entail the abolition of any discrimination based on nationality between workers of the Member States as regards employment, remuneration and other conditions of work and employment. [...].

Article 49 is interesting in relation to Article 48. It is obvious that this Article anticipates forthcoming obstacles to free movement, and it hence describes the processes to be taken in order to discern these obstacles to free movement and counteract them. Article 49 explicitly names the EEC's institutions and their tasks:

> As soon as this Treaty enters into force, the Council shall, acting on a proposal from the Commission and after consulting the Economic and Social Committee, issue directives or make regulations setting out the measures required to bring about, by progressive stages, freedom of movement for workers, as defined in Article 48, in particular:
>
> [...]
>
> (b) by systematically and progressively abolishing those administrative procedures and practices and those qualifying periods in respect of eligibility for available employment, whether resulting from national legislation or from agreements previously concluded between Member States, the maintenance of which would form an obstacle to liberalisation of the movement of workers; (c) by systematically and progressively abolishing all such qualifying periods and other restrictions provided for either under national legislation or under agreements previously concluded between Member States as imposed on workers of other Member States conditions regarding the free choice of employment other than those imposed on workers of the State concerned [...].

The Treaty of Rome also defines another cornerstone of EU Citizenship, namely the core of the right to equal treatment and non-discrimination. At first, it extended to equality of men and women and their right to equal pay. This is defined in Article 119:

> Each Member State shall during the first stage ensure and subsequently maintain the application of the principle that men and women should receive equal pay for equal work. For the purpose of this Article, "pay" means the ordinary basic or minimum wage or salary and any other consideration, whether in cash or in kind,

which the worker receives, directly or indirectly, in respect of his employment from his employer. Equal pay without discrimination based on sex means:

a) that pay for the same work at piece rates shall be calculated on the basis of the same unit of measurement;
b) that pay for work at time rates shall be the same for the same job.

As said above, both the right to free movement and the right to equal payment for women and men relate to market or more concretely labour market participation. Nevertheless, these rights created a direct link between EEC citizens in their role as market participants and the EEC, since they were directly applicable and citizens were able to claim them before the Court of Justice (formerly European Court of Justice, ECJ, today CJEU).

The Court, in the following years, became an important agent in developing EEC and later EU Citizenship rights further. While the Court does not make the laws itself, it interprets them in its judgements. As discussed in Chapter 7, the Court has a margin of interpretation in this, that is, it can interpret laws in a rather broad or a rather narrow manner. In the case of citizenship, the Court interpreted the Treaties' regulations very broadly and by and by a broad EEC-related catalogue of rights in the areas of work, healthcare, or consumer protection developed.

However, it has to be underlined that the Court has been restricting other parts of citizenship rights in its judgements, namely social rights. The Court's judgements tend to weigh the principle of freedom of movement much more strongly than the protection of national social standards, to the extent that it de facto limited the rights of Trade Unions and national social standards in several cases (Wiesner 2019b, pp. 249–260).

While the Court had a clear agenda in favour of abolishing obstacles to free movement even if this meant cutting down social standards, in other respects the Court was very proactive. In particular, over the years the Court and the Commission acted as agents of non-discrimination policy. The Commission regularly suggested new laws, and the Court interpreted the existing EU laws in the broadest possible way.

A crucial case in this respect is the "Defrenne" case. Gabrielle Defrenne was a Belgian stewardess. Belgium until the 1970s had obliged female flight attendants to retire at 40, unlike male flight attendants. Defrenne therefore had been forced to retire, and accordingly received a lower pension than her male colleagues would receive after a longer working period. She complained that the lower pension resulting from this violated her right to equal treatment under Article 119 (Court of Justice of the European Union 1976).

In 1976, the Court judged that equal payment and equal treatment of women and men had to be enacted in practice and for individuals. The Court made a point of Article 119 being directly applicable and having immediate consequences for the member states. It argued in its judgement that

> The principle that men and women should receive equal pay, which is laid down by Article 119, may be relied on before the national courts. These courts have a duty to ensure the protection of the rights which that provision vests in individuals, in particular in the case of those forms of discrimination which have their origin in legislative provisions or collective labour agreements, as well as where men and women receive unequal pay for equal work which is carried out in the same establishment or service, whether private or public. (Court of Justice of the European Union 1976, pp. 418–481)

The judgement means that Gabrielle Defrenne individually claimed her right to equal treatment with regard to retirement age and pension level. It also marks two other decisive developments: the Court specified that EEC law was directly applicable in the member states, and it laid the ground for an extensive, broad and proactive interpretation of EU antidiscrimination laws. This became particularly evident from the 1990s onwards (see below).

UNION CITIZENSHIP

The Treaty of Maastricht (1993) more than 35 years after the Treaty of Rome, marked another decisive step. It decoupled rights from sole market participation and created citizenship rights valid for all member states nationals by introducing Union Citizenship or "Citizenship of the Union". The Treaty of Maastricht is the first EU Treaty that uses the concept "citizenship" with regard to the EU. It hence applies a key concept of nation-state representative democracy to the EU.

Articles 8 to 8e in The Maastricht Treaty define Union Citizenship rights (all quotes taken from Council of the European Communities and Commission of the European Communities 1992). Article 8 states:

> 1. Citizenship of the Union is hereby established.
>   Every person holding the nationality of a Member State shall be a citizen of the Union.
> 2. Citizens of the Union shall enjoy the rights conferred by this Treaty and shall be subject to the duties imposed thereby.

The key innovation Union Citizenship brought about is to create *political* citizenship rights that were directly related to the EU and not only to member states, and to extend the right to free movement to any citizen of a member state, irrespective of the fact that he or she participated in the inner market. Article 8a states:

1. Every citizen of the Union shall have the right to move and reside freely within the territory of the Member States, subject to the limitations and conditions laid down in this Treaty and by the measures adopted to give it effect. [...].

Article 8b defines a right to vote and a right to stand as a candidate in municipal and EP elections:

1. Every citizen of the Union residing in a Member State of which he is not a national shall have the right to vote and to stand as a candidate at municipal elections in the Member State in which he resides, under the same conditions as nationals of that State. [...]
2. Without prejudice to Article I3s(3) and to the provisions adopted for its implementation, every citizen of the Union residing in a Member state of which he is not a national shall have the right to vote and to stand as a candidate in elections to the European Parliament in the Member State in which he resides, under the same conditions as nationals of that State.

Subsequently, Articles 8c and 8d define the right to diplomatic and consular protection of EU citizens and the right to petition to the EP and to apply to the European Ombudsman.

Union Citizenship therefore introduced general citizen rights for every national of a member state. While these were (and are) far from the range of rights national citizenship provides, they represent a major historical step – that was introduced in a new Treaty that was concluded by the heads of state and government of the then 15 member states. A closer look at the background of Union Citizenship rights shows that these rights were not invented spontaneously in Maastricht. Instead, ideas that had been developed for more than 20 years by the Commission, EP, and the Council were finally adopted (Wiener 1998, p. 84). As the Treaty of Rome, the Maastricht Treaty had been prepared by extensive negotiations. The EU's "innovating ideologists" (Skinner 2002, p. 142) had for a long time developed their political ideas on creating an EU Citizenship. Maastricht was only a window of opportunity for realising these existing ideas. The background, again, relates to the strategic interests of the heads of state and government and the EU legitimacy crisis of the 1990s: Weiler (1996, p. 9) states that the Spanish Prime Minister Felipe Gonzalez in the very final stage of the Maastricht negotiations suggested countering a growing Euroscepticism in the population by "doing something about citizenship". The chapter on Union Citizenship, based on the existing preparations, was drafted in record time.

After Union Citizenship had been fixed in the Treaties, the interesting part was yet to come: the political and legal interpretation and hence the development of these laws. Since the Maastricht Treaty came into force in 1993, all

EU citizens, in addition to their national citizenship, are citizens of the Union – but what does this concretely entail in political and legal practice?

One key feature of Union Citizenship is that it is *derived* from the possession of the nationality of an EU member state. There is no proper EU nationality. Union Citizenship does not interfere with the member states' classical sovereign right to determine their nationals. Interestingly, this point had not been made explicit in the Maastricht Treaty. The legal loophole this omission offered led to the status of Union Citizenship becoming the object of an interpretative struggle between the Council of the EU and the Commission immediately after it had been created. The Council stated in Birmingham in October 1992

> [...] that Union citizenship brings additional rights and additional protection for our citizens, but in no respect takes the place of their respective nationality. [...] The nationality of a person will only be ruled by the respective domestic laws of the member states. (European Union 2001, p. 2; own translation C. Wiesner)

As opposed to this, the Commission had another interpretation, as the following statement from an official commission report on Union Citizenship underlines:

> Citizenship of the Union is both a source of legitimation for the process of European integration, by reinforcing the participation of citizens, and a fundamental factor in the creation among citizens of a sense of belonging to the European Union and of having a genuine European identity. (European Commission 2001, p. 7)

The Commission furthermore highlighted that Union Citizenship concerns both the EU and the member states:

> Because of its origins and the rights and duties associated with it, Citizenship of the Union is sui generis and cannot be compared to national citizenship in a member state. In this new type of multiple citizenship on different levels, Citizenship of the Union complements national citizenship and does not replace it. (European Commission 2001, p. 7)

The controversy was settled as it is often the case in the EU. The status of Union Citizenship was explicated in the Treaty of Amsterdam that was concluded in 1997 and entered into force in 1999. Since then, the Treaties underline that Union Citizenship must complement but not replace national citizenship. Article 9 of the TEU states:

> Every national of a Member State shall be a citizen of the Union. Citizenship of the Union shall be additional to and not replace national citizenship. (European Union 2016)

Union Citizenship thus is a sort of hybrid compared to nation state citizenships. The EU does not have its own nationality, and hence Union Citizenship is derived from member state nationalities. Nevertheless, Union Citizenship creates EU-related citizenship rights which counteract former sovereign rights of the member states when it comes to free movement or elections.

Union Citizenship rights today are defined in Articles 20–25 TFEU: the right to free movement and residence all over the EU (but only for EU citizens that can assure the means for living), active and passive election rights in local and municipal as well as in EP elections in their country of residence, the right to diplomatic and consular protection outside the EU by embassies of all EU member states, the right to petition to the EP, and the right to write in one of the 23 official EU languages to EU institutions and receive answers in the same language (TFEU, Articles 20–25). The expression "Citizenship of the Union" since the Maastricht Treaty is explicitly used as a headline in the Treaties. Today it is fixed in the TFEU as part of the headline "Non-discrimination and Citizenship of the Union" (European Union 2016).

IMPLEMENTING UNION CITIZENSHIP: THE EXAMPLE OF THE RIGHT TO FREE MOVEMENT

The legal and institutional framework of Union Citizenship also represents an innovation. After it had been introduced in Maastricht, Union Citizenship became part of the policy field of the internal market. This meant practically that all further decisions in this field became subject to co-decision of the Council and EP, as at the time of the Maastricht Treaty only decisions in the field of the internal market were subject to co-decision. The choice was decisive: as will be discussed below, a number of new laws on citizenship were made in the following years, and this could happen in the framework of co-decision, that is, via including the EP that usually supports the broadening of EU Citizenship rights.

This was also interesting as putting Union Citizenship rights into practice happened not without problems. This fact indicates a general problem: the fact that rights are fixed in Treaties or conventions does not mean they will also be enacted. Rights are not "just there" but need to be respected and put into practice. One decisive question is what happens if they are not put into practice or disregarded. A violation of Treaties or conventions is a regular problem in transnational politics. In order to counteract such breaches, the EU disposes of more and different means than the UN. In the case of Union Citizenship, the European Commission stepped in and used its role as Guardian of the Treaties as well as its law-initiating competencies.

After Union Citizenship rights had been introduced in Maastricht and the Treaty came into force, it soon became obvious that the new rights interfered with established competencies and routines in the nation states. The implementation of Union Citizenship rights led to political and conceptual struggles carried out via policy documents and laws, until finally a new practice developed (Wiesner 2007, pp. 154–195; Wiesner 2014). The related struggles are illustrated by the course of events in the field of the free movement of persons.

The right to free movement proved a particularly conflicting issue when it was put into practice. In 1997, 5.5 million EU citizens lived in member states that were not their home countries. A Commission report revealed a number of problems with regard to their right to free movement that were mostly related to unclear, incomplete or contradictory laws. Moreover, national, regional, or local government institutions sometimes put obstacles to the full implementation. The Commission therefore established an expert group which analysed the practice of the application of Union Citizenship after four years. The report (European Commission 1997) indicates that national authorities' reaction to the new rights was part of a political struggle around the interpretation and the implementation of the new Union Citizenship rights – and about the classical sovereign rights of a nation state. Problems were related to the practice of residence permits, the acceptance of foreign degrees, employment in the public sector, and social and family related rights. For example, regarding residence permits, EU citizens only needed to have a valid ID in order to *enter* into another EU member state. However, in order to become *resident* in this state, a residence permit was required if the EU citizen stayed for more than three months. But there was no particular permit for stays between four months and a year – theoretically EU citizens then needed to apply for a long-term residence permit. Many EU citizens in this situation omitted to do so and hence got into an irregular situation after three months. Students in most cases could not apply for a residence permit that exceeded one year, so they often had serial residence permits (European Commission 1997, pp. 17–29). In cases where such obstacles hindered the obtention of a residence permit, EU citizens were threatened by expulsion, or had to endure difficulties in access to services of general interest like drinking water, electricity, heating, or telecommunication.

The Commission reacted to the report and used the full range of its legal and political means to counter such problems. It began with legal means, that is, it led several infringement procedures before the Court of Justice against all member states. Most of them then changed the situation, but only after some years (European Commission 2001, p. 10).

The Commission's next move in the political struggle with the member state authorities and governments was communication via policy documents. It issued several documents and declarations that claimed improvements and announced the changes that had to take place. The Commission announced it wanted a uniform regulation of the right to free movement and residence for all EU citizens and their family members; it wanted to reduce the requirement for residence permits to a minimum of cases, and it wanted a concretisation of the conditions of expulsion (European Commission 2001).

The third step of the Commission was to propose new EU laws.

> The proposal for a Directive is a product of the legal and political environment created by the introduction of citizenship of the Union. It takes account of the results of the report of the high-level panel on the free movement of persons, the Commission Communication on the follow-up to the recommendations of the highlevel panel, 12 the Second Report on Citizenship, the European Parliament resolutions and the past rulings of the Court of Justice. (European Commission 2001, p. 8)

The respective law initiatives followed until 2004, and subsequently, the laws were concluded.

One decisive legal step is Directive 2004/38/EC (European Union 2004), voted upon by the Council and the EP. As other EU directives in the area of EU Citizenship rights (see below), it begins with a number of declarations which aim at clarifying aspects that had been the subject of controversy before. It is interesting to notice that in the wording, the EP and Council also take on the role of agents who claim a broadening and strengthening of EU-related citizenship rights when they are implemented:

> (1) Citizenship of the Union confers on every citizen of the Union a primary and individual right to move and reside freely within the territory of the Member States, subject to the limitations and conditions laid down in the Treaty and to the measures adopted to give it effect.
> (2) The free movement of persons constitutes one of the fundamental freedoms of the internal market, which comprises an area without internal frontiers, in which freedom is ensured in accordance with the provisions of the Treaty.
> (3) Union citizenship should be the fundamental status of nationals of the Member States when they exercise their right of free movement and residence. […]
> (11) The fundamental and personal right of residence in another Member State is conferred directly on Union citizens by the Treaty and is not dependent upon their having fulfilled administrative procedures. (European Union 2004)

The directive thus emphasises a number of keywords with regard to the status of EU Citizenship, naming it "a primary and individual right" and a "fundamental status", underlining that it is "conferred directly on Union citizens", rather than emphasising the dependence on the member states.

Among other aspects, the law text itself then fixes unified rules of residence. It declares that Union citizens may stay in another member state for three months without any residence permit. After three months, member states may require one. But then employees, self-employed persons, persons in education or studies, and their family members can require a permit on the basis of their ID, a working contract or a certificate of training, a proof of self-employed status, a proof of sufficient means for living, and health insurance. The regulation states that a declaration is sufficient as proof for the means for living and no fixed sum can be required. Union citizens can only be expelled in cases of severe threats to inner security, with an exclusion of minors and persons that have been resident for more than ten years in the respective state. The regulation also requires the member states to inform EU citizens of their rights (European Union 2004).

SHAPING THE PRINCIPLE OF ANTIDISCRIMINATION

Free movement was not the only area of citizenship rights in which the EU made new laws. After the groundwork was done in the 1970s by the Court in the Defrenne case, several other non-discrimination rights have been added to the catalogues. The EU not only introduced many new rights in the fields of anti-discrimination and equal treatment – the rights that were thus created were also further-reaching than in most national citizenship right catalogues. Since they had to be applied in all member states like all other EU legislation, the EU thus extended the former catalogue of citizenship rights.

The principle of non-discrimination and equal treatment had been first introduced in the Treaty of Rome, as explained above, with regard to the right to equal payment for women and men. The Treaty of Rome moreover had interdicted any discrimination based on nationality. Afterwards, as said above, the Commission and the Court interpreted existing EU laws in the broadest possible way and forced member states as well as employers to the largest possible extent of equal treatment enabled by the EU laws. Policy documents, laws, and declarations again were their tools in these political struggles (for further detail see Wiesner 2007, pp. 223–225), as explained above with regard to the Defrenne case.

In developing antidiscrimination rights further, again the first step was a Treaty. After decades of active non-discrimination policies, the Amsterdam Treaty in 1999 considerably enlarged the legal base and defined a political goal of equal treatment and non-discrimination. Article 19 of the TFEU now states, in the current version of the Lisbon Treaty:

> 1. Without prejudice to the other provisions of the Treaties and within the limits of the powers conferred by them upon the Union, the Council, acting unanimously in accordance with a special legislative procedure and after obtaining the consent of the European Parliament, may take appropriate

> action to combat discrimination based on sex, racial or ethnic origin, religion or belief, disability, age or sexual orientation.
>
> 2. By way of derogation from paragraph 1, the European Parliament and the Council, acting in accordance with the ordinary legislative procedure, may adopt the basic principles of Union incentive measures, excluding any harmonisation of the laws and regulations of the Member States, to support action taken by the Member States in order to contribute to the achievement of the objectives referred to in paragraph 1. (European Union 2016)

Referring to this newly introduced legal base, the Commission developed the principle of antidiscrimination. It proceeded similarly to the case of free movement, by first suggesting a policy package (European Commission 1999). The package mainly consisted of a proposal of two EU directives that aimed at putting the article cited above into political practice. Referring to the principles of freedom, democracy, human rights, rule of law, as well as the four freedoms of the inner market, the Commission communication underlines very clearly the aim to create a political practice that was further reaching than in the member states. It also becomes evident that the Commission wanted to force the member states to change their legal and political practices:

> In more general terms, a number of Member States do not have comprehensive legislation (other than isolated provisions contained in various labour or criminal codes) to combat discrimination on the grounds of racial or ethnic origin, religion or belief, age and sexual orientation. (European Commission 1999, p. 4)

The law project in question was not subject to co-decision and hence concluded by the Council only. The Council followed the Commission's initiative and voted two new antidiscrimination directives in 2000. The second one, COUNCIL DIRECTIVE 2000/78/EC of 27 November 2000, interdicts any discrimination on ethnic grounds and fixes equal treatment as a leading principle regarding employment, education, social security, and access to products and services (European Council 2000b). The first directive, COUNCIL DIRECTIVE 2000/43/EC of 29 June 2000, is even more far-reaching: it interdicts any discrimination in employment and profession that is based on race, ethnic origin, religion, ideology, age, or sexual orientation (European Council 2000a).

This general antidiscrimination directive again represents a clear political statement. The first part of the directive consists of a declaration which lists 28 arguments on why the Council did adopt the directive – including references to the EP. The list is very exhaustive and includes not only several value-oriented statements and reasons in favour of the EU's non-discrimination policies, it also indicates future perspectives, and last but by no means least, it underlines the norms and values of the EU (all quotes taken from European Council 2000a):

> (2) In accordance with Article 6 of the Treaty on European Union, the European Union is founded on the principles of liberty, democracy, respect for human rights and fundamental freedoms, and the rule of law, principles which are common to the Member States, and should respect fundamental rights as guaranteed by the European Convention for the protection of Human Rights and Fundamental Freedoms and as they result from the constitutional traditions common to the Member States, as general principles of Community Law.

There is also a reference to other international Treaties and the Human Rights:

> (3) The right to equality before the law and protection against discrimination for all persons constitutes a universal right recognised by the Universal Declaration of Human Rights, the United Nations Convention on the Elimination of all forms of Discrimination Against Women, the International Convention on the Elimination of all forms of Racial Discrimination and the United Nations Covenants on Civil and Political Rights and on Economic, Social and Cultural Rights and by the European Convention for the Protection of Human Rights and Fundamental Freedoms, to which all Member States are signatories.

Later in the list of arguments, several future-oriented declarations follow, which underline that other measures and policy initiatives are in planning:

> (12) To ensure the development of democratic and tolerant societies which allow the participation of all persons irrespective of racial or ethnic origin, specific action in the field of discrimination based on racial or ethnic origin should go beyond access to employed and self-employed activities and cover areas such as education, social protection including social security and healthcare, social advantages and access to and supply of goods and services.
>
> (24) Protection against discrimination based on racial or ethnic origin would itself be strengthened by the existence of a body or bodies in each Member State, with competence to analyse the problems involved, to study possible solutions and to provide concrete assistance for the victims.

The directive itself defines a far-reaching purpose. Article 1 states:

> The purpose of this Directive is to lay down a framework for combating discrimination on the grounds of racial or ethnic origin, with a view to putting into effect in the Member States the principle of equal treatment.

Some member states were very reluctant to transfer these directives into national legal practice. Germany was one of the last states to do so, already under pressure of an infringement procedure.

IN CONCLUSION

What can be learned from the above on political processes in the EU in general? The example of EU Citizenship underlines what has been emphasised in Chapters 7 and 9, namely, EU politics do not only lead to making simple laws that are immediately effective in the member states, but they shape the EU's political system and its key concepts – in the above case, they led to establishing an independent EU Citizenship.

The actors that invented and shaped EU Citizenship over the decades have mostly been based in EU institutions or have been national and EU politicians, but there were also national authorities involved. The processes sketched above underline that there were differing and sometimes even contradicting opinions on how far-reaching EU rights should be and whether they should be applied in broad or narrow interpretations. The documents quoted above do document these controversies. They indicate the intentions of the respective actors, document the various steps of the related controversies, and fix the (interim) outcomes of these steps and controversies in laws and Treaties. These, once fixed, need to be implemented, and the implementation often laid the ground for new controversies and a new round of conceptual innovations.

The processes and conflicts related to the introduction, interpretation and implementation of EU Citizenship rights, as well as the interests of the agents, can be traced in the studied documents. The Commission apparently was the major driving force behind the creation and the implementation of the new EU-related citizenship rights. It seems to be in the Commission's interest that EU Citizenship rights are practised smoothly and in a broad way. In relation to the institutional and conceptual context of the EU that was discussed in Chapter 7, it is a possible explanation that enlarging EU-related citizenship rights and breaking up the member state's monopoly in this field strengthens the EU and its supranational dimension. What strengthens the supranational dimension per definition strengthens one of the two supranational institutions, that is, the Commission. Strengthening EU Citizenship rights in that sense can be interpreted as symbolically creating subjects to the Commission and the EP.

The Commission has been seconded by the Court, which not only led infringement procedures where the new rights were not satisfyingly complied with, but also interpreted the new rights as broadly as possible in its judgements. The member states' governments have been acting in ambivalent ways. On the one hand, the national ministers voted in favour of the new rights in the Council decisions, even if these new laws impeded their sovereign powers.

On the other hand, the national authorities were often reluctant when it came to their implementation. This means that there is a tension between what the heads of the executive branches decide upon and what the lower levels of the executive do in carrying these decisions out. Importantly, the controversies around the interpretation and implementation of the new rights were not fully, or not at all, carried out before drafting the laws and voting on them – they seem to have been carried out in the majority after the laws had been decided upon and in the course of implementation. Moreover, those agents that are the most concerned by the new rights, the EU's citizens, were not included in shaping the new rights. EU citizens just benefit from the new rights, without having fought for them.

REFERENCES

Arendt, Hannah (1973). The Origins of Totalitarianism. Orlando, Harcourt.

European Commission (1985). The Relaunching of Europe. From the Messina Conference to the Treaties of Rome, 1955–1957. Luxembourg, Office for Official Publications of the European Communities.

European Union (2001). Der Vertrag von Amsterdam: Gebrauchsanweisung Unionsbürgerschaft. Available online at http//europa.eu.int/scadplus/leg/de/lvb/a1 2000.htm (accessed 8/25/2005).

Koselleck, Reinhart (2006). Drei bürgerliche Welten. Zur vergleichenden Semantik der bürgerlichen Gesellschaft in Deutschland, Frankreich und England. In: Reinhart Koselleck (Ed.). Begriffsgeschichten. Frankfurt am Main, Suhrkamp, 402–463.

Küsters, Hanns Jürgen (1990). Fondements de la Communauté économique européenne. Bruxelles/Luxembourg, Labor; EUR-OP.

Pocock, John (1998). The Ideal of Citizenship since Classical Times. In: Gershon Shafir (Ed.). The Citizenship Debates. Minneapolis, University of Minnesota Press, 31–41.

Skinner, Quentin (1993). Two Concepts of Citizenship. Tijdschrift voor Filosofie 55, 403–419.

Skinner, Quentin (2002). Moral Principles and Social Change. In: Quentin Skinner (Ed.). Visions of Policics Vol. 1. Regarding Method. Cambridge [u.a.], Cambridge University Press, 145–157.

Weber, Max (1978). Economy and Society: An Outline of Interpretative Sociology. Berkeley, California, University of California Press.

Weiler, Josef H.H (1996). The Selling of Europe. Jean Monnet Working Papers 3. Available online at https://jeanmonnetprogram.org/archive/papers/96/9603.html (accessed 2/12/2013).

Wiener, Antje (1998). European Citizenship Practice. Boulder, Westview Press.

Wiesner, Claudia (2007). Bürgerschaft und Demokratie in der EU. Münster, Lit.

Wiesner, Claudia (2008). Women's Partial Citizenship. In: Kari Palonen/Tuija Pulkkinen/José María Rosales (Eds.). The Ashgate Research Companion to the Politics of Democratization in Europe. Farnham, Surrey and Burlington, VT, Ashgate, 235–250.

Wiesner, Claudia (2014). The Europeanisation of Citizenship: Conceptual Innovations, Legal Changes, and Development of New Institutional Practices. Contributions to the History of Concepts 9 (1), 88–104.

Wiesner, Claudia (2018). Shaping Citizenship Practice Through Laws: Rights and Conceptual Innovations in the EU. In: Claudia Wiesner/Anna Björk/Hanna-Mari Kivistö et al. (Eds.). Shaping Citizenship. A Political Concept in Theory, Debate and Practice. London, Routledge, 159–174.
Wiesner, Claudia (2019a). Citizens of a Polity Without Politics? The European Union, Concepts of Federalism and Citizenship. In: Skadi Krause (Ed.). Theories of Federalism. Baden-Baden, Nomos, 310–323.
Wiesner, Claudia (2019b). Inventing the EU as a Democratic Polity. Concepts, Actors and Controversies. Cham, Springer International Publishing; Imprint Palgrave Macmillan.
Wiesner, Claudia (2022). Between Conceptual Innovation and "There is No Alternative": Conceptual Politics and the Building of the EU as a Polity. In: Niilo Kauppi/Kari Palonen (Eds.). Rhetoric and Bricolage in European Politics and Beyond. Cham, Switzerland, Palgrave Macmillan, 89–116.
Wiesner, Claudia (2023). Actors, Concepts, Controversies: The Conceptual Politics of European Integration. Political Research Exchange 5 (1), 145. https://doi.org/10.1080/2474736X.2023.2258173
Wiesner, Claudia (2025). (Non)Political Citizenship? Federalism, Rights, Democracy and Politicisation in the EU. In: Skadi Krause (Ed.). Theories of Federalism. Baden-Baden, Nomos.
Wiesner, Claudia/Haapala, Taru/Palonen, Kari (2017). Debates, Rhetoric and Political Action. Practices of Textual Interpretation and Analysis. London, Palgrave Macmillan UK; Imprint Palgrave Macmillan.
Wiesner, Claudia/Björk, Anna/Kivisto, Hanna-Mari/Mäkinen, Katja (2018). Introduction: Shaping Citizenship as a Contested Concept. In: Claudia Wiesner/Anna Björk/Hanna-Mari Kivistö et al. (Eds.). Shaping Citizenship. A Political Concept in Theory, Debate and Practice. London, Routledge, 1–16.

EU Documents

Council of the European Communities/Commission of the European Communities (1992). Treaty on European Union. Luxemburg, Office for Official Publications of the European Communities.
Court of Justice of the European Union (1976). Judgment of the Court of 8 April 1976. Gabrielle Defrenne v Société anonyme belge de navigation aérienne Sabena. Reference for a preliminary ruling: Cour du travail de Bruxelles – Belgium. The principle that men and women should receive equal pay for equal work. CASE 43/75. Available online at https://eur-lex.europa.eu/legal-content/EN/TXT/PDF/?uri=CELEX:61975CJ0043 (accessed 4/24/2025).
European Commission (1997). Bericht der hochrangigen Arbeitsgruppe zu Fragen der Freizügigkeit unter dem Vorsitz von Frau Simone Veil. Available online at http://www.uni-mannheim.de/edz/pdf/1997/hlpde.pdf (accessed 2/12/2013).
European Commission (1999). Communication from the Commission to the Council, the European Parliament, the Economic and Social Committee and the Committee of the Regions on certain Community measures to combat discrimination. Available online at http://eur-lex.europa.eu/LexUriServ/LexUriServ.do?uri=COM:1999:0564:FIN:EN:PDF (accessed 2/12/2013).

European Commission (2001). Third Report from the Commission on Citizenship of the Union, COM (2001) 506 final. Available online at http://eur-lex.europa.eu/LexUriServ/LexUriServ.do?uri=COM:2001:0506:FIN:EN:PDF (accessed 2/12/2013).

European Council (1957). The Treaty of Rome. Available online at http://ec.europa.eu/economy_finance/emu_history/documents/treaties/rometreaty2.pdf (accessed 2/11/2013).

European Council (2000a). COUNCIL DIRECTIVE 2000/43/EC of 29 June 2000 implementing the principle of equal treatment between persons irrespective of racial or ethnic origin. Available online at https://eur-lex.europa.eu/legal-content/EN/TXT/PDF/?uri=CELEX:32000L0043 (accessed 4/24/2025).

European Council (2000b). COUNCIL DIRECTIVE 2000/78/EC of 27 November 2000 establishing a general framework for equal treatment in employment and occupation. Available online at https://eur-lex.europa.eu/legal-content/EN/TXT/PDF/?uri=CELEX:32000L0078 (accessed 4/24/2025).

European Union (2004). Directive 2004/38/EC of the European Parliament and of the Council of 29 April 2004 on the right of citizens of the Union and their family members to move and reside freely within the territory of the Member States amending Regulation (EEC) No 1612/68 and repealing Directives 64/221/EEC, 68/360/EEC, 72/194/EEC, 73/148/EEC, 75/34/EEC, 75/35/EEC, 90/364/EEC, 90/365/EEC and 93/96/EEC (Text with EEA relevance). European Parliament; Council of the European Union. Available online at https://eur-lex.europa.eu/eli/dir/2004/38/oj/eng (accessed 2/12/2013).

European Union (2016). Consolidated versions of the Treaty on European Union and the Treaty on the Functioning of the European Union – Consolidated version of the Treaty on the Functioning of the European Union – Protocols – Annexes – Declarations annexed to the Final Act of the Intergovernmental Conference which adopted the Treaty of Lisbon, signed on 13 December 2007 – Tables of equivalences. Official Journal C 326, 26/10/2012 P. 0001 – 0390. Available online at https://eur-lex.europa.eu/eli/treaty/tfeu_2012/oj/eng (accessed 6/6/2025).

PART IV

Learning to practise transnational politics

12. Preparing MUN and MEU: course plan, teaching materials and teaching modules

Clara Umstätter, Muriel Cathérine Wenzel and Claudia Wiesner

Participating in a Model United Nations (MUN) or in a Model European Union (MEU) requires thorough preparation. One has to learn about the conference flow and the rules of procedure, know the basics of international law, and be prepared for negotiations and public speaking. All of this requires time, effort, and the willingness to learn more about international politics. Preparation for a MUN or MEU, as already explained in Chapters 2 and 3, can either take place online or in presence, be integrated into a course or semester plan within a study programme, be done by a MEU / MUN-club which follows the character of peer-to-peer teaching, or on an individual basis.

No matter how and in whatever format you want to implement the preparation, this chapter and its teaching modules for MUN or MEU training seminars will provide a vital overview of what to keep in mind and offer a great variety of teaching activities. The content of the teaching modules relates to all the previous chapters in providing the background and basic knowledge to prepare students for participation in simulations. The below describes how teaching these topics can be structured and what is necessary to be implemented within a preparatory course on simulations.

To simulate the United Nations (UN) or the European Union (EU), it is necessary to understand their institutional design (see Chapters 6 and 7), the function of international law (Chapter 8), and the rules of procedure and internal political processes (Chapter 9). Before attending a simulation, participants should learn about the mandates and competencies of the UN's or the EU's central bodies and gather an understanding of their structures. Furthermore, they will need various soft skills such as teamwork, public speaking, or negotiating to participate successfully. Moreover, knowledge about the outcome documents and rules of procedure is of the utmost importance.

Therefore, teaching modules and training seminars should teach students that the UN and the EU are arenas of politics. They will also learn how political processes take place in these arenas when they take part in a simulation as delegates of an assigned member state.

The teaching modules presented here can be adapted to the given circumstances, such as online or offline teaching and teaching by university staff or among peers. They provide a basis and guidelines for teaching and include the most important aspects to be taken into account in preparation for simulations. It is perfectly possible to adapt the teaching modules to your specific situation.

In the following, each teaching module follows the same structure. The points in the checklists allow you to tick off those tasks that have been completed already. They support the teacher in communicating what is expected from the students and ensure that all necessary steps have been taken in order to achieve the goals of the respective session. Please note that we will be using the terms teacher and students throughout to distinguish between two roles: the role of the person who is responsible for the preparation seminars and the preparation of a delegation for a MEU or MUN, and the role of delegates wishing to participate. The teacher does not necessarily have to be a professor or faculty member, but could also be a peer, a UN club member, or a faculty advisor.

Furthermore, we would like to refer to the glossary in Chapter 14, which provides a basic overview of MUN-specific terms and explains them in detail. It serves as orientation and as a means to look up terms during teaching or participating in a MUN. The glossary can and should be used in combination with the teaching modules to avoid confusion and misunderstandings with regard to the specific MUN terms.

LEARNING GOALS

Before we start, we want to provide a number of learning goals. These goals give an overview and hint at the most important topics students should know before participating in their first simulation. These learning goals entail the following points that can be checked by each student individually or by the teacher for the whole class at the end of the training seminar:

- Know about international law, including its status, differences between hard and soft law, the pressure on states, different forms of resolution and treaties, and the role of nation states.
- Know the UN and/or the EU, their history and contemporary role, central organs, internal processes as well as decision-making processes.
- Be familiar with UN and EU documents.

- Have looked at case studies to see how the UN's and the EU's impact is in reality and how processes and decisions come about.
- Distinguish outcome documents at MUN and MEU, such as working papers, draft resolutions, or resolutions, and their content and structures.
- Know how to research to prepare for representing a member state.
- Be able to write a position paper in the correct formatting.
- Know the rules of procedure and code of conduct.
- Be able and confident to hold (spontaneous) speeches.
- Know how to negotiate and stand in for one's position successfully.
- Be prepared for the conference's topics.

MODULES

The following presents 16 teaching modules. Importantly, the modules do not necessarily have to be arranged in the order of numbering. It is possible to both start with the institutional background and reading and then go on to the practical aspects such as speech training – but it is also possible to mix sessions on institutional backgrounds and practice training. The two seminar plans provided below, one on a MUN training seminar and one on a MEU and MUN training seminar, follow these different patterns.

It is possible to combine modules and fill whole days as a block seminar or to go through them on a weekly/bi-weekly basis in shorter seminar sessions. A recommended duration is provided for each module in the sections to follow to facilitate timing.

- 0 – Pre-meeting
- Modules 1–6 – Building the foundation
- Module 7 – Discussion and reflection
- Module 8a – Outcome Documents Part 1 – Working papers
- Module 8b – Outcome Documents Part 2 – Draft resolutions
- Module 8c – Outcome Documents Part 3 – Resolutions
- Module 8d – Outcome Documents Part 4 – EU regulations
- Module 9 – Position paper
- Module 10 – Research
- Module 11 – Rules of procedure
- Module 12 – Speeches
- Module 13 – Position paper (2)
- Module 14 – Negotiations
- Module 15 – Fill in the blanks
- Module 16 – Topic preparation

The teaching modules can be implemented both onsite and online, as mentioned above. Depending on the format, different aspects need to be considered. For an online seminar, we recommend using an online conference tool that offers a stable connection, can host the number of participants inscribed for the seminar, and enables screen sharing and breakout rooms. There are various tools available; for example, Zoom, WebEx, Microsoft Teams; however, pricing differs among them.

Another important aspect to think about before starting the seminar concerns the sharing of the seminar material. It is helpful to rely on an e-mail list or make use of an online platform that allows up- and downloading and offers the necessary data protection. Such tools might already exist at your institution.

SAMPLE SEMINAR PLANS

Based on the 16 modules, we provide two sample seminar plans.

The first (Table 12.1) is based on MUN preparatory seminars that were taught online in the PATRAPO project at Fulda UAS, UAM and UNiZG in the winter terms 2021/2022 and 2022/2023 and in following seminars at Fulda UAS. Those seminars were taught as block seminars. This means that instead of regular sessions each week, full days throughout the semester were chosen and teaching went from 9am to 4.30pm, including shorter coffee breaks and a longer lunch break. However, the seminar does not have to be implemented in this form but can be taught weekly or in a different rhythm as is most appropriate for each institution.

Table 12.1 Seminar plan for MUN block seminars

Time	Content / To dos	Literature/Notes/Homework
0	**Pre-meeting**	-
-	Introduction, expectations, organisational issues	-
First Day	**Modules 1–7**	-
09:00am	Opening	-

Time	Content / To dos	Literature/Notes/Homework
First session (2h) 09:10am – 11:10am	UN presentation plus discussion Method: student group presentations to be prepared before the seminar, each presentation 15min + 20min discussion	International law (status of international law, difference between soft/hard law, pressure on states), different resolution/treaties (declaration), role of nation states a) Simpson, Gerry. 2012. International Law in Diplomatic History. In The Cambridge Companion to International Law, ed. James Crawford and Martti Koskenniemi, pp. 25–46. Cambridge: Cambridge University Press. b) Koskenniemi, Martti. 2012. International Law in the World of Ideas. In The Cambridge Companion to International Law, ed. James Crawford and Martti Koskenniemi, pp. 47–63. Cambridge: Cambridge University Press. c) Mégret, Frédéric. 2012. International Law as Law. In The Cambridge Companion to International Law, ed. James Crawford and Martti Koskenniemi, pp. 64–92. Cambridge: Cambridge University Press. History (in which context founded, goals of the UN) a) Morris, Justin. 2018. Origins of the United Nations. In The Oxford Handbook on the United Nations, ed. Thomas G. Weiss and Sam Daws, pp. 40–58. Oxford: Oxford University Press. b) Klabbers, Jan. 2009. An Introduction to International Institutional Law, pp. 16–41. Cambridge: Cambridge University Press. Contemporary Role of UN today (concentration on crucial points and conflicts, what is the UN working on?) a) United Nations. 2017. Basic Facts about the United Nations, 42nd edn. New York: United Nations Department of Public Information, pp. 58–67 (Peace). Access via: https://www.un-ilibrary.org/content/books/9789210584906/read b) United Nations. 2017. Basic Facts about the United Nations, 42nd edn. New York: United Nations Department of Public Information, pp. 105–113 (Disarmament). Access via: https://www.un-ilibrary.org/content/books/9789210584906/read c) United Nations. 2017. Basic Facts about the United Nations, 42nd edn. New York: United Nations Department of Public Information, pp. 117–127 (Decolonisation). Access via: https://www.un-ilibrary.org/content/books/9789210584906/read

Time	Content / To dos	Literature/Notes/Homework
First session (2h) 09:10am – 11:10am	UN presentation plus discussion Method: student group presentations to be prepared before the seminar, each presentation 15min + 20min discussion	d) United Nations. 2017. Basic Facts about the United Nations, 42nd edn. New York: United Nations Department of Public Information, pp. 128–167 (Development). Access via: https://www.un-ilibrary.org/content/books/9789210584906/read e) United Nations. 2017. Basic Facts about the United Nations, 42nd edn. New York: United Nations Department of Public Information, pp. 197–221 (Human Rights). Access via: https://www.un-ilibrary.org/content/books/9789210584906/read
Second session (2h) 11:30am – 01:30pm (1h lunch break)	UN presentation plus discussion Method: student group presentations to be prepared before the seminar, each presentation 15min + 20min discussion	Structure and function (UN main organs: Security Council, General Assembly, ECOSOC Council, Secretariat, International Court, Trusteeship Council, agencies) a) Koskenniemi, Martti. 1995. The Police in the Temple Order, Justice and the UN. A Dialectical View. European Journal of International Law (6), 325–348. b) United Nations. 2017. Basic Facts about the United Nations, 42nd edn. New York: United Nations Department of Public Information, pp. 3–29 (UN-Charter, Structure and System). Access via https://www.un-ilibrary.org/content/books /9789210 584906/read c) Peterson, M. J. 2018. General Assembly. In The Oxford Handbook on the United Nations, ed. Thomas G. Weiss and Sam Daws, pp. 119–139. Oxford: Oxford University Press. d) Newman, Edward. 2018. Secretary-General. In The Oxford Handbook on the United Nations, ed. Thomas G. Weiss and Sam Daws, pp. 231–249. Oxford: Oxford University Press. e) Einsiedel, Von, and David M. Malone. 2018. Security Council. In The Oxford Handbook on the United Nations, ed. Thomas G. Weiss and Sam Daws, pp. 140–164. Oxford: Oxford University Press. Important documents (UN case studies: e.g. Women's rights/women's security, climate change, war crime/ conflict resolution) and how they were implemented

Time	Content / To dos	Literature/Notes/Homework
Second session (2h) 11:30am – 01:30pm (1h lunch break)	UN presentation plus discussion Method: student group presentations to be prepared before the seminar, each presentation 15min + 20min discussion	a) Riles, Annelise. 2006. [Deadlines]: Removing the Brackets on Politics in Bureaucratic and Anthropological Analysis. In Documents. Artifacts of Modern Knowledge, ed. Annelise Riles. Ann Arbor: University of Michigan Press. b) The Beijing Platform (document Riles refers to), see https://beijing20.unwomen.org/en/about c) United Nations 1995. Beijing Declaration and Platform for Action, for download at https://www.unwomen.org/en/digital-library/publications/2015/01/beijing-declaration preamble, Chapters 1, 2 and 3 Decision-making process (within the different UN committees, role of observer states) a) Rules of procedure of the General Assembly. https://www.un.org/en/ga/about/ropga/
Third session (2h) 03:00pm – 04:30pm	UN presentation plus discussion	-
-	-	Homework: • Read *Rules of Procedure Guide* (available at nmun.org) and note 2–3 questions/possible problems on the platform. • Read *Delegate Preparation Guide* (available at nmun.org) and note 2–3 questions/possible problems on the platform.
Second Day	**Modules 8a, 8b, 8c, 9, 10, 11**	-
First session 09:00am – 10:45am (90min + 15min break)	Outcome documents	-
Second session 10:45am – 12:15am (90min + 1h 15min lunch break)	Position papers and research	-

Time	Content / To dos	Literature/Notes/Homework
Third session 01:30pm – 04:00pm (90min)	Rules, voting	-
-	-	Homework: • Read *Position Paper Guide* (available at nmun.o rg) and note 2–3 questions/possible problems on the platform. • Write a preambular clause on your own research.
Third Day	**Modules 12, 13, 14**	**-**
First session 09:00am – 10:45am (90min + 15min break)	Speeches and speech training	-
Second session 10:45am – 12:15am (90min + 1h 15min lunch break)	Negotiation training	-
Third session 01:30pm – 04:00pm (90min)	Position paper	-
-	-	Homework: • Post questions/topics you want to focus on more on the project platform. • 3min – max 5min video recording of oneself (if I were China, preambular clause, make operative claims as a specific country, can be hypothetical). • Continue writing the hypothetical resolution by adding some hypothetical operative clauses.

Time	Content / To dos	Literature/Notes/Homework
Fourth Day	**Module 15**	**-**
First session 02:00pm – 03:45pm (90min + 15min break)	"Fill in blanks"	-
Second session 03:45pm – 05:15pm (90min + 15min break)	Conference dynamics	-
Third session 05:30pm – 07:00pm (90min)	Conclusion Evaluation Further procedure	-
-	-	Homework: • Work on position paper. • Find out possible allies and dependencies of your delegation (if assigned yet).
Additional sessions	**Modules 16, 17**	**-**
#1	Position paper edits and corrections	Peer review (one or two rounds of edits) and get feedback.
#2	Opening speech training	Practice opening speech and get feedback.

The second seminar plan (Table 12.2) is based on a preparatory seminar for MUN and MEU that was taught at Fulda UAS in the summer term 2025. The seminar had weekly sessions of 90 minutes in the first term to do the basic preparation. In the second term, which is not shown on this seminar plan, students prepare for specific simulations in block sessions. Again, the seminar does not have to be implemented in this form but can be taught in blocks or in a different rhythm as is most appropriate for each institution.

Table 12.2 Seminar plan for MUN and MEU seminars

Session	Content	Literature/Homework
Session 1	**Introduction**	-
-	Introduction Expectations Organisational issues	Welcome + Introductions Simulation script and discussion Read through simulation script in plenary (included in *Rules of Procedure Guide*)
-	-	*Students have to each select and present a text with a short (1 page) handout in groups of 2 students.*
Session 2	**What is the UN?**	-
-	Short presentations by students	Morris, Justin. 2018. *Origins of the United Nations.* In The Oxford Handbook on the United Nations, ed. Thomas G. Weiss and Sam Daws, pp. 40–58. Oxford: Oxford University Press. United Nations. 2017. *Basic Facts about the United Nations*, 42nd edn. New York: United Nations Department of Public Information, pp. 3–29 (UN-Charter, Structure and System). Access via https://www.un-ilibrary.org/content/books/9789210584906/read Newman, Edward. 2018. *Secretary-General.* In The Oxford Handbook on the United Nations, ed. Thomas G. Weiss and Sam Daws, pp. 231–249. Oxford: Oxford University Press. Von Einsiedel, Sebastian, and David M. Malone. 2018. *Security Council.* In The Oxford Handbook on the United Nations, ed. Thomas G. Weiss and Sam Daws, pp. 140–164. Oxford: Oxford University Press.
-	-	*Homework: Read the Delegate Preparation Guide and add 3 important questions/findings/things to remember in Moodle.*
Session 3	**The UN, its institutions and its procedures**	-
-	Rules, voting	-
-	UN Institutions continued – short presentations	Peterson, M. J. 2018. *General Assembly.* In The Oxford Handbook on the United Nations, ed. By Thomas G. Weiss and Sam Daws, pp. 119–139. Oxford: Oxford University Press.
-	-	*Homework: Read the Rules of Procedure Guide and add 3 important questions/findings/things to remember to the glossary in Moodle.*

Session	Content	Literature/Homework
Session 4	**Negotiation training**	-
-	Negotiations Lost at Sea	Lost at Sea
Session 5	**What is the EU?**	-
-	Short presentations by students	Hix, Simon, and Bjørn Høyland. 2022. *The Political System of the European Union*. 4th ed. London: Bloomsbury. Introduction Tömmel, Ingeborg. 2014. *The European Union: What It Is and How It Works*. Houndsmills: Palgrave Macmillan, Chapter 4 Costa, Olivier, and Brack, Nathalie. 2019. *How the EU Really Works*. London/New York, Routledge. Chapter 3–5
Session 6	**The UN, the EU and international law**	-
-	Short presentations by students	Klabbers, Jan. 2009. *An Introduction to International Institutional Law*, pp. 16–41. Cambridge: Cambridge University Press. Koskenniemi, Martti. 1995. *The Police in the Temple Order, Justice and the UN. A Dialectical View*. European Journal of International Law (6), 325–348. Azoulai, Loïc. 2016. "Integration Through Law" and Us. *IJCLAW* 14 (2), 449–63. https://doi.org/10.1093/icon/mow024. Tömmel, Ingeborg. 2014. *The European Union: What It Is and How It Works*. Houndsmills: Palgrave Macmillan, Chapter 5
Session 7	**The UN today**	-
-	Short presentations by students	United Nations. 2017. *Basic Facts about the United Nations*, 42nd edn. New York: United Nations Department of Public Information, pp. 58–67 (Peace). Access via: https://www.un-ilibrary.org/content/books/9789210584906/read United Nations. 2017. *Basic Facts about the United Nations*, 42nd edn. New York: United Nations Department of Public Information, pp. 128–167 (Development). Access via: https://www.un-ilibrary.org/content/books/9789210584906/read United Nations. 2017. *Basic Facts about the United Nations*, 42nd edn. New York: United Nations Department of Public Information, pp. 197–221 (Human Rights). Access via: https://www.un-ilibrary.org/content/books/9789210584906/read

Session	Content	Literature/Homework
-	-	*Homework: Find one UN resolution, EU directive or EU legislation online and note 3 findings on the formatting and structure in Moodle.*
Session 8	**Outcome documents**	-
-	Presentations and quizzes	Working papers Draft resolutions Resolutions EU regulations
Session 9	**The EU today**	-
-	Short presentations by students	Knodt, Michèle and Wiesner, Claudia. 2024. Introduction, in Wiesner, Claudia, and Michèle Knodt, eds. *The War Against Ukraine and the EU: Facing New Realities.* [S.l.]: Palgrave Macmillan. https://doi.org/10.1007/978-3-031-35040-5. European Commission: *Commission's Priorities 2024–2029*, https://commission.europa.eu/priorities-2024-2029_en
Session 10	**What is transnational politics?**	-
-	Short presentations by students	Riles, Annelise. 2006. *[Deadlines]: Removing the Brackets on Politics in Bureaucratic and Anthropological Analysis.* In Documents. Artifacts of Modern Knowledge, ed. Annelise Riles. Ann Arbor: University of Michigan Press. The *Beijing Platform* (document Riles refers to), see https://beijing20.unwomen.org/en/about United Nations 1995. *Beijing Declaration and Platform for Action*, for download at https://www.unwomen.org/en/digital-library/publications/2015/01/beijing-declaration preamble, Chapters 1, 2 and 3
-	-	*Homework: Read the Position Paper Guide and add 3 important questions/findings/things to remember to Moodle.*
Session 11	**Position papers & research**	-
-	Presentations Students' task	Position paper Research mission Research

Session	Content	Literature/Homework
-	Presentations Students' task	*Homework: Write at least three hypothetical preambular clauses on the topic you were assigned in the research activity. Follow the correct format and use the correct verbs provided in the Delegate Preparation Guide. The committee for this assignment is the General Assembly. Hand your sentences in via Moodle.*
Session 12	**Speeches and speech training**	-
-	Short speeches by students (to be continued in Session 13)	Speeches Input about speeches in general and structure of speeches Spontaneous speech training with feedback by peers and teachers
Session 13	**Closure and conference dynamics**	-
-	Second round speech training Wrap up and open questions Next semester	Useful tips

TEACHING MODULES

The following teaching modules indicate how to structure the training seminars. They also contain the necessary information to teach the modules and implement a thorough preparation seminar for a MEU or MUN.

Each module of the seminar is structured in the following way:

Goal: At the beginning of each module, we explain its goal or the aspired learning outcomes and the idea behind it, as well as the content that it should include in detail.

Structure of the session: This section provides an overview of the steps conducted in the module. The steps combine various teaching methods, from lectures to discussions in groups or plenum and group work to active learning measures and individual learning.

Teaching materials: This part contains presentation slides and links to material. The content for each presentation is shown in a table. It can be copied and pasted into your individual presentation.

Recommended duration: The timeframe for the module.

Checklists

We provide two checklists for each module: a student's checklist, including the preparation necessary for the module, and a teacher's checklist to prepare and teach the module. The checklists below may also support the teachers in communicating what is expected from the students and ensuring that all necessary steps have been taken in the preparation in order to achieve the goals of the respective session.

0 – PRE-MEETING

Goal: It is highly important to have a pre-meeting with the students before the actual start of the class. This pre-meeting mainly aims at introducing the seminar, discussing the goals and necessities, and allowing students and teachers to get acquainted. The pre-meeting should take place prior to the seminar, preferably two or three weeks before the start. However, the timing might be adjusted depending on your seminar plan.

During the pre-meeting, the students should understand what is expected from them in a simulation and what the seminar will look like in detail. All organisational issues regarding the seminar and the simulation should be presented. Assignments should be announced and the students' obligations for participation should be clearly communicated. Another aim is to create a respectful atmosphere where students can feel empowered and comfortable as some of the exercises required to prepare for a simulation, like public speaking, may push some students out of their comfort zone.

Structure of the session: Presentation "Pre-Meeting" – Read through NMUN code of conduct together – Provide assignments.

Teaching materials: Presentation "Pre-Meeting" (Table 12.3).

Recommended duration: 90 minutes.

Table 12.3 *Presentation "Pre-Meeting"*

Slide	Content
Slide 1	Model United Nations (MUN) = worldwide simulation of the work of the UN, in which students from all over the world participate and represent an assigned country in current political issues in one of the UN committees. It consists of formal debates and informal work phases and often a cultural programme. Today, more than 400,000 students from high school to university level participate in MUNs each year.

Slide	Content
Slide 1	National Model United Nations (NMUN): "The world's largest and oldest ongoing intercollegiate MUN." Originated as a Model Assembly of the League of Nations at Syracuse University in New York in 1927 and was re-established in 1946. UN participation: "NMUN has been a recognized non-governmental organisation (NGO) formally associated with the United Nations Department of Global Communications since 1982, and a UN Academic Impact Member since 2013" (NMUN 2020).
Slide 2	Model European Union (MEU) = a simulation of EU decision-making, e.g. the ordinary legislative procedure, or of EU negotiations in the Council. Duration from 45 minutes to three days. Roles such as Members of the European Parliament, ministers in the Council, commissioners, lobbyists, journalists.
Slide 3	What is at stake? Understand the nature of international, transnational, and global phenomena, develop a capacity for critical and autonomous thinking in relation to international events, debates and policies, and be sensitive to the dynamics of historical change. Critically analyse specific cases in the field of International Relations, apply the theoretical instruments acquired, be aware of the limitations of the theories that assume the existence of unitary actors, and defend the strict separation of the domestic sphere from the international. Learn the main theoretical currents that address the ethical dilemmas of International Relations and acquire instruments to analyse from the ethical point of view international problems. Gain basic knowledge of the EU and UN, the international Human Rights system, and international humanitarian law. Understand the role of institutions in the development of international action and politics. Acquire tools of applied research, preparation of reports, teamwork, work in a professional environment and knowledge of the internal functioning of the organisation, its tasks, and functions. Carry out with autonomy an activity of the professional world, either research or activities related to their area of study. NMUN code of conduct https://www.nmun.org/nmun-conduct-expectations.html
Slide 4	Introduction of the teachers to be assembled individually.
Slide 5	Detailed programme of the seminar, including dates. The programme should be provided in a PDF for the students and, if possible, be added to the institution's and/or student's electronic calendar.
Slide 6	Information about the MUN/MEU to be attended at the end of the seminar. To be selected individually by each student or for the whole group by the teacher.
Slide 7	Assignments for Modules 1–6.

Checklists

Tick off the following points on both checklists to check if the steps of the first module 0-Pre-meeting have been reached.

Students' checklist:

- Think about your own expectations for this MUN training seminar.
- Be aware of the assignments and what you have to hand in during the seminar.

Teacher's checklist:

- Start advertising the MUN training seminar at your institution and set a deadline for applications if those are necessary to participate in the seminar.
- Select the students by reading the applications (one page letter of motivation) if necessary.
- Divide the students into groups and assign texts to each group for the task to create a one-pager with the most essential points of a given text for the subsequent sessions (see also Modules 1–6).
- If online: Online conference tool to be set up beforehand and links for all sessions to be distributed to the students either via e-mail or via a joint platform.
- Provide the students with a list of references and literature based on the topic for their one-pager. Texts to be provided as copy or online for download.
- Edit/add/amend the presentation "Pre-Meeting".
- Coordinate and fix the dates for the seminar days and the MUN.
- Think about your own expectations for this seminar.

MODULES 1–6 – BUILDING THE FOUNDATION

Based on Module 0-Pre-meeting, the seminar starts with Modules 1–6 on topics regarding the EU, UN, and international law. Details, outlines, materials, and tips on these modules are provided below.

Goal: The main goal of Modules 1–6 is building a solid foundation. More specifically, students shall learn about international law, including its status, differences between hard and soft law, the pressure on states, different forms of resolution and treaties, and the role of nation states. They should get to know the UN and the EU, their history and contemporary role, their main organs, internal processes, as well as decision-making processes. Furthermore, they should become familiar with UN and EU documents such as resolutions, and take a look at case studies to see how the UN's and the EU's impact is in reality. Hence, these six modules lay out the vital basis for the next modules and provide the required background knowledge for the students to understand and contextualise the following content and activities. The content can be adjusted depending on the previous knowledge the students bring to the table. Nevertheless, if it is a diverse group or a group that has yet to study these aspects in detail, we recommend focusing on these topics.

Please note that for Modules 1–6, students were given reading lists with relevant literature in advance (see 0-Pre-meeting). They were divided into groups and assigned one text. Each group had to create a one-pager with the most important points of the given texts and upload it on a joint platform or hand it in via email.

Structure of the sessions: Reading texts in groups and preparing a one-pager in advance – Group discussion moderated by students – Collection of results in plenum.

Teaching materials: Reading list: This list can be updated or changed based on the teachers' background and the knowledge considered important for the seminar (as outlined in Table 12.4).

Recommended duration: 90 minutes per session (six in total).

Table 12.4 *Reading list for MUN/MEU seminars*

Topic	Texts
What is the UN?	Morris, Justin. 2018. Origins of the United Nations. In The Oxford Handbook on the United Nations, ed. Thomas G. Weiss and Sam Daws, pp. 40–58. Oxford: Oxford University Press. United Nations. 2017. Basic Facts about the United Nations, 42nd edn. New York: United Nations Department of Public Information, pp. 3–29 (UN-Charter, Structure and System). Access via https://www.un-ilibrary.org/content/books/9789210584906/read Newman, Edward. 2018. Secretary-General. In The Oxford Handbook on the United Nations, ed. Thomas G. Weiss and Sam Daws, pp. 231–249. Oxford: Oxford University Press. Von Einsiedel, Sebastian, and David M. Malone. 2018. Security Council. In The Oxford Handbook on the United Nations, ed. Thomas G. Weiss and Sam Daws, pp. 140–164. Oxford: Oxford University Press. Peterson, M. J. 2018. General Assembly. In The Oxford Handbook on the United Nations, ed. By Thomas G. Weiss and Sam Daws, pp. 119–139. Oxford: Oxford University Press.

Topic	Texts
What is the EU?	Hix, Simon, and Bjørn Høyland. 2022. The Political System of the European Union. 4th ed. London: Bloomsbury. Introduction Tömmel, Ingeborg. 2014. The European Union: What It Is and How It Works. Houndsmills: Palgrave Macmillan, Chapter 4 Costa, Olivier/Brack, Nathalie (2019). How the EU really works. London/New York, Routledge, Chapter 3–5.
The UN, the EU, and international law	Klabbers, Jan. 2009. An Introduction to International Institutional Law, pp. 16–41. Cambridge: Cambridge University Press. Koskenniemi, Martti. 1995. The Police in the Temple Order, Justice and the UN. A Dialectical View. European Journal of International Law (6), 325–348. Azoulai, Loïc. 2016. "Integration Through Law" and Us. IJCLAW 14 (2), 449–63. https://doi.org/10.1093/icon/mow024. Tömmel, Ingeborg. 2014. The European Union: What It Is and How It Works. Houndsmills: Palgrave Macmillan, Chapter 5.
The UN today	United Nations. 2017. Basic Facts about the United Nations, 42nd edn. New York: United Nations Department of Public Information, pp. 58–67 (Peace). United Nations. 2017. Basic Facts about the United Nations, 42nd edn. New York: United Nations Department of Public Information, pp. 128–167 (Development). United Nations. 2017. Basic Facts about the United Nations, 42nd edn. New York: United Nations Department of Public Information, pp. 197–221 (Human Rights).
The EU today	Knodt, Michèle and Wiesner, Claudia (2024): Introduction, In Wiesner, Claudia, and Michèle Knodt, eds. The War Against Ukraine and the EU: Facing New Realities. [S.l.]: Palgrave Macmillan. European Commission: Commission's Priorities 2024–2029, https://commission.europa.eu/priorities-2024-2029_en
What is transnational politics?	Riles, Annelise. 2006. [Deadlines]: Removing the Brackets on Politics in Bureaucratic and Anthropological Analysis. In Documents. Artifacts of Modern Knowledge, ed. Annelise Riles. Ann Arbor: University of Michigan Press. The Beijing Platform (document Riles refers to), see https://beijing20.unwomen.org/en/about United Nations 1995. Beijing Declaration and Platform for Action.

Checklists

Student's checklist:

- Get in touch with your group members for the assigned text.
- Read through assigned text(s).

- Produce a one-pager with your group members.
- Upload the one-pager on the joint platform or hand it in as explained by the teacher.
- Prepare important points for the group discussion on your assigned topic.

Teacher's checklist:

- Check if all groups found each other and handed in a one-pager.
- Provide one-pagers for everyone on the joint platform or in print.
- Prepare important points of each text for the discussion in the plenum.

MODULE 7 – DISCUSSION AND REFLECTION

Goal: The goal of Module 7 is to collect learning results and open questions from Modules 1 to 6, and to answer any open questions. This module is used as an opportunity for reflection to see if any issues that need further attention throughout the training seminar or any repetitions of already discussed content arose. It is also a way to ensure that the students have understood the main takeaways from Modules 1–6, thus have the required background knowledge, and are ready to continue with the seminar. Depending on the background knowledge the students may already have, this session can be used to refresh their memory and ensure they remember all the important takeaways outlined in Modules 1–6.
Structure of the session: Group discussion – Collection of results in plenum.
Teaching materials: None necessary.
Recommended duration: 45 to 60 minutes.

Checklists

Student's checklist:

- Think of questions or things that are left unclear after Modules 1–6.

Teacher's checklist:

- Think of probable questions from the students and possible answers as well as the most important aspects in your opinion.

MODULE 8A – OUTCOME DOCUMENTS PART 1 – WORKING PAPERS

Goal: The aim of Module 8a is to introduce working papers as the first phase of outcome documents at MUN simulations. Furthermore, students should know the differences between sponsors and signatories. They should be able to answer some basic questions in a quiz (example questions to be found in the Annex) at the end of the session to evaluate their learning progress and help memorise the content.
Structure of the session: Presentation "Working papers" – Quiz – Collection of questions in plenum.
Teaching materials: Presentation "Working papers" (Table 12.5).
Recommended duration: 45 to 60 minutes.

Table 12.5 Presentation "Working papers"

Slide	Content
Slide 1	Outcome documents at (N)MUN: working paper–draft resolution–resolution
Slide 2	What is a working paper? The document is still a work in progress and has not been accepted or coded by the dais (except perhaps informally during the editing process). The dais often has begun to make comments and edits to it. Working papers are not distributed to the committee formally by the dais. Delegates cannot lobby for specific working papers in formal speeches or refer to them by the informal code. As delegates work on working papers and receive edits from the dais, changes can be incorporated directly.
Slide 3	Working paper process: Once the agenda is adopted and the committee begins discussing a specific topic in both formal and informal sessions, groups of delegations will begin to work together on writing resolutions. During the initial writing and revision stages, these documents are referred to as working papers. They are drafted within a working group, and then discussed with a larger number of delegations and revised or merged as needed according to their input. Working papers are submitted to the dais for review and feedback. They may go through several revisions before being approved as a draft resolution. Changes can be incorporated directly into the working paper by the working group as the dais has not yet approved it. In order to ensure correct formatting and to discourage pre-written resolutions, delegates are required to use provided templates. The (N)MUN secretariat will not accept documents using a different template.

Slide	Content
Slide 4	Sponsors and signatories: The required number of signatures for a paper to be submitted is equivalent to 20% of the membership in attendance during the first committee session, or five – whichever is greater. The number of signatures can be any combination of sponsors and signatories, with at least one sponsor. The dais will provide the required number after the first session's roll call. When a working group feels that the working paper is complete, in the correct format, and ready to be considered by the entire body, they may submit it to the dais.
Slide 5	**Sponsors**: These are member states who created the content of a working paper, which means those who have actively contributed, e.g. added a clause, did additional work throughout the writing process. All sponsors must agree on any changes made to the paper. Sponsors can approve friendly amendments. They are responsible for ensuring that it will be voted on as a draft resolution and should be able to answer questions regarding it during session hours. Sponsors have to vote in favour of their working paper. Sponsorship has no other advantages at (N)MUN and is not an award criterion. Be careful of delegates who try to leech off your working paper as a sponsor but have not contributed anything. Do not hesitate to address this in a professionally and diplomatically way.
Slide 6	**Signatories**: These are member states or observers who are interested in bringing a working paper forward for consideration. They have not contributed anything but support the idea. May vote in favour of, against, or abstain on draft resolution during the voting procedure. It is important to have signatories and keep communication with them.
Slide 7	**Mergers**: Keeping your paper unique and specific is a way to avoid mergers. Mergers can be high-stress and much work, especially when merging with a large group. If you have to merge, make sure you go into it with a plan. Keep you work from being lost during the merger. You need to have all the sponsors agree with the merger.
Slide 8	Helpful Tips: • Working papers will be written on days 1–3 of the conference. • Once you have a working group, you can begin the writing process. • The dais will set deadlines for edits. There will be multiple rounds. • The first submission you send in may be basic, and that is okay. • Be realistic with your ideas and solutions. • Stay informed of the other working papers in the committee. There will not be multiple groups working on similar ideas, but you will be merged. • Be careful with how you share your working paper with other people. • Try to be on more than just one working paper. • Divide up the work so everyone has something to work on.

Checklists

Student's checklist:

- Have a first look at working papers in the *Delegate Preparation Guide* (available at nmun.org).

Teacher's checklist:

- Edit/add/amend the presentation "Working papers".
- Prepare questions and answers for the quiz (to be found in the Annex). The quiz can either be added to an online programme, to a Moodle course, or done in written and/or printed form.

MODULE 8B – OUTCOME DOCUMENTS PART 2 – DRAFT RESOLUTIONS

Goal: Module 8b aims to introduce draft resolutions as the second phase of outcome documents at MUN simulations. Students should know about the three main parts of a draft resolution and be able to distinguish friendly from unfriendly amendments. The students should be able to answer some basic questions in a quiz (example questions to be found in the Annex) at the end of the session to evaluate their learning progress and help memorise the content.
Structure of the session: Presentation "Draft resolutions" – Quiz – Collection of questions in plenum.
Teaching materials: Presentation "Draft resolutions" (Table 12.6).
Recommended duration: 45 to 60 minutes.

Table 12.6 Presentation "Draft resolutions"

Slide	Content

Slide 1	What is a draft resolution?
	All resolutions that have not yet been voted on
	One long sentence with sections separated by commas and semicolons
	Three main parts to a draft resolution:
	• Heading: committee and topic, signatories
	• Preamble: describes the current situation
	  • Preambulatory clauses: historical justifications for action
	• Operative section: describes actions to be taken
	  • Operative clauses: policies that the resolution is designed to create

Slide	Content
Slide 1	The second stage of the resolution writing process in which the committee may formally debate the merits of the document and begin the amendment process. Draft resolutions have been accepted by the dais, coded, and distributed to the committee for consideration before a substantive vote. Draft resolutions can only be altered through amendments.
Slide 2	Draft resolution process: After approval, the working paper is considered a draft resolution, assigned a number, and sent to the dais for posting online. At this time, the names of all sponsors and signatories are removed from the document by the secretariat. The electronic distribution of a draft resolution is considered its formal introduction to the committee – no procedural motion or reading of the draft resolution by a sponsor is necessary. All draft resolutions will be made available electronically. Once a draft resolution has been introduced, it is formally debated as part of the topic area, and amendments may be proposed. It can also be referred to in speeches made during formal debates. Process: working paper is approved – draft resolution is posted online – draft resolution is considered introduced.
Slide 3	**Amendment** = A clarification or a change in a draft resolution that incorporates additional interests or concerns after a working paper has been formally submitted to a committee. Preambular clauses of draft resolutions cannot be amended. There are two types of amendments: friendly and unfriendly.
Slide 4	**Friendly amendment**: A friendly amendment is proposed by any member of the body in writing and accepted by all original sponsors of the document (before voting). It is typically used to clarify the point. Upon agreement of all of the original sponsors, the change is incorporated into the proposal without a vote by the committee. If a sponsor of a working paper is not in the room to approve an amendment, even if every other sponsor approves, the amendment becomes unfriendly. Withdrawal of a paper is only possible through a friendly amendment.
Slide 5	**Unfriendly amendment**: An unfriendly amendment is a modification that does not have the support of all the sponsors. Unfriendly amendments must be formally submitted to the dais prior to the voting procedure, with the requisite number of signatures (20% or five) for the committee. A debate and a vote will be held on all unfriendly amendments to a draft resolution immediately before voting on the entire draft resolution. If multiple unfriendly amendments are submitted, the dais will call for a vote on each unfriendly amendment in order of most to least severe.
Slide 6	What can or cannot be amended? Amendments can be written to add, change, or remove one or several operative clauses or sub-clauses; they may add and/or strike words, phrases, or whole clauses. Amendments cannot be written to remove all operative clauses. Amendments cannot be written to add, change, or remove preambular clauses from draft resolutions. The secretariat will correct all spelling, format, and grammatical errors without an amendment.

Slide	Content
Slide 7	Helpful Tips: "Advertise" and gain support for your draft resolution to pass as a resolution: Communication skills are essential! Formal session: Highlight the key actions your draft resolution is proposing in speeches. Informal session: Go around and mingle with other delegates, present your draft resolution, and encourage their support. Preambles cannot be edited anymore. Only operatives can be amended. Be aware of any issues/concerns any countries have with your draft resolution, and make sure to address these as soon as possible.
Slide 8	There is a deadline for submitting papers to become draft resolutions, so be aware of your time and work efficiently. Once the dais has recognised all working papers as draft resolutions, you will enter the voting procedure to vote on them. You will be given some time before the voting procedure to review and discuss the draft resolutions, but after that time, there is no more discussing the draft resolutions with people in your committee. This is the time when unfriendly amendments come into play. Your committee will vote on the draft resolution presented. If it passes, it will be recognised as a resolution. If it fails, then it will not be recognised. It is important to discuss with your body any concerns with your paper prior to voting. Try to make amendments prior to the voting procedure.

Checklists

Student's checklist:

- Have a look at draft resolutions in the *Delegate Preparation Guide* (available at nmun.org).

Teacher's checklist:

- Edit/add/amend the presentation "Draft resolutions".
- Prepare questions and answers for the quiz (to be found in the Annex). The quiz can either be added to an online programme, to a Moodle course, or done in written and/or printed form.

MODULE 8C – OUTCOME DOCUMENTS PART 3 – RESOLUTIONS

Goal: The aim of Module 8c is to introduce resolutions as the third phase of outcome documents at MUN. Students should know the exact formatting

and structure of a resolution and distinguish between preambular and operative clauses. The students should answer some basic questions in a quiz (example questions to be found in the Annex) at the end of the session to evaluate their learning progress and help memorise the content.
Structure of the session: Presentation "Resolutions" – Quiz – Collection of questions in plenum.
Teaching materials: Presentation "Resolutions" (Table 12.7).
Recommended duration: 45 to 60 minutes.

Table 12.7 Presentation "Resolutions"

Slide	Content
Slide 1	What are resolutions? = Formal expressions of the opinion or will of United Nations organs/formal recommendations and/or decisions of the committee on the conference's topic. Used to apply political pressure on member states, express an opinion on an important issue, or recommend action to be taken – a form of political commitment. Only the Security Council may produce resolutions which are binding upon the member states (e.g. Chapter VII of the Charter and renewing mandates). Multiple resolutions may be adopted on a topic. At (N)MUN, all committees write resolutions and pre-written resolutions are forbidden. **Working paper**: Work-in-progress document; not accepted or coded by the dais; not distributed to the committee formally by the dais; delegates cannot lobby for specific working papers in formal speeches or refer to them by the informal code; changes can be incorporated directly. **Draft resolution**: Accepted by the dais, coded, and distributed to the committee for consideration ahead of a substantive vote; can only be altered through amendments. **Resolution**: Adopted by a substantive vote of the committee or adopted by acclamation; include all friendly and unfriendly amendments the committee has accepted in a substantive vote; reflect all successful divisions of the question.
Slide 2	Structure of a resolution: Three parts: • Heading • Preamble: background and foundation of a topic • Operative section: information on what action the body believes should be taken Header, resolution code, date, and committee are clearly labelled. One long sentence with commas and semicolons throughout. Only one period at the very end. Single spaced.

Slide	Content
Slide 3	**Preambular clauses** = framework through which the problems of the topic are viewed. To support the solutions proposed + to supply historical background for the issue + to justify the action to be taken. "Lack of precision" is appropriate, e.g. pointing to general ideas related to certain issues. Elements: • Charter of the United Nations: to establish the basis for the committee's approach to the topic; Charter generally and/or to specific articles or chapters. • Relevant international legal precedents/resolutions from UN entities: to summarise the existing efforts to address the topic at hand, e.g. conventions, resolutions, international documents. • Observations regarding the topic under discussion: to provide an overview of the content or driving ideas of the resolution; specifically refer to factual situations/statistics/incidents. Begin with present participles (written in italics) and are always followed by a comma, e.g. *Recognising* that poverty eradication and the achievement and preservation of peace are mutually reinforcing and also recognising that peace is inextricably linked to equality between women and men and to development Listed with no numbers or bulletins. A single line between each clause. List of preambular clauses in the *Delegate Preparation Guide* (available at nmun.org).
Slide 4	**Operative clauses** = what the committee is going to do on the topic. A logical progression of sequentially numbered operative clauses. Language should suggest action going forward: vague, e.g. denunciation of a particular situation or a call for negotiations; specific, e.g. as a call for a ceasefire or a monetary commitment for a particular project. Clauses may recommend, urge, condemn, encourage, request specific actions, or state an opinion regarding an existing situation. Sub-clauses to provide further detail for complex ideas: Augment an operative clause to explain a whole idea/proposal and form a complete clause; Each sub-clause must logically continue the parent operative clause and exhibit a parallel structure; At least two sub-clauses if employed.Begin with an active, present tense verb (in italics) followed by a semicolon, with a period placed after the final clause, e.g. 1. *Urges* all Governments to fully implement Security Council resolution 1325 (2000) by: 1. Developing national action plans with budgetary allocations that identify concrete strategies for national-level implementation; 2. Developing formal consultation mechanisms to support civil society engagement and capacity-building in post-conflict peacebuilding processes, with a particular focus on women's organisations. List of operative clauses in the *Delegate Preparation Guide* (available at nmun .org).

Slide	Content
Slide 5	Example *Recognising* that Public-Private Partnerships (PPPs) are significant and that relevant private actors that can contribute their knowledge, competencies, and expertise to solve sustainability challenges *Proposes* a framework to include marginalised groups in entrepreneurial activities through cooperating with PPPs in areas including, but not limited to: a. Incentivising private firms to foster a positive environment for marginalised communities, as well as a business framework based on inclusion, equal opportunity, and transparency b. Providing education on business skills and professional development through various mechanisms, such as i. Mobile workshops ii. Teleconferencing iii. Webinars iv. Grassroots Programs c. Providing institutional support to ensure that formal barriers are not barring marginalised communities from participating, basing itself on human rights and equality of opportunity d. Incorporating the individuals from these marginalised groups into their own business activities as well as in the formal and informal economies
Slide 6	**Do's**: Double-check grammar, punctuation, spelling; Format your position paper to the associated template; Do plenty of research; Stay within the character of your country; Be proactive. Whether it be during committee or the writing process; Be respectful; Remain in decorum during all committee sessions. **Don'ts**: Repeat things that have already been done; Be vague; Break character; Try and do things that are outside your committee's mandate; Mix up your preambles and operatives; Attack any member state in your papers; Argue with your dais over any edits; Steal ideas or plagiarise; DO NOT GO TO CONFERENCE WITH ANY SORT OF PRE-WRITTEN CLAUSES/ RESOLUTION.
Slide 7	Helpful Tips: If using Google docs, be very aware of who has access and what sort of access they have. The editing, suggesting, and view-only features of Google docs are great. Bring a USB stick! Use your research binder. You can get overwhelmed during the entire process, so take care of yourself. Stay in contact with your head delegate, and communicate if you have any problems or concerns. REVIEW! REVIEW! REVIEW! Do your ideas make sense? Are they new ideas? Are they realistic? Are you within committee mandate? Country character? Is your solution one that the entire international body can adopt? Does it flow and make sense?

Checklists

Student's checklist:

- Have a first look at resolutions in the *Delegate Preparation Guide* (available at nmun.org).

Teacher's checklist:

- Edit/add/amend the presentation "Resolutions".
- Prepare questions and answers for the quiz (to be found in the Annex). The quiz can either be added to an online programme, to a Moodle course, or done in written and/or printed form.

MODULE 8D – OUTCOME DOCUMENTS PART 4 – EU REGULATIONS

Goal: The aim of Module 8d is to introduce EU regulations and get to know the EU's ordinary legislative procedure. Students should know the exact formatting and structure of an EU regulation. They should furthermore be able to explain the ordinary legislative procedure and the various players participating in it.
Structure of the session: Presentation "EU Regulations" – Collection of questions in plenum.
Teaching materials: Presentation "EU Regulations" (Table 12.8).
Recommended duration: 45 to 60 minutes.

Table 12.8 Presentation "EU Regulations"

Slide	Content
Slide 1	Ordinary legislative procedure Based on Article 294 Treaty on the Functioning of the European Union (TFEU) European Parliament and Council adopt law together. Commission has the right to initiative and proposes a legislative proposal for a regulation, directive, or decision. Up to three hearings are possible.

Slide	Content
Slide 2	What are regulations? Part of the EU's secondary law, derive from EU treaties as primary law To distinguish fromdirectives or white papers Legal acts defined in Article 288 TFEU. Regulations are binding in their entirety to EU institutions, member states, and individuals. Addressed to abstract categories of persons. Directly applicable in all member states: no need for transposing into national law; directly invocable rights and obligations before national courts (EUR-Lex 2025). Article 290 TFEU: "1. A legislative act may delegate to the Commission the power to adopt non-legislative acts of general application to supplement or amend certain non-essential elements of the legislative act." Article 291 TFEU: "2. Where uniform conditions for implementing legally binding Union acts are needed, those acts shall confer implementing powers on the Commission, or, in duly justified specific cases and in the cases provided for in Articles 24 and 26 of the Treaty on European Union, on the Council."
Slide 3	Formal structure of an EU directive: Preamble: explanation of the background, objectives and legal basis. Articles (1) ongoing: justification of the need for the directive and the expected effects. Second set of articles: the actual provisions of the regulation in chapters, sections, and articles. Annexes (optional): additional documents, such as forms, tables or instructions. Date of adoption and signatures.
Slide 4	Other possible outcome documents of MEU could be: White Papers Proposals of the European Council Conclusions of the European Council Newspaper articles or other journalistic artifacts

Checklists

Student's checklist:

- Have a look at the EU's ordinary legislative procedure by doing a search on the internet.

Teacher's checklist:

- Edit/add/amend the presentation "EU regulations".

MODULE 9 – POSITION PAPER

Goal: Module 9 provides all the information necessary to write a position paper. Students should know what a position paper is, how it is formatted and structured, and what information it has to contain. This session is vital as it provides the necessary background knowledge and foundation needed for a follow-up module on position papers.
Structure of the session: Presentation "Position Paper" – Collection of open questions in plenum.
Teaching materials: Presentation "Position Paper" (Table 12.9).
Recommended duration: 45 to 60 minutes.

Table 12.9 Presentation "Position Paper"

Slide	Content
Slide 1	What is a position paper? = A paper in which a member state or observer sets out its position on a set of topics. Based on the topics that are outlined in the Committee Background Guide (if available). Only one position paper per committee – even if there are two delegates. After the deadline: All submitted position papers will be posted online, and delegates should read all position papers from their committee! Includes recommendations for actions to be taken by the committee in addressing the topic moving forward. In addition, it may include new information regarding the member state's history with the issue; endorsed conventions and/or resolutions; quotes taken from speeches by heads of government/member state documents.
Slide 2	Solution thinking: What is being done to address the issue? What more can be done? How can the international community work in unity to address these issues? What can your member state do? Have they addressed the issue? Where are the areas of improvement? What systems or organisations are already set up that address this topic? Are there any areas they can expand on?
Slide 3	Begin with a brief introduction Structure for each topic: 1. Importance of the topic (provide the context): Describe the context, explain international and national precedents, work of the international community (international and regional conventions, treaties, declarations, resolutions, and other precedents).

Slide	Content
Slide 3	2. International and national precedents: Clear and concise policy statement representing the relevant views, positions, aims, and actions of your assigned member state. 3. Solutions, actions, and recommendations: Give specific proposals and suggestions on how to address the topic going forward.
Slide 4	Your member state's position / Your member state's history relating to the issue / Areas for negotiation and recommendations for change.
Slide 5	**Do's**: Be specific and direct with your argument; Be action and solution orientated; Use relevant resolutions; Analyse; Use the appropriate language; Follow the correct format. **Don'ts**: Be fluffy; List irrelevant information and resolutions; Go outside your member states and committee's mandates; Reiterate the Background Guide; Use less than two pages.

Checklists

Student's checklist:

- Read the *Position Paper Guide* (available at nmun.org).

Teacher's checklist:

- Edit/add/amend the presentation "Position Paper".

MODULE 10 – RESEARCH

Goal: The goal of Module 10 is that students should conduct a short research project on their own to gather experience. They should know the difference between research for a term/written paper and a position paper, as well as where to find the necessary information to conduct the research for a position paper.

Structure of the session: Research activity – Presentation "Research" – Collection of questions in plenum.

Teaching materials: Presentation "Research"; Position Paper Research Checklist (Table 12.10).

Recommended duration: 45 to 60 minutes.

Table 12.10 Presentation "Research"

Slide	Content
Slide 1	Research Process United Nations or European Union – General background member state – Committee – Committee's topics – Member state's position
Slide 2	Research for (N)MUN and MEU: No classical literature or information research, like for a term paper. Gathering information about your assigned country to prepare your part in the simulation. One specific research question vs. background and context of your country's positions. Results are used as the background for your position-taking.
Slide 3	Documents to do research: UN or EU documents and information UN resolutions and reports on the issues under discussion EU white papers and laws Other articles, periodicals, books, and internet resources (e.g. databases) Contacting the delegation's permanent mission to the UN Contacting EU contact points or EU institutions
Slide 4	Useful documents and links – United Nations United Nations Website: https://www.un.org/ United Nations Today: https://untoday.org/ UN digital Library: https://digitallibrary.un.org UN global issues overview: https://www.un.org/en/global-issues Various research Guides: http://research.un.org/en?b=s&group_id=2087 The World Fact Book (CIA): https://www.cia.gov/the-world-factbook/ Permanent Missions to the United Nations: https://www.un.org/dgacm/en/content/protocol/permanent-missions United Nations Department of Global Communications: https://www.un.org/en/sections/departments/department-global-communications/ The Europa World Yearbook: https://www.europaworld.com/ United Nations Handbook: https://www.mfat.govt.nz/en/peace-rights-and-security/our-work-with-the-un/un-handbook?m=72857#search:dW4gaGFuZGJvb2s= GA Handbook: https://unitar.org/sites/default/files/media/publication/doc/un_pga_new_handbook_0.pdf United Nations Chronicle: https://www.un.org/en/chronicle/ New York Times: https://www.nytimes.com/ The Economist: https://www.economist.com/ Member States on the Record: https://www.un.org/en/library/unms
Slide 5	Useful documents and links – European Union Official website: https://european-union.europa.eu/index_en EU document register: https://www.consilium.europa.eu/en/documents/public-register/public-register-search/ EUR-Lex: https://eur-lex.europa.eu/homepage.html?locale=en EU law tracker: https://law-tracker.europa.eu/homepage Publications Office of the European Union: https://op.europa.eu/en/home

Slide	Content
Slide 5	EU countries: https://european-union.europa.eu/principles-countries-history/eu-countries_en News and Events page of the EU: https://european-union.europa.eu/news-and-events_en EU Parliament Research Service: https://epthinktank.eu/ Joint Research Centre: https://commission.europa.eu/about/departments-and-executive-agencies/joint-research-centre_en European Council for Foreign Relations: https://ecfr.eu/ Politico EU: https://www.politico.eu EUobserver: https://euobserver.com/ Euractiv: https://www.euractiv.com/ Euronews: https://www.euronews.com/ New Eastern Europe: https://neweasterneurope.eu/ New Europe: https://www.neweurope.eu/ Financial Times: https://www.ft.com/europe

Checklists

Student's checklist:

- Read the *Position Paper Guide* again (available at nmun.org).

Teacher's checklist:

- Edit/add/amend the presentation "Research".
- Provide various research links in a link list or upload them on the joint platform.

MODULE 11 – RULES OF PROCEDURE

Goal: The rules of procedure are to be explained in Module 11. Students should know what happens at an MUN and MEU and get a first impression by reading a simulation script. They should know the differences between formal and informal sessions, between being "present" and "present and voting" at roll call, and between substantive and procedural votes. Furthermore, they should be informed about etiquette and proper behaviour at an MUN and MEU.
Structure of the session: Presentations "Rules of procedure" – Read through simulation script in groups – Discussion in plenum.
Teaching materials: Presentation "Rules of procedure" (Table 12.11).
Recommended duration: 45 to 60 minutes.

Table 12.11 Presentation "Rules of procedure"

Slide	Content
Slide 1	MUN conference flow Opening ceremony Committee called in session Roll call The speakers list opened Agenda-setting speeches Motion for informal session Motion for setting the agenda Speakers list is cleared, and a new list is created
Slide 2	Formal session: • Motions are used. • No talking to other delegates/partner. • No technology of any kind is allowed to be opened and used. • The only person allowed to be talking is either the dais or the delegate giving a speech. • Delegates must be seated. • Delegates must have your blazers or jackets on at all times. Informal session: • Motions are not used. • Delegates can walk around in the room and talk to other delegates. • This is where a large majority of the writing will take place. • Bilateral negotiations. • Lobbying for one's draft resolutions. • Delegates remain in decorum and character throughout all sessions. They can only break character when your committee session is on a lunch break or has ended for the day.
Slide 3	Roll call: Multiple times throughout the conference • Two ways to answer roll call: "Present": You can vote, YES or NO or ABSTAIN. • "Present and Voting": You can only vote YES or NO. Your voting status mainly depends on your member state. It is very crucial to note who is "Present and Voting" during the voting procedure. If you are ever late and miss roll call, you will need to send a note to the dais and let them know.
Slide 4	Placard (only for physical conferences): Always know where your placard is. Without your placard you will not be able to vote, make any motions, etc. If you lose it, you will have to pay to get a new one. Be sure to take care of it so it always looks presentable. Communicate with your partner who has the placard. Remember to bring it with you when you leave in the morning for committee.

Slide	Content
Slide 5	Making Motions: Be sure you know what you want to say. Once you are called, stand up, speak loud and clear, with a levelled voice. Always begin with mentioning your member state, e.g. "France moves to…" or "Thank you, Honourable Chair, the French Republic moves to…" Keep it short! When motioning for an informal session, be mindful of your committee schedule. Listen to what other motions have been made, so you are not repeating something already motioned or something that the dais has already denied. Motions at (N)MUN see *Rules of Procedure Guide* (available at nmun.org).
Slide 6	MEU often bases its rules on Robert's Rules (https://robertsrules.com/). See also Administration Team of the EU Delegation to the United States (2022) and Buonanno et al. (2025) for MEU specific guides.
Slide 7	Voting: Procedural: YES or NO. Abstentions are not allowed. For Motions. Substantive: YES or NO or ABSTAIN. For Resolutions. Division of the question. You MUST vote at all times. Votes are taken by placard unless a roll call vote is requested.
Slide 8	Technology (only for physical conferences). Formal sessions: Absolutely no technology opened or being used. Use a research binder! Informal sessions: Free to use any technology.
Slide 9	Communication with the dais: Send notes, e.g. to be added to the speakers list. Always ask: "Permission to approach…" Approach from the front of the table. After the session has ended for the day, you will have to approach them during the next session. If you happen to run into your dais outside of committee, do not talk about committee.
Slide 10	Committee etiquette: Always be on time (early). Sit front and centre or fairly close to that area. Always have your placard. Be quiet during formal sessions. Do not talk to other delegates, and refrain from speaking to your partner. Use notes to communicate. Clean up any garbage you have. Always abide by the dress code.

Slide	Content
Slide 11	Speech procedure: Begin all speeches with "Thank you, Honourable Chair…" or "Honourable Chair." Structure your speeches so they flow and are as straightforward as possible. Avoid too much fluffy material or talking too much about things that are not important to your speech. It should be structured similarly to how you would structure an essay. Beginning (intro), middle (main and most important part of speech), and end (thank-you). The intro and outro should be short so they do not use too much time from your speaking time.

Checklists

Student's checklist:

- Read the *Rules of Procedure Guide* (available at nmun.org).

Teacher's checklist:

- Edit/add/amend the presentation "Rules of procedure"
- Upload simulation script on a joint platform for the students or print it out for the students.
- Prepare the simulation script which is included in the *Rules of Procedure Guide* (available at nmun.org) by marking important passages that should be highlighted.

MODULE 12 – SPEECHES

Goal: Gaining a first experience in public speaking is the aim of Module 12. Students should know the structure of a speech and the differences between various types of speeches at an MUN and MEU. In spontaneous speech training, they will be able to get first-hand experience in public speaking with only short preparation and constructive feedback from their peers and their teacher to improve their skills.
Structure of the session: Presentation "Speeches" – Speech training in groups – Collection of open questions in plenum.
Teaching materials: Presentation "Speeches" (Table 12.12).
Recommended duration: 45 to 60 minutes.

Table 12.12 Presentation "Speeches"

Slide	Content
Slide 1	Speech structure **Intro**: "Thank you, Honourable Chair…" or "Honourable Chair…"; "Fellow delegates…"; Mention your country's name (mention the full name once, use a short name afterward). **Middle**: Largest and most important part of your speech; Ideas, solutions, things you are working on. **Outro**: Always thank the body; Can conclude by inviting delegates to approach you during the next informal session.
Slide 2	Agenda-setting speech: Know the order you want to set the agenda and stick with it. Make sure your speech clearly communicates the order. Explain why the topic you want to discuss first is the most important. Invite other member states to approach you during the next informal session to discuss further. Note: Once you have set the agenda order, you should not be referring to the other topics presented to the body to discuss.
Slide 3	Speeches at the beginning of the conference: Once you have set the agenda order, you will begin with speeches on the first topic. Avoid reiterating why the topic is important. Introduce your ideas. Invite delegates to approach you during the next informal session to discuss your ideas further. Listen to the speeches being made by other delegates. A good way to find out if other delegations have similar ideas.
Slide 4	Speeches during working paper/groups: Mention your working group and the direction that your working paper is going. Make sure to communicate with your sponsors about what they are talking about in their speeches to avoid repetition. Gain support from the body for your working paper (signatories), but do not refer to your paper by the informal code (if the dais assigned one)! You can give recognition to the other sponsors from your group for their efforts on the working paper. If you have an area (or a breakout room) your group is meeting to work, invite member states to meet there. Once you have submitted your working paper, and it has been given a code, check with your dais if it is okay to refer to it by that code.
Slide 5	Draft resolution speeches: Sell your draft resolution! Gain support from the body. Highlight the importance of your draft resolution. Communicate with sponsors to avoid repetition. You can divide the draft resolution between the sponsors, and everyone highlights a different part. Invite member states to read over your draft resolution and approach you with any questions or concerns.

Slide	Content
Slide 6	Public speaking tips Three parts of a speech: 1. **Hook**: An engaging way to grab your audience's attention. The Question, quote, statistic, story. 2. **Point**: Your country's policy on the topic. State your country's policy on the topic. Offer 2–3 reasons explaining why your country has adopted this policy. 3. **Call** to Action: Possible solutions to the topic. Explain your specific solution to the problem. (Source: https://www.carthage.edu/community/model-un/high-school-conference/conference-training-resources/public-speaking-tips/)
Slide 7	Confidence: Research and prepare well and speak as if you know you are undoubtedly right. Stand up straight, shoulders back and keep eye contact with the audience. Clear: Always speak slowly at a levelled tone with a loud voice and use the total amount of time. Know your terminology. Try to enunciate words properly. Concise: Present in a clean and clear-cut fashion. Be brief and to the point: Do not use unnecessary words and information. Do not ramble on about the topic. Constructive Start with a solid foundation that brings together all of your ideas. Present your points, and then connect them by reviewing what you said. Say it once, say it and review it, then say it again.
Slide 8	"Con Passion": Speak from the heart and with passion. Critique: It is better to offer constructive critique than to criticise. Remember that this is a diplomatic speech. Avoid using filler words such as "umm," "well," "it is sort-a like," "it's kinda like", "you know," "I think," "I'm sorry," "just," "but," "should," "like," "um," and, "a," etc. Make use of pauses: A pause after a thought and prefacing a response to a question holds the attention of the listener and allows you to take a deep breath. Breathe from the diaphragm. Breathe deeply and often. Pace yourself: Do not talk too fast or too slow. Practice your speech and take your time. Position yourself powerfully: No slouching, tilting your head, and crossing your arms or legs. Stand up straight, shoulders back, feet firmly planted and knees unlocked. Project your presence: Speak from your diaphragm not your throat. Keep the sound in the low to medium range. Speak loudly enough to be easily heard. Focus on speaking with enthusiasm and energy and create colour with your voice. Use gestures: Do not be a statue. Consider occasionally exaggerating a gesture if it feels natural to you. Connect: Use a lot of eye contact. Be confident: If a mistake happens, do not let it irritate you too much.

Slide	Content
Slide 9	Tips for when you are flustered: Whatever you do, do not apologise if you stumble on a word or mess something up. Take a second, collect your thoughts, and continue. If you are flustered to the extent, you think you need to end your speech, have your emergency line ready. E.g. "Please approach us during the next informal session if you would like to discuss these ideas further. Thank you!" Always thank the body before taking your seat.
Slide 10	Helpful links Speaking during formal session: http://srmun.org/videos.php https://bestdelegate.com/how-to-write-an-opening-speech/ Videos: 3 Tips to Improve Your Body Language When Giving MUN Speeches + 3 Tips to Improve the Way You Sound When Giving MUN Speeches: https://mun.bestdelegate.com/video-gallery/

As this session foresees speech training, we have provided potential topics for you below. However, you may choose different topics as this exercise mainly aims at practicing the students' public speaking skills. Nevertheless, we have chosen the topics below to help the students in quickly drafting a speech that refers to topics which may be addressed at a MUN. As this will potentially be the first exercise of this kind, the topics shall be broad and the questions not too long to ensure that students do not get overwhelmed. If you are planning on conducting this exercise several times, or if the students are already trained in public speaking and speech writing, feel free to use more complex questions or provide additional information, for example, already assign the students a specific country and let them argue the question from this perspective. We recommend implementing this practice throughout the course to build on the developed skills and further strengthen the students' experience and confidence.

Topics for Speech Training

- What is international justice?
- Why do we need the UN?
- Why do we need the EU?
- Why do we need more multilateralism?
- Why do we need less multilateralism?
- Why is state sovereignty important?
- Why should states interfere in other states' issues?

- Why do we need more representation of marginalised groups within the UN?
- How should we deal with power imbalances in the EU?
- What is the importance of the UN General Assembly?
- What is international peace?
- What is the Common Market?
- What are the challenges the UN is facing?
- What are the challenges the EU is facing?

Checklists

Student's checklist:

- Watch short speeches by politicians at International Organisations.

Teacher's checklist:

- Edit/add/amend the presentation "Speeches".
- Prepare topics and a stopwatch for speech training.

MODULE 13 – NEGOTIATIONS

Goal: The goal of Module 13 is to introduce negotiations. Students will be given tips to negotiate successfully in an international environment. In an activity called "Lost at Sea", they will experience negotiations themselves and gather important personal insights into negotiations.
Structure of the session: Presentation "Negotiations" – Discussion in plenum – "Lost at Sea" – Reflection in plenum.
Teaching materials: Presentation "Negotiations" (Table 12.13); "Lost at Sea": To be found here: https://insight.typepad.co.uk/insight/2009/02/lost-at-sea-a-team-building-game.html for download.
Recommended duration: 45 to 60 minutes.

Table 12.13 Presentation "Negotiations"

Slide	Content
Slide 1	Negotiating Tips • Do not be afriad to ask for what you want. • Be assertive and challenge everything. • Practice expressing your feelings without anxiety or anger.

Slide	Content
Slide 1	• Use "I" statements. • Use your right to question. • Be quiet and listen. • Ask probing questions and then shut up. • Follow the 70/30 Rule. The others speak 70% of the time, you only 30%. • Ask open-ended questions.
Slide 2	• Do your homework. • Gather as much pertinent information as possible prior to your negotiation.Always be willing to walk away. • Never negotiate without options. • Do not be in a hurry. • The other negotiator might offer concessions to provide you with an incentive to say YES. • Aim high and expect the best outcome. • Open up with an extreme position. Sellers should ask for more than they expect to receive, and buyers should offer less than they are prepared to pay.
Slide 3	• Focus on the other side's pressure, not yours. • Ask, "What is the pressure on the other side in this negotiation?" • Look for ways to exploit that pressure to achieve a better result for yourself. • Show the other person how their needs will be met. • Seek to understand the other negotiator and show them ways to feel satisfied. • Do not give anything away without getting something in return. • Always tie a string: "I will do this if you do that." • Do not take the issues or the other person's behaviour personally. • If someone is rude or difficult to deal with, try to understand their behaviour and do not take it personally.

Checklists

Student's checklist:

- Watch/read news on current international negotiations.

Teacher's checklist:

- Edit/add/amend the presentation "Negotiations" (example can be found in the Annex).
- Prepare "Lost at Sea" activity by either printing the instructions to distribute in the session or uploading them on the joint platform.

MODULE 14 – POSITION PAPER (2)

Goal: Module 14 is a repetition of position papers. Based on their knowledge from Module 9, students will correct example position papers to become familiar with structure and formatting and to know more about possible pitfalls and mistakes.
Structure of the session: Position paper correction activity – Reflection in plenum – Collection of open questions in plenum.
Teaching materials: Position papers to correct, for example, from previous MUN conferences or examples from the NMUN website.
Recommended duration: 45 to 60 minutes.

Checklists

Student's checklist:

- Read through the *Position Paper Guide* (available at nmun.org) again to refresh your memory.
- Have another look at the presentation "Position Paper" from Module 9.

Teacher's checklist:

- Look for position papers from previous MUNs and provide them on the joint platform or print them for your students.

MODULE 15 – FILL IN THE BLANKS

Goal: Module 15 consists of a reflection on the whole preparation seminar. Students should reflect on what is still unclear and where they need more information or practice. This will allow the teachers to adapt the last sessions accordingly or provide additional resources on a joint platform or via email.
Structure of the session: Group work and collecting open questions – Answering questions in plenum – Providing information about further steps.
Teaching materials: None needed.
Recommended duration: 45 to 60 minutes.

Checklists

Student's checklist:

- Think of your major learnings from the whole seminar.
- Think of open questions and additional resources that might be helpful for you.

Teacher's checklist:

- Prepare the further planning for MUN or MEU participation.

MODULE 16 – TOPIC PREPARATIONS

Goal: The aim of Module 16 is to prepare the students for the conference topics. In a simulation, the topics can be chosen either by the students themselves, by the dais, by the teachers, or can be given when participating in an already organised MUN or MEU. Students should know the basics of the topic (What is it about? Why is it essential? What are current developments? What does it relate to?) and where/how to conduct more research for their position paper on the topic. Additional short speech training will help students become more confident in public speaking. It is recommended to do a second preparatory session in case there is more than one conference topic.
Structure of the session: Reading of material and answering questions – Group discussion on the assignments – Collection of results in plenum – Input from teachers – Speech training in groups – Concluding discussion in plenum.
Teaching materials: Important material to be read for the second conference topic and questions related to it. Further input on the first topic.
Recommended duration: 120 minutes.

Checklists

Student's checklist:

- Read the material provided on the conference topic.
- Do additional research on the conference topic on the internet.

Teacher's checklist:

- Choose/find out and prepare the conference topic and research material for it.

REFERENCES

Administration Team of the EU Delegation to the United States (2022). Organising a Model EU: Guide for Educators. Available online at https://www.eeas.europa.eu/sites/default/files/documents/2024/Organising%20a%20Model%20EU_%20Guide%20for%20Educators.pdf (accessed 6/5/2025).
Buonanno, Laurie/Cugleşan, Natalia/Nugent, Neill/Rabb, Gregory/Rushboldt, Raymond/Smith, Derek (2025). The IEUSS Guide to the Saturday Suny Model European Union 2nd edition. Available online at https://ieuss.buffalostate.edu/sites/ieuss/files/documents/SATURDAY%20SUNYMEU_Guidelines_2025_FINALVer.pdf (accessed 6/5/2025).
National Model United Nations (2020). Mission & History. Available online at https://www.nmun.org/about-nmun/mission-and-history.html (accessed 10/19/2020).
National Model United Nations (2022). Delegate Preparation Guide. National Model United Nations. Available online at https://www.nmun.org/conferences/new-york/prepare-for-committee/committee-materials.html (accessed 2/7/2023).

ANNEX

Quizzes with Example Questions

In Modules 8a, 8b, and 8c we propose to make use of a quiz to evaluate the students' learning progress. The quiz also serves as a repetition of the content and facilitates memorising the different outcome documents. We provide questions as well as correct and false answers for three quizzes: a quiz on working papers, a quiz on draft resolutions, and a quiz on resolutions. The questions can either be imported into an online programme, printed on paper or used orally in the session. X marks a correct answer, O marks an incorrect answer.

Quiz Working Papers

1. What are the outcome documents of a (N)MUN conference? (Multiple correct answers)
   a) Working papers X
   b) Position papers O
   c) Draft resolutions X
   d) Resolutions X
2. True or false? Delegates can already lobby for specific working papers in their formal speeches.
   - False!
3. How can changes be incorporated into the working paper?
   a) By a vote in formal session O
   b) Without a vote, directly into the working paper X
   c) Only by the dais O
4. Write answer yourself: Who creates the content of a working paper?
   - Sponsors
5. What are the characteristics of a signatory? (Multiple correct answers)
   a) They support the content of the working paper X
   b) They did not play an instrumental role in creating the content X
   c) They may ultimately disagree with the content X
   d) They are interested in bringing the working paper forward for consideration by the committee X

Quiz Draft Resolutions

1. What has to happen in order for a working paper to be accepted as a draft resolution? (Multiple correct answers)
   a) Accepted by the dais X

   b) Majority vote O
   c) Coded X
   d) Distributed to the committee X
2. Write answer yourself: How can draft resolutions be altered?
   - Through amendments
3. When is a draft resolution considered to be formally introduced to the committee?
   a) After a formal reading by one of the sponsors O
   b) After the dais has announced it O
   c) After the electronic distribution X
   d) After a procedural vote O
4. Which part of a draft resolution can be amended?
   a) The whole document O
   b) Only the preambular clauses O
   c) Only the operative clauses X
   d) Draft resolutions can't be amended anymore O
5. Amendments can be written to… (multiple correct answers)
   a) Add/change/remove operative sub-clauses X
   b) Remove all operative clauses O
   c) Correct spelling or grammar errors O
   d) Strike word, phrases or whole clauses X

Quiz Resolutions

1. Which resolutions are legally binding? (Write answer yourself)
   - Resolutions from the Security Council
2. What is not a part of a resolution?
   a) Heading O
   b) Subordination clauses X
   c) Operative clauses O
   d) Preambular clauses O
3. How many periods does a resolution have?
   a) 2 O
   b) 1 X
   c) 3 O
4. What elements can be used in a preambular clause? (Multiple correct answers)
   a) Conventions X
   b) UN Charter X
   c) Other resolutions X
   d) Statistics X

5. What is the minimum of operative sub-clauses in a resolution?
   a) 1 O
   b) 2 X
   c) 3 O
   d) 4 O

Position Paper Research Checklist

Research for the Position Papers can be overwhelming for the students. They might not know where to start and what to research exactly. Therefore, we provide a research checklist. This checklist provides useful links to possible online sources, information and aspects that should be considered and looked up regarding the committee of the MUN, the member state assigned, and more ideas for sources to gather information. The research checklist can be printed or distributed in a PDF. It is not final, but information and sources, as well as other aspects deemed relevant, can be added.

United Nations

- United Nations Website: https://www.un.org/
- United Nations Today: https://untoday.org/
- UN Digital Library: https://digitallibrary.un.org
- UN Global Issues overview: https://www.un.org/en/global-issues
- Various Research Guides: http://research.un.org/en?b=s&group_id=2087
- The World Fact Book (CIA): https://www.cia.gov/the-world-factbook/
- Permanent Missions to the United Nations: https://www.un.org/dgacm/en/content/protocol/permanent-missions
- United Nations Department of Global Communications: https://www.un.org/en/sections/departments/department-global-communications/
- The Europa World Yearbook: https://www.europaworld.com/
- United Nations Handbook: https://www.mfat.govt.nz/en/peace-rights-and-security/our-work-with-the-un/un-handbook?m=72857#search:dW4gaGFuZGJvb2s=
- GA Handbook: https://unitar.org/sites/default/files/media/publication/doc/un_pga_new_handbook_0.pdf
- United Nations Chronicle: https://www.un.org/en/chronicle/
- New York Times: https://www.nytimes.com/
- The Economist: https://www.economist.com/
- Member States on the Record: https://www.un.org/en/library/unms

European Union

- Official Website: https://european-union.europa.eu/index_en
- EU Document Register: https://www.consilium.europa.eu/en/documents/public-register/public-register-search/
- EUR-Lex: https://eur-lex.europa.eu/homepage.html?locale=en
- EU Law Tracker: https://law-tracker.europa.eu/homepage
- Publications Office of the European Union: https://op.europa.eu/en/home
- EU Countries: https://european-union.europa.eu/principles-countries-history/eu-countries_en
- News and Events Page of the EU: https://european-union.europa.eu/news-and-events_en
- EU Parliament Research Service: https://epthinktank.eu/
- Joint Research Centre: https://commission.europa.eu/about/departments-and-executive-agencies/joint-research-centre_en
- European Council for Foreign Relations: https://ecfr.eu/
- Politico EU: https://www.politico.eu
- EUobserver: https://euobserver.com/
- Euractiv: https://www.euractiv.com/
- Euronews: https://www.euronews.com/
- New Eastern Europe: https://neweasterneurope.eu/
- New Europe: https://www.neweurope.eu/
- Financial Times: https://www.ft.com/europe

Committee

- Read the Committee Background Guide provided by NMUN.
- Research resources:
  - Committee's website
  - Other UN resources (including the UN System Chart books and scholarly articles)
  - Important past decisions or resolutions of your committee often shed important light on its powers, the types of actions it takes, and the methods by which it acts
- Make sure to have a thorough understanding of:
  - The foundational documents (the resolution(s) that established the body, and its foundational governing document, such as a charter or treaty)
  - The evolution and changes in mandate over time
  - Other key international documents that underpin the mandate
- Find out about:
  - History
  - Governance
  - Structure

    - Membership
    - Mandate
    - Functions
    - Powers
    - Recent sessions
    - Current priorities
    - Important past decisions or resolutions of your committee
- Committee's topics
- Look to the mandate of your committee (it will give you an idea of the tone and type of work done within your committee)
- Research what is currently in place and what is planned for the future
- It is also important to examine successes and failures, and to attempt to determine why those approaches have succeeded or failed
- Search for:
    - Speeches made by your country on the topic
    - Important resolutions discussed and adopted in your committee

Research using the Committee Background Guide and answer the following questions

- What essential questions are being raised in each topic?
- What important documents are essential to your research?
- What actions have various international bodies taken in the past regarding these issues?
- In your opinion as a diplomat, why are these issues important?
- Why do you believe these issues remain unresolved?
- What actions are currently being taken and/or what committees or entities exist to address these issues?
- What should be done from the perspective of your member state or observer to resolve these issues?

Research other sources and answer the following questions

- What has been done internationally, nationally, regionally, and locally to address the topics?
- What should be done going forward on each topic (which you can understand from reading about proposals that others have suggested in relation to a topic and by forming your own innovative solutions to the issues at hand)?

Research your committee's website and answer the following questions

- What resolutions/reports has it published on the topic?
- What conferences or events has it held to address the topic?

- What are recent news items on the committee's website in relation to the topic?

Other sources for your research

- Websites and other resources from other UN bodies that may have addressed each topic; for example, topics related to population may have been addressed by the Commission on Population and Development and the UN Population Fund (as well as other UN bodies), while topics related to gender equality may have been addressed by UN-Women, the Commission on the Status of Women, and the General Assembly Third Committee (as well as other UN bodies).
- The UN News Centre, which publishes information regarding recent UN efforts on different topics, allowing you to search for key words regarding your topic to find relevant articles on recent UN events or publications.
- The UN's Meetings Coverage and Press Releases website, which provides UN press releases and information regarding UN meetings.
- Research into how other intergovernmental, regional or local organisations, and non-governmental organisations (NGOs) have addressed the topic and what they propose as effective strategies to approach the topic going forward.
- Books, reports, and scholarly articles on the topic from reputable sources (often professors, scientists, NGOs, or think tanks).

Research how your topic may be addressed on the international, regional, and local levels of the international community member state

- Most member states of the UN have their own UN website; check it out.
- Understand the foreign policies of their country's government (as you are expected to act within those).
- Research the problems within your state regarding ethnic and religious minorities, suppression of dissent, division of wealth, freedom of the press, development, health care, education, poverty, the environment, human rights, and so on. Also, do not overlook the more nuanced aspects of your state's domestic and foreign policies.

Research your assigned member state

- Political structure
- Economic conditions
- Religion(s)
- History
- Culture
- Population and demographics
- Geography

- Ethnic and religious minorities
- Development
- Healthcare
- Educational access
- Division of wealth and poverty
- Environmental policies
- Freedom of the press
- Key domestic policies
- Key foreign policies
- Your state's allies and member states it may not regularly work with (for various reasons)

Member state's positions on committee's topics

- Look for resources that:
  - share what your member state or observer has already done in relation to the topic;
  - what it proposes to be done on the topic;
  - and/or its national policies on issues related to the topic.
- If there is not a lot of information available, you may need to infer how your member state or observer would approach a given topic based on what you have learned about your member state generally.
- Search for speeches made by representatives of your member state or observer on the topic and important resolutions discussed and adopted in your committee that were supported or not supported by your member state or observer.
- Check voting records via UNBISNET or Member States on the Record (a valuable resource managed by the UN) to see whether your member state supported the latest resolutions on a specific item.
- Research national laws and discussions on each topic within your member state or observer.
- Look at reports published by regional organisations, NGOs, and think tanks about your member state or observer in relation to the issues at hand.

Research Activity: Countries and Topics

In Module 10 – we propose doing a research activity. This allows for a first research as it is necessary for the position paper but on a smaller scale to practice. We provide member states and possible topics that can be distributed among the students to do this research activity. Please note that these are only examples. Other member states and other topics are possible and could be added based on, for example, a special focus of the seminar or a specific background of students.

- USA – Countering the Threat Posed by Improvised Explosive Devices
- Jamaica – Reducing Nuclear Danger
- Norway – The Convention on Biological Diversity and Its Contribution to Sustainable Development
- Sao Tome and Principe – Ensuring Equitable and Inclusive Access to Education
- Australia – The Right to Privacy in a Digital Age
- Estonia – Eliminating Human Trafficking of Women, Girls, and Gender and Sexual Minorities
- Russia – Promoting and Protecting the Rights and Dignity of Older Persons
- Thailand – Ensuring Access to Affordable, Reliable, Sustainable, and Modern Energy for All
- France – Meeting the Fast-Track Commitments to Eradicate HIV/AIDS
- Somalia – Climate Change: Mitigating its Economic, Environmental and Social Effects
- Nigeria – Countering the Threat Posed by Improvised Explosive Devices
- Serbia – Reducing Nuclear Danger
- New Zealand – The Convention on Biological Diversity and Its Contribution to Sustainable Development
- Rwanda – Ensuring Equitable and Inclusive Access to Education
- Guinea-Bissau – The Right to Privacy in a Digital Age
- Afghanistan – Eliminating Human Trafficking of Women, Girls, and Gender and Sexual Minorities
- Iraq – Promoting and Protecting the Rights and Dignity of Older Persons
- Bolivia – Ensuring Access to Affordable, Reliable, Sustainable, and Modern Energy for All
- Brazil – Meeting the Fast-Track Commitments to Eradicate HIV/AIDS
- Egypt – Climate Change: Mitigating its Economic, Environmental and Social Effects
- Japan – Countering the Threat Posed by Improvised Explosive Devices
- Syria – Reducing Nuclear Danger
- Saudi Arabia – The Convention on Biological Diversity and Its Contribution to Sustainable Development
- United Kingdom – Ensuring Equitable and Inclusive Access to Education
- Portugal – The Right to Privacy in a Digital Age
- Panama – Eliminating Human Trafficking of Women, Girls, and Gender and Sexual Minorities
- Mexico – Promoting and Protecting the Rights and Dignity of Older Persons
- Africa – Ensuring Access to Affordable, Reliable, Sustainable, and Modern Energy for All
- Colombia – Meeting the Fast-Track Commitments to Eradicate HIV/AIDS

- Ireland – Countering the Threat Posed by Improvised Explosive Devices
- Finland – Reducing Nuclear Danger
- Denmark – The Convention on Biological Diversity and Its Contribution to Sustainable Development
- Italy – Ensuring Equitable and Inclusive Access to Education

13. Preparing and doing a UN or EU simulation

Muriel Cathérine Wenzel, Clara Umstätter and Claudia Wiesner

This chapter guides you through the most important steps and provides an overview of what you have to consider when self-organising a simulation, be it a Model United Nations (MUN) or a Model European Union (MEU). Furthermore, the chapter will differentiate between the organisational issues of organising an in-person conference versus a solely virtual one as the conference format has a rather big influence on the organisational issues. For example, all travel and accommodation related tasks can be omitted if the conference is solely virtual. However, a virtual conference will still require specific points to consider, like the technical tools and the flow of the conference in a virtual room.

Please note that MUN-specific terms, for example, dais, motions, head delegates, are explained in the glossary in Chapter 14.

BENEFITS AND PITFALLS

Before we proceed to the organisation as such, we would like to stress some benefits and pitfalls of self-organising a simulation.

First of all, self-organising a simulation in your institution allows for greater flexibility regarding dates, schedule, venue, and choice of committee, member states, as well as conference topics. However, if you are planning on organising and hosting a MUN or MEU for the first time, it can be quite overwhelming to think of all the necessary details. Usually, this sort of conference is characterised by a complex set of tasks due to its specific requirements and the rather fixed schedule. In addition, organising conferences in general usually means a high workload that requires a whole team to manage all the different tasks. Hence, depending on the size of the conference and how many participants (called delegates as they are the individual representatives of a country in a MUN/MEU) are taking part, it is vital to ensure that the workload is distributed among a sufficient number of people and that the budget will cover all costs. However, there are no blueprints for a standard simulation. Depending on the number of participants and the length of the conference as well as any additional programme, the workload may vary. A conference with only 20 participants who live nearby and a duration of only one evening entails a much lower workload and could probably be organised by one person more or less for free, while a simulation with 500 participants, a duration of five days and an additional programme may need ten to 15 staff members and a budget of some thousand euros.

Therefore, the following points will have to be considered in advance and before the decision to organise a simulation is taken: Where will the conference take place? How many participants are to be expected? Will additional staff be required to support in organising the conference? How and by whom will food and drinks be supplied? and so on. All of these aspects will raise questions about the funding which will have to be discussed. Of course, the organisational tasks and the budget may vary greatly, depending on, for example, where the participants will come from, or if their travel and accommodation will have to be provided. If there are not enough capacities and resources available to organise a simulation, and for carrying it out, we advise visiting an organised MUN or MEU as participation entails only the preparatory parts (see Chapter 12) for the students and not the organisation of the whole conference. There is an excellent variety of options when it comes to attending a (N) MUN or MEU conference. You may check out the mymUN[1] website which offers a comprehensive overview of MUN conferences throughout the year, or then consult GlobalMEU.[2]

Nevertheless, if the budget will suffice and enough resources and capacities are available, we can recommend and encourage you to host your own simulation, even if it is a small one, as the experience can be truly enriching and offers a great set of learning skills for your staff and students.

If you decide on self-organising a conference, you will find all the necessary information in the following. The conference planning we propose is divided into three phases: before the conference, during the conference, and after the conference. These phases are explained in detail below. Similar to the teaching modules (see Chapter 12), this chapter also entails checklists to support you in following up on all tasks and provides an overview of what needs to be accomplished. These checklists will guide you through every aspect and may be adopted accordingly depending on your specific circumstances.

1 mymUNhttps://mymun.com/conferences/list
2 https://globalmodeleuropeanunion.org/

CONFERENCE ORGANISATION IN PRESENCE

To begin with, we will talk about organising a simulation in presence. Later on, we will solely address the organisation of a virtual conference. However, if vital differences between an in-person and a virtual conference are drawn, they will be pointed out in this section as well.

The following will outline the different steps and tasks needed to organise an in-person simulation. As discussed above, the layout of the section is threefold: first, the organisational issues that have to be addressed before the conference are explained which mainly focus on the topics of venue, timeline, topics, speeches, dais, participants, fees, travel, cultural programme, programme of the conference, advertisement, equipment, printing, and food and drinks. Second, the tasks that arise during the conference are outlined. This part addresses rule training, organisation team, and awards. Third, all tasks in regard to after the conference are explained. The main areas in this section are the closing ceremony, debriefing, and additional post-conference tasks. Lastly, this section entails a checklist for each of the three areas which will lay out all the tasks needed to organise a successful simulation.

Before we continue, we would like to present a possible programme for a MUN (as outlined in Table 13.1). This programme is based on the Fulda MUN 2023 that was organised among the partners of the PATRAPO project. It may serve as a blueprint to be adapted for any other simulation.

Table 13.1 Fulda MUN 2023 programme

Sunday	Monday	Tuesday	Wednesday	Thursday	Friday
-	-	09.00 faculty feedback session	09.00 faculty feedback session	09.00 faculty feedback session	-
Arrival	09.30–12.30: Training + Repetition of Rules of Procedure + Conference-Flow	09.30–12.30: MUN-Conference ((in)formal sessions, Working Papers)	09.30–12.30: MUN-Conference ((in)formal sessions, Working Papers)	09.30–12.30: MUN-Conference ((in)formal sessions, Working Papers)	Return home
-	12.30–02.00: Lunch	12.3002.00: Lunch	12.30–02.00: Lunch	12.30–02.00: Lunch	-

Sunday	Monday	Tuesday	Wednesday	Thursday	Friday
-	02.00–03.00: Opening Ceremony Speeches + Keynote 03.30–06.00: Dais to open conference, Roll Call and Agenda-Setting	02.00–06.00: MUN-Conference ((in)formal sessions, Working Papers)	02.00–06.00: MUN-Conference ((in)formal sessions, Working Papers)	02.00–04.00: MUN-Conference - Voting 04.30–06.00: Awards + Debriefing	-
Sightseeing	Evening free	07.00: MUN-Reception	Evening free	07.00: Grill event or formal dinner	-

Before the Conference

As discussed above, the tasks to prepare a simulation may be divided into three steps. The first and most comprehensive one is outlined in this section. It entails all areas which have to be considered when organising a simulation and outlines all vital tasks which have to be thought about and completed prior to the conference. We will talk in detail about aspects such as the venue, the timing, the topics, speakers, the dais, participants, fees and the budget, travel or advertising.

First, the most important point on which everything else depends is the budget.

Budget: If you decide to self-organise a simulation, you need to know your budget beforehand. All decisions, for example, choice of venue or duration, depend on the question of how much money is available. Money is needed for such things as to pay for staff (if there are no volunteers), to rent rooms, to provide snacks, to travel to the simulation and stay overnight. In our experience, organising a five-day simulation with an additional programme requires at a minimum a budget for one staff member working full time for three months. More budget is needed to pay for at least three student assistants who work during the five days of the conference. And last but by no means least, hotel, travel, and snacks have to be paid. Probable options for funding may be an institutional budget, a project budget, public or private funding, and fundraising.

Another way to tackle the budget question is to have participants' fees. What you should keep in mind when having them is explained in detail in the following.

Fees: You will have to decide on this early and consider it when calculating your budget for the conference if you need fees. The fee may depend first of all on your contributed budget but also on rent for the venue, the number and content of the coffee breaks you plan to offer, whether lunch or dinner is provided, and many other factors that may vary for each conference. The participants' fee and payment should be communicated from the beginning as it might hinder participants from participating in the conference. In such a case, funding options should be available.

The location where the simulation will take place is another important point. Therefore, the following will dive deeper into the venue and other aspects resulting from the chosen location, like the travel and accommodation of the participants.

Venue: If one wants to organise a simulation in presence, thorough attention has to be paid to the venue. The venue must offer enough space for all participants, the technical equipment (e.g. projectors, outlets, microphones) and enough additional rooms or space for students to work on their resolution in groups. Furthermore, it has to have sufficient access to Wi-Fi and an area where students may eat and drink during their breaks. An appropriate venue can be on campus, in buildings belonging to the host institution, in public buildings such as the city hall, or in private buildings such as conference centres. However, additional costs should be considered if the rooms are booked elsewhere than at the institution.

After you have decided where the conference should take place, it is crucial to discuss the timeline as several points will have to be taken care of several months before the conference begins. However, this aspect also depends on the location of the conference as in some cities it may be more difficult to find appropriate accommodation than in others or the timeline to reserve hotels might differ.

Timing: We advise organising at least half a year before the conference is going to take place because accommodations need to be booked in advance and travel arrangements have to be made. If it is necessary and possible to hire additional staff, preparation should start at least eight months prior to the conference. If there is a cultural programme, this needs to be planned well in advance as well, for example, renting buses to drive to touristic sites or booking field trips. The first step is to form a team of people responsible for the organisation as well as decide on one primary coordinator who will keep an eye on the whole planning process and assign tasks. Including students in these tasks either as student assistants or as volunteers might also be an option – they will gain valuable experience from being part of an organisational team. In the first team meeting, everyone involved should be briefed about the timelines, given the information necessary to perform the tasks, and open questions should be answered. Ideally, at least one person of this team should have experience with simulations and know what this kind of conference requires, in order to have a better overview of the set-up and procedures.

It is helpful to develop and follow a shared list of tasks so that everyone can track the progress of the planning. Online tools might be helpful for this. Furthermore, a shared folder for all the documents needed for organising is useful. During the first meeting of the preparatory team, a timeline and deadlines/milestones should be set so that everyone knows what has to be done and until when. For this part, it is crucial to include additional time and flexibility in the planning process, as things might not go according to plan. Keep in mind that a few things need to be taken care of during the conference which will be elaborated on below. Therefore, at least two people should be present at the conference at all times for emergencies and questions, but also a clear division of responsibilities between the organisation team members should be made beforehand so that everyone knows whom to approach if an issue arises.

The following points address the necessary tasks that have already been outlined roughly in the sections. They will be explained in more detail below. Keep in mind that this area will require many resources, personnel-, time- and budget-wise, depending on how much you will be involved in booking processes and travel planning and whether you are going to (co-)fund it. Of course, you may hire a travel agency or leave the planning and booking to the students or their faculty members. However, we recommend planning for additional resources in this regard.

Travel: In case students from other universities or institutions participate, it is important to arrange and book travel and accommodation early. Hotels often allow booking a contingent of rooms which is useful when the number of participants still needs to be fixed. However, make sure that there is an option for free cancellation of the rooms if participants get sick at short notice. The same goes for flights, trains, and buses, which should be booked with a free cancellation option if possible. It is also possible to leave the planning of travel and accommodation to the participants. Options for hotels and travel instructions (nearest airport or train station, …) should be provided in that case. Who is paying for travel and accommodation should be clearly stated from the beginning to budget it accordingly.

After the logistical issues have been discussed and it has been ensured that the budget will suffice, the planning process moves on to the content of the conference.

Topics: When the planning process has started, it is a good idea to decide about the conference topics right away. This way, they can be integrated into the preparatory course, giving students more time to conduct their research. Most of the MUN conferences offer a variety of two to three current political topics. The topic of your conference has to be chosen and communicated accordingly. When thinking about which topics to choose, we advise looking at current debates at the United Nations (UN) and the European Union (EU), at recent events that are discussed worldwide, or choosing them according to the team members' main foci and research interests to provide enough information on them.

Notably, one does not have to choose several topics for a simulation. It is common to have two at MUN, but smaller conferences only have one, and the biggest conference (NMUN New York) sometimes has three. However, having two topics, even though it requires more work and research from the students, offers a greater dynamic at the conference as there will have to be debates and negotiations about which topic to address at the conference.

Speakers: If you wish to invite speakers to give a keynote speech during the opening ceremony of the conference or provide input on the chosen topics, searching for and inviting potential speakers would be the next step to think about. Speakers for the opening and closing ceremony who can give an informed and inspiring input on the topics should be decided on early and contacted/invited. Such speakers could, for example, be diplomats, authors of relevant literature, work in the field the conference topics revolve around, or hold official positions in your city. If necessary, travel and accommodation should be organised and paid for them.

As mentioned above, MUN and MEU conferences have rather specific characteristics. For example, you will need to appoint a dais/chair (see glossary in Chapter 14) for the conference.

Dais/chair: Crucially, a dais or chair (either of those terms might be used) should be found early on as they might want to be part of the planning process and course. The dais can either consist of one to three experienced students from their own or other (partner) universities or of people from the organisation team who know the exact procedures. Here, it is crucial to choose people with a lot of experience and knowledge about MUN or MEU as they will moderate and facilitate the whole conference, which means they are responsible for procedures being carried out correctly and for the general atmosphere at the conference and learning outcomes of the students.

States to be represented: Regardless of where the participants will come from in real life, you will have to choose the member states that will be represented in the simulation, and also the UN and EU bodies or part institutions that will be the object of the simulation, for example, committees, Council configurations. Furthermore, the delegations will have to be assigned and additional information, such as deadlines, will have to be communicated to the participants.

Participants: Regarding the participants, the planning depends on whether only students from your own course/university or also from other institutions are invited to join. The latter would necessitate a registration form and intensified advertising activities. Furthermore, there are different options of either letting the participants choose the represented member state and/or delegation themselves or assigning member states and forming delegations. There are advantages for each option, and we recommend that one should make sure particular member states who are vital for the dynamic of the conference (this mainly refers to an equal geographical distribution and the permanent member states of the Security Council) and for the set topic are represented. It is a good idea to keep a constantly updated participants' list from the beginning to know the exact number of students. This list should include at least names and contact details (e-mail). Information can be added to it as necessary, for example, dietary preferences, study programme, assigned member state/delegation, gender if relevant for rooming.

Position papers: As for the deadline for position papers, we advise setting it three to four weeks before the conference as the students will have to read all the other position papers to learn about the countries' positions on the topic and prepare for the conference by thinking about possible allies with whom they could work with during the simulation. Therefore, the submitted position papers should be distributed virtually to all participating students. The deadline should be communicated as early as possible to enable a thorough editing process and feedback, for example, from the dais or teachers.

Cultural programme: A physical simulation can entail a cultural programme (mandatory or voluntary) that would have to be planned. Such a cultural programme can play a vital role as it provides an opportunity for the students and the teachers to network and get to know each other on a deeper level. Students will have to stick to their character as a representative of a particular country during the conference, which might make it harder for the ones representing certain "non-sympathetic" countries to make friends. A cultural programme enables them to leave their role and get to know their peers privately.

Offering a cultural programme thus may present many advantages. However, it requires resources to plan and organise the respective activities. The cultural programme could include touristic visits, dinner, lunch, or other joint events such as bowling or minigolf. It could also include low-key activities such as a sightseeing tour in the city or on campus or joined walks in breaks. All this needs to be carefully organised by at least one member of the preparatory team, and the funding or payment needs to be clarified.

Programme for the conference: Another crucial point that has to be prepared prior to the conference is the conference programme which entails vital information for all participants.

We advise that the programme of the conference should at least include the parts mentioned below. In addition, we have included recommendations that have proven to be helpful:

1) a short rules training to refresh the students' memories and ensure that everyone understands the rules of procedure, which are crucial for a successful conference. This rules of procedure training should last for approximately 60–180 minutes;
2) an opening ceremony with speakers or a keynote, as well as administrative information to be given by the organisation team;
3) the simulation, that is,
   a) the MUN as such, which includes roll call, formal and informal sessions in different committees;
   b) the MEU as such, which is usually less formalised and often based on Robert's Rules (https://robertsrules.com/);
4) voting procedure;
5) a closing ceremony with awards; and
6) regular debriefings and feedback sessions. We learned that a faculty session each morning is helpful for finding out and speaking about any issues that arose during the simulation and discussing how to approach and solve them.

Depending on how long the simulation lasts, this programme can be stretched over just a few hours up to a whole week. Three to four days of conference, including one to three days of cultural programme, are a good timeframe, but it depends on how many students participate and on several other resources like the budget.

One part of organising a simulation that is often forgotten about or not considered carefully enough, is the advertising. Depending on your specific case, there might be more or less need for advertisement and more or less support from respective departments at institutions. Nevertheless, we recommend planning for additional resources both in terms of workforce and budget as it can be underestimated how much work and how much costs advertisement may require. You can find areas of advertisement and additional recommendations below.

Advertising the simulation: Regarding the advertisement of the simulation, a variety of options, such as social media, websites, e-mails, flyers, posters, and so on, can be used. An invitation with all the information and the programme in PDF format is a good way to distribute the information quickly and also to invite local/national press to attend the simulation and write pre-/post-reports to generate greater awareness of the simulation, and thus already start the advertisement process for the next conference. Some institutions offer help from a press or communication department. Others rely on own measures to be taken.

Equipment at the venue: At the venue, there should be free Wi-Fi for all participants to use online programmes to work on working papers together and conduct additional research. Power outlets should be available to charge laptops during formal sessions. A projector, computer, and black-/whiteboard should be available to share the speakers list and the current motions on the floor, as well as to provide additional information during the simulation, such as the times of the informal sessions (see glossary in Chapter 14). It would help if one person ensures that all technical equipment is set up and everything works properly. Furthermore, it would be good to check the equipment a few days ahead to avoid technical issues, especially if the conference is hybrid or completely virtual.

Certain documents and items may have to be printed. You can find recommendations below. However, we would like to emphasise that the less paper, the better. Therefore, you should carefully consider which documents really have to be printed. However, as MUN and MEU conferences typically do not allow students to use their laptops during formal sessions (where speeches and voting take place), it may be helpful for the students to have certain documents on paper or in a binder.

Printing: We recommend printing the following documents in advance: name tags including the delegates' names, represented country and committee, placards (see glossary in Chapter 14), data protection consent forms, signs for video and audio recording, and signs to find the venue and rooms. Furthermore, drafts for outcome documents (e.g. resolutions; see glossary in Chapter 14) should also be prepared and distributed to participants before the simulation virtually and, if necessary, in print.

Snacks and drinks: The last preparatory measures are ordering snacks and drinks. As already addressed before, you will have to consider if, when, and how you will provide food. In addition to lunch, you should discuss the items of snacks and drinks. As the days can get quite long, fresh fruit and vegetables, cookies, sweet and savoury snacks are a good option to be offered during the informal sessions and breaks. Coffee, tea, and cold drinks should be provided. Breaks for lunch and dinner should be included in the programme. You can either recommend restaurants or you can organise joint lunches or dinners. If you do not plan to organise snacks, drinks and food, communicate it clearly to the participants so that they can prepare and bring their own drinks/bottles and snacks.

Conference guide: Lastly, all the necessary information should be provided clearly arranged. This is possible with a conference guide. We advise including a guide for the city/venue. This guide should include restaurants, cultural and tourist attractions, and events, as well as insider tips and a map of the city and venue. Information on public transport, medical emergencies, and the dress code should be included as well. The guide can be used to inform the participants and facilitate their planning. The conference programme and the optional cultural programme should also be included in the guide. Times and meeting points need to be named clearly.

During the Conference

As all tasks prior to the conference have been covered now, we would like to move on to the ones that will arise during the conference.

Organisation team: As outlined above, it is vital to include enough supporting staff for all the tasks that may arise spontaneously. Generally, the organisation team is responsible for taking care of the venue and guiding everyone through the conference as well as the cultural programme. As already mentioned, at least two organisation team members should always be present for questions and in case of an emergency. The conference organisation team should support the dais during the conference, for example, for technical and administrative issues. If snacks and drinks are provided, the organisation team has to take care of these. As mentioned previously, regular feedback sessions with faculty advisors and head delegates (if there are such in your conference) are a good idea to discuss things that can be improved upon during the conference.

Please find below further details on the specific steps of a conference, that is, rule training and awards.

Rule training: We strongly advise that each simulation starts with rule training so that all participants are on the same page and know the rules enforced at this conference. This rule training can cover the most important rules only, or go more in depth and explain details as well as provide room for questions. Its length might vary between 45 minutes and up to three hours. A short break usually follows this before the opening ceremony starts. It is possible to welcome the participants and inform them about the venue and administrative questions before/after the rule training or during the opening ceremony.

Awards: Most MUN conferences will provide awards to students who have done exceptionally well in the conference. Of course, it is your decision if you would like to hand out awards. If you decide to do so, there are several options for awards but common ones are: best position paper, best delegation, best speech, and the peer award, which the participating students vote on. If required, the awards can be printed and handed out on the last day of the conference. Keep in mind that a template for the awards should be at hand and prepared in advance. If one decides to hand out awards, they should be decided on at the end of the conference in close cooperation with the dais, who will have observed the work of the students the closest.

Post-Conference

Even after you have successfully conducted the simulation, the tasks are not done yet. Some might arise directly after the last conference session and others might have to be addressed in the following days and weeks. This section aims at outlining these tasks and specifically focuses on the closing ceremony, the debriefing, and additional post-conference tasks.

Closing ceremony: Of course, it is up to you whether you would like to have an official closing ceremony but we highly recommend having at least a short one. It will take place after the voting procedure and the last formal session. In a MUN, the conference is then declared adjourned until the next year. The closing ceremony should include at least one speaker, for example, a delegate summarising the experience and briefly referring back to the topics and learning outcomes. We also advise having a short speech by an invited speaker, such as in the opening ceremony. The awards can be distributed in the closing ceremony as well.

The next point is also voluntary but highly recommended as a thorough evaluation is vital to improve if you are planning on organising another simulation.

Debriefing: We suggest doing a short debriefing and collecting feedback before the participants leave. This can be done anonymously (e.g. through a survey or by providing paper where the students can note their feedback) or in an open discussion.

Post-conference: After the participants have left, several organisational issues still have to be taken care of. In the days following the simulation, the adopted resolutions or decisions should be published online, and a conference report with pictures should be written and published, for example, on the websites or with local press. Lastly, receipts should be handed into financial management if necessary. In addition, it would be tremendously useful to have an evaluation session with all members of the organisation team to discuss the challenges and collect ideas on how to further improve the processes and the general planning for the following conference.

CHECKLISTS FOR CONFERENCE ORGANISATION IN PRESENCE

To organise a simulation in presence, we have provided checklists that address the three different areas of organisation (before, during, after). These checklists provide an overview of the most important tasks and can be extended, shortened or adjusted to one's own needs and circumstances. They shall help to guide you through the processes of organising a simulation and support you in keeping track of what still has to be done.

Before the Conference

The following checklist includes all tasks that should be done before the conference starts. You can use it to tick off the single preparatory steps and to gain an overview of what is required before the conference. It addresses all the areas outlined in the respective sections above.

- Decide on a budget and a funding source
- Set and collect participants' fee
- Find people to organise and assign responsibilities
- Decide who is going to lead the team as the main coordinator
- Start with a first team meeting to discuss open questions and get everyone on board
- Provide training and information for the organisation team so that they can do their tasks
- Set up joint folders and task lists for the team
- Set a timeline for all the tasks and a deadline when everything should be prepared
- Decide on one or two conference topics
- Find a suitable dais for the conference
- Marketing measures to be taken, for example, social media, websites, e-mails, ...
- Gather participants and constantly update the participants list
- Assign countries to the participants and form delegations
- Set and communicate deadlines for position papers
- Book rooms for the committees at the venue
- Organise a cultural programme if necessary
- Organise lunch and dinner options/events
- Decide on and distribute the conference programme
- Inform the participants about the setting, venue, and dress code
- Book travel and accommodation if necessary
- Look for and invite speakers for the opening and closing ceremony
- Organise travel and accommodation for the invited speakers
- Prepare a guide for the city, including restaurants, cultural attractions, medical info
- Invite local/national press to attend and report
- Make sure that there is free Wi-Fi for all participants
- Do a technical check before the conference
- Print name tags, placards, data protection consent forms, video/audio recording, photography signs, and signs for the venue and rooms
- Prepare drafts for outcome documents

- Correct and publish position papers
- Order snacks and cold as well as hot drinks
- Organise cups and plates if necessary
- Assign tasks to the organisation team during the conference

During the Conference

The following checklist includes all tasks and steps that arise during the conference. You can use it to tick off the single preparatory steps and to gain an overview of what is required before the conference. It addresses all the areas outlined in the respective sections above.

- Organise opening ceremony
- Welcome participants and inform them about the venue and administrative issues
- Be present for any questions and in case of an emergency
- Support the dais
- Provide snacks and drinks during breaks
- Take care of the venue and the technical equipment
- Guide through the conference and cultural programme
- Hold regular feedback sessions with faculty advisors and head delegates

Post-Conference

The following checklist includes all tasks and steps that should be done after the conference. You can use it to tick off the single preparatory steps and to gain an overview of what is required before the conference. It addresses all the areas outlined in the respective sections above.

- Organise closing ceremony
- Decide on, print, and grant awards
- Collect feedback from participants
- Publish resolutions (online)
- Write and publish conference reports
- Pay open invoices
- Hand in receipts to financial management if necessary
- Note possible improvements for the next conference

ORGANISATION OF A VIRTUAL CONFERENCE

After having laid out in detail how to organise a simulation in presence, we will now proceed to the organisation of a virtual conference. The primary tasks of organising a virtual simulation are the same as for a conference in presence. However, some additional aspects should be taken into account, and others, such as the cultural programme, can be left out.

A virtual conference offers several advantages over a physical one. First, the required budget is significantly lower as costs for travel, accommodation, food, additional activities, and so on, will be dropped. Furthermore, it allows for more inclusive and international participation as students will not have to travel. But not only will the budget be lower in comparison to an in-person conference, the workload will also be reduced as the tasks regarding the topics above will be omitted. However, a solely virtual conference also has its disadvantages. The experience of a virtual conference will be different and may not be as dynamic and fruitful as the open exchange students will have in additional activities on venue when the conference is not in session. Furthermore, the conference flow will be slightly different as a virtual room has some limitations over a physical one. Lastly, it has to be considered that virtual conferences and using a computer for several hours at a time may pose certain challenges in regard to concentration for the students.

All in all, it should be carefully considered which format fits your circumstances best. In order to gain a deeper understanding and draw a thorough comparison to a physical conference, the sections below follow the same structure as the ones at an in-person conference (before the conference, during the conference and after the conference), while focusing on the tasks specifically required for a virtual conference.

First, the tasks prior to the conference will be discussed. More specifically, the areas of software, fees, programme, breaks, marketing, and equipment will be covered. Secondly, the tasks during the conference will be addressed and lastly the post-conference tasks will be covered.

Before the Conference

Some aspects are similar to a physical conference and some might be less complex due to the virtual character. Therefore, find below further explanations on tasks you will have to consider when planning a virtual conference.

The first steps to start the organisation process are the same for a virtual conference as for a conference in presence: deciding on a budget. What you should keep in mind in this regard is explained in the following.

Budget and fees: As explained above, compared to a physical conference, the budget for a virtual simulation is significantly lower. There is no need to pay for travel, accommodation, a cultural programme, or food during the conference. However, costs for software licenses for an online conference tool might arise and some costs such as the personal cost, for example, for the staff organising the conference, persist and need to be calculated carefully beforehand. These costs depend on whether you employ institutional staff or the students, or your institution's UN club organise the simulation on a voluntary basis. If necessary, participants' fees can be used to cover the arising costs. However, keep in mind that the willingness to pay for an online simulation might be lower than to pay for a simulation in presence. Anyhow, the participants' fee and payment should be communicated from the beginning as it might hinder participants from participating in the conference. In such a case, funding options should be available.

Taking place online, some aspects regarding localities become mostly irrelevant for organising a virtual simulation. However, other questions connected to these might pop up.

Travel, accommodation and venue: The invitation of speakers for the opening and closing ceremonies related to the conference topics might be easier for a virtual conference because there is no need to travel. The same applies to the participants. Nevertheless, if speakers or participants come from a country in another time zone, the time difference should be kept in mind, and the programme adjusted accordingly. You should also be prepared in case of energy cuts or internet problems such as unstable connections that could arise for the participants when participating from their home.

One of the advantages of virtual conferences is that there is no need to think too much about the tasks related to venue and accommodation. However, the physical room has to be replaced by a virtual one which requires appropriate software or tool.

Software: Usually, a virtual conference will depend on a software license for an online conference tool. This tool should provide breakout rooms, screen-sharing, and a large enough number of participants to log in simultaneously. Furthermore, you should check requirements regarding data protection. Possible examples for such software are WebEx, Zoom, or Microsoft Teams. The license is the most significant cost factor next to organisation team cost to be considered for the budget and participants' fee.

Programme: The conference programme is also different in a virtual conference. For a virtual simulation, neither a cultural programme nor a guide for the city is necessary. However, the conference programme as such is quite similar. It should include the same parts: in a MUN, a short rules training for repetition of 45–60 minutes, an opening ceremony with speakers or a keynote, technical information to be given by the organisation team, formal and informal sessions (including agenda-setting and voting), a closing ceremony with awards and a debriefing. The feedback session can be substituted by a link to an online feedback/evaluation survey. A faculty feedback session each morning is helpful, only if the virtual conference lasts longer than one day. However, the faculty members can go to a breakout room any time during the conference to discuss current difficulties and issues.

One part of the conference programme that becomes even more crucial in virtual conferences is the aspect of breaks. Below you may find our recommendations on how to schedule breaks and how long a virtual conference shall be.

Breaks: As online meetings are much more tiring, we advise providing enough breaks (shorter and longer ones) during which the monitors can be switched off. For a one-day conference, such breaks could be every 90 minutes for 15 minutes for coffee and a longer lunch break of 90 minutes. Furthermore, the simulation should be shorter than in presence. A few hours up to two days maximum are sufficient. The same is true for the rules training, which is much more tiring online and should be kept shorter.

Marketing: Similar to physical conferences, virtual ones also benefit from marketing. While marketing is almost the same for a virtual simulation, the press or staff might not be able to take pictures. Therefore, screenshots can be provided, and the press can join the online conference for a short time. This might facilitate reporting because no travel to the venue is necessary, and the costs (time, money) are lower than in presence. Students can be asked before the conference whether they would do interviews and sent to breakout rooms with the journalists.

Equipment: A technical check is necessary before the virtual simulation. This check should include the cameras and microphones of the participants as well as the tools used, for example, the conference tool, whiteboard, note-taking applications, and screen sharing. Participants should sign data protection consent forms either in a scanned or electronically signed form. Drafts for outcome documents can also be prepared and distributed to the participants ahead of the simulation. Links to these documents can also be provided via the chat during the conference, and screen sharing may be used.

During the Conference

Even though a virtual conference differs from a physical one, the conference programme itself remains the same. However, it will have to be adapted to the virtual space and circumstances, and certain procedures will have to be conducted differently (e.g. voting through raising placards versus voting through raising virtual hands or writing in the chat). Further information on the tasks involved during the conference may be found below.

As explained before, a virtual simulation also starts with a rule training followed by a short break and then an opening ceremony. It is possible to welcome the participants and inform them about technical issues such as being on mute during formal sessions before/after the rule training or during the opening ceremony. Name tags are not possible online, but participants can rename themselves appropriately, for example with "Country, Name." The organisation team should support the chair(s) during the conference, for example, for technical and administrative issues such as breakout rooms or screen sharing. At least two organisation team members should be present at all times for questions and in case of an emergency, as for the simulation in presence.

Regarding the speakers list (see glossary in Chapter 14) in a virtual conference, we advise using a shared document and providing a link to it. On this document, the current motions on the floor, additional information during the conference such as the times of the informal sessions, and links to important documents or e-mail addresses to hand in working papers and draft resolutions can be provided, too.

Post-Conference

Even after you have successfully conducted the virtual conference, the tasks are not done yet. Some might arise directly after the last conference session and others might have to be addressed in the following days and weeks. This section aims at outlining these tasks and specifically focuses on the closing ceremony, the debriefing and additional post-conference tasks.

After the voting procedure, which can be done by reaction buttons such as raising a hand, and the last formal session, where the simulation is finished or the MUN/MEU is adjourned until the next year, the closing ceremony will take place in a virtual format. After the closing speech, awards are distributed virtually. A tip is to have everyone switch off their cameras, and only the award winners and speakers have their cameras on so that they are clearly visible. We advise doing a short debriefing and collecting feedback before the participants log out. This can be done anonymously (e.g. by providing a link to an online evaluation or feedback form) or in an open discussion.

Just like the conference in presence, in the days following the simulation, the adopted resolutions or decisions should be published online, and a conference report with pictures should be written and published for example, on the websites or with local press. Lastly, receipts should be handed into financial management if necessary. In addition, it would be tremendously useful to have an evaluation session with all members of the organisation team to discuss the challenges and collect ideas on how to further improve the processes and the general planning for the following conference.

CHECKLIST FOR ORGANISATION OF VIRTUAL SIMULATIONS

To organise a virtual simulation, we have provided checklists that address the three different areas of organisation (before, during, after). These checklists provide an overview of the most important tasks and can be extended, shortened and adjusted to one's own needs and circumstances. They shall help to guide you through the processes of organising a virtual simulation and support you in keeping track of what still has to be done.

Before the Conference

The following checklist includes all tasks that should be done before the conference starts. You can use it to tick off the single preparatory steps and to gain an overview of what is required before the conference. It addresses all the areas outlined in the respective sections above.

- Decide on a budget and on a funding source
- Set and collect participants' fee
- Find people to organise and assign responsibilities
- Decide who is going to lead the team as the main coordinator
- Start with a first team meeting to discuss open questions and get everyone on board
- Provide training and information for the organisation team so that they can do their tasks
- Set up joint folders and task lists for the team
- Set a timeline for all the tasks and a deadline when everything should be prepared
- Decide on one or two conference topics
- Find a suitable dais for the conference
- Marketing measures to be taken, for example, social media, websites, e-mails, ...
- Gather participants and constantly update the participants list
- Assign countries to the participants and form delegation
- Set and communicate the deadline for position papers
- Get a license for an online conference tool
- Look for and invite speakers for the opening and closing ceremony
- Decide on and distribute the conference programme
- Inform the participants about the programme, times, and provide links
- Assign tasks to the organisation team during the conference
- Invite local/national press to attend

- Prepare drafts for outcome documents
- Do a technical check before the conference (conference tool, other applications)
- Correct and publish position papers
- Assign tasks to the organisation team during the conference

During the Conference

The following checklist includes all tasks and steps that arise during the conference. You can use it to tick off the single preparatory steps and to gain an overview of what is required before the conference. It addresses all the areas outlined in the respective sections above.

- Organise opening ceremony
- Welcome participants and inform them about the programme and data protection consent
- Be present for questions and in case of an emergency
- Support the dais
- Manage technical issues, for example, breakout rooms
- Hold regular feedback sessions with faculty advisors and head delegates

Post-Conference

The following checklist includes all tasks and steps that should be done after the conference. You can use it to tick off the single preparatory steps and to gain an overview of what is required before the conference. It addresses all the areas outlined in the respective sections above.

- Organise closing ceremony
- Decide on, prepare and grant awards virtually and in written form via email
- Collect feedback from participants
- Publish resolutions (online)
- Write and publish conference reports
- Pay open invoices
- Hand in receipts to financial management if necessary
- Note possible improvements for the next conference

14. Tutorials, practical advice, do's and don'ts

Muriel Cathérine Wenzel and Clara Umstätter

Based on Chapters 12 and 13 on teaching preparative seminars, including teaching modules and the organisation of Model United Nations (MUN) or Model European Union (MEU) simulations virtually or in presence, this chapter provides various practical support tools, such as a glossary, including the most important MUN-specific terms, practical tips, or do's and don'ts. It is based on the experience of the PATRAPO project members and aims to help with possible difficulties and caveats in training seminars as well as in organising or participating in simulations. Thereby, it provides additional information, material and support for anyone teaching, organising, or participating in a simulation.

CHECKLISTS

The chapter begins with checklists for MUN and MEU conferences. This checklist provides the most basic overview of what simulations could look like. Please note that each conference looks a bit different, which means that there is no exact blueprint or single structure. However, the most basic parts of an MUN and MEU can be broken down into the steps below.

An MUN Conference Step by Step

- Arrival (in presence or virtually)
- Cultural programme (not mandatory)
- Rules training (not mandatory)
- Opening ceremony
- Roll call
- Agenda-setting (including opening of the speakers list, agenda-setting speeches, closing of the speakers list, voting for the agenda)
- Opening of discussion on the first topic
- Opening of the speakers list

- Opening speeches
- Formal and informal sessions
- Closure of debate or closure of speakers list
- Voting procedure
- Closing ceremony and awards
- Departure (in presence or virtually)
- Publishing of resolutions

An MEU Conference Step by Step

- Arrival (in presence or virtually)
- Cultural programme (not mandatory)
- Rules training (not mandatory)
- Opening ceremony / plenary meeting
- Opening of discussion on the first topic
- Opening of the speakers list
- Formal and informal sessions
- Press briefings
- Closure of topic one or closure of speakers list
- Voting procedure
- Closing ceremony / plenary meeting
- Departure (in presence or virtually)
- Publishing of Council conclusions

MUN GLOSSARY

The following glossary provides a basic overview of MUN-specific terms and explains them in detail. It serves as orientation and as a means to look up terms during teaching or participating in a MUN. The glossary in its original form is to be found at Wisemee. We have adapted and extended it for the purposes of our handbook. It can be copied and printed out to be distributed to MUN participants or used by students as well as teachers in MUN preparative seminars. This glossary is not exhaustive, but more terms can be added at any time.

Agenda-Setting: First part of a simulation, when the delegates choose which of the agenda topics they wish to discuss first.

Amendment: A written change made to an operative clause. Amendments can change an existing clause, add a new one, or delete a section or an entire clause.

Chair/Director/Dais: Consists of usually three students and is seated at the front of the room. The chair facilitates debate according to the rules of procedure and provides help and feedback to the delegates.

Decorum: A call to order by the chair.

Delegate: An individual representative of a country in a MUN committee. The aim of the delegate is to represent the assigned country as best as possible and not to fall back on his/her individual view.

Delegation: A group of usually two delegates who represent a country in a MUN committee together.

Draft Resolution: The final draft of a working paper properly formatted and approved by the chair for both content and format. Once approved by the chair, draft resolutions can be discussed in formal session and, when debate is closed, voted upon.

Formal Session/Debate: Time of a MUN in plenum where speeches are held, motions can be raised and voting takes place. Usually technical devices are not allowed during this time.

Friendly Amendment: A change to a clause approved by all the sponsors. These are automatically added to the draft resolution.

Head Delegate: The student head of a delegation.

Informal Session/Debate: Motion needed for a specific time to talk to and negotiate among delegates and work on working papers. Technical devices may be used during this time.

Member State: A country that has ratified the UN Charter and has voting rights.

Merger: When two or more draft resolutions are combined.

Moderated Caucus: A less formal discussion on a subtopic within the general topic, chosen by a delegate and passed by a majority. Delegates raise their placards to offer moderated caucuses when the chair opens the floor for motions. Moderated caucuses need to offer overall time, individual speakers time, and topic of discussion.

Motion: Official request at a MUN.

Motion for Adjournment: A motion to end the committee session until the next MUN.

Motion for Closure of Debate: A motion for the committee to end debate and move into voting procedure. If this passes, the speakers list is closed and the only motions allowed are those that pertain to the voting procedure.

Motion for Suspension of the Meeting/Debate: A motion to put the session on hold, for example, for lunch or coffee break.

Motion to Divide the Question: A motion to vote separately on a set of specifically chosen operative clauses.

Motion to Reorder Draft Resolutions: To change the order of the draft resolutions, which is different from the one where the one introduced first is voted on first.

Observer: A delegate who is not a natural member of the committee and can only vote on procedural matters.

On the Floor: When a motion, working paper or draft resolution is open to discussion and voting.

Operative Clause: Clauses that detail the policies or explain what the draft resolution is going to do. Operative clauses can go into detailed sub-clauses to properly convey the idea. The first words are italicised and each clause is numbered.

Out of Order: Actions that are not allowed according to the rules of procedure.

Page: A volunteer who passes notes between the delegates and to the chair during a MUN.

Preambulatory Clause: Clauses that explain why you are implementing the policies described in the operative clauses. They can provide a background to the problem, legal precedent, and other supporting data. Preambulatory clauses are usually italicised and not numbered.

Placard: Cardboard or paper sign with the country name written on it. It is used to identify presence, vote, and signal to the chair.

Point of Information: Used to ask a question during formal debate.

Point of Order: Called by a delegate on another delegate or on the chair, when the rules of procedure are not being followed.

Position Paper: A summary of the country's position on the conference topics to be submitted before the MUN.

Present: What a delegate says during roll call when they are present in the committee and want to reserve the right to abstain on the final vote.

Present and Voting: What a delegate says during roll call when they forgo their right to abstain. This means they can only vote for or against the draft resolution. This is usually done when they feel strongly about the topic.

Procedural Voting: Voting on something that does not impact the world outside.

Quorum: The minimum number of delegates needed to be present for the debate to take place.

Roll Call: A procedure performed by the chair at the beginning of each committee session to know how many delegates are present in the room (for a simple majority and 2/3 majority voting) and to know who is "present" and who is "present and voting".

Rules of Procedure: The rules which dictate how to run a MUN.

Secretariat: The organisers of a MUN.

Secretary-General: The head of the secretariat or of a UN club.

Signatories: Delegates who support a draft resolution.

Simple Majority: A vote that requires at least one over 50 per cent of the vote to pass.

Speakers List: A list of delegates who have been recognised to speak in a specific order.

Sponsors: Delegates who were major contributors to the draft resolution.

Substantive Voting: Voting on something that has a real-world impact, for example, on a draft resolution.

Unfriendly Amendment: A change to a clause that at least one sponsor does not agree to. These go to vote and are only added to the draft resolution if passed with a majority in favour of the amendment.

Vote by Acclamation: A motion which means that a draft resolution can pass as long as no delegate objects. If one delegate objects, the motion moves to a simple majority vote.

Vote by Roll Call: A motion to have each country declare verbally: "In Favour", "Against", "Abstain".

Vote Clause by Clause: A motion to vote on each clause individually instead of all together.

Voting Procedure: At the end of a committee session. Once the debate is closed, delegates will vote on amendments and then on draft resolutions. During the voting procedure, nobody may enter or leave the room.

Working Paper: The first draft of ideas in writing which is compiled by the delegates during an informal session.

TERMS NOT TO USE AND THINGS TO REMEMBER OR AVOID AT MUN OR MEU

In the following, we want to point out some terms and things that should be remembered or avoided when participating in MEU/MUN or teaching preparation seminars. This overlaps in parts with the etiquette and code of conduct of an MUN that may differ from conference to conference.

"Teacher": Delegates should not call the chair "teacher", but use "chair" or a correct title. The same goes for the organisation team and other delegates who should also be addressed properly.

Avoid "I": Use "we" or the country's name as a delegate.

Breaking character: Delegates should avoid breaking character and standing in for their personal opinion instead of the member states' position.

Swearwords: Everyone should communicate diplomatically.

Foreign languages other than English: Everyone should be fair and communicate completely in English during the conference. Other delegates might not understand one's own mother tongue and feel offended or left out when speaking over their head.

Emotions are possible: Students might get emotional, especially if the days are long. Faculty advisors, as well as the organisation team, should be prepared to keep calm and attend to their needs if necessary.

No stress: Not everything will work out the way it was planned. Finding alternative solutions and trying to do creative solution thinking is part of organising and participating in a simulation.

Platforms: Using a platform or an online board to provide information to participants as well as interested people is useful. It should be updated regularly.

Disputes with other delegates: Everyone should be aware of the code of conduct and of proper manners at a MUN/MEU. If somebody gets into a dispute, he/she should try to get help from the chair or the secretariat to solve the issue.

Pre-written working papers: Delegates are not allowed to write or formulate/format any working papers or phrases to be included in resolutions before the conference. Writing the working papers is only done at the conference during informal sessions and goes hand in hand with negotiating and working with other delegates.

VIDEO LINKS

There are a number of videos available online for free that can be used for preparation or during the preparatory MUN seminar. Some of these are below and can be provided in class for further practice.

- Various training videos: SRMUN has created several training videos on important procedural questions: http://srmun.org/videos.php
- MMUN provides short training videos on various topics: https://mmun.org/delegate-resources/training-videos/
- MUN Institute Training Videos: https://mun.bestdelegate.com/video-gallery/
- Movies including MUN:
    - *Winning London* is a 2001 direct-to-video comedy film directed by Craig Shapiro and starring Mary-Kate and Ashley Olsen. https://www.imdb.com/title/tt0272360/
    - *"Never Have I Ever" ...started a nuclear war ...* is the fifth episode in Season 1 of the Netflix series, Never Have I Ever. It includes participation at a MUN. https://neverhaveiever.fandom.com/wiki/..._started_a_nuclear_war

INFORMATION LINKS

This section includes links to various institutions or websites for research as well as conference preparation. The list can be provided to the participants or used in preparatory seminars. It is not exhaustive. Further sources can and should be added to it. Please note that links might change with time; therefore, we provide the name of the websites to search for them online if necessary.

UN Specific Sources

- UN databases to do research and to get familiar with UN documents: https://data.un.org/

- To do better research see the FAQ here: https://data.un.org/Host.aspx?Content=FAQ#Searching
- UN digital library: https://digitallibrary.un.org
- UN global issues overview: https://www.un.org/en/global-issues
- United Nations Department of Global Communications: https://www.un.org/en/department-global-communications
- Sustainable Development Goals: https://sdgs.un.org/goals
- United Nations Handbook: https://www.mfat.govt.nz/en/peace-rights-and-security/our-work-with-the-un/un-handbook/
- United Nations Chronicle: https://www.un.org/en/chronicle/
- United Nations Today: https://www.un.org/en/events-and-news
- The World Factbook: https://www.cia.gov/the-world-factbook/
- Permanent Missions to the United Nations: https://www.un.org/dgacm/en/content/protocol/permanent-missions
- The Europa World Yearbook: http://www.europaworld.com/pub/
- New York Times: https://www.nytimes.com/
- The Economist: https://www.economist.com/
- Various research guides: http://research.un.org/en?b=s&group_id=2087
- Member States on the record: https://www.un.org/en/library/unms
- More links to conduct research: https://www.un.org/en/mun/resources/research-resources

EU Specific Sources

- Official website: https://european-union.europa.eu/index_en
- EU document register: https://www.consilium.europa.eu/en/documents/public-register/public-register-search/
- EUR-Lex: https://eur-lex.europa.eu/homepage.html?locale=en
- EU law tracker: https://law-tracker.europa.eu/homepage
- Publications Office of the European Union: https://op.europa.eu/en/home
- EU countries: https://european-union.europa.eu/principles-countries-history/eu-countries_en
- News and Events page of the EU: https://european-union.europa.eu/news-and-events_en
- EU Parliament Research Service: https://epthinktank.eu/
- Joint Research Centre: https://commission.europa.eu/about/departments-and-executive-agencies/joint-research-centre_en
- European Council for Foreign Relations: https://ecfr.eu/
- Politico EU: https://www.politico.eu/?no-geo-redirect
- EUobserver: https://euobserver.com/
- Euractiv: https://www.euractiv.com/
- Euronews: https://www.euronews.com/

- New Eastern Europe: https://neweasterneurope.eu/
- New Europe: https://www.neweurope.eu/
- Financial Times: https://www.ft.com/europe

IMPORTANT DOCUMENTS FOR DELEGATES

This section includes important documents for delegates to be downloaded and printed out or distributed electronically before the MUN. It provides a vital overview in preparation for an in presence MUN or MEU (see Chapter 12) and can be used in the planning to gather all pertinent information.

Content:

- MUN Rules of Procedure long and short form
  - https://www.nmun.org/assets/documents/nmun-rules.pdf
  - https://www.nmun.org/assets/documents/nmun-rules-short.pdf
- MEU Rules of Procedure
- Comments on the EU Council's Rules of Procedure
  - https://www.consilium.europa.eu/en/resources/publications/council-rules-procedure-comments/
- Voting Calculator EU
  - https://www.consilium.europa.eu/en/council-eu/voting-system/voting-calculator/
- Delegate Preparation Guide
  - https://www.nmun.org/assets/documents/nmun-delegate-prep-guide.pdf
- Conduct expectations
  - https://www.nmun.org/nmun-conduct-expectations.html
- Draft for working paper
- Glossary
- Venue information
- Programme
- Important contacts

REFERENCE

Wisemee (2023). MUN Glossary & Terms. Available online at https://www.wisemee.com/mun-glossary/ (accessed 10/9/2023).

Index

active learning 1, 7–8, 13, 14, 18, 47–50, 53, 56, 67–70, 72, 77, 79–80, 209
advisory opinion 85, 131
agenda 8, 20–21, 26, 37, 41, 54, 56, 63, 95, 97, 108, 117, 128, 145–6, 159–162, 168, 170–72, 182, 216, 230, 233, 270–71
agenda-setting 15, 20–21, 56, 145, 230, 233, 253, 266, 270–71
amendment 54, 99, 217–21, 242, 271–2, 274–5
Annan, Kofi 19, 161, 168–9, 171
antidiscrimination 183
arena of politics 8, 106–7, 110
assessment 31–2, 43, 89, 129
Autonomous University Madrid (UAM) 2, 200
awards 21, 51, 60, 217, 252–3, 258, 260–61, 263, 266–7, 269, 271

blended learning ix, xi–xii, 48, 52, 64
Boutros-Ghali, Boutros 19, 95
budget 2, 4, 8, 10, 23, 33, 85, 89–93, 95–96, 100, 110–113, 117, 152, 251, 253–5, 258, 262, 264–5, 268
Bush, George H.W. 19

ChatGPT 55
China 18, 36, 86, 89–90, 92, 146, 166, 204
Churchill, Winston S. 85
citizenship xi, 9, 16, 18, 71, 74, 76, 78, 176–89, 192
civic education 8, 67, 72, 75–8, 80
climate change 36, 98, 100, 172, 202, 248
closing ceremony 21, 252, 256, 258, 261–3, 266–9, 271
code of conduct 199, 210–11, 275
Cold War 87, 92, 108, 130, 160–62
collaborative online international learning (COIL) xii, 49, 52–3, 62–3
committee x, 1, 14, 16, 20–22, 48, 53, 55–6, 58, 62, 87, 91–2, 97–8, 124, 126, 144, 147, 154, 160, 171, 181, 209, 216–23, 226, 228, 230–31, 241–7, 250, 259, 272–5
conceptual politics 9, 176
conference x, xii–xiii, 1, 4, 14, 16–22, 26, 29, 31–5, 37, 41, 49–53, 55–7, 59–61, 64, 77–9, 85–6, 93, 97–8, 123–4, 126, 131, 159–60, 168, 172, 197, 199–200, 205, 209, 212, 217, 221, 223, 230–31, 233–4, 238–41, 245, 250–71, 273, 275–6
consensus xi–xii, 8, 16, 39, 47, 54, 59, 91, 112, 168
contingency 106, 142
cosmopolitanism 73
Council of Europe 87
Council of the European Union 99
Court of Justice of the European Union (CJEU) 110–11, 113, 176, 179, 182
COVID-19 xi, 18, 48, 100
cultural programme 4, 20, 22, 210, 252, 254, 257–8, 260, 262–5, 270–71

dais 20–22, 48–9, 51, 53, 58–9, 61–2, 145–6, 216–17, 219–21, 223, 230–31, 233, 239, 241–2, 250, 252–3, 256–7, 260, 262–3, 268–9, 272
debate 9, 20–21, 56, 58, 73, 75, 91, 97, 99, 129–30, 132, 140–42,144–7, 149, 156, 159–72, 176, 178, 210–11, 219, 256, 271–5
debriefing 32, 41–3, 72, 252–3, 258, 261, 266–7
decision-making ix–x, 1, 8, 14–15, 24, 26, 30, 34, 36, 42, 50, 71, 92, 129,

140–41, 143, 147–51, 162, 179, 198, 203, 211, 213
Declaration by United Nations 85
decorum 22, 223, 230, 272
Defrenne, Gabrielle 182–3, 189
delegate x, xii, 1, 5–7, 14–22, 35, 49–59, 61, 71, 110, 114, 130, 132, 140, 143, 145, 149, 152, 159, 164, 166–7, 169–70, 198, 203, 206, 209, 216–18, 220–26, 230–31, 233, 235, 240–41, 250, 259–61, 263, 269, 271–6, 278
delegation 3–4, 14, 16, 22, 26, 33, 36, 50, 56, 60, 62, 99, 124, 126–7, 146, 150, 159, 166–7, 198, 205, 216, 228, 231, 233, 240, 256–7, 260, 262, 268, 272
development 3, 8, 36, 59, 69, 74, 84, 95–8, 107–9, 112, 116–18, 126, 151–3, 164, 166, 169–70, 177, 179, 184, 191, 202, 207, 211, 214, 222–3, 246–9
digital diplomacy xii, 23, 58, 62
diplomacy ix–xiii, 5, 7–8, 15, 17–18, 23–4, 47–8, 50–52, 54, 57–8, 60–64, 91, 85, 106, 123, 132–3
diplomat ix–xiii, 15–17, 19, 23, 47, 50, 53–4, 57, 59, 79, 99, 125–6, 132, 164, 172, 245, 256
director 19, 59, 272
Director-General 52–3
documents xii, 5, 9, 21, 39, 43, 62, 98, 115, 141, 143–4, 146–7, 153, 156, 161, 164, 176, 179–80, 187, 189, 192, 197–9, 202–203, 208, 213, 216, 218, 220, 222, 224–6, 228, 241, 244–5, 255, 259, 262, 266–7, 269, 276, 278
draft resolution x, 20–21, 56–9, 99, 145–6, 199, 208, 216–21, 230, 233, 241–2, 267, 272–5
Dumbarton Oaks Proposals 86

Economic and Social Council (ECOSOC) 90, 93, 100, 127, 131, 149, 202
education 8, 14–15, 18, 22, 24, 28, 67–8, 71–2, 74–8, 80, 189–91, 223, 246, 248–9
educational xi–xii, 1, 6, 8, 16, 34, 47, 59–60, 67–8, 74–5, 78–9, 93, 127, 247
Eliasson, Jan 19
Erasmus+ 2–3
EU Citizenship 176–7, 179–82, 184, 186, 188, 192
Euratom 108, 153
European Coal and Steel Community (ECSC) 87
European Commission (Commission) 7, 26, 34–5, 37, 99, 110–14, 116–19, 150, 152–6, 179–90, 192, 208, 224–5
European Communities 108, 152, 183
European Community of Defence 108
European Council (EC) 26, 34–5, 37, 99, 109, 111–17, 143, 150, 151, 225, 244, 277
European Court of Justice (ECJ) 182
European Economic Community (EEC) 108–10, 152–3, 177, 179–83
European integration 5, 107–10, 116, 179, 185
European Parliament (EP) 9, 27, 34, 37, 108–19, 140, 143, 148, 150–56, 179–80, 184, 186,
188–90, 192, 224
European Political Community (EPC) 108
European Union (EU) ix,1, 26, 71, 79, 84, 99, 106–19, 141–4, 147–51, 153, 176–7, 179–80, 182–93, 197–9, 207, 211–14, 224–5, 228–9, 235–6, 244, 256, 277
evaluation 34, 62, 69, 72, 97, 205, 261, 266–7
executive 90, 106, 113, 115, 117, 119, 130, 150, 152, 171, 193
experiential learning xi, 8, 14, 16, 18, 26, 29, 31–4, 37, 42–3, 47, 49–50, 59

faculty 3, 19, 29, 35, 49, 55, 60–62, 64, 252, 258, 266
  advisor 22, 35, 47–9, 53, 198, 260, 263, 269, 275
  attendee 22
  members 20–22, 48, 51–2, 59, 198, 255, 266
federalism 107, 109, 117–118

federalists 107–108
feedback 19, 21–22, 31–2, 42, 49, 52, 55, 58, 205, 209, 216, 232, 252, 257–8, 260–61, 263, 266–7, 269, 272
First World War 84, 178
Food and Agriculture Organisation of the United Nations (FAO) 95
formal session 20–22, 216, 220, 229–31, 235, 241, 252–3, 258–9, 261, 266–7, 271–2
France 86–7, 92, 108–109, 165, 231, 248
free movement 109, 180–83, 186–90
free trade agreement (FTA) 27, 36
Fulda University of Applied Sciences (UAS) 2–4, 61, 200, 205, 252

General Assembly (GA) 7, 14, 18–20, 50, 62, 84, 87–100, 116, 123, 125–8, 130–32, 140, 142, 146–51, 159–60, 162, 171, 202–203, 209, 228, 236, 243, 246
Global Citizenship Education 71, 74
global governance x, xiii, 15–17, 47, 50–51, 62, 101, 124, 128–9, 131, 133
glossary 10, 198, 206, 250, 256, 267, 269, 270–71, 278

Hammarskjöld, Dag 84, 95
hard law 5, 201
head delegate 22, 223, 250, 260, 263, 269, 272
high school 8, 14, 16, 27, 32, 34, 210
Human Rights Council 98–100, 160
Human Rights Council Advisory Committee 98
hybrid 2–4, 7, 20, 38, 61, 186, 259
hybrid diplomacy xii–xiii, 17, 23, 48, 61, 63–4

informal session 20–22, 59, 61, 145, 216, 220, 229–31, 233, 235, 252–3, 258–9, 266–7, 271–2, 275–6
infringement 2, 114, 180, 187, 192
institutions xi–xii, 1, 3, 5–9, 17, 26, 29–30, 33–8, 40, 42, 47, 50, 52, 55, 60, 62–3, 71, 73–6, 78–80, 84, 106–107, 109–15, 118–19, 122–3, 128, 132, 140–44, 146–50, 155–6, 160–61, 164–5, 169, 171, 176, 180–81, 186–7, 192, 206, 211, 225, 228, 255–6, 258, 276
instructors 31–34, 37, 43
intergovernmental 2, 8, 47, 55, 106, 108–109, 116, 118, 141, 148, 150–51, 153, 246
intergovenmentalism 29, 107, 109, 118
International Court of Justice (ICJ) 85, 90, 93–4, 128, 149, 162
International Criminal Court (ICC) 94
International Covenant on Economic, Social and Cultural Rights 98
International Covenant on Civil and Political Rights 98
International Labour Organisation (ILO) 95
international law ix, 2, 9, 84, 87, 98, 122–4, 126, 128–9, 131, 148–9, 159, 166–7, 169, 197–8, 201, 207, 212, 214
International Monetary Fund (IMF) 95
International Organisation (IO) ix–xi, xiii, 2, 5, 8–9, 14–17, 23, 28, 47–51, 57, 59, 62–4, 84, 86, 95, 106–107, 125, 127, 129–30, 141, 143, 145, 147–8, 150, 236
international politics ix–xiii, 6, 8, 14–15, 17, 59, 63–4, 85, 197
International Relations ix, xiii, 3, 5–6, 9, 14, 16–18, 23, 47–51, 53, 60, 63–4, 67, 71, 78–9, 88, 164–7, 170, 172, 211

judicative 106, 115, 150

knowledge x, xii–xiii, 1, 4–7, 10, 15–17, 20, 23, 28, 30–33, 39, 42, 47–8, 50, 55, 57–8, 62, 64, 67–72, 74–77, 79–80, 168, 197, 211, 213, 215, 223, 226, 238, 256

law-making 9, 114, 122–7, 129–31, 152, 177
leadership x, xii–xiii, 8, 14, 19, 23, 24, 30, 32, 42–3, 48–53, 55, 61, 63, 64, 95
League of Nations 9, 15, 18, 67, 85, 93, 123, 125–7, 129, 133, 211
legislative 106, 109, 111–17, 119, 150–51, 153–5, 183, 189–90, 211, 224–5

MacEwan University 2–3, 49–50, 52, 61–63
Member of the European Parliament (MEP) 26, 111, 113, 117, 149, 151, 153–6, 211
member states 2, 9, 20, 28, 33, 35, 39, 41, 57, 75, 84–5, 87–101, 106, 109–10, 112–15, 117–19, 124, 129–32, 141, 148–52, 160, 164, 168, 172, 177, 179–81, 183–92, 217, 221, 225, 227–8, 233, 243, 246–7, 250, 256–7, 275, 277
merger 21, 59, 217, 272
micropolitics 5–7, 9, 118, 140–148, 150–151, 153–154, 156, 176
  interinstitutional micropolitics 107, 110, 118
Millennium Declaration 88–89
Millennium Development Goals (MDGs) 95, 97
Model European Union (MEU) xi–xii, 1, 3–8, 10, 26–38, 40–44, 72, 75, 77, 79, 80, 118–19, 144, 197–9– 205–206, 209, 211, 213, 225, 228–9, 231–2, 239, 250–51, 256, 258–9, 267, 270–71, 275, 278
Model United Nations (MUN) ix, xi–xiii, 1–10, 14–24, 26, 31, 34, 38–40, 42, 49, 52, 59–60, 62, 67, 72, 75, 77–80, 144–5, 159–60, 168, 172, 197–200, 205–206, 209–13, 216–18, 220–21, 228–32, 235, 238–9, 241, 243, 250–52, 255–6, 258–61, 265, 267, 270–78
Mohammed, Amina 19
Moon, Ban Ki 19
Moscow Declarations 86
motion 21–22, 40, 113, 144–7, 155 219, 230–31, 250, 259, 267, 272–4
multilateralism x, 2, 15, 50, 51, 78, 86–7, 99, 122, 124, 167, 170, 235
multilevel system 9, 176

National Model United Nations (NMUN) xii, 3–4, 8, 14, 18–19, 49, 51–3, 55–62, 210–11, 238, 244, 256
National University Kyiv Mohyla Academy (NaUKMA) 49, 52, 59–60, 62
negotiation x–xiii, 5–6, 8–9, 14–17, 20, 23, 26, 28–30, 32, 34–5, 37, 40–43, 47, 49–52, 54–9, 62, 64, 70, 78, 80, 96, 98, 100, 106, 125, 131, 133, 140–43, 148–51, 154–6, 180, 184, 197, 199, 204, 207, 211, 222, 227, 230, 236–7, 256
Nobel Peace Prize 84, 95
Non-Governmental Organisation (NGO) 18–19, 93, 100, 125, 130, 211, 246–7
North Atlantic Treaty Organisation (NATO) 84, 87

observer 99, 170, 203, 226, 245, 247, 273
opening ceremony 20, 230, 253, 256, 258, 260–61, 263, 265, 267, 269–71
Organisation for Economic Co-operation and Development (OECD) 76
outcome documents 146, 197, 199, 203, 208, 216, 218, 220, 224–5, 241, 259, 262, 266, 269

peace x, xii, 2, 18, 28, 71, 84–90, 92, 95–6, 99–100, 125–6, 128–9, 147, 160–63, 165–6, 171–2, 201, 207, 214, 222, 236
peacebuilding 96, 161, 171, 222
peacekeeping 84, 89–90, 92, 96, 99, 130, 160–62, 168, 171
peer-to-peer training 8, 48–9, 51–4, 56–7, 59–63
placard 21, 230–31, 259, 262, 266, 272–3
policy-making 15, 23, 29, 112, 177
political
  action 1, 9, 79, 106, 110, 141, 143, 145, 147, 153, 156
  practices 9, 140–41, 144, 147–51, 190
  processes 1, 9, 140–41, 146–7, 176–7, 192, 197–8
Political Science 3, 5, 23, 29, 67, 70, 77, 106–107, 141, 177
politics 2, 4–9, 15, 18, 29, 30–31, 37, 64, 73, 77–8, 92, 106–107, 110, 124, 140–47, 149–50, 176–7, 180, 192, 198, 211
position paper 5, 16, 21–22, 55–7, 62, 199, 203, 204–205, 208, 223, 226–7, 229, 238–9, 241, 243, 247, 257, 260, 262–3, 268–9, 273

post-conflict states 165, 168
Power, Samatha 19
power relations 5, 149
practice-oriented xi, 7–8, 18
Practising Transnational Politics (PATRAPO) ix, 1–4, 7, 10, 24, 52, 61, 200, 252, 270
presentation 8, 23, 32, 42–43, 201–203, 206–10, 212, 216, 218, 220–21, 224–30, 232–3, 236–8
pro et contra 145
procedural knowledge 62, 70–71, 79
procedure xii, 2–3, 5, 7–9, 14, 17, 21, 23, 31, 39–40, 47, 54, 59, 63, 80, 95, 114, 117, 124, 129, 140–41, 144–5, 147, 149–53, 155, 179–81, 187–90, 192, 205–206, 211, 217, 219–20, 224–5, 230, 232, 255–6, 258, 261, 266–7, 271, 273–5
protocol xii, 50, 80, 146–7
public speaking xii, 8, 32, 42–3, 49–50, 56, 62, 71, 197, 210, 232, 234–5, 239

quorum 274

research x, xii, 4, 6, 8, 16, 22, 29–31, 35, 38–40, 42–3, 49–50, 55–6, 62, 95, 147, 153, 199, 203–4, 208–9, 211, 223, 227–9, 231, 234, 239–40, 243–7, 255–6, 259, 276–7
resolution 2, 5, 7, 16, 21–2, 42, 57–9, 62, 84, 89–90, 93, 96–7, 99–101, 131, 143, 145–7, 160, 162–3, 188, 198–9, 201, 204, 208, 212–13, 216, 218–24, 226–8, 231, 241–5, 247, 254, 259, 261, 263, 267, 269, 271, 276
Responsibility to Protect (R2P) 95, 100, 161, 171
rhetoric, 7, 9, 132
Rice, Susan 19
role play 26, 28, 30, 32, 34, 36, 39, 41–2, 80
roll call 20, 58, 90, 217, 229–31, 253, 258, 270, 273–4
Roosevelt, Franklin D. 85
rule of law 9, 159–61, 163–72, 190–91
rules training 20, 258, 265–6, 270–71
rules of procedure xi, xiii, 16, 19–20, 22, 26, 32, 34–5, 40, 54–5, 57, 61–3, 71, 75, 77, 84, 110, 125, 143–7, 150, 197, 199, 203, 206, 229–32, 252, 258, 272–4, 278
Russia 36, 49, 52, 60–61, 63, 92, 146, 166–7, 178, 248

Second World War 2, 9, 18, 84–6, 99, 107–108, 125, 127, 133, 178
secretariat 22, 51, 90, 94, 127–8, 149, 168, 172, 202, 216, 219, 274, 276
Secretary-General (SG) 19, 52, 84, 93–7, 127–8, 130, 161, 168, 171, 274
Security Council 7, 9, 20, 59, 86, 90–96, 100, 124, 126, 143, 149, 151, 159–72, 202, 221–2, 242, 257
seminar plan 3, 199–200, 205–6, 210
signatories 58, 85, 88, 98, 191, 216–19, 233, 274
simulation ix–xiii, 1, 4–10, 14–21, 23–4, 26–43, 47–64, 67–8, 70–72, 75–80, 118–19, 159, 197–8, 205–6, 210–11, 216, 218, 228–9, 232, 239, 250–61, 264–8, 270–71, 275
Single European Act (SEA) 109
skills x, xii–xiii, 5, 7–8, 14, 19, 23–4, 26, 29–32, 42,43, 49, 52–3, 55–7, 60, 63–4, 69–72, 79, 220, 223, 232, 235, 251
social practice 8, 48
soft law 198, 212
soft skills x 14, 16, 23, 197
speakers list 20–22, 57, 230–31, 259, 267, 270–71, 273–4
speech 5, 21, 43, 56, 60, 144, 165, 199, 204–5, 209, 230, 232–6, 239, 256, 260–61, 267
sponsors 58, 216–17, 219, 233, 241–2, 272, 274
State University of New York at Cortland (SUNY Cortland) 3, 29
Steinmeier, Frank-Walter 60
support 10, 22–23, 30–31, 36, 52, 60, 63, 96, 98–9, 116, 118, 132, 144, 152, 166, 186, 190, 198, 210, 217, 219–20, 222–3, 233, 241, 247, 251, 258, 260–61, 263, 267–70, 273–4
supranational 2, 9, 84, 106, 108–9, 118, 140–41, 143, 147–53, 156, 192
supranationalism 107

Sustainable Development Goals (SDGs) 96, 277

teaching
material 1–2, 5–7, 10, 197, 209–10, 212, 215, 216, 218, 221, 224, 226, 227, 229, 232, 236, 238–9
modules 10, 197–200, 209, 251, 270
thematic debates 160, 162–163, 168, 171–2
theory 29, 68, 73, 80, 169, 177–8
Thomas-Greenfield, Linda 19
time 2–4, 9, 21–2, 28, 32–5, 37–8, 40–41, 59, 62, 67, 78–80, 86–8, 92, 100, 106–9, 114, 122, 127, 132–3, 142, 144–6, 152, 160–61, 163, 167, 176–8, 182, 184, 186, 197, 200–205, 209, 219–20, 230–32, 234–5, 237, 244, 250, 253, 255, 259–60, 264–8, 271–2, 276
training seminar 3, 10, 197–9, 209, 212, 215, 270
transnational politics 1, 4–5, 7–8, 186, 208, 214
Treaty of Lisbon, Lisbon Treaty 39, 109–12, 114, 116–17, 153, 177, 189
Treaty of Maastricht, Maastricht Treaty 109–110, 114, 152–3, 177, 179, 183–6
Treaty of Rome 108–9, 152, 177, 179–81, 183–4, 189
Treaty on European Union (TEU) 111–13, 116, 151, 153, 177, 185, 191, 225
Treaty on the Functioning of the European Union (TFEU) 177, 186, 189, 224–5
Trusteeship Council 90, 93, 127, 149, 202

Ukraine 4, 36, 49, 52, 59–61, 63, 92, 146
Ukraine Resource Development Centre 59
Ukrainian Catholic University 2, 49, 52, 59–62
UN club 2, 23–4, 48–50, 52–4, 56, 59, 61, 197–8, 265, 274
UN High Commissioner for Human Rights 98
UN Human Rights Council 98–100, 160
Union Citizenship 183–188
Union of Soviet Socialist Republics (USSR) 60, 86–7
Unionists 107
United Kingdom of Great Britain and Northern Ireland (UK) 76, 86–7, 90, 92, 110, 163–6, 168
United Nations (UN) ix–xiii, 1–2, 4–9, 14–20, 23–4, 40, 50–51, 55, 58–9, 62–3, 71, 78–9, 84–100, 106–8, 114, 118, 122–33, 140–43, 146–51, 159–64, 166–7, 169–71, 197–9, 201–3, 206–8, 210–13, 228, 235–6, 243–4, 246, 256, 276–7
budget, 8, 85, 89–91, 93, 95–6, 100
Charter 8, 18, 53, 55, 84–8, 90–96, 114, 123, 125–30, 133, 143, 149, 159–63, 166–7, 170, 180, 202, 206, 213, 221–2, 242, 244, 272
conferences 93, 97–8
organs 8, 14, 84–6, 90–91, 93–5, 97, 124–32, 148–9, 159, 198, 202, 213, 221
United Nations Children's Fund (UNICEF) 84, 95
United Nations Educational, Scientific and Cultural Organization (UNESCO) 72, 74
United States of America (USA) 1, 15, 18, 24, 26, 29, 49, 51, 85–7, 89–90, 92, 98, 100, 117, 124, 165, 167, 248
Universal Declaration of Human Rights (UDHR) 96, 98, 131, 191
university ix, 1 3–4, 6, 8, 14, 16, 18, 20, 22–3, 26, 29, 31–5, 37, 48–9, 51–2, 59, 198, 210–11, 256
University of Zagreb (UNiZG) 2, 200

vote 20, 22, 57–8, 90–93, 99, 108, 112–14, 117, 123, 125, 130, 142–7, 149, 151, 153–6, 178, 184, 217, 219–21, 229–31, 241–2, 260, 273–5
voting 20–21, 39, 41, 48, 57, 62, 88, 90, 93, 95, 99, 125, 143–4, 149–51, 155, 193, 204, 206, 217, 219–20, 229–31, 247, 253, 258–9, 261, 266–7, 270–75, 278

Waldheim, Kurt 19
Warsaw Pact 87

Wilson, Woodrow 85, 123
working paper 16, 20–22, 49, 56–9, 61, 76, 199, 208, 216–21, 233, 241, 252–3, 259, 267, 272–3, 275–6, 278
World Bank 95
World Health Organisation (WHO) 84, 131
World Trade Organisation (WTO) 84

Yalta Conference 86

Printed and bound by CPI Group (UK) Ltd, Croydon, CR0 4YY

17/06/2026

14902647-0003